Crime, Victims and Policy

Palgrave Studies in Victims and Victimology

Series editors:

Matthew Hall
School of Law, University of Lincoln, UK

Pamela Davies
Department of Social Sciences and Languages, Northumbria University, UK

In recent decades, a growing emphasis on meeting the needs and rights of victims of crime in criminal justice policy and practice has fuelled the development of research, theory, policy and practice outcomes stretching across the globe. This growth of interest in the victim of crime has seen victimology move from being a distinct subset of criminology in academia to a specialist area of study and research in its own right.

Palgrave Studies in Victims and Victimology showcases the work of contemporary scholars of victimological research and publishes some of the highest-quality research in the field. The series reflects the range and depth of research and scholarship in this burgeoning area, combining contributions from both established scholars who have helped to shape the field and more recent entrants. It also reflects both the global nature of many of the issues surrounding justice for victims of crime and social harm and the international span of scholarship researching and writing about them.

Titles include:

Dean Wilson and Stuart Ross (*editors*)
CRIME, VICTIMS AND POLICY
International Contexts, Local Experiences

Palgrave Studies in Victims and Victimology
Series Standing Order ISBN 978–1–137–55702–5 hardback
(*outside North America only*)

You can receive future titles in this series as they are published by placing a standing order. Please contact your bookseller or, in case of difficulty, write to us at the address below with your name and address, the title of the series and the ISBN quoted above.

Customer Services Department, Macmillan Distribution Ltd, Houndmills, Basingstoke, Hampshire RG21 6XS, England

Crime, Victims and Policy

International Contexts, Local Experiences

Edited by

Dean Wilson
University of Sussex, UK

and

Stuart Ross
University of Melbourne, Australia

First published 2015 by
PALGRAVE MACMILLAN

Palgrave Macmillan in the UK is an imprint of Macmillan Publishers Limited,
registered in England, company number 785998, of Houndmills, Basingstoke,
Hampshire RG21 6XS.

Palgrave Macmillan in the US is a division of St Martin's Press LLC,
175 Fifth Avenue, New York, NY 10010.

Palgrave Macmillan is the global academic imprint of the above companies
and has companies and representatives throughout the world.

Palgrave® and Macmillan® are registered trademarks in the United States,
the United Kingdom, Europe and other countries.

ISBN: 978–1–137–38392–1

This book is printed on paper suitable for recycling and made from fully
managed and sustained forest sources. Logging, pulping and manufacturing
processes are expected to conform to the environmental regulations of the
country of origin.

A catalogue record for this book is available from the British Library.

A catalog record for this book is available from the Library of Congress.

Contents

Acknowledgements

The idea behind this volume had its gestation in 2009 at a victimology conference held at the University of South Australia in Adelaide. In conversation, it was quickly apparent to us that there was a wealth of innovation, theoretical and practical, evident in Australasia. Aware of the international context, we were also cognizant that while there were many similarities and continuities, local contexts were something that really mattered. They mattered in a way that made our own research, and that of many other scholars and practitioners we knew, more than simply case studies of international trends. There were examples of practice and theory that could not only contribute to international debates but also open up new vistas of theory and practice. It was from these initial thoughts that this collection emerged, and we have subsequently been extremely privileged to work with an exemplary group of authors who have all contributed in the creation of a book that extends those early conversations in exciting and informed directions. It almost goes without saying – but it nevertheless needs to be said – that we wish to sincerely thank all of the authors who have contributed to this volume. The high standard of writing, research and scholarship; the responsiveness to deadlines and emails; and their willingness to incorporate suggestions has made the task of editing this collection a very rewarding one for us both.

We must also thank the generous support of the Australia Research Council because it was through involvement in funded research projects that interrogated questions of victims' experiences that we arrived at the concept of this collection. Both projects, one touching upon policing and victims of crime (ARC LP0775304) and another investigating victims' perceptions of the criminal justice process (ARC DP0665417) are represented in the chapters in this volume. We would also like to acknowledge the great debt that we both owe to the late Adam Sutton, an inspirational scholar, colleague and friend, who was involved with some of this research in its early stages. Much of Adam's thinking continued to influence the direction of our research and the collection as we progressed with the project.

We are also exceptionally grateful for the support of commissioning editor Julia Willan and to editorial assistants Harriet Barker and Dominic Walker at Palgrave Macmillan. They have been helpful, endlessly patient, and also 'firm but fair' when it was called for to keep things moving along in the production process. Their professionalism and dedication to publishing the products of our research has been greatly valued.

Lastly, we must express our deepest thanks to our respective families: Sophie Coutand-Marin and Fiona Ellis. Thanks are due not only for the comforts and support of home but also for providing that invaluable perspective and reminder that there are other aspects of life that are important beyond the academic world.

Notes on Contributors

Tracey Booth is an associate professor in the Faculty of Law at the University of Technology, Sydney. She has researched and published widely in the areas of bail, victim participation in criminal justice processes and the restorative capacities of victim impact statements. Tracey recently completed a qualitative study investigating victim participation, particularly via oral victim impact statements, in the sentencing of homicide offenders, drawing on data from interviews with crime victims and observation of sentencing hearings in the New South Wales Supreme Court. Her current research explores the reconceptualisation of the contemporary sentencing hearing as a forum that both preserves the offender's entitlements to a fair hearing and promotes a restorative approach to dealing with the consequences of crime.

Chris Cunneen is Professor of Criminology at the University of New South Wales, Sydney, Australia. He has a conjoint appointment with the Cairns Institute, James Cook University. He has published widely in the areas of juvenile justice, policing, criminal justice policy, restorative justice and Indigenous legal issues. Recent books include *Penal Culture and Hyperincarceration* (2013, co-authored with E. Baldry, D. Brown, M. Brown, M. Schwartz and A. Steel), *Juvenile Justice, Youth and Crime in Australia* (2011, co-authored with Rob White) and *Debating Restorative Justice* (2010, co-authored with Carolyn Hoyle).

Robyn Holder is a research fellow at the Key Centre for Ethics, Law, Justice and Governance at Griffith University, in Brisbane, Australia, and was previously a visiting fellow at the Regulatory Institutions Network, The Australian National University. She has nearly 30 years of experience in research, public policy and law reform in Australia and the UK, particularly on system reform. Her areas of research interest include victims, rights and justice; violence against women and justice responses; and the relationship between political theory and justice. More recently she has explored justice for victims in conflict and post-conflict settings. For over 15 years she was an independent statutory advocate for victims' rights.

Jan Jordan is an associate professor at the Institute of Criminology, Victoria University of Wellington, New Zealand. She has over 20 years of experience teaching and researching in the area of women and crime, and she has been a member of government committees such as the Prostitution Law Review Committee. Her principal research focus is on women as victim/survivors of sexual violence, and she is a regular presenter to police training courses on adult sexual assault investigation. Her books include *Serial Survivors: Women's Narratives of Surviving Rape* (2008) and *The Word of a Woman? Police, Rape and Belief* (Palgrave Macmillan, 2004).

Michael O'Connell is South Australia's first Commissioner for Victims' Rrights. Before this appointment, he was that state's first victims of crime coordinator and a strategic policy officer. He served over 20 years as a police officer, during which time he was the inaugural victim impact statement coordinator. He teaches and writes on victimology and victim assistance, and he has taught criminology, crime prevention and Australian politics. Michael is the Secretary-General and life member of the World Society of Victimology. He chairs the Society's Communications Committee and is a consulting editor for International Perspectives on Victimology. In 1995 he was awarded the Australian Police Medal for his work for victims of crime; and, in 1999 the Institute of Justice Studies made him a life member to honour his activities to advance justice administration. He was a finalist in the 2004 South Australia division of the Australian of the Year; and in 2010 Victim Support Australasia presented him its national award for his contribution to advancing victimology, victims' rights and victim assistance.

Rebecca Powell is Managing Director of the Border Crossing Observatory, an innovative virtual research centre based at Monash University that connects international stakeholders to high quality, independent and cutting edge research on border crossings. She has worked in the field of human trafficking prevention from a law enforcement and criminal justice perspective for international organisations including the United Nations Office on Drugs and Crime (UNODC) at headquarters in Vienna, the Regional Centre of East Asia and the Pacific and Lao PDR country office and the Asia Regional Trafficking in Persons Project (ARTIP).

Stuart Ross is a senior fellow in the School of Social and Political Sciences at the University of Melbourne. His research interests include sentencing decision making, criminal justice population modelling and the evaluation of criminal justice programs. His recent work includes evaluations of release transition programs, court programs (community justice and client services) and the development of an instrument for assessing risk and need in Victorian prisoners and offenders. He is currently chief investigator on an Australian Research Council Discovery project on procedural justice for victims of crime and three linkage projects on mentoring of women released from prison, over-representation of indigenous offenders in the justice system and the integrated reform of responses to family violence. Prior to joining the Department of Criminology, he was Director of the National Centre for Crime and Justice Statistics in the Australian Bureau of Statistics. He is the co-author of *Sentencing Reform and Penal Change: The Victorian Experience* (1999).

Simone Rowe is a research officer at the University of New South Wales, and adjunct research fellow at James Cook University. Her recently completed research thesis explores the increasing criminalisation and incarceration of Indigenous women in Western settler societies through the lens of Indigenous and critical theory. Her publications include research on the impact of epistemic and physical dimensions of colonialism on the nature of violence in contemporary Indigenous communities; decolonising approaches to research; and the decolonisation of criminological and social work approaches to Indigenous people involved in criminal justice systems.

Marie Segrave is a senior lecturer in criminology at Monash University. She researches a wide range of areas across regulation, globalisation, exploitation, policing and criminalisation. Her current research projects include an analysis of temporary labour exploitation, funded by an Australia Research Council Discovery Early Career Researcher Award (DECRA). She also continues to research and publish in the area human trafficking, security and migration, imprisonment and the police provision of victim support.

Julie Stubbs is a professor in the Faculty of Law, University of New South Wales. Her research focuses primarily on women and criminal justice, including domestic violence law reforms, defences to homicide, battered woman syndrome, restorative justice, sexual assault, justice reinvestment and women's imprisonment. She also has published research concerning juvenile justice and cross-cultural issues in the legal system. She is co-editor (with Stephen Tomsen) of *Australian Violence* (2015).

Jane Wangmann is a senior lecturer in the Faculty of Law, University of Technology, Sydney. Her research focuses on primarily legal responses to domestic violence, particularly civil protection orders. Her doctorate (2009) examined the use of cross applications in NSW civil protection order proceedings. Most recently she has been exploring the use of sociological research on typologies of intimate partner violence in the context of family law. She has worked in legal practice, community legal education, government policy and law reform in the area of violence against women.

Rob White is Professor of Criminology in the School of Social Sciences at the University of Tasmania. Recent books include *Environmental Harm: An Eco-Justice Perspective* (2013), *Green Criminology: An Introduction to the Study of Environmental Harm* (with Di Heckenberg, 2014) and *Innovative Justice* (with Hannah Graham, forthcoming).

Dean Wilson is Professor of Criminology in the School of Law, Politics and Sociology, University of Sussex, UK. Dean's research interests include surveillance practices and security networks, policing and victims of crime and histories of criminal justice. His recent work includes an ethnographic study of CCTV control rooms in Australia, qualitative research into the victimisation of persons experiencing homelessness, a project funded by the British Academy that examines internal immigration policing and a major study involving interviews with 200 officers across Victoria investigating their experiences and perceptions of dealing with victims of crime (with Dr Marie Segrave). He is a director of the Surveillance Studies Network and an associate editor of *Surveillance and Society*. Between 2007 and 2011, he was the chief investigator on a major Australia Research Council Linkage Project with Victoria Police (LP0775304) examining the interactions of police with victims of crime and developing targeted recommendations to improve policing practice.

Introduction

Victims Research, Theory and Policy: The Role of Local Contexts

Stuart Ross and Dean Wilson

In the weeks leading up to the end of 2014, Australians were confronted with a series of events where victims played a central role. Thousands of floral tributes filled Martin Place in Sydney at the site of a siege where two hostages were murdered. In North Queensland, the Manoora community was the focus for condolence, counselling and support in response to the murder of eight children. Australia was one site for responding to victims at an international level when memorial services for the hundreds of thousands of victims of the 2004 tsunami were held at the Boxing Day cricket match in Melbourne, as well as throughout the region. Also in Victoria, the new Labour government announced its intention to establish a royal commission into family violence. These responses – emotional, spontaneous, symbolic, practical and institutional – show the depth and reach that victims have in contemporary society.

While all of these events involved Australians as victims and participants in the responses to victimisation, none of them are in any sense distinctively Australian. Public tributes, memorial services, commissions and inquiries, as well as personal responses to victimisation, transcend national boundaries. However, at the same time there is no 'universal' experience of being a victim or of responding to victimisation as an individual or a community. Each of these events was framed or shaped by circumstances that were locally specific. The tributes in Martin Place reflected public anxieties associated with the impact of terrorism on ordinary life, as exemplified by the site of the siege at a coffee shop used by morning commuters. The process of grieving in the Torres Strait Islander community was central to the responses to the Manoora tragedy. The decision to establish a royal commission on family violence reflects both the raised community expectations and the failure of previous public policy responses in Victoria.

This book is about the way that local circumstances – places, communities, legal and physical environments – shape both the experiences of victims and the policy responses and practical actions intended to prevent victimisation or ameliorate its harms. The local experiences here are predominantly Australasian, although the issues that are addressed are in no sense parochial. Rather, the aim of this collection is to examine how some of the global themes in victimology play out in specific social, legal and institutional contexts.

Our intention is not to present a 'national' handbook on victimology or to argue for some kind of distinctly Australian experience of victimisation. Recent years have seen a number of significant monographs that to varying degrees attempt to locate victimology within national, cultural and institutional frameworks in India (Rajan 1995), South Africa (Peacock 2013), Canada (Scott 2010) and a number of Southern and East Asian countries (Lui et al. 2013). While there is merit in this kind of analysis, readers looking for details of victimisation rates or accounts of victims' services should go to the excellent library of data, agency reports and summaries maintained by the Australian Institute of Criminology.

Our contributors are primarily concerned with the way that local experiences illuminate or add explanatory depth to issues of international significance. In this sense, this collection is an attempt to confront the problem identified nearly ten years ago by Paul Rock (2006), namely that the Australian literature on victimology is primarily an institutional literature of reports about victims' experiences or of agency responses. The chapters in this collection approach key criminological issues – the experience of criminal justice agencies, the policy formulation process, the construction of victim identities and the 'discovery' of new victims – with the aim of showing how the local contexts of postcolonial societies within the southern hemisphere both reflect and diverge from global developments in victims' experience, policy and practice.

This collection is also about the relationship between, on the one hand, research and theory development on crime victims, and on the other the policy actions that are taken to respond to or provide resources that rectify problems that victims experience as the direct and continuing consequences of crime, as well as the secondary trauma associated with their involvement in the criminal justice system. However, any thoughtful consideration of victims' policy must acknowledge that the evidence for the contribution of research and theory to effective policy is contestable. Despite several decades of progress in victims' policy reform, profound challenges remain in addressing the harms experienced by victims of crime.

These challenges remain even in relation to long-standing problems where policy is informed by mature theory and a substantial body of practical experience and research. The problem of child sexual abuse has been known for at least 50 years, and mandatory reporting has been a requirement in many jurisdictions for at least 20 years (James 1994). However, the exposure of widespread sexual abuse of children by priests and other authority figures in over 20 countries has highlighted glaring inadequacies across the spectrum of systems that are intended to protect and support victims (United Nations Committee on the Rights of the Child 2014).

Innovations in research, theory and practice are also challenged by new problems of victimisation that emerge. The spread of Internet-based communications has created new forms of fraud, harassment and exploitative crime. Identity crime is emerging as a major threat with the potential to have widespread impacts on the lives of many people. The impact of this form of crime is usually described in purely financial terms, but it is becoming apparent that it may also give rise to profound emotional harm to victims (Wall 2013). Despite the media attention devoted to 'cybercrime', one of the barriers to assisting victims is that many do not understand that they have experienced fraud or theft. In this respect some of the same policy challenges associated with educating the community about the true nature of family violence and sexual assault also arise in relation to online crime.

Even where research has been instrumental in designing more effective policy models, these can test our capacity to turn them into practical and effective practice responses. In the case of domestic violence services, there is strong research evidence to support the use of integrated service approaches. However the creation of demonstrably effective integrated service models remains at best a work in progress (Klevens and Cox 2008). Recent work by the New South Wales Bureau of Crime Statistics and Research shows that becoming a victim of violent crime results in a decline in mental health (Freeman and Smith 2014), with important implications for the way that support services are delivered to victims. Trauma-informed care models demonstrate the need to respond to victims of sexual and domestic violence, natural disasters and terrorism in ways that integrate traditional victim support with mental health and other specialised trauma-informed services (Mental Health Coordinating Council [MHCC] 2013).

Thus, in providing a new contribution to the field of victimology, it is important that we ask what kind of role this can play in responding to these old and new challenges. Our intention in preparing this edited collection was to focus on the local context of victims' policy and to ask what is distinctive about the way these issues play out in these local contexts – in effect, to ask what kinds of solutions work and under what kind of circumstances. While the contributions in this volume recognise the role of existing theory, they also recognise that it is not sufficient to simply force new problems into the framework of existing theory. In victimology, as in many other areas, effective policy responses have to be designed and adapted to respond to the local circumstances – crime, law, social systems, governance arrangements and resources.

This focus on the local speaks to a wider tension inherent in criminology between a predilection for general theories and a focus on more reflexive modes of enquiry. The attractions of general theories are manifold: they make broad-ranging statements about fundamental issues of crime and deviance and locate criminology in relation to comparably general, social and psychological theories. In a sense, general theories have *weight* – they aim to position criminology as a significant form of social science with important claims to make about the world, as a discipline to be taken seriously by decision makers. However, it is notable that general theories in criminology have been concerned mainly with criminal behaviour and have had relatively little to say about victimisation.

In contrast to the philosophical and methodological certainties inherent in general theories of criminology, reflexive modes of inquiry attempt to capture the complexity and interactional nature of social problems. This is partly a rejection of the claims of positivist and normative criminology as an 'adjunct of government' (Muncie 2000) and partly a recognition that social realities are constructed and that knowing about social systems requires an approach that recognises and accords with their contingent and interdependent nature. Reflexive criminology has a long history. It has its origins in the critical criminology of the 1970s with its focus on race, gender and class inequalities, and it continues to reverberate through the work of feminist and postmodern theorists in the 1980s and 1990s. A key theme in critical criminology has been the idea that social justice is a fundamental requirement for effective criminal justice and that this in turn requires a focus on the social harms associated with crime (Muncie 2000). Critical criminology is sometimes associated with a concern with the way that social and other forms of inequality – and the use of power and language – give rise to and institutionalise criminality. However critical approaches have also involved an acknowledgement that crime does real harms to victims and that many of the same inequalities associated with offenders apply equally to victims (Young 1997).

A key theme in this book is how victimisation is experienced within specific local contexts, in particular how these local contexts both echo and depart from global developments in victim experience, policy and practice. The link between reflexivity and local context is made by Watts et al. (2008) when they argue that criminologists should be 'paying attention to the kind of society of which they are a part' (p. 237). The contributors to this book share a common interest in the particularities of crime victimisation issues and the ways that these are affected by specifics of context. Context can involve physical locality but is more usefully constructed in terms of local contexts of power, politics and meaning. The intersection between these ideas is illustrated by two recent examples of responses to crises of victimisation that have been driven by social movements: the campaigns by Broken Rites and other activist groups in relation to the sexual abuse by Catholic clergy and the social network campaigns that now follow some serious sexual and violent crimes. Established in 1993, Broken Rites has provided a vehicle for individuals hurt by sexual abuse in the Catholic Church to work together to advocate for reform and to support other victims. It is a process that deliberately distances itself from the formal institutional responses (the Catholic Church Towards Healing process and state and federal royal commissions) in order to better maintain its relationship with victims. The emergence of social network campaigns and support groups in response to serious crimes also illustrates the power of local context. While the Facebook sites associated with the murders of Jill Meagher and Luke Batty are available to anyone, it is clear that there are distinctively local dimensions to the involvement that people have with them.

These social movements manage to be influential in terms of institutional reform processes while maintaining their sense of connection with a well-defined community of people affected by the crimes that give rise to them. There is a strong argument that these processes have resulted in enduring cultural change in the perceptions about the standing and motivation of the churches, the depiction of women and children in the media and sentencing. While the idea that cultural and social changes have been important in shaping attitudes about criminal justice and via that the policy settings for policing and sentencing, these recent events seem to represent a much more direct linkage of social and cultural responses to victimisation and legal and societal responses.

This collection

The essays in this collection are diverse; each represents a distinctive contribution to a specific set of issues, and they have a common thread: the local experience of victimological issues that are international in scope are consistently interrogated. The first two chapters challenge conventional victimology. Chris Cunneen and Simone Rowe (Chapter 1) put forward an alternative critical Indigenous framework that takes us beyond the limitations of traditional Eurocentric victimology, and they call for a foregrounding of the coloniality of power in governmental responses to Indigenous victimisation and crime. While Indigenous involvement in the justice system is frequently configured in terms of crime and punishment, Cunneen and Rowe draw attention to the equally high and distressing rates of victimisation in Indigenous communities. In their analysis, the experience of victimisation needs to be understood in relation to the history of Indigenous contact with police and justice institutions and the continuing discrimination and denial of sovereign and human rights. Another contribution that challenges the boundaries of conventional victimological theory is provided by Rob White's contribution (Chapter 2) on developments in environmental criminology. While many of his examples are drawn from his Tasmanian context, White asks us to examine the ways that we construct ideas about criminal harm and victimisation when the harm arises from environmental degradation and when the victims of this harm include people and nonhuman entities – examples of the latter include rivers or animals. White provides a boundary challenging analysis, in part because it considers the issues of victimisation arising from legal as well as illegal behaviour.

Another area of victimology requiring substantial reconsideration of how we conceptualise categories of crime and victims involves human trafficking and migration. In Chapter 3 Marie Segrave and Rebecca Powell examine the way that conceptions of victims shape institutional and regulatory responses to irregular migration and human trafficking, as illustrated by counter-trafficking efforts in Thailand, Australia and the United Kingdom. Their chapter aims to give voice to the broader experiences of victimisation and exploitation in trafficking and shows how local and global responses are shaped by gendered understandings of victimisation that are unresponsive to victims' needs. While the regulatory response to human trafficking appears to be straightforward and based on constructions of 'ideal victims' who need rescuing from harm and exploitation, Segrave and Powell argue that the reality is considerably more complex and that these regulatory responses both deny agency to trafficked persons and fail to take into account the broader social, political, economic and institutional processes that give rise to harm.

Sexual assault victimisation is a long-standing area of focus for victimology, and the last two decades have seen significant changes in policing and prosecutorial practice driven by a growing awareness of the inadequacies of these systems in responding to victims. Nevertheless, the process of reform has proven to be highly problematic. Jan Jordan (Chapter 4) examines police and public reactions to a high-profile case of rape in New Zealand, demonstrating how – despite decades of inquiries and reform – police and societal attitudes about rape remain fundamentally unchanged. Jordan links the experiences of victims and responses by police in New Zealand to similar systemic failures in the United Kingdom and the United States, and she contrasts the formal rhetoric regarding the importance of victims' rights and victim care with the continuing existence of barriers to transforming social and institutional attitudes.

Domestic violence is another long-standing, well-documented and serious issue that poses a profound challenge for anyone concerned about victim policy. Recent years have seen significant change in policing practices, increases in the funding of support services and the widespread adoption of integrated service models. However, Julie Stubbs and Jane Wangmann (Chapter 5) argue that victims of domestic violence continue to be subjected to conflicting and competing requirements and obligations. Stubbs and Wangmann invite us to consider how the law constructs domestic violence victims as a single idealised entity and to contrast this with the different ways in which women victims seek a response to the gendered harm of domestic violence. They examine the pathways that victims must navigate their way through in the legal domains of child protection, criminal law and family law, where varying constructions and interpretations are applied to their experiences.

Police are the frontline agents in dealing with victims of crime, and understanding the way that interactions with victims are framed by police work and culture is fundamental to improving victims policy. Dean Wilson and Marie Segrave interviewed police in a range of training and operational posts, and in Chapter 6 they show how disparate viewpoints regarding the importance of victims of crime arise out of different conceptions about the meaning and significance of policing. They find that a predilection for 'action-oriented' policing, in combination with competing pressures from other tasks, often leads to a down-playing of victim services. Nevertheless, there is also evidence that many police place a high value on their interactions with victims of crime and see police–victim interactions as an integral element of building trust in communities.

One of the important developments intended to improve victims' experiences in the courts has been victim impact statements (VIS). In Chapter 7 Tracey Booth considers the legal and ethical issues associated with the introduction of VIS into the New South Wales court system. She argues that the use of VIS is not intrinsically incompatible with the interests of offenders and that the availability of VIS is not in itself sufficient to ensure fairness to victims in the sentencing hearing. Courts must also demonstrate awareness of, and respect and sensitivity for, the interests of the victims in order for victims to experience procedural justice.

A central idea in reflexive criminology is that methodology itself should also be the subject of critical inquiry. In Chapter 8 Robyn Holder considers one of the most common metrics of victimisation studies – 'satisfaction' – and asks what this really means in the experiences and constructions of victims of crime. Her analysis of the narratives and survey responses of a sample of male and female victims provides evidence of a richness and complexity all too often absent from conventional constructions of victims as satisfied or dissatisfied consumers of services.

The political dimension of policy is a persistent theme in victimology, and the book ends with two chapters that consider victims' policy in Australia in its wider context as a branch of social and criminal justice policy. Australian justice systems have been moving steadily in the direction of greater punitiveness and populism with an inevitable carry-over into victim policy. In Chapter 9 Stuart Ross examines how the rights-based reform movements of the last century have been overtaken by policies informed by neoliberal perspectives on justice policy – perspectives that frequently represent victims' rights and interests as inevitably and diametrically opposed to those of offenders.

New Zealand and Australia were leaders in the creation of victim assistance services, and the last chapter provides an overview of the history of victims' policy in Australia. As Commissioner for Victims' Rights in South Australia, Michael O'Connell has had the opportunity to observe at first hand the shifts and developments in victim policy. He traces the way these service systems responded to the recognition of problems of violence against women and the injustices experienced by victims in their dealings with the justice system. More latterly, he describes the way that increased political and funding pressure on victims' services has led to them becoming viewed as another arm of the criminal justice system.

References

Freeman, K. and Smith, N. 2014. *Understanding the Relationship Between Crime Victimisation and Mental Health: A Longitudinal Analysis of Population Data.* Contemporary Issues in Crime and Justice No. 177. Sydney: NSW Bureau of Crime Statistics and Research.

James M. 1994. *Child Abuse and Neglect: Incidence and Prevention.* NCPC Issue No. 1. Melbourne: Australian Institute of Family Studies.

Klevens, J. and Cox, P. 2008. Coordinated Community Responses to Intimate Partner Violence: Where Do We Go From Here? *Criminology and Public Policy* 7(4), pp. 547–556.

Lui, J., Jou S. and Hebenton, B. 2013. *Handbook of Asian Criminology.* New York: Springer.

Mental Health Coordinating Council (MHCC) 2013. *Trauma-Informed Care and Practice: Towards a Cultural Shift in Policy Reform across Mental Health and Human Services in Australia, A National Strategic Direction, Position Paper and Recommendations of the National Trauma-Informed Care and Practice Advisory Working Group*, Authors: Bateman, J. and Henderson, C. (MHCC) Kezelman, C. (Adults Surviving Child Abuse, ASCA). http://mhcc.org.au/media/32045/ticp_awg_position_paper__v_44_final___07_11_13.pdf

Muncie, J. 2000. *Decriminalising Criminology.* British Criminology Conference: Selected Proceedings. Vol. 3. British Society of Criminology Conference, Liverpool, July 1999. htttp://lboro.ac.uk/departments/ss/bsc/bccsp/vol03/Muncie.html&

Peacock, R. 2013. *Victimology in South Africa: An Introduction.* 2nd ed. Hatfield, SA: Van Schaik.

Rajan, V.N. 1995. *Victimology in India: Perspectives Beyond Frontiers.* New Delhi: APH Publishing.

Rock, P. 2006. Aspects of the Social Construction of Crime Victims in Australia. *Victims and Offenders* 1(3), pp. 289–321.

Scott, H. 2010. *Victimology: Canadians in Context.* Don Mills, ON: Oxford University Press Canada.

United Nations Committee of the Rights of the Child 2014. Concluding observations on the second periodic report of the Holy See. CRC/C/VAT/CO/2. http://apps.washingtonpost.com/g/documents/world/un-issues-scathing-report-on-vatican-handling-of-sex-abuse/777/Wall, D.S. 2013. *The Future Challenges of Identity Crime in the UK* DR20. Future Identities: Changing identities in the UK – the next 10 years. London: Foresight Project. www.foresight.gov.uk

Watts, R., Bessant, J. and Hil, R. 2008. *International Criminology: A Critical Introduction.* Milton Park, Abingdon: Routledge.

Young, J. 1997. Left Realist Criminology: Radical in its Analysis, Realist in its Policy. In: Maguire M., Morgan R. and Reiner, R. eds. *The Oxford Handbook of Criminology.* Second Ed. Oxford: Oxford University Press, pp.473–498.

1
Decolonising Indigenous Victimisation

Chris Cunneen and Simone Rowe

> There is no form of knowledge to which we can attribute, in general, an epistemological privilege.... There is no global social justice without global cognitive justice.
>
> – Boaventura de Sousa Santos,
> in Dalea and Robertson 2004, pp. 58–60.

This chapter is part of a broader project we refer to as the 'penal/colonial complex' – a project that seeks to delineate, decentre and challenge the dominant mechanisms through which law, policy and practice continue to subjugate Indigenous peoples, their cultures and their knowledges (Cunneen et al. 2013, pp. 186–187; Cunneen and Rowe 2014). We see the need to decentre victimology at both a theoretical and policy level as an important component of the broader project. Our intentions in this chapter are fivefold: to consider the current status of the victimisation (and, we argue, concomitant criminalisation) of Indigenous peoples in postcolonial Western settler societies; to establish the limitations of Eurocentric victimological approaches to understanding this phenomenon; to clarify how an alternative critical Indigenous analytic framework can transgress these limitations; to contrast Indigenous and state policy responses to Indigenous victimisation; and thereby to establish the analytical and decolonising[1] significance of critical Indigenous approaches.

Introduction: Indigenous victimisation

In the postcolonial Western settler societies of Australia, Canada, New Zealand and the United States, Indigenous peoples are grossly over-represented as victims[2] of crime. In Australia, rates of violent victimisation for Indigenous peoples are two to three times higher than for non-Indigenous Australians; the rates are four to six times higher in the case of family violence (AIC 2013). In Canada, some 35 per cent of Aboriginal people report being a victim of crime, compared to 26 per cent of non-Aboriginal people. Aboriginal Canadians are nearly three times more likely to be victims of violent crime than non-Aboriginal Canadians; they are five times more likely to be the victims of sexual offending (Department of Justice Canada 2012). In New Zealand, numerous surveys have shown that Maori peoples are more likely to be victims of a violent crime than non-Maori peoples (Statistics New Zealand 2010, pp. 20–30). And in the United States, rates of violent victimisation, for both males and females, are higher among Native Americans than among any other racial or ethnic group (CFCC 2012, p. 1).

Indigenous women's victimisation rates are particularly high. To take Canada as an example, Aboriginal women are three and a half times more likely than non-Aboriginal women to be victims of violence. Aboriginal women ages 25–44 are five times more likely to die as a result of violence (Wesley 2012, p. 5). Violence against Aboriginal women in the home is prevalent: spousal violence against Aboriginal women and girls in Canada is more than three times higher than for other Canadian women; Aboriginal women are eight times more likely to be a victim of spousal homicide (HRW 2013, p. 25; Wesley 2012, pp. 5–6). Similarly in Australia, Indigenous women are disproportionately represented as victims of crime: they are more than ten times as likely to be a victim of homicide than other women are; 45 times more likely than non-Indigenous women to be a victim of domestic violence; and more than twice as likely to be the victim of sexual assault (ATSISJC 2006, pp. 337–341).

In the context of victimisation, one must also consider the over-representation of Indigenous children in child protection systems. In Australia, for example, Indigenous children are more likely to be the subject of a notification to a child protection agency (this rate is nearly six times greater than the one for non-Indigenous children); their cases are much more likely to be substantiated after a child protection agency investigation (this rate is eight times greater than the one for non-Indigenous children); and they subsequently have much higher rates of removal from their family and placement in care (at a rate 11 times higher than the one for non-Indigenous children). It is also important to recognise that these rates have been increasing over the last decade (SCRGSP 2014, pp. 15.12–15.15). Similarly in Canada and the United States, evidence suggests that Aboriginal and Native American children are disproportionately represented among child welfare reports, investigations, and out-of-home placements (Fallon et al. 2013, pp. 48–49). In the United States, despite representing just one per cent of the urban child population, urban Native American children under age 18 represent two per cent of all children placed in out-of-home care. This disparity is much higher in particular states (Carter 2010, p. 657).

Coinciding with an increased awareness of Indigenous victimisation rates has been the growth in Indigenous criminalisation and incarceration. Over the last two decades, the Australian Indigenous imprisonment rate has doubled, while the non-Indigenous rate has been both significantly lower and increasing at almost half the Indigenous rate (Baldry and Cunneen, 2014). There is evidence to suggest that the high levels of over-representation of Indigenous peoples in prison in Canada, the United States and New Zealand have remained constant or worsened over recent years (Cunneen 2014, p. 389).

Of particular interest in the context of the current chapter is the extraordinary growth in Indigenous women's imprisonment rates, which has far outstripped the growth in Indigenous men's imprisonment rates. It is a phenomenon explored by a growing number of critical scholars (see,e.g. Baldry and Cunneen 2014; Pollack 2013; Dell and Kilty 2013; Marchetti 2013; Ross 1998, 2004; Stubbs 2011). From these explorations, several key theoretical insights have emerged, including the inextricable connections between the categories of race, gender and class (see, e.g. Ross 1998, p. 264); the related importance of a nuanced intersectional analysis (see, e.g. Stubbs, 2011, p. 59); the enduring underestimation of the effects of colonisation, patriarchy and violence on the lives of victimised, criminalised and incarcerated Indigenous women (see, e.g. Baldry and Cunneen 2014); and the significance of the feminist notion of the victimisation-criminalisation continuum in explaining the over-representation of Indigenous women, both as victims and as offenders (see, e.g. Pollack 2013).

All of the above insights are important, however, with respect to understanding the over-representation of Indigenous women *and* men, both as victims *and* offenders, we wish to highlight the analytic significance of the victimisation-criminalisation continuum.[3] To clarify, while we acknowledge the importance of the increasing emphasis on the disproportionate victimisation and criminalisation of Indigenous women, our focus henceforth is on the disproportionate contact of *both* Indigenous women and men with the criminal justice system – an issue all too frequently neglected in the theory and practice of victimology. In relation to Indigenous men and women, evidence continues to suggest that the separation between the categories of victim and offender are not at all clear. 'In reality many Indigenous people in the criminal justice system are both offenders and victims' (ATSISJC 2002, p. 149).

The analytic importance of this concept becomes especially salient when one broadens current conceptualisations of Indigenous victimisation beyond the narrow confines of *criminal* victimisation, a practice we argue that is crucial to understanding and responding to the broader victimisation of Indigenous peoples. Indeed, it is only when we broaden our focus beyond criminal victimisation that we begin to see how discriminatory, unjust and oppressive colonial processes are in fact a form of victimisation. Similarly, when one broadens the category of Indigenous criminalisation, we begin to see Indigenous peoples' law-breaking not as an indication of their so-called criminality, but rather as resistance to ongoing colonisation (Blagg 2008; Cunneen 2001; Ross 1998). The continuing criminalisation of Indigenous peoples' survival strategies is thereby rendered problematic. Thus, a critical stance on the causes and categorisation of Indigenous victimisation and criminalisation and on the functions of criminal law in controlling Indigenous peoples is required. Achieving this aim, we contend, requires challenging the 'epistemological privilege' (de Sousa Santos, in Dalea and Robertson 2004, pp. 58–60) of Eurocentric approaches.

This then is the principal agenda of our chapter: to advance critical consideration and analysis of the victimisation and criminalisation of Indigenous peoples living in postcolonial Western settler societies. The discussion below unfolds in four sections. First, we establish the limitations of dominant Eurocentric victimological approaches to understanding and responding to the complex forms by which colonisation continues to impact the extraordinary over-representation of Indigenous peoples, both as victims and offenders. Building on the work of Indigenous scholars, we propose an alternative critical Indigenous analytic framework. The chapter proceeds by clarifying how a critical Indigenous lens can help decolonise hegemonic constructions of Indigenous victimisation and criminalisation by re-centring Indigenous peoples' worldviews, understandings and responses. We then contrast these with an analysis of an Australian Government response to Indigenous victimisation – a policy initiative commonly known as 'The Northern Territory Intervention' (hereinafter the 'NT Intervention'). We conclude that understanding and responding to the alarming rates of Indigenous victimisation demands recognition of critical Indigenous approaches, alongside a commitment to enhance Indigenous agency and control.

Limitations of Eurocentric victimology

Paul Rock (2012, p. 55) recently noted that 'the poverty of victimological theory is a reiterated complaint', and there is much that victimological theory cannot and does not reveal. For the increasing number of Indigenous victims living and dealing with the consequences of ongoing colonisation, there is much that a mainstream Eurocentric victimological lens serves to conceal. This concealment is further exacerbated when public policy actively derides Indigenous voices – a point we will return to later.

As a sub-discipline of criminology, victimology suffers from many of the same conceptual limitations underlying mainstream positivist/ conventional approaches to the investigation of crime. Critical scholars have documented the broader conceptual limits of mainstream criminological and victimological approaches for at least four decades (see, e.g. Cunneen and Rowe 2014; Taylor et al. 1973; Stubbs 2008; Walklate 1990). Rather than rehearse these here, we wish to focus on the comparatively less developed conceptual restraints arising from the assumed superiority of Eurocentric approaches to the investigation of the victimisation and criminalisation of Indigenous peoples.

As many Indigenous and non-Indigenous scholars have argued, paradigm change is crucial to transgressing Eurocentric conceptual frames (see, e.g. Cunneen and Rowe 2014; Denzin and Lincoln 2008; Kincheloe 2006; Moreton-Robinson 2009a; Moreton-Robinson and Walter 2009). Such change can occur only when colonisation is brought 'front and centre and named as the root cause' of Indigenous over-representation, both as victims and as offenders (McCaslin and Breton 2008, p. 518). As Dipesh Chakrabarty (2006, p. iv) argues, 'the colonial model' should not be abandoned; it remains crucial to making sense of the position of Indigenous peoples.

While the process in which colonisation occurred and ultimately impacted the Indigenous peoples of Australia, Canada, New Zealand and the United States differed in some respects (see, e.g. Marchetti and Downie 2014, pp. 362–366), there are also manifold commonalities in the experiences of Indigenous peoples in Western settler societies derived from English common law traditions (Cunneen 2014, pp. 386–387). A significant part of this shared experience stems from the history of colonisation and the profound disruption caused to pre-existing traditional societies. In short, *every* part of Indigenous society was attacked during the colonial process. The long history of confining and imprisoning Indigenous peoples in Australia, Canada, New Zealand and the United

States, denying their civil and political rights, and controlling behaviour both through and outside the law is far from finished. Rather, as Indigenous scholar Aileen Moreton-Robinson explains, 'Colonisation has not ceased to exist; it has only changed in form from that which our ancestors encountered' (2009, p. 11).

Perhaps one of the most underexplored forms through which colonisation continues to occur in criminological and victimological discussions of Indigenous peoples is the epistemic violence (Spivak 1995, pp. 24–25) arising from entrenched beliefs in the superiority of Eurocentric epistemologies and the concomitant marginalisation of the 'subjugated knowledges' (Foucault 1980, pp. 81–85) of Indigenous peoples. In the context of continuing colonisation, epistemic violence, or the violence of knowledge, operates 'not by military might or industrial strength, but by thought itself' (Chatterjee 1986, p. 11). In the case of criminalised and victimised Indigenous peoples, the epistemic violence that occurs through the ongoing imposition of Western conceptual frames on Indigenous contexts 'risks reproducing the very colonial discourse we might have set out to unseat' (Blagg 2008, p. 201).

The imposition of the dominant Eurocentric episteme to the issue of domestic violence in Indigenous contexts exemplifies this concern. Understanding the inappropriateness and inadequacy of these initiatives requires recognising the incongruity between Indigenous and Western ontological understandings of the self. Indigenous peoples understand the self as being centrally defined by relationships to kinship groups and the natural world. Western understandings by contrast generally see the nature of self in an individualised and autonomous context (Moreton-Robinson and Walter, 2011; Wilson, 2001). Indigenous people often define domestic violence in the broader and relational concept of *family violence*, a term reflective of the centrality of the relationality to Indigenous worldviews (for a discussion of the distinction, see Memmott et al. 2001, p. 34). Nevertheless, Eurocentric domestic violence, law and policy imposed in Indigenous contexts is often predicated on an incongruent ontological and epistemological reality – a reality based on the potential for autonomous and individualised decision making.

Another important example is the difference between Western and Indigenous concepts of self-determination: from a Western perspective, self-determination is usually viewed as an individual concern; from an Indigenous perspective, self-determination is usually viewed as a collective concern (Green and Baldry 2008, pp. 398–399). It is also seen as a fundamental collective human right, as evidenced in the United Nations *Declaration on the Rights of Indigenous Peoples* 2007. Again, such differences have important implications for the development of specific public policy responses to both victimisation and criminalisation. Criminal justice policies must begin with the recognition of this fundamental human right if they are to be aligned with the broader political and social imperatives of Indigenous peoples. As discussed in the ensuing section on the NT Intervention, Indigenous responses rooted in these understandings continue to be marginalised by state policy initiatives.

We argue that the silencing of Indigenous worldviews, voices and perspectives through the imposition of Eurocentric conceptual frames has been central to perpetuating an image of Indigenous dysfunction and to reproducing the assumed 'criminogenic' features of Indigenous peoples through various 'risk' technologies. As exemplified in Pollack's (2013, p. 107) critical analysis of racialised women in correctional systems in Canada, epistemic violence also occurs through the eradication of the 'perspectives and subjectivities of criminalised women whose experience of self, criminalisation and imprisonment may not be measurable through the ideological tools of evidence-based research and practice'.

However, not only is the Eurocentric victimological imagination limited by its failure to conceptualise and interrogate the impact of ongoing colonisation (both in its practical and epistemological manifestations); as we noted earlier, it is also restricted by its inability to conceptualise and interrogate the complex forms of victimisation to which Indigenous peoples are subjected. So, when viewed through a Eurocentric victimological lens, the focus remains almost exclusively on Indigenous peoples as victims of crime. Alternative categories of victimisation – such as the victimisation of Indigenous peoples through the continued denial of their sovereign and human rights by the state (a point to which we will return) – are largely ignored. We argue that such limitations call for a decentring of Eurocentric constructs and knowledge from their privileged place at the centre of all inquiry and a re-centring of the subjugated knowledges of Indigenous peoples.

An alternative analytic framework: Critical Indigenous approaches

As a mode of analysis stemming from the work of Indigenous scholars, critical Indigenous theory 'offers the possibility for a transformative agenda' (Smith 2005, p. 88) – an agenda that 'necessarily speaks to Indigenous people living in postcolonial situations of injustice'

(Denzin and Lincoln 2008, p. xii). Critical Indigenous approaches can, we contend, be put to advantage by non-Indigenous victimologists and Indigenous victimologists to interrogate and explain how colonialism connects to the neo-colonial social worlds where Indigenous men and women continue to be both victimised and criminalised. As the Indigenous scholar Jelena Porsanger (2004, p. 109) makes clear, Indigenous approaches do not reject non-Indigenous researchers and scholars, nor do they simply reject Western canons of academic work. Furthermore, we suggest that critical Indigenous scholarship is fundamental to decolonising dominant understandings and responses to the disproportionate over-representation of Indigenous victimisation. The ensuing discussion considers salient features of critical Indigenous approaches relevant to our focal concern: the extreme over-representation of Indigenous peoples, both as victims and offenders.

As we suggested earlier, the 'colonial model' is crucial to conceptualising and explaining the extraordinary rates of Indigenous victimisation. Problematising the enduring role that colonising processes continue to have in the lives of Indigenous peoples is also fundamental to critical Indigenous inquiry (see, e.g. Denzin and Lincoln 2008; Moreton-Robinson and Walter 2011; Sherwood 2010; Smith 2012). Taking colonialism as our point of departure, and thereby coming to terms not only with the specificity of Indigenous peoples as colonised peoples but also with the vested interest of neo-colonial institutions in maintaining their dominant role vis-à-vis Indigenous peoples, has significant ramifications for how we understand Indigenous victimisation. This is especially so in relation to the dominant representations and interpretations of violence in contemporary Indigenous communities.

In recent years the problem of violence in Indigenous communities has attracted considerable focus in Australia, New Zealand and North America, as have the corresponding high levels of violent victimisation and the high rates of violent offences of Indigenous men and women (see, e.g. Bartels 2012; Blagg 2000; CFCC 2012; Davis 2000; Deer 2004; HRW 2013; Macklin and Gilbert 2011; Memmott et al. 2001; Ramirez 2004). It is well understood that violent behaviour involving Indigenous people (including homicide and serious assaults) is most frequently directed towards intimates rather than strangers, more often than is the case in non-Indigenous communities (Chan and Payne 2013, p. 20; Memmott et al. 2001). A preoccupation with measuring Indigenous violence means that there is no shortage of statistical data pertaining to Indigenous peoples' 'problem' with violence (as was demonstrated in the earlier sections of this chapter).

The pathologising and individualising discourses that flow from this data subsequently inform various policy initiatives that continue to negatively impact Indigenous communities. For example, the plethora of uncritical interpretations of such data has been central to the mainstreaming of Indigenous violent offenders in criminal justice treatment programmes. These programmes are underpinned chiefly by the Eurocentric belief in cognitive behavioural therapy (CBT) and are overwhelmingly designed for non-Indigenous violent offenders. Ontologically, CBT is premised on the notion of western Cartesianism that separates the individual from the natural world (Kincheloe 2006). This is a position entirely antithetical to an Indigenous ontology that privileges the importance of relationality. Unsurprisingly, evidence continues to suggest that such programs fail to address the unique circumstances and needs of Indigenous offenders (see, e.g. Bartels 2012; Day et al 2006; Lawrie 2003; Stubbs 2011; VEOHRC 2013).

Through a critical Indigenous lens, the problems associated with quantifying Indigenous violence through Eurocentric scientific frames are made manifest. As Indigenous scholar Maggie Walter (2010) has revealed, the production, analysis and presentation of statistical data pertaining to Indigenous concerns are not neutral interpretations of numerical accounts. Rather, 'the unstated epistemological, ontological and axiological certainties of scientific frameworks have long been used by anthropologists, historians and others to bolster white possession and nullify Indigenous humanity under a carapace of objectivity' (Walter 2010, p. 52).

So, in the case of statistical accounts of the 'problem' of Indigenous violence, through a critical Indigenous lens one sees first how the production, analysis and presentation of such data inescapably renders invisible the impact of ongoing colonisation on the causation and perpetuation of such violence. Furthermore, a critical Indigenous analytic frame alerts one to the Eurocentric tendency to present and analyse the high rates of violent victimisation and violent offences of Indigenous peoples to an automatic rating of the problematic Indigenous 'other' alongside that of the comparatively lower rates of violent victimisation and violent offences of non-Indigenous peoples – a process that inescapably has the effect of perpetuating a pejorative image of Indigenous dysfunction and, as a consequence, the problematic Indigenous 'other' (Walter 2010, pp. 51–52; see also Jackson 1995). This depreciatory effect is magnified by the comparatively smaller representation of Indigenous peoples in the general population. Finally, a critical Indigenous lens makes evident the problems ensuing from an over-reliance of data generated by non-Indigenous organisations (Tauri and Webb 2012). Indeed, data on Indigenous violence, victimisation, criminalisation and incarceration continues to be sourced almost exclusively from non-Indigenous government-funded criminal justice institutions, the very institutions that have evolved to resolve the 'Aboriginal problem' (Blagg 2008, p. 2). Caught within broader dominant epistemological frameworks, cultural values and political relationships, such institutions can be seen as complicit in reproducing Indigenous men and women as dysfunctional criminal subgroups (Blagg and Smith 1989, pp. 138–139; see also Cunneen 2006). Thus, while it is true that statistics do not lie, 'neither do they always tell the same truth' (Walter 2010, p. 53). Rather, the political and social reality of data is 'framed by how they are garnered and interpreted, by whom, and for what purpose' (Walter 2010, p. 53).

In contradistinction, a critical Indigenous theoretical approach asserts the need to foreground the voices, worldviews, subjectivities and perspectives of Indigenous peoples (see, e.g. Moreton-Robinson and Walter 2011; Sherwood 2010; Smith 2012) – a process through which an entirely different view of Indigenous peoples' *so-called* problem with violence, both as offenders and victims, is revealed. In the words of two victimised and criminalised Aboriginal Canadian women,

> There is no accidental relationship between our convictions for violent offences, and our histories as victims. As victims we carry the burden of our memories: of pain inflicted on us, of violence done before our eyes to those we loved, of rape, of sexual assaults, of beatings, of death. For us, violence begets violence: our contained hatred and rage concentrated in an explosion that has left us with yet more memories to scar and mark us. (Aboriginal Justice Inquiry 1990, cited in Wesley 2012, p. 23)

Indeed violence was at the foundational core of the colonising process. Thus, to analytically neglect the significance of the colonial model – the enduring impact of the history of terror, torture, violence and ill-treatment on the disproportionate numbers of victimised and criminalised Indigenous peoples – is to collude with the reproduction of colonising discourses. It also reinforces the dominant position of the coloniser vis-à-vis the colonised, a dominant position where 'expert others' continue to speak and plan on behalf of victimised and criminalised Indigenous peoples living and dealing with the consequences of ongoing colonisation. As many Indigenous people have noted, when colonial violence, the genocidal propensities of colonial powers, the theft of land, dispossession, forced relocations, forced removals and the mass control of Indigenous people through and beyond the law are properly considered, then the answer to the questions 'who is criminal?' 'who is victimised?' and 'what is justice?' take on an entirely different meaning (see, e.g. Barsh and Youngblood Henderson 1976; Davis 2000; Langton 1992; Jackson 1995; O'Shane 1992; Ross 1998; Tauri 1998). Indeed, the criminalisation of Indigenous peoples' resistance to colonisation continues to silence criticism of the complex forms by which neo-colonial powers continue to victimise Indigenous peoples through such factors as social and political exclusion, economic immiseration and the denial of rights.

A brief example serves to elucidate these points further. It is well known that colonial authorities forcibly removed Indigenous children from their families in a direct effort to eradicate Indigenous culture and identity and to remake citizens in the interests of colonial society. The effects of these policies have contemporary tangible outcomes in terms of victimisation and criminalisation. The intergenerational effects on many of those removed have included the loss of culture; loss of parenting skills; mental illness; self-harm; unresolved grief and trauma; drug and alcohol problems; poorer educational and employment outcomes; criminalisation; and further interventions by child protection agencies (see, e.g. NISATSIC 1997). The effect of colonial policies directly affects Indigenous people *irrespective* of whether they had been personally removed. For example, it has been shown that some Indigenous women who have been subjected to domestic and family violence will not report the violence to state authorities because of a direct fear, if police are called, that their children will be removed by child protection agencies (Cunneen 2009, p. 326). It is a graphic example of how the effects of colonial policies structure contemporary Indigenous decision making.

Decentring Eurocentric constructs and knowledge and instead privileging Indigenous worldviews offer a very different interpretation of 'child protection'. Not a single submission to the Australian National Inquiry into the Separation of Aboriginal and Torres Strait Islander Children from Their Families 'saw intervention by welfare departments as an effective way of dealing with Indigenous child protection needs' (NISATSIC 1997, p. 454). Perhaps more important was the understanding by many Indigenous people that separation of Indigenous children from their land, culture and kin constituted emotional, physical and mental child abuse (NISATSIC 1997, pp. 455–456). Put bluntly, privileging an Indigenous perspective completely inverts state classifications, statistics and responses to Indigenous 'child protection'. It is from this position that one begins to appreciate that it is not the colonisers but the colonised who are the experts in finding solutions to their 'problems' (Briskman 2007, p. 3), a position all too frequently lacking in policy responses to Indigenous victimisation.

Responding to Indigenous victimisation and criminalisation

Blagg (2008, pp. 143–145) has identified a multiplicity of structural factors that continue to prevent mainstream criminal justice systems from responding appropriately to Indigenous victims. These include embedded systemic racism; problematic constructions of Aboriginal criminality; massive under-reporting of Indigenous victims; the inappropriateness of Eurocentric models of victim support; and a lack of investment in Indigenous community-owned solutions. He notes that programs are 'delivered on the whole by agencies that have no roots in the communities they serve, and in the capacity of what is – from an Aboriginal perspective – a wholly alien system of justice' (Blagg 2008, p. 143).

Indigenous and critical scholars and activists in Western settler societies have repeatedly named the importance of Indigenous autonomy in decision making and the right to self-determination as fundamental principles to engaging with the problems of victimisation and criminalisation. These fundamental principles have epistemological and praxis implications for research and policy. How Indigenous people 'know' violence in their communities impacts on the understanding of the causes and remedies for violence. In the first instance, as Native American scholar Ramirez (2004, p. 103) has argued, it is important to use 'Native rather than Eurocentric philosophy and viewpoints to begin to move beyond colonial hierarchies' in understanding Indigenous cultural approaches to healing both offenders and victims. Others have noted, 'true justice and healing will only be possible when the victims can seek accountability within their own judicial systems' (Deer 2004, p. 18; see also Ross 1998, p. 267). Deer goes on to argue that the laws and policies of the United States play 'a significant role in the high rate of victimisation, because they have inhibited the ability of tribal communities to respond to and address crime in a culturally appropriate way' (2004, p. 19). The problems of state law and policy responses to Indigenous violence have been noted in Australia (e.g. Cunneen 2011, 2014)'; we explore this further in the following section on the NT Intervention.

If we turn specifically to the question of violence against Indigenous women, Indigenous perspectives are based largely on different under-standings and explanations for the violence. They thus demand law and policy interventions that are different from mainstream approaches to domestic violence. Indigenous approaches do not necessarily rely on a criminalisation approach. Self-determination, community development and capacity building are all acknowledged as aspects to dealing with domestic and family violence. Furthermore, the acknowledgement of the links between colonial experiences of violence and contemporary violence are emphasised (ATSISJC 2002, p. 165; Cunneen 2011, p. 322; Deer 2004, p. 25).

There is a perception that Western criminal justice interventions are 'extremely poor at dealing with the underlying causes of criminal behav-iour and make a negligible contribution to addressing the underlying consequences of crime in the community' (ATSISJC 2004, p. 21). The failures of these interventions are manifold. They fail at the symbolic level because there is little or no ownership of the institutions (i.e. they lack legitimacy); they fail by escalating the violence against women and children (imprisoned men return more damaged and violent); and they fail by continuing to separate Indigenous families (which is seen as an ongoing strategy of colonialism) (Cunneen 2011, p. 323).

The contrast between Western and Indigenous ontologies and epis-temologies, and the practical policy interventions that flow from these differing positions, can be seen in the divergent responses to both victim-isation and criminal offending. If we reflect on Indigenous-developed interventions based on healing, it is evident that they start at a different place to conventional programmes aimed at individualised victims and offenders:

> Indigenous concepts of healing are based on addressing the rela-tionship between the spiritual, emotional and physical in a holistic manner. An essential element of Indigenous healing is recognising the interconnectedness between, and the effects of, violence, social and economic disadvantage, racism and dispossession from land and culture on Indigenous peoples, families and communities. (ATSISJC 2004, p. 57)

As we have explored in more detail elsewhere (Cunneen 2014, pp. 399—401; Cunneen and Rowe 2014), Indigenous programmes start with the collective Indigenous experience. Inevitably, that involves an understanding of the collective harms and outcomes of colonisation, including genocidal policies and practices, the loss of lands, the disruptions of culture, the changing of traditional roles of men and women, the collective loss and sorrow of the removal of children and relocation of communities. Not only is the continuum of victimisation and offending understood as an outcome of disadvantage and marginalisation, but it is also linked to non-economic deprivation 'such as damage to identity and culture, as well as trauma and grief' (ATSISJC 2002, p. 136). Healing is not simply an individualised response. It is fundamentally about addressing trauma in a range of areas from the personal, social and intergenerational to the historical. Healing is quintessentially and simultaneously an individual and collective experience.

The Northern Territory Intervention: contemporary colonialism in action

Violence in Indigenous communities has become the focal point of governmental concern and in many cases the major rationale for significant shifts in criminal justice and social policy. We use the example of the Northern Territory Emergency Response[4] (also commonly referred to as 'the Intervention') initiated by the Australian Government, as a contemporary example of 'patriarchal white sovereign' power being used 'to regulate and manage the subjugation of Indigenous communities' in the name of protecting Indigenous women and children from sexual assault and violence (Moreton-Robinson 2009b, p. 68).

Critical Indigenous theory provides a useful lens through which to consider contemporary understandings of violence and the nature of government intervention. In the governmental rhetoric surrounding the Intervention, Indigenous law and culture was presented as a significant part of the problem of violence. Indigenous women were presented as victims and Indigenous men as inherently violent, thus confirming 'the superiority of white men' (Watson 2007, p. 102). Aboriginal culture was presented as a largely worthless male-dominated collection of primitive beliefs – a view that evidenced the continuing pervasiveness of a patriarchal colonial consciousness (Baldry and Cunneen 2014).

The government's legislative and policy response to violence against women and child abuse which underpinned the Intervention brought together particular racialised and gendered understandings of Aboriginality: 'traditional' Aboriginal men were particularly to blame for abuse and violence, and Aboriginal women and children were seen as passive and hapless victims. Presented as a response to family violence in Indigenous communities, the Commonwealth *Crimes Amendments (Bail and Sentencing) Act 2006* restricted the courts from taking customary law into consideration in bail applications and when sentencing. The legislation drew an incontrovertible link between Indigenous culture and gendered violence. A raft of other legislation was introduced criminalising alcohol possession and consumption and possession of pornography in designated Aboriginal communities, as well as an increased police presence in many communities. As Moreton-Robinson (2009a, p. 68) has noted, the 'impoverished conditions under which Indigenous people live [were] rationalised as a product of dysfunctional cultural traditions and individual bad behaviour'; Indigenous pathology was to blame for the situation of violence and abuse, 'not the strategies and tactics of patriarchal white sovereignty'. The construction of Aboriginal culture in the NT as supporting violence and sexual abuse was the reinvention of a well-established colonial trope: Aboriginal people represented the 'new barbarism' (Cunneen 2007).

The Intervention was also a clear example of Chatterjee's (1993) notion of the rule of colonial difference. Aboriginal people in the NT were placed outside the framework of civil society because of their racially constructed difference. Their most important legal protection against racial discrimination, the Commonwealth *Racial Discrimination Act 1975*, was suspended by parliament to allow the racially discriminatory aspects of the Intervention to occur without challenge to the courts. In a further sign of Aboriginal removal from civil society, the Australian military was used to support the Intervention. In addition to new forms of criminalisation, various extensive forms of surveillance and control were introduced over a range of matters from medical records and school attendance to social security entitlements, all of which impacted Indigenous women, men and children.

The immediate rationale for the Federal government intervention in the NT was the *Little Children are Sacred* report on Aboriginal child sexual assault. Similar reports, mostly written by Indigenous taskforces, had emerged around the same time in New South Wales, Western Australia, Victoria and Queensland on Aboriginal child sexual assault and family violence (Cunneen 2007). What these inquiries have in common is that they reiterate the importance of the following:

- the significance of Indigenous self-determination and developing negotiated responses to violence and abuse with Indigenous communities;
- strengthening Indigenous culture is the answer, not the barrier, to improving the situation in relation to violence;

- developing and extending Aboriginal law is part of the solution to the problem, and not a cause of the problem;
- the need to see the current problems of abuse and violence as directly connected to the trauma caused by successive colonial policies;
- the need to trust Indigenous families and communities to look after their own children;
- the need to reengage Indigenous men (Cunneen 2007, p. 44).

In responding to the Intervention, a coalition of Aboriginal organisations called for governments to identify, support and extend community capacities to respond to the issue of violence. In particular the organisations noted the opportunity to develop existing community-driven, but largely underfunded, initiatives such as Indigenous night patrols, safe houses, safe family programs, community justice groups, and mediation services (Cunneen 2007, p. 45). These demands by Aboriginal organisations in the NT were largely ignored.

The impact of the NT Intervention

A consistent criticism of the Intervention has been its suspension of human rights and its neo-paternalism (Altman 2007) – a colonial strategy harking back to earlier approaches of direct and unambiguous racialised control of Indigenous peoples. In relation to human rights, there is little contention that the Intervention breached Australia's international human rights obligations, particularly in relation to the racial discriminatory aspects of income management, alcohol and pornography restrictions, the special powers of the Australian Crime Commission and other matters (Anaya 2010, p. 45–49). More generally, Aboriginal people in the NT have subsequently reported increased levels of racial discrimination (Cunneen et al. 2014, p. 227).

However, the effects of a reinvigorated colonial approach to Indigenous people extend well beyond discrimination. And given that the rationale for the Intervention was the protection of victimised women and children, what have been the consequences for them? We argue that in fact government policy has created a range of secondary victimisation effects. Following the Intervention there was a new level of penal punitiveness in the NT. Imprisonment rates grew by 34 per cent between 2008 and 2012 (ABS 2012, p. 56). It is clear that the increase in imprisonment was *much greater* for Aboriginal women than for Aboriginal men.[5] The removal of Aboriginal children from their families by child protection agencies also escalated in the years following the Intervention (Northern Territory Government 2010, p. 21).

The Intervention introduced significant changes to social policy governed by increased state regulatory processes, such as housing tenancy leases, requirements around antisocial behaviour, school attendance and social security income management. Indigenous people were ill-equipped to respond to these new demands, and the Intervention generated a raft of new legal and social problems for Indigenous people in the NT. Research has indicated that Indigenous women in particular have been negatively impacted because of these changes (Cunneen et al. 2014). For example, in relation to housing, school attendance requirements, social security payments and income management, Indigenous women are *more likely* to identify a problem than are Indigenous men (Cunneen et al. 2014, pp. 223–224).

The Intervention showed clearly the denial of Indigenous knowledge and understanding of violence in their communities. It consistently subjugated the voices of Indigenous people and their demands for appropriate responses to Indigenous victims and offenders. Finally, it actively reinscribed systems of domination and control through criminal justice and social policy that further marginalised, institutionalised and criminalised the very victims it ostensibly set out to save: Indigenous women and children.

Conclusion

The inadequacy of relying on dominant Eurocentric approaches in order to understand and respond to the over-representation of Indigenous peoples, both as victims and offenders, indeed confirms that the 'master's tools will never dismantle the master's house' (Lorde 1984, cited in Denzin 1997, p. 53). Rather, the pressing quest to delineate, decentre and challenge the epistemological privilege of colonising paradigms and processes demands that paradigms shift. As inferred by our use of de Sousa Santos's quote at the beginning section of our chapter, achieving global social justice for the growing number of victimised and criminalised Indigenous peoples rests upon achieving global cognitive justice. In other words, for laws, policies and practices to shift, we need to reinscribe an Indigenous understanding of the world.

We argue in conclusion that such a reinscription requires at a minimum three features.First, there is a need to foreground an understanding of the coloniality of power[6] which is both implicit and explicit in governmental responses to Indigenous peoples' victimisation and criminalisation. There is also a requirement to understand how the coloniality of power influences Indigenous peoples' reactions to the way the state defines and responds to victimisation and criminalisation. Alternative and broader categories of victimisation are important, in particular in relation to the role of colonial states in abrogating Indigenous human rights.

Second, there is a need for a much deeper understanding of Indigenous ontologies and the way the 'self' is understood in connectivity to the social, physical and spiritual world. The centrality of interrelationality to Indigenous worldviews means that the understandings of particular situations and contexts, and the decisions which people make, are formed from within a worldview that is in strong contrast to colonising assumptions regarding individual decision making based on autonomous self-interest.

Finally, there is a need to respect Indigenous political demands for self-determination. Understanding self-determination requires cognisance of the scepticism which many Indigenous people have in the ability of the colonial state to deliver just outcomes. The demand for self-determination is a demand for greater control in decision making over how best to deal with problems of crime and victimisation that beset many communities. Self-determination in this context also requires a move away from linking victimisation and criminalisation with portrayals of Indigenous dysfunction to seeing problems through the definitions from Indigenous people themselves. In this way, academics and allies to Indigenous people become not experts; rather, they become facilitators who assist in the promotion of Indigenous peoples' knowledges, voices, perspectives and aspirations for social justice and self-determination.

Notes

1. Throughout this chapter, the term *decolonisation* is used in its broadest sense for denoting the unmasking and deconstruction of imperialism, both in its old and new formations, alongside a search for sovereignty; for reclamation of knowledge, language and culture; and for the social transformation of the colonial relations between the colonised and the coloniser (Smith 2005, p. 88). We use the term *decolonising victimisation* to refer to the many critical, emancipatory and reflexive analytic processes and practices used to disrupt, interrogate, expose and transform the complex and oppressive social forces contributing to the victimisation of Indigenous peoples.
2. We are aware that the term victim 'is a word that evokes strong images of submissiveness, pain, loss of control and defeat' (Rock 2012, p. 41) – images that fail to capture the enduring resilience, resistance and strength of Indigenous peoples. Following Cornel West (1993, cited in Agozino 1997, p. 18), we reject the notion of passive victimhood; rather we assert the notion of victims as survivors who possess individual agency and 'who fight militantly against victimization' (Agozino 1997, p. 18).

3. Pollack (2013, p. 104) notes that the victimisation-criminalisation continuum 'challenged the prevailing victim-offender dichotomy by conceptualizing women's law-breaking as resistance to gender oppression and violence. The underlying assertion was that these coping strategies often propelled women into situations that put them at risk of being criminalized'. (See also Balfour 2012.)

4. The NT Emergency Response, initiated in 2006 and with a raft of legislation passed in 2007, used the army, social and welfare workers and the police to impose significant controls on many Aboriginal communities in the NT. This was claimed by the government of the day, led by Prime Minister John Howard, to be necessary to manage behaviour and respond to the victimisation of Aboriginal women and children.

5. Australian Bureau of Statistics (ABS) data is available on the number of Aboriginal men and women in NT prisons from 2010 to 2012. During this period the number of Aboriginal men imprisoned increased by 24 per cent; for Aboriginal women, the increase was 59 per cent (ABS 2010, Supplementary Data Cubes, Table 13; ABS 2012, Supplementary Data Cubes, Table 13).

6. We take the phrase from de Sousa Santos, who points to the colonialist nature of the modern world system – one of the implications of which is that the end of colonialism (in its official form) has not meant the end of colonial relations; the latter go on 'reproducing themselves as racist disqualifications of the other' (de Sousa Santos in Dalea and Robertson 2004, p. 159).

References

Agozino, B. 1997. *Black Women and the Criminal Justice System*. Aldershot: Ashgate.

ABS (Australian Bureau of Statistics) 2010. *Prisoners in Australia*. Canberra: ABS.

ABS (Australian Bureau of Statistics) 2012. *Prisoners in Australia*. Canberra: ABS.

Altman, J.C. 2007. *The Howard Government's Northern Territory intervention: Are neo-paternalism and Indigenous development compatible?*. Topical Issue No. 16/2007. Canberra: Centre for Aboriginal Economic Policy Research. http://caepr.anu.edu.au/Publications/topical/2007TI16.php [Accessed: 09 March 2014].

Anaya, J. 2010. *The Situation of Aboriginal Peoples in Australia*, New York, United Nations Human Rights Council. http://www2.ohchr.org/english/issues/indigenous/rapporteur/docs/ReportVisitAustralia.pdf [Accessed: 09 March 2014].

ATSISJC (Aboriginal and Torres Strait Islander Social Justice Commissioner) 2002. *Social Justice Report 2002*. Sydney: Human Rights and Equal Opportunity Commission.

ATSISJC (Aboriginal and Torres Strait Islander Social Justice Commissioner) 2004. *Social Justice Report 2004*. Sydney: Human Rights and Equal Opportunity Commission.

ATSISJC (Aboriginal and Torres Strait Islander Social Justice Commissioner) 2006. *Social Justice Report 2006*. Sydney: Human Rights and Equal Opportunity Commission.

Australian Institute of Criminology (AIC) 2013. *Indigenous Justice*. http://www.aic.gov.au/crime_types/in_focus/indigenousjustice.html [Accessed: 05 March 2014].

Baldry, E. and Cunneen, C. 2014. Imprisoned Indigenous Women and the Shadow of Colonial Patriarchy. *Australian and New Zealand Journal of Criminology* 47(2), pp. 276–298..

Balfour, G. 2012. Do Law Rreforms Matter? Exploring the Victimisation-Criminalisation Continuum in the Sentencing of Aboriginal Women in Canada. *International Review of Victimology* 19(1), pp. 85–102.

Barsh, R. and Youngblood Henderson, J. 1976. Tribal Courts, the Model Code, and the Police Idea in American Indian Policy. *Law and Contemporary Problems* 40(1), pp. 25–60.

Bartels, L. 2012. Violent Offending By and Against Indigenous Women. *Indigenous Law Bulletin* 8(1), pp. 19–22.

Blagg, H. 2000. *Crisis Intervention in Aboriginal Family Violence, Summary Report*. Partnerships Against Domestic Violence. Canberra: Commonwealth of Australia.

Blagg, H. 2008. *Crime, Aboriginality and the Decolonisation of Justice*. Sydney: Hawkins Press.

Blagg, H. and Smith, D. 1989. *Crime, Penal Policy and Social Work*. Essex: Longman.

Briskman, L. 2007. *Social Work with Indigenous Communities*. Sydney: Federation Press.

Carter, V.B. 2010. Factors Predicting Placement of Urban American Indian/ Alaskan Natives into Out-of-Home Care. *Children and Youth Services Review* 32, pp. 657–663.

Centre for Families, Children and the Courts (CFCC) 2012. *Native American Statistical Abstract: Violence and Victimisation*. http://www.courts.ca.gov/documents/Tribal-NAmericanStatsAbstract.pdf [Accessed: 05 March 2014].

Chakrabarty, D. 2006. Forward. In: Lea, T. et al. eds. *Moving Anthropology: Critical Indigenous Studies*. Darwin: Charles Darwin University Press, pp. iii–iv.

Chan, A. and Payne, J. 2013. *Homicide in Australia: 2008–09 to 2009–10 National Homicide Monitoring Program Annual Report*. Canberra: Australian Institute of Criminology.

Chatterjee, P. 1986. *Nationalist Thought and the Colonial World: A Derivative Discourse?* London: Zed Books.

Chatterjee, P. 1993. *The Nation and its Fragments. Colonial and Postcolonial Histories*. Princeton, NJ: Princeton University Press.

Cunneen, C. 2001. *Conflict, Politics and Crime*. St Leonards: Allen and Unwin.

Cunneen, C. 2006. Racism, Discrimination and the Over-Representation of Indigenous People in the Criminal Justice System: Some Conceptual and Explanatory Issues. *Current Issues in Criminal Justice* 17(3), pp. 329–346.

Cunneen, C. 2007. Assimilation and the Re-Invention of Barbarism. *Australian Indigenous Law Review* 11, pp. 42–45.

Cunneen, C. 2009. Criminology, Criminal Justice and Indigenous People: A Dysfunctional Relationship? *Current Issues in Criminal Justice* 20(3), pp. 323–336.

Cunneen, C. 2011. Indigeneity, Sovereignty and the Law: Challenging the Processes of Criminalisation. *South Atlantic Quarterly* 110(2), pp. 309–327.

Cunneen, C. 2014. Colonial Processes, Indigenous Peoples, and Criminal Justice Systems. In: Bucerius, T. and Tonry, M. eds. *The Oxford Handbook of Ethnicity, Crime, and Immigration*. Oxford: Oxford University Press, pp. 386–407.

Cunneen, C., Baldry, E., Brown, D., Brown, M., Schwartz, M. and Steel, A. 2013. *Penal Culture and Hyperincarceration. The Revival of the Prison.* Farnham: Ashgate.

Cunneen, C., Allison, F. and Schwartz, M. 2014. Access to Justice for Aboriginal People in the Northern Territory. *Australian Journal of Social Issues* 49(2), pp. 219–240.

Cunneen, C. and Rowe, S. 2014. Changing Narratives: Colonised Peoples, Criminology and Social Work. *International Journal for Crime, Justice and Social Democracy* 3(1), pp. 49–67.

Dalea, R. and Robertson, S. 2004. Interview with Boaventura de Sousa Santos. *Globalisation, Societies and Education* 2(2), pp. 147–160.

Davis, A. 2000. *Keynote Address: Color of Violence Conference Proceedings.* http://colorlines.com/archives/2000/10/the_color_of_violence_against_women.html [Accessed: 05 March 2014].

Day, A., Davey, L., Wanganeen, R., Howells, K., DeSantolo, J. and Nakata, M. 2006. The Meaning of Anger for Australian Indigenous Offenders: The Significance of Context. *International Journal of Offender Therapy and Comparative Criminology* 50(5), pp. 520–539.

Deer, S. 2004. Federal Indian Law and Violent Crime: Native Women and Children at the Mercy of the State. *Social Justice* 31(4), pp. 17–30.

Dell, C.A. and Kilty, J.M. 2013. The Creation of the Expected Aboriginal Woman Drug Offender in Canada: Exploring Relations between Victimisation, Punishment, and Cultural Identity. *International Review of Victimology* 19(1), pp. 51–68.

Denzin, N. 1997. *Interpretive Ethnography: Ethnographic Practices for the 21st Century.* London: Sage.

Denzin, N.K. and Lincoln, Y.S. 2008. Introduction. In: Denzin, N.K. et al. eds. *Handbook of Critical and Indigenous Methodologies.* London: Sage, pp. ix–20.

Department of Justice Canada 2012. *A Review of Research on Criminal Victimization and First Nations, Métis and Inuit Peoples 1990 to 2001.* http://www.justice.gc.ca/eng/pi/rs/rep-rap/2006/rr06_vic1/p5.html [Accessed: 05 March 2014].

Fallon, B., Chabot, M., Fluke, J., Blackstock, C., MacLaurin, B. and Tommyr, L. 2013. Placement Decisions and Disparities among Aboriginal Children: Further Analysis of the Canadian Incidence Study of Reported Child Abuse and Neglect Part A: Comparisons of the 1998 and 2003 surveys. *Child Abuse and Neglect* 37, pp. 47–60.

Foucault, M. 1980. *Power/Knowledge: Selected Interviews and Other Writings 1972–1977,* Translated by Colin Gordon et al. In: Gordon, C. ed. New York: Pantheon.

Green, S. and Baldry, E. 2008. Building Indigenous Australian social work. *Australian Social Work* 61(4), 389–402.

HRW (Human Rights Watch). 2013. *Those Who Take Us Away: Abusive Policing and Failures in Protection of Indigenous Women and Girls in Northern British Columbia, Canada.* http://www.hrw.org [Accessed: 05 March 2014].

Jackson, M. 1995. Justice and Political Power: Reasserting Maori Legal Processes. In: Hazlehurst, K. ed. *Legal Pluralism and the Colonial Legacy: Indigenous Experiences of Justice in Canada, Australia, and New Zealand.* Aldershot: Averbury Ashgate, pp. 243–263.

Kincheloe, J.L. 2006. Critical Ontology and Indigenous Ways of Being: Forging a Postcolonial Curriculum. In: Kanu, Y. eds. *Curriculum as Cultural Practice: Postcolonial Imaginations.* Toronto: University of Toronto Press, pp. 181–202.

Langton, M. 1992. The Wentworth Lecture: Aborigines and Policing, Aboriginal Solutions from Northern Territory Communities. *Australian Aboriginal Studies* 2, pp. 2–14.

Lawrie, R. 2003. *Speak Out, Speak Strong.* Sydney: Aboriginal Justice Advisory Committee.   http://www.communitybuilders.nsw.gov.au/893033_3.html [Accessed: 05 March 2014].

Macklin, A. and Gilbert, R. (2011). Working with Indigenous Offenders to end Violence. *Indigenous Justice Clearinghouse*, Brief 11, pp. 1–8.

Marchetti, E. and Downie, R. 2014. Indigenous People and Sentencing Courts in Australia, New Zealand, and Canada. In: Bucerius, S. and Tonry, M. eds. *The Oxford Handbook of Ethnicity, Crime, and Immigration.* Oxford: Oxford University Press, pp. 360–385.

McCaslin, W.D. and Breton, D.C. 2008. Justice as Healing: Going Outside the Colonisers' Cage. In: Denzin, N.K. et al. *Handbook of Critical and Indigenous Methodologies.* London: Sage Publication, pp. 511–530.

Memmott, P., Stacy, R., Chambers, C. and Keys, C. 2001. *Violence in Aboriginal Communities.* Canberra: Attorney-General's Department.

Moreton-Robinson, A. 2009a. Introduction: Critical Indigenous Theory. *Cultural Studies Review* 15(2), pp. 11–12.

Moreton-Robinson, A. 2009b. Imagining the good indigenous citizen: Race War and the Pathology of Patriarchal White Sovereignty. *Cultural Studies Review* 15(2), pp. 61–79.

Moreton-Robinson, A. and Walter, M. 2009. Indigenous Methodologies in Social Research. In: Walter, M. eds., *Social Research Methods.* Oxford: Oxford University Press, pp. 95–109.

Moreton-Robinson, E. and Walter, M. 2011. *Leadership in Indigenous Research Capacity Building: Implementing and Embedding an Indigenous Research Methodologies Masterclass Module.* Sydney: Australian Learning and Teaching Council.

NISATSIC (National Inquiry into the Separation of Aboriginal and Torres Strait Islander Children from their Families). 1997. *Bringing Them Home.* Sydney: Human Rights and Equal Opportunity Commission.

Northern Territory Government. 2010. *Growing Them Strong Together*, Summary Report of the Board of Inquiry into the Child Protection System in the NT. Darwin: Northern Territory Government.

O'Shane, P. 1992. Aborigines and the Criminal Justice System. In Cunneen, C. ed. *Aboriginal Perspectives on Criminal Justice.* Sydney: The Institute of Criminology, pp. 3–7.

Pollack, S. 2013. An Imprisoning Gaze: Practices of Gendered, Racialised and Epistemic Violence. *International Review of Victimology* 19(1), pp. 103–114.

Porsanger, J. 2004. *An Essay about Indigenous Methodology.* http://septentrio.uit. no/index.php/nordlit/article/viewFile/1910/1776 [Accessed: 05 March 2014].

Ramirez, R. 2004. Healing, Violence, and Native American Women. *Social Justice* 31(4), pp. 109–116.

Rock, P. 2012. Theoretical Perspectives on Victimisation. In: Walklate, S. ed. *Handbook of Victims and Victimology.* Hoboken: Taylor and Francis, pp. 37–61.

Ross, L. 1998. *Inventing the Savage: The Social Construction of Native American Criminality.* Austin: University of Texas Press.

Ross, L. 2004. Native Women, Mean-Spirited Drugs, and Punishing Policies. *Social Justice* 31(4), pp. 54–62.

32 *Chris Cunneen and Simone Rowe*

SCRGSP (Steering Committee for the Review of Government Service Provision) 2014. *Report on Government Services 2014*. Melbourne: Productivity Commission. http://www.pc.gov.au/__data/assets/pdf_file/0004/132358/rogs-2014-volumef-chapter15.pdf [Accessed: 05 March 2014].

Sherwood, J. 2010. *Do No Harm: Decolonising Aboriginal Health Research*. PhD Thesis, University of New South Wales. http://www.library.unsw.edu.au [Accessed: 05 March 2014].

Smith, L.T. 2005. On Tricky Ground: Researching the Native in the Age of Uncertainty. In: Denzin, N.K. and Lincoln, Y.S. eds. *The Sage Handbook of Qualitative Research*. 3rd ed. London: Sage, pp. 85–107.

Smith, L.T. 2012. *Decolonising Methodologies: Research and Indigenous Peoples*. 2nd ed. London: Zed Books.

Spivak, G.C. 1995. Can the Subaltern Speak? In: Ashcroft, B. et al. eds. *The Post-Colonial Studies Reader*. London: Routledge, pp. 24–28.

Statistics New Zealand 2010. Crime Victimisation Patterns in New Zealand. http://www.stats.govt.nz/browse_for_stats/people_and_communities/crime_and_justice/crime-victimisation-patterns-nz.aspx [Accessed: 05 March 2014].

Stubbs, J. 2008. Critical Criminological Research. In: Anthony, T. and Cunneen, C. eds. *The Critical Criminological Companion*. Sydney: Federation Press, pp. 6–17.

Stubbs, J. 2011. Indigenous Women in Australian Criminal Justice: Over-Represented but Rarely Acknowledged. *Australian Indigenous Law Review* 15(1), pp. 47–63.

Tauri, J. 1998. Family Group Conferencing: A Case Study of the Indigenisation of New Zealand's Justice System. *Current Issues in Criminal Justice* 10(2), pp. 168–182.

Tauri, J.M. and Webb, R. 2012. A Critical Appraisal of Responses to Maori Offending. *The International Indigenous Policy Journal* 3(4), pp. 1–16.

Taylor, I. Walton, P. and Young, J. 1973. *The New Criminology: For a Social Theory of Deviance*. London: Routledge.

Victorian Equal Opportunity and Human Rights Commission (VEOHRC) 2013. *Unfinished Business: Koori Women and the Justice System*. Carlton, VIC: VEOHRC. http://www.humanrightscommission.vic.gov.au [Accessed: 05 March 2014].

Walklate, S. 1990. Researching Victims of Crime: Critical Victimology. *Social Justice* 17(3), pp. 25–42.

Walklate, S. 2012. Conclusion. In: Walklate, S. ed. *Handbook of Victims and Victimology*. Hoboken: Taylor and Francis, pp. 484–494.

Walter, M.M. 2010. The Politics of the Data: How the Australian Statistical Indigene is Constructed. *International Journal of Critical Indigenous Studies* 3(2), pp. 45–56.

Watson, I. 2007. Aboriginal Women's Laws and Lives: How Might We Keep Growing the Law?. *Australian Feminist Law Journal* 26, pp. 95–107.

Wesley, M. 2012. Marginalised: The Aboriginal Women's experience in Federal Corrections. http://www.publicsafety.gc.ca. [Accessed: 05 March 2014].

Wilson S. 2001. What is Indigenous Research Methodology? *Canadian Journal of Native Education* 25(1), pp. 175–179.

2
Environmental Victimology and Ecological Justice

Rob White

Environmental victimology refers to the study of the social processes and institutional responses pertaining to victims of environmental crime. It is a new area of criminological concern (Hall 2013), and it can be intellectually located as a subset of 'green criminology', itself a relatively new development (White and Heckenberg 2014). This chapter provides a broad overview of environmental victimology and, in particular, how research in this area is engaging with both human and nonhuman environmental victims.

Students of environmental victimology face two key issues at the outset. The first issue relates to the fact that many environmentally destructive practices are quite legal (such as use of clear-felling techniques in forestry) and the law is frequently utilised to regulate but not prevent environmentally damaging activities (such as land, air and water pollution). Carbon emissions and the trading of wild animals, for example, are not in themselves criminal activities. It is only under certain conditions that they are deemed to be so. The first part of the chapter therefore discusses the differences between 'environmental crime' and 'environmental harm' and addresses the question of legality in the construction of environmental victims.

The second issue relates to who or what is being victimised and how this is construed in law as well as in popular consciousness. From the point of view of green criminology, adequate analysis of the 'subjects' of environmental victimisation must extend beyond just consideration of humans as victims. Accordingly, the chapter incorporates consideration of both specific matters arising from the study of human environmental victims and those that pertain specifically to the nonhuman environmental victims. Before doing this, however, it charts out some of the

33

key dimensions of environmental victimology as a distinctive form of analysis.

The conceptual parameters of environmental victimology

The key focus of green criminology is environmental crime. For some writers, environmental crime is defined narrowly within strict legal definitions – it is what the law says it is. For others, however, the question arises whether the focus of study should be solely that which is 'criminal' or legally defined or whether other actions and activities that can be argued or proven to be harmful or worthy of concern should also be embraced (Beirne and South 2007; White 2013a). In fact, for a green perspective this is fairly easy to answer if the primary aim is to engage with damage, degradation and depletion affecting the earth, environment and all species because much of this is caused by *legal* behaviour. Legal harms are therefore of central interest to green criminologists, as much as is formally specified illegal activity.

Specific types of harm as described in law include things such as illegal transport and dumping of toxic waste; the transportation of hazardous materials, such as ozone depleting substances; the illegal traffic in real or purported radioactive or nuclear substances; the illegal trade in flora and fauna; and illegal fishing and logging. A more expansive definition of environmental crime or harm includes transgressions that are harmful to humans, environments and nonhuman animals, regardless of legality per se and includes environmental-related harms that are facilitated by the state, as well as corporations and other powerful actors, insofar as these institutions have the capacity to shape official definitions of environmental crime in ways that allow, condone or excuse environmentally harmful practices (White 2011).

Green criminology therefore provides an umbrella under which to theorise about and critique both *illegal* environmental harms (i.e. environmental harms currently defined as unlawful and therefore punishable) and *legal* environmental harms (i.e. environmental harms currently condoned as lawful but which are nevertheless socially and ecologically harmful). How harm is conceptualised is thus partly shaped by how the legal–illegal divide is construed within specific research and analysis.

This approach to environmental harm mirrors that offered in the 'social harm' literature. One of the hallmarks of 'social harm' as a concept is that it directs writers to critically consider wider social contexts and the limitations of conventional approaches, particularly criminological, to harm (Hillyard et al. 2004; Hillyard et al. 2005; Hillyard and Tombs

2007). Indeed, for some, a standard criminological approach to harm is inherently limiting and should be eschewed in favour of an alternative discipline, sometimes referred to as 'zemiology' (Hillyard and Tombs 2007). Others are less convinced that criminology ought to be left behind, highlighting the long tradition within criminology of challenges to legalistic, narrow definitions of crime and harm (Friedrichs and Schwartz 2007; Matthews and Kauzlarich 2007).

Social harms are ubiquitous precisely because they stem from and are ingrained in the structures of contemporary societies (Pantazis and Pemberton 2009). However, whereas social harm is generally defined in terms of *human* needs, rights and being, the subject matter of green criminology, and more specifically environmental victimology, is concerned with the *nonhuman* as well as the human (White 2013a). To approach and appreciate concern for both of these demands a different kind of analytical framework than what is usually provided within the social harm literature.

There are three important dimensions to the study of environmental victims that provide context for the specific discussions to follow. First, much environmental harm has traditionally been ignored, downplayed or trivialised. This has had ramifications for analysis of environmental victims. For example, in a report that maps the contours of environmental crime and victimisation, Skinnider (2011, p. 2) observes that 'historically, research on environmental crime has lacked the theoretical and methodological depth applied to other traditional crimes'. In part, this is the result of perceptions of environmental crime as 'victimless' to the extent that 'they do not always produce an immediate consequence [and] the harm may be diffused or go undetected for a lengthy period of time' (Skinnider 2011, p. 2). This is further compounded by the condoning of environmentally harmful activities by governments, industry and in some cases particular communities and society as a whole. As a result, 'victims of environmental harm are not widely recognised as victims of "crime" and thus are excluded from the traditional view of victimology which is largely based on conventional constructions of crime' (Skinnider 2011, p. 2).

Second, taking into account both the human and the nonhuman necessarily complicates the study of environmental harm and its effects. It also throws up intriguing questions about how environmental victimhood is socially constructed and how it might best be addressed concretely. Environmental victimisation is not a solely human experience, and this is acknowledged in recent commentaries that argue that 'the biosphere and non-human biota have intrinsic value independent of their utilitarian or instrumental value for humans' (Preston 2011, p. 143). Rivers, mountains, animals and plants, specific ecosystems, all of these can be considered victims in particular circumstances.

More expansive definitions of rights and justice thus extend the definition of 'victim' to include the nonhuman in the moral equation. From an eco-justice perspective, there are three broad conceptualisations of harm (White 2013a). Each of these is construed in relation to particular notions of rights and justice: with variable focus on humans, environments and animals. Justice within an eco-justice perspective is initially framed in terms of the subject or victim that is liable to be harmed.

- *Environment justice* – the victim is humans
  environmental rights are seen as an extension of human or social rights so as to enhance the quality of human life, now and into the future.
- *Ecological justice* – the victim is specific environments
  human beings are merely one component of complex ecosystems that should be preserved for their own sake.
- *Species justice* – the victim is animals and plants
  animals have an intrinsic right to not suffer abuse and plants have an intrinsic right to not suffer the degradation of habitat to the extent that threatens loss of biodiversity.

The investigation of environmental crime and the victims of environmental crime therefore have to contend with relative disinterest in the topic area, until very recently, within criminology and the complexities that arise when questions of environmental, ecological and species justice are taken seriously.

Third, to fully appreciate the nature of global environmental crimes and environmental victimisation, it is essential to consider the physical location of harms within particular geographical contexts. Varying types of environmental harm pertain to different geographical levels. Some issues are on a planetary scale (e.g. global warming); others on a regional scale (e.g. oceans and fisheries); some are national in geographical location (e.g. droughts in particular African countries); and others are local (e.g. specific oil spills). Similarly, laws tend to be formulated in particular geographically defined jurisdictions. The priority issues at any point in time will depend in part upon local contexts and both local environmental and criminogenic factors (e.g. rare species living in particular kinds of habitat). At the country level, different kinds of crimes and harms are linked to specific national contexts and to particular geographical regions. For example, threats to biodiversity have been associated with illegal logging and deforestation in the Atlantic Forest of Brazil; illegal wildlife hunting and trade in Chiapas, Mexico; the commercial-scale illegal logging and shipment of illegal logs in Papua Province, Indonesia; and illegal fishing with dynamite and cyanide in Palawan, the Philippines (Akella and Cannon 2004).

Environmental harm may originate in a specific location, but due to natural processes of water and air movement and flow, it can spread to other parts of a city, another region, another country or another continent. A localised problem thus contains the seeds of a global dilemma. Environmental harm such as dioxins in water is both temporal and spatial in nature. That is, the harm itself actually moves across time and space, covering wide areas and with long-lasting effects. Moreover, toxins accumulate over time. In other words, there is a cumulative impact on waterways and aquatic life, and small amounts of poison may eventually lead to great concentrations of toxicity in fish and other living creatures of the water, with major social consequences for fishers and human consumers of fish.

It is likewise important to appreciate the interrelationship between built and natural environments. On the one hand, it long recognised that the lungs of the planet are its forests, and therefore wilderness areas need to be protected not only for intrinsic but instrumental reasons. What happens to the global forests affects how humans, among other creatures, live in the built environments of the city. On the other hand, even where 'natural' areas are subject to conservation orders and state protection, as in the case of national parks, problems may flow from the cities to these areas. For example, some national parks in the United States are more polluted than cities; they have ozone levels that are higher than some major metropolitan areas. The source of the problem tends to be located elsewhere and takes the form of power-plant emissions, among other causes (Cooper 2002).

Specific incidents, trends and issues can be analysed, therefore, in terms of local conditions and international influences. Worthy of concern, for example, are issues pertaining to the ownership and control over heavily polluting factories in Mexico, the transfer of toxic waste to the Ivory Coast due to lax regulation and state corruption, the impact of forest sequestration schemes on local communities in Africa, the involvement of mafia in waste and pollution control in Naples, and the BP oil spill off the coasts of Louisiana and Florida in the Gulf of Mexico. Each case deserves close attention to the specific factors arising from the particular 'spaces' in which they have emerged (White 2008; White and Heckenberg 2014).

Environmental victimology and the human factor

In its narrow formulations, environmental victimisation refers to specific forms of harm which are caused by acts or omissions leading to the presence or absence of environmental agents which are associated with *human* injury (Williams 1996). According to Williams (1996 p. 21), environmental victims are 'those of past, present, or future generations who are injured as a consequence of change to the chemical, physical, microbiological, or psychosocial environment, brought about by deliberate or reckless, individual or collective, human act or act of omission'. In response to a growing body of literature on nonhuman victims, within green criminology and other disciplines and fields, this definition of 'victim' is now being extended to include animals, plants and ecosystems. This is discussed at greater length later on.

As noted, in the specific area of environmental victimology, the literature to date has tended to focus on humans as victims rather than other on species or particular environments (see, e.g.Jarrell and Ozymy 2012; Hall 2013; Williams 1996). This is not surprising, given that the complexities and development of victimology as a specific sub-discipline of criminology has primarily been due to the attention given to the dynamic nature of relationships between human actors as perpetrators, as victims, and as observers (Fattah 2010; Rock 2007). It also reflects the concerns and campaigns of the environmental justice movement, which tend to focus attention on particular human population groups and specific human communities (Bullard 2005; Pellow 2007; Pezzullo and Sandler 2007). As our collective knowledge of global environmental harm increases, so too is there a growing appreciation that those who suffer environmental victimisation deserve sustained analysis and strategic interventions in their own right (see Hall 2013).

Environmental victimology, as such, has until recently been less concerned with nonhuman animals and specific biospheres than with the interests and well-being of humans in specific circumstances. In this regard it is useful to heed the lessons of mainstream victimology, that being and becoming a victim is never socially neutral. This holds true for environmental victimisation as it does for other sorts of victim making. Fattah (2010, p. 46) makes the comment that

> In most instances victims are not chosen at random, and in many cases the motives for the criminal act develop around a specific and non-exchangeable victim. Therefore, an examination of victim

characteristics, of the place the victim occupies, and the role the victim plays in these dynamic processes is essential to understanding why the crime was committed in a given situation, at a given moment, and why a particular target was chosen.

This should not be interpreted as suggesting that somehow the victim is responsible in some way for their targeting. Rather, it is an acknowledgement that the more one examines specific actions that produce and involve environmental victims, the greater the consensus that those who suffer harm do so because of their specific proximity and/or relationship to perpetrators of the harm. Largely these consist of relations of power, domination and exploitation. It is the social, economic and political characteristics of victim populations that make them vulnerable to victimisation in the first place. Some people suffer more than others when it comes to poor environmental living conditions and/or events that are disastrous to their lives. The majority of human victims of environmental degradation – stemming from industrial and commercial activities, global warming, loss of biodiversity and increased waste and pollution – are the poor and the dispossessed. While all of us are threatened by global environmental disaster, there remain large social differences in the likelihood of exposure and subsequent resilience to injury, harm and suffering.

When it comes to measuring the value of human life some people count more than others, and in some circumstances the health and wellbeing of certain people will be sacrificed in favour of business profits and 'national' interests. This can be quantified in terms of United Nations figures on world poverty, on disease, on illnesses related to indoor and outdoor air pollution, on life expectancy and on other similar data sets (see, e.g. the differential impact of air pollution, as discussed by Walters 2013).

Victimisation is also measurable in terms of production processes worldwide in which destruction of local environments is part and parcel of resource extraction, the recycling of commodities and expanding forms and mountains of waste (Stretesky et al. 2014). In Asia, for example, 'recycling' of e-waste presents certain types of opportunities:

> The open burning, acid baths and toxic dumping pour pollution into the land, air and water and exposes the men, women and children of Asia's poorer peoples to poison. The health and economic costs of this trade are vast and, due to export, are not born by the western consumers nor the waste brokers who benefit from the

trade. (Basel Action Network/Silicon Valley Toxics Coalition [BAN/ SVTC] 2002, p. 1)

For that which is not 'recycled', the solution is simply disposal, however and wherever local conditions allow: 'Vast amounts of E-waste material, both hazardous and simply trash, is burned or dumped in the rice fields, irrigation canals and along waterways' (BAN/SVTC 2002, p. 2). The problems of waste and of trade thus feed into each other, compounding already difficult circumstances. Recent research on e-waste confirms the vast extent of the transfers from developed countries to less developed countries and the considerable harms to which local communities are exposed in Africa and Asia (Bisschop 2012; Gibbs et al. 2010; Lundgren 2012). Meanwhile, in developed countries such as the United States, the United Kingdom, Canada and Australia, mining activities, and especially 'fracking', have emerged as major public issues due to concerns about pollution, greenhouse gas emissions and contamination of groundwater (Cleary 2012; Klare 2012).

Who is affected by activities carried out by powerful industries is also partly a matter of where and when. For example, the Arctic region is inhabited by some 4 million people, including more than 30 different Indigenous communities. Eight states – Canada, Denmark/Greenland, Finland, Iceland, Norway, the Russian Federation, Sweden and the United States – have territories in the Arctic region. While ostensibly a pristine environment where local peoples rely upon traditional food sources, for decades numerous pollutants have been impacting the Arctic and the people and animals that live there (European Environment Agency 2010; United Nations Environment Programme, 2007). This pollution originated elsewhere, especially in industrial heartlands such as the United States, but the effect of transference has been devastating. In some parts of the Arctic, for example, breastfeeding mothers have been advised to supplement breast milk with powdered milk in order to reduce exposure to noxious chemicals (European Environment Agency 2010).

Denial of harm on the part of the advantaged and socially privileged is easier when stereotypes, denigrating images and self-interest are mobilised in order to ignore such harms. This has long been the substantive concern of environmental justice movements (see Bullard 2005; see also Hall 2013). Environmental injustice is accomplished precisely through the devaluing of those who suffer the consequences of environmental harms, not of their own making but stemming from decisions made by someone else, elsewhere in the world, in the interests of those who will never share their environmental risks and harms.

The subjective disposition and consciousness of people is also crucial to perceptions of threat, risk and imminent danger. The unequal distribution of exposure to environmental risks, whether in relation to the location of toxic waste sites or proximity to clean drinking water may not always be conceived as an 'environmental' issue, nor indeed as an environmental 'problem'. For instance, Harvey (1996) points out that the intersection of poverty, racism and desperation may occasionally lead to situations where, for the sake of jobs and economic development, community leaders actively solicit the relocation of hazardous industries or waste sites to their neighbourhoods. On the other hand, the underlying reasons may be cultural, as noted by Waldman (2007), who describes a local community in South Africa that saw the contamination effects of asbestos as 'natural'. This was due to a combination of religious beliefs (that stressed a passive stance to the world around them) and the fact that often harms that are imperceptible to the senses only exist as a problem if they are constituted as such in public discourse (and in particular, the public discourse of the village community). Sometimes, too, governments and regulatory agencies alike ignore near misses and early warnings, despite strong evidence to take precautions.

Consciousness of risk can also be studied from the point of view of differential risk within at risk populations. A particular suburb or city may be placed in circumstances that heighten risks to well-being and health for everyone (e.g. dumping of toxic waste in Abidjan, Ivory Coast, or the spraying of chemical pesticides in New York City). However, particularly where heightened risk is deemed to be 'acceptable' in terms of cost-benefit analysis, as in the use of pesticides to prevent the spread of disease borne by mosquitoes, there are 'hidden' costs that may not be factored in. For instance, children and those with chemical sensitivities will suffer disproportionately if chemicals are sprayed, since they are more vulnerable than others to ill effects arising from the treatment. In such circumstances, the crucial questions are not only 'how many will be harmed' but also 'who will be harmed'? (Scott 2005, p. 56).

To take another example of how distribution of risk impacts different groups in at risk populations, consider the case of Environmental Protection Agency (EPA) standards in the United States that limit the level of dioxin releases from paper mills into rivers and streams:

> These releases are known to contaminate fish, and so the EPA based its release levels on the average consumption of such fish. Yet Native American consumption is well known to be higher than the average

American, making the dioxin release a much greater health risk to Native Americans. (Schlosberg 2007, p. 60)

Vulnerability to environmental harm, therefore, is also due to social differences in how people utilise or interact with nature based on certain perceptions. All those who consume fish under the above circumstances may be at risk of dioxin poisoning, but certain groups are more vulnerable because of their particular cultural prescriptions and traditions.

For those who engage in systematic study of such questions, it is clear that, regardless of intent, the practical outcome of corporate and government action has been to ensure that disadvantaged groups end up living in the most hazardous and environmentally poor areas (Pellow 2007). This is so whether it is in the United States (Bullard 2005), Canada (Chunn et al. 2002), India (Engel and Martin 2006) or Australia (White, 2013b). Moreover, it is these communities that also suffer most from the extraction of natural resources. Specifically, in many places around the globe where minority or Indigenous peoples live, oil, timber and minerals are extracted in ways that devastate local ecosystems and destroy traditional cultures and livelihoods (Schlosberg 2004, 2007). In the United States, for example, the Chippewa people have fought against mining operations on their lands, knowing that mining on their ceded lands would lead to environmental destruction of the land and water, thereby destroying their means of subsistence (Clark 2002). As with similar activities elsewhere, contamination of the natural world constitutes an assault that goes to the heart of Indigenous culture and identity.

The context of global warming, declining oil resources and food crises puts even more of the world's ecological and economic burdens on the backs of the poor. As Shiva (2008, pp. 5–6) observes:

> First, they are displaced from work; then they bear a disproportionate burden of the costs of climate chaos through extreme droughts, floods, and cyclones; and then they lose once more when pseudo-solutions like industrial biofuels divert their land and their food. Whether it is industrial agriculture or industrial biofuels, car factories or superhighways, displacement and forced evictions of indigenous peoples and peasants from the land are an inevitable consequence of an economic model that creates growth by extinguishing people's rights.

Displacement from homeland is accelerating through the acquisition of large areas of arable land in developing countries by foreign governments and private companies (see White 2012). These land acquisitions are having major negative impacts on local people who are losing access to and control over the resources on which they depend and which are the rightful inheritance of future generations.

Vulnerabilities to environmental victimisation are not only due to geographical location but also due to other inequalities. For example, many countries have coastal areas that, especially in the context of climate change, are vulnerable to sea-level rise. But the Netherlands has the technological and financial capacity to protect itself to a greater extent than does Bangladesh. Thus, not only are poorer countries less responsible for the problem, they are simultaneously less able to adapt to the climate impacts they will suffer because they lack the resources and capacity to do so. This raises three key questions surrounding matters of justice: the question of responsibility (e.g. the North owes the South an 'ecological debt'); the question of who pays for action on mitigation and adaptation; and the question of who bears the costs of actions and inactions (see Bulkeley and Newell 2010).

Environmental victimisation may be direct or indirect, immediate or long-lasting, local or regional. It may involve lead in soils, dioxins in water and radioactivity in the atmosphere. It may be based upon routine industrial practices or stem from specific events such as climate-related disasters. The threat may be realised (due to actual presence or absence of something in the environment) or be potential (as in e.g. a proposed privatisation of drinking water or development plans to build a dam or pulp mill). Children are much more vulnerable to some types of environmental harm (e.g. toxic chemicals) than adults are. In other cases, victimisation is more a question of proximity to the harm (e.g. death and maiming related to explosions, poisoning related to industrial emissions).

Ecological justice and nonhuman environmental victims

A more expansive definition of environmental victimisation alludes to the inclusion of the nonhuman into the moral equation. For example, ecological notions of rights and justice see humans as but one component of complex ecosystems that should be preserved for their own sake, as supported by the notion of the rights of the environment. As Smith (1998, p. 99) puts it:

> By extending the moral community we are attributing intrinsic value to creatures and other natural things, as ends in themselves rather

than the means to some set of human ends.... In ethical terms, any set of moral rules should consider these duties toward non-human animals, the land, forests and woodland, the oceans, mountains and the biosphere.

This perspective asserts notions of interconnectedness and human obligations to the nonhuman world. All living things are bound together, and environmental matters are intrinsically global and trans-boundary in nature. Ecological justice demands that how humans interact with their environment be evaluated in relation to potential harms and risks to specific creatures and specific locales as well as the biosphere generally. This involves critical analysis of human intervention in the affairs of the natural world (White 2013a).

Consider, for example, the choices made by humans about which species receive human protection and which do not (see Sollund 2012). Endemic species (i.e. those which have an historical relationship with particular ecosystems in particular geographical areas) are not always the species that are most valued and most likely to gain support from human backers when it comes to situations of species competition. In this context, human decisions trade-off one species against another. The galaxias fish is a case in point. A number of types of this species of fish are unique to the island state of Tasmania in Australia. However, due to the destruction of habitat and the introduction of non-native species, they are now under serious threat.

The key problem is introduced trout species. Galaxias not only are forced to compete for food (insects that fall or land on the surface of the water) but are also preyed upon by non-native predators such as the brown trout and rainbow trout (Threatened Species Unit, Parks and Wildlife Service Tasmania 1998). Trout were introduced into Tasmania in the mid-1800s, primarily for the purposes of recreational fishing. Today they are also a valued part of the aquaculture industry. Almost all of government and private attention has been on protecting the trout, regardless of the consequences of this for the galaxias. This is because the trout is deemed a valued and valuable species (for tourism and for commercial food markets), while the plight of the galaxias is ignored since they have no economic value. Laws have been designed to protect the trout (e.g. catch limits, closed seasons and licences). While officially the galaxias is classified as 'protected', the fact is that its main predator has been encouraged to flourish regardless of the ecological outcome and the predator's impact on the future viability of the galaxias species. They are thus 'victims' (of policy and introduced predators) but not recognised as such.

The status and value of animals – of particular species and of individual animals – varies greatly according to circumstance and larger ecological patterns and trends (see White 2013a). Likewise, appreciation of rivers, mountains and oceans is contingent upon how these are conceptualised in popular discourse and legal opinion (Stone 1972). Whether and how the nonhuman is viewed as victim is a relatively new area of investigation within green criminology. Yet, environmental victimology cannot afford to omit such considerations as it develops further.

The law does allow for a modicum of protection for the nonhuman as well as the human. This is reflected in legislation pertaining to endangered species (e.g. particular animals, such as tigers) and to conservation more generally (e.g. in the form of national parks). Harm is central to these forms of social regulation as well; however, whether 'harm to the environment' is of consequence *unless* it is measured with reference to human values (e.g. economic, aesthetic and cultural) is of ongoing concern in regard to legal decision making (Lin 2006). In essence, natural objects (such as trees and forests) lack legal rights (and agency or volition), and so they must rely on humans to bring actions to protect them. Some argue that the inherent interests of 'natural objects' ought to be protected through legal actions by the objects themselves, with humans serving as their guardians or trustees (Stone 1972; Lin 2006).

To date, most judicial and legal attention has been on humans as environmental victims. The definition of 'victim' is, however, evolving and expanding. Public interest law, for example, has been utilised to give standing to human representatives of nonhuman entities, such as rivers and trees. For example, a river was represented at a restorative justice conference in New Zealand by the chairperson of the Waikato River Enhancement Society (Preston 2011, p.144, fn53). In an increasing number of cases, there are 'surrogate victims' who are recognised as representing the community affected (including harms to particular biotic groups and abiotic environs) for the purpose of the restorative process. Public trust and public interest law have been used to establish future generations as victims of environmental crime (Preston 2011; Mehta 2009): the victims include human as well as the environment and nonhuman biota, for which surrogate victims (such as parents or non Government Organisations (NGOs)) have provided representation. Who speaks for whom or what is nevertheless still controversial, especially when it comes to natural objects such as trees, rivers and specific ecosystems.

Acknowledgement of 'victim' status is crucial to understanding the ways in which environmental harm affects both the human and the nonhuman. This means locating creatures and environments within their unique ecological niche and context. It also means examining events and contemporary human practices from the vantage point of history and geography. For environmental victimology, a major challenge is to develop conceptual and scientific tools whereby 'value' and 'harm' can be measured, compared and evaluated. There are, invariably, conflicts involving the different interests and rights of humans, specific ecosystems and animal and plant species. How best to respond to these conundrums is precisely the main task of environmental victimology in the future.

For example, if analysis of victimisation is pitched at too high a level of abstraction, this will only reinforce rigid definitions and absolutist positions (e.g. humans come first; the earth is most important; any harm to animals is bad). Reinforcing these can preclude closely considered analysis of specific situations. An absolutist approach may contend, for instance, that humans should not, in any way, interfere with animals. This approach may be appropriate when dealing with a situation involving dingoes and kangaroos in the wilds of the Northern Territory in Australia but inappropriate when dealing with wandering polar bears in Churchill, Manitoba. Specific and situational analysis is required to fully elaborate the nature of a problem and the grounds for developing a reasonable solution and/or compromise to it. Context is crucial in this regard.

Bennison (2010) observes that conflicts of interest – between environments, humans and animals – ought to be evaluated from the point of view of not only moral criteria (such as animal rights or animal welfare) but also ecological criteria and by considering the total environment:

> killing domesticated animals that have escaped and established themselves in ecologically destructive nonendemic wild populations should only occur if it can be justified scientifically, culturally, ethnically, and morally. That justification is dependent on the protection of, for example, an endangered species in an area where that species has little chance of survival, and only upon ensuring that the nonhuman animals killed would not suffer in any way. Taking the life of any individual is in reality a denial of their intrinsic value, and denying such value in any individual should not be taken lightly. (Bennison 2010, pp. 194–195)

For environmental victimology, this implies several interrelated tasks. What needs to be considered is not only the type and degree of harm as this pertains to humans, ecosystems and animals but also the type and degree of harm, in particular places (including global spaces), and how these harms impact humans, ecosystems and animals over time. To not kill the seal at point A is to ensure the demise of fish at point B and the desolation of human communities at point C. To kill seals may be 'wrong' in absolutist terms, but what if the failure to cull seal herds compounds the suffering of human and nonhuman alike into the future, including members of the seal colony itself (White 2013a)?

Close scrutiny of the conditions pertaining to the human and the nonhuman also reveal instances of shared victimisation, as in the cases of climate change, illegal fishing and air pollution, in which many different species and ecosystems are somehow affected. There are also instances of specific victimisation, as in the case of some plant and animal species being vulnerable to harm but which may be unacknowledged due to remoteness of location or general human devaluation of species. As with humans, there will be differing degrees and durations of harm, injury and, in some cases, suffering as this pertains to animals and natural objects.

The distinctions between and among species and their relative status in legal and philosophical terms have ramifications for whom or what is defined as a victim. For example, the absence of animal considerations within mainstream victimology is due in part to the absence of legal status as 'persons' and thus the treatment of nonhuman animals as outside the usual realms of ordinary law and legal decision making. The difference in analytical approach is also the result of species differences in the exercise of agency, relating to issues of consciousness, response and social dynamics (including e.g. victim precipitation). Humans may be treated like animals (i.e. treated badly), but traditional victimology would nonetheless see human victims not as objects of harm (i.e. as victims of cruelty) but subjects with rights (i.e. victims of human rights violations).

As indicated above, inclusion of advocates who can speak on behalf of those who cannot – that is, those who voice concern about what is happening to trees, to soils, to bees and to orchids – is inherently problematic. There may be broad agreement that advocacy should also involve active listening, by humans, to the nonverbal communication from nature – the signals emanating from the natural world and its inhabitants – that denote things such as the impacts of climate change (e.g. oceans warming and insect eggs hatching earlier) (see Schlosberg 2007; Besthorn 2013). There is much to learn by bringing the nonhuman into the dialogue about ecological health and wellbeing that affects all.

Yet, who speaks for whom is nevertheless still controversial, especially when it comes to natural objects such as trees, rivers and specific biospheres. For instance, the 'voice' that gets heard when it comes to restoration policy is too often that of the human, not that of the nonhuman (Besthorn 2013). This raises important and fascinating issues regarding the criteria by which judgements around restoration are to be made and the kind of ecological and zoological expertise required to adequately be a surrogate victim for the nonhuman. These are matters that warrant much greater attention as environmental victimology continues to develop. They are also integral to the further development of effective policy and legal responses to the phenomenon of environmental victimisation.

Conclusion

In responding to environmental harm and victimisation, there are inevitably a range of vested interests and 'discourses' that contribute to the shaping of perceptions and issues (see Hannigan 2006). This implies differences among perspectives and a certain contentiousness of knowledge about the nature of the harm or crime.

Consider, for example, the variety of players who might be associated with disputes over toxic landfills or stockpiled mining tailings in a residential community adjacent to a mining operation. Because victimisation is a contestable social process that involves a wide range of individuals, it is important to identify stakeholders and their specific interests (e.g. workers and jobs as well as residents and amenity). It is useful to explore the diverse and often conflicting discourses around 'risk' and 'harm' by different stakeholders (e.g. medical practitioners' consciousness of risk in relation to the health department; loss of livelihood in the case of farmers; and limited perception that there is a problem from local miners).

Moreover, the marshalling of particular types of evidence is typically driven by very specific requirements for criteria (and forms of evidence) dictated by institutions and groups. Who says what and why is linked to specific social purposes and interests and to particular discursive domains. The language of crime and victimisation is reflective of how an environmental problem (in this case toxic landfills) is socially constructed depending upon how it is being considered, who is considering it and who is potentially affected and how.

As recent commentary also points out, policies and laws addressing environmental harms (such as carbon emissions) can have the consequence

of shutting down industries and destroying jobs, processes which disproportionately affect already deprived local and regional communities
(Davies 2014). Issues of social and ecological justice demand approaches
and responses that are sensitive to the conflicts over policy objectives
and communal needs. Pitting jobs against the environment, however,
reproduces false dichotomies in which conflicting human needs are
each put in jeopardy. Such a view ignores the substantive reality that
the dominant system of production is fundamentally intertwined with
the exploitation of both humans and nature (see Stretesky et al. 2014;
White 2013c).

Moreover, the setting up of the debate in this way reinforces an anthro-
pocentric interpretation of the issues. It is humans who count, one way
or the other (i.e. as being engaged in productive labour or not and as
being exposed to particular environmental hazards or not). But what
should we do about instances in which environmental victims who do
not have a 'voice' – such as animals, plants and particular ecosystems –
are under threat? Proof of harm still necessarily rests with human protec-
tors and advocates in this situation. Even so, there is plenty of scope to
take into account stakeholder interests, and even to some extent stakeholder 'perspectives', in cases involving nonhuman victimisation and
exploitation. As this chapter has argued, taking all of these interests
into account is also part of the ongoing challenge facing environmental
victimology now and into the future.

References

Akella, A. and Cannon, J. 2004. *Strengthening the Weakest Links: Strategies for Improving the Enforcement of Environmental Laws Globally*. Washington, DC: Conservation International.
Basel Action Network/Silicon Valley Toxics Coalition (BAN/SVTC). 2002. *Exporting Harm: The High-Tech Trashing of Asia*. Seattle and San Jose: BAN/SVTC.
Beirne, P. and South, N. eds. 2007. *Issues in Green Criminology: Confronting Harms against Environments, Humanity and Other Animals*. Cullompton: Willan.
Bennison, R. 2010. Ecological Inclusion: Unity Among Animals. In: Bekoff, M. ed. *Encyclopedia of Animal Rights and Animal Welfare, Volume 1*. Santa Barbara, CA: Greenwood Press, pp. 194–198.
Besthorn, F. 2013. Speaking Earth: Environmental Restoration and Restorative Justice. In: van Wormer, K. and Walker, L. eds. *Restorative Justice Today: Practical Applications*. Los Angeles: Sage, pp. 233–239.
Bisschop, L. 2012. Is It All Going To Waste? Illegal transports of e-waste in a European trade hub. *Crime, Law and Social Change* 58(3), pp. 221–249.
Bullard, R. ed. 2005. *The Quest for Environmental Justice: Human Rights and the Politics of Pollution*. San Francisco, CA: Sierra Club Books.
Bulkeley, H. and Newell, P. 2010. *Governing Climate Change*. London: Routledge.

Chunn, D., Boyd, S. and Menzies, R. 2002. 'We all live in Bhopal': Criminology Discovers Environmental Crime. In: Boyd, S., Chunn, D. and Menzies, R. eds. *Toxic Criminology: Environment, Law and the State in Canada.* Halifax, NS: Fernwood Publishing, pp. 7–24.

Clark, B. 2002. The Indigenous Environmental Movement in the United States. *Organization and Environment* 15(4), pp. 410–442.

Cleary, P. 2012. *Mine-Field: The Dark Side of Australia's Resources Rush.* Collingwood, Victoria: Black Inc.

Cooper, M. 2002. Bush and the Environment: Are the President's Policies Helping or Hurting? *The CQ Researcher* 12(7), pp. 865–896.

Davies, P. 2014. Green Crime and Victimization: Tensions between Social and Environmental Justice. *Theoretical Criminology* 18(3), pp. 300–316.

Engel, S. and Martin, B. 2006. Union Carbide and James Hardie: Lessons in Politics and Power. *Global Society* 20(4), pp. 475–490.

European Environment Agency. 2010. *EEA Signals: Biodiversity, Climate Change and You.* Copenhagen: European Environment Agency.

Fattah, E. 2010. The Evolution of a Young, Promising Discipline: Sixty Years of Victimology, a Retrospective and Prospective Look. In: Shoham, S., Knepper, P. and Kett, M. eds. *International Handbook of Victimology.* Boca Raton, FL: CRC Press, pp. 43–94.

Friedrichs, D. and Schwartz, M. 2007. Editor's Introduction: On Social Harm and a Twenty-First Century Criminology. *Crime, Law and Social Change* 48(1–2), pp. 1–7.

Gibbs, C., McGarrell, E. and Axelrod, M. 2010. Transnational White-Collar Crime and Risk: Lessons from the Global Trade in Electronic Waste. *Criminology and Public Policy* 9(3), pp. 543–560.

Hall, M. 2013. *Victims of Environmental Harm: Rights, Recognition and Redress Under National and International Law.* London: Routledge.

Hannigan, J. 2006. *Environmental Sociology.* 2nd ed. London: Routledge.

Harvey, D. 1996. *Justice, Nature and the Geography of Difference.* Oxford: Blackwell.

Hillyard, P. and Tombs, S. 2007. From "crime" to social harm? *Crime, Law and Social Change* 48(1–2), pp. 9–25.

Hillyard, P., Pantazis, C., Tombs, S. and Gordon, D. eds. 2004. *Beyond Criminology? Taking Harm Seriously.* London: Pluto Press.

Hillyard, P., Pantazis, C., Tombs, S., Gordon, D. and Dorling, D. 2005. *Criminal Obsessions: Why Harm Matters More Than Crime.* London: Crime and Society Foundation.

Jarrell, M. and Ozymy, J. 2012. Real Crime, Real Victims: Environmental Crime Victims and the Crime Victims' Rights Act (CVRA). *Crime, Law and Social Change* 58(4), pp. 373–389.

Klare, M. 2012. *The Race For What's Left: The Global Scramble for the World's Last Resources.* New York: Metropolitan Books, Henry Holt and Company.

Lin, A. 2006. The Unifying Role of Harm in Environmental Law. *Wisconsin Law Review* 3, pp. 898–985.

Lundgren, K. 2012. *The Global Impact of E-waste: Addressing the challenge.* Geneva: International Labour Organization.

Matthews, R. and Kauzlarich, D. 2007. State Crimes and State Harms: A Tale of Two Definitional Frameworks. *Crime, Law and Social Change* 48(1–2), pp. 43–55.

Mehta, M. 2009. *In the Public Interest: Landmark Judgements and Orders of The Supreme Court of India on Environment and Human Rights* (volume 1). New Delhi: Prakriti Publications.

Pantazis, C. and Pemberton, S. 2009. Nation States and the Production of Social Harm: Resisting the Hegemony of 'TINA'. In: Coleman, R., Sim, J., Tombs, S. and Whyte, D. eds. *State, Power, Crime.* London: Sage, pp. 214–233.

Pellow, D. 2007. *Resisting Global Toxics: Transnational Movements for Environmental Justice.* Cambridge, MA: MIT Press.

Pezzullo, P. and Sandler, R. 2007. Introduction: Revisiting the Environmental Justice Challenge to Environmentalism. In: Sandler, R. and Pezzullo, P. eds. *Environmental Justice and Environmentalism: The Social Justice Challenge to the Environmental Movement.* Cambridge, MA: MIT Press, pp. 1–24.

Preston, B. 2011. The Use of Restorative Justice for Environmental Crime. *Criminal Law Journal* 35(3), pp. 136–145.

Rock, P. 2007. Theoretical Perspectives on Victimization. In: Walklate, S. ed. *Handbook of Victims and Victimology.* Cullompton: Willan, pp. 37–61.

Scholsberg, D. 2004. Reconceiving Environmental Justice: Global Movements and Political Theories. *Environmental Politics* 13(3), pp. 517–540.

Schlosberg, D. 2007. *Defining Environmental Justice: Theories, Movements, and Nature.* Oxford: Oxford University Press.

Scott, D. 2005. When Precaution Points Two Ways: Confronting 'West Nile Fever'. *Canadian Journal of Law and Society* 20(2), pp. 27–65.

Shiva, V. 2008. *Soil Not Oil: Environmental Justice in an Age of Climate Crisis.* Brooklyn, NY: South End Press.

Skinnider, E. 2011. *Victims of Environmental Crime – Mapping the Issues.* Vancouver: The International Centre for Criminal Law Reform and Justice Policy.

Smith, M. 1998. *Ecologism: Towards Ecological Citizenship.* Minneapolis, MN: University of Minnesota Press.

Sollund, R. 2012. Speciesism as Doxic Practice Versus Valuing Difference and Plurality. In: Ellefsen, R., Sollund, R. and Larsen, G. eds. *Eco-global Crimes: Contemporary Problems and Future Challenges.* Farnham: Ashgate.

Stone, C. 1972. Should Trees Have Standing?: Toward Legal Rights for Natural Objects. *Southern California Law Review* 45, pp. 450–487.

Stretesky, P., Long, M. and Lynch, M. 2014. *The Treadmill of Crime: Political Economy and Green Criminology.* London: Routledge.

Threatened Species Unit, Parks and Wildlife Service Tasmania (1998). *Listing Statement – Swan Galaxias (Galaxias Fontanus).* www.dpiw.tas.gov.au/inter.nsf/attachment/rlig-5428gn/$file/swan.pdf.

United Nations Environment Programme 2007. *Global Environment Outlook.* New York: UNEP.

Waldman, L. 2007. When Social Movements Bypass the Poor: Asbestos Pollution, International Litigation and Griqua Cultural Identity. *Journal of Southern African Studies* 33(3), pp. 577–600.

Walters, R. 2013. Air Crimes and Atmospheric Justice. In: South, N. and Brisman, A. eds. *Routledge International Handbook of Green Criminology.* London: Routledge, pp. 134–149.

White, R. 2008. *Crimes Against Nature: Environmental Criminology and Ecological Justice.* Cullompton: Willan.

White, R. 2011. *Transnational Environmental Crime: Toward an Eco-Global Criminology*. London: Routledge.

White, R. 2012. Land Theft and Rural Eco-Crime. *International Journal of Rural Criminology* 1(2), pp. 203–217.

White, R. 2013a. *Environmental Harm: An Eco-Justice Perspective*. Bristol: Policy Press.

White, R. 2013b. Resource Extraction Leaves Something Behind: Mining and Environmental Justice. *International Journal for Crime and Justice* 2(1), pp. 50–64.

White, R. 2013c. Eco-Global Criminology and the Political Economy of Environmental Harm. In: South, N. and Brisman, A. eds. *Routledge International Handbook of Green Criminology*. London: Routledge, pp. 243–260.

White, R. and Heckenberg, D. 2014. *Green Criminology: An Introduction to the Study of Environmental Harm*. London: Routledge.

Williams, C. 1996. An Environmental Victimology. *Social Justice* 23(4), pp. 16–40.

3
Victimisation, Citizenship and Gender: Interrogating State Responses

Marie Segrave and Rebecca Powell

For over two decades human trafficking has been a high priority on the international agenda, attracting significant investment in legal and policy infrastructure across the globe (Lee 2011; Segrave 2013). This continues apace. As a consequence of such interest, a counter-trafficking industry has emerged – one stretching from the international to the local context that relies predominantly upon the traditional criminological configuration of crime: featuring victims (innocent women and children, most often) and offenders (traffickers) and the need for intervention in the form of rescue and justice for victims (most often conducted by the state via the criminal justice system). Such linear, black-and-white responses to trafficking are embedded in the three-Ps approach (prevention, protection and prosecution) that recently grew into the four-Ps approach (with the addition of partnerships), which is upheld by the United States as the 'fundamental framework' to address the problem of human trafficking globally (United States Department of State [hereinafter USDOS] 2014). Key national and international counter-trafficking instruments, such as US Department of State's *Trafficking in Persons Report*, the UN *Protocol to Prevent, Suppress and Punish Trafficking in Persons, Especially Women and Children*, the UN *Model Law against Trafficking in Persons*, and others further reiterate 'best practice' in addressing trafficking as a 'law and order' one, erected on 'ideal victim' and 'ideal offender' stereotypes (Christie 1986; see also Milivojevic and Pickering 2013; Segrave et al. 2009). The counter-trafficking industry that has being borne out of this context, as Weitzer and Ditmore argue (2010, pp. 325–326), is founded upon a moral equation that defines human trafficking 'as an unqualified evil and sees its mission as a righteous enterprise with both symbolic goals (attempting to redraw or bolster normative boundaries and moral standards) and instrumental ones (providing relief to victims, punishing evildoers)'. However, the clarity of the counter-trafficking rhetoric belies the complexity and the lived experiences of exploitation.

While narratives of extreme victimisation offer a straightforward response in terms of rescuing victims and acknowledging the harm that has taken place, human trafficking is challenging to detect and consequently the majority of victims remain largely unseen and unheard. Difficulties identifying and responding to victims' needs is due in part to the complexity of human trafficking cases. They rarely involve extreme forms of exploitation, such that it may not always be immediately clear that abuse has taken/is taking place (Hoyle et al. 2011 O'Brien 2013; Segrave et al. 2009). Another layer of complexity is the often complicated migration status of victims; in many cases, victims of human trafficking are also irregular non-citizens (and/or non-citizens who are working in breach of visa conditions) (O'Connell Davidson 2010; Segrave et al. 2009; Simeunovic-Patic 2005). Thus, victims of trafficking may also be non-citizens at risk of deportation. While counter-trafficking commitments often articulate that migration status is not an issue when victimisation is present, implementing this commitment poses challenges for authorities. In addition, while irregular migration status may be addressed via creating accessible short-term visas for potential victims of trafficking, the *limits* of this visa system and the absence of the broader support measures indicate that migration status and citizenship *do* ultimately matter and inform the boundaries of what is provided for and expected of victims of trafficking (Andrijasevic 2010).

For criminologists concerned with the study of victims and the analysis of how we define and respond to victim experiences, human trafficking has been an important location for the application of emerging critical criminological critiques pertaining to gender, victimisation and borders (Pickering and Ham 2014; Segrave et al. 2009). The analysis within this chapter offers some expansion of these areas of scholarship through bringing recent critiques together when considering local and global responses to human trafficking and victimisation. In this chapter, we examine the ways in which dominant gendered understandings of victimisation can and have been translated into responses to victims that are both narrow and largely unresponsive to victims' needs. We also consider the ways in which this reinforces gendered notions of victimisation that serve to undermine efforts to recognise and give voice to the broader experiences of victimisation and exploitation in trafficking. We reveal the pertinence of the emerging fields of criminological analysis of borders via an examination of the ways in which migration controls are intimately connected to the logic that underpins and justifies both the recognition and identification of victims and support provisions for victims.

Specifically, this chapter draws on Australia, Thailand and the UK as three case study nations to offer insight into the points of connection and diversion between local (national) contexts and the international context of counter-trafficking. It will examine these country's provisions for victims of trafficking, following the identification of victims by authorities,[1] with a focus on support and what happens when a case is closed from the perspective of authorities as defined by the policy and legislation in place (i.e. closed when it is determined there is no case to investigate or closed following a prosecution). We draw on publicly available information (including government policy documents, inquiries and reports, departmental annual reports and media releases in addition to non-governmental reports, submissions and media releases), to examine these processes.

Background: human trafficking as a contemporary international concern

In order to examine contemporary responses to human trafficking in various national contexts, we need to first canvass the international frameworks that have been formulated in response to human trafficking because they have been influential in the design of national responses implemented across the globe. While there has been considerable scholarly examination of the international covenants and conventions pertaining to human trafficking as they manifested prior to the contemporary emergence of this issue in the late 1990s (Doezema 2000; Kempadoo 2005; Saunders and Soderlund 2003; Segrave et al. 2009; Spencer and Broad 2012), for the purposes of this chapter we are concerned with the response of the international community over the past 15 years, focussing particularly on the recognition of victims and the response to victimisation.

In the year 2000 the primary international agreement on human trafficking came into being as a supplementary protocol of the UN *Convention against Transnational Organized Crime*. The *Protocol to Prevent, Suppress and Punish Trafficking in Persons, Especially Women and Children* (also referred to as the Palermo or Trafficking Protocol, hereinafter the Trafficking Protocol) came into effect in December 2003 (Krieg 2009) and was the culmination of extensive campaigns and activism around the contemporary emergence of human trafficking (Doezema 2002; Milivojevic and Pickering 2013; Pickering 2011). The aim of the Protocol is to assist in defining a 'comprehensive international approach' to trafficking and to provide a 'universal instrument that addresses all aspects of trafficking in persons' (Preamble: 1). The purpose of the Trafficking Protocol is:

(a) to prevent and combat trafficking in persons, paying particular attention to women and children;
(b) to protect and assist the victims of such trafficking with full respect for their human rights;
(c) to promote cooperation among state parties in order to meet those objectives (Article 2).

While victims appear to be an intended primary focus of the Trafficking Protocol, the design of and emphasis throughout the Trafficking Protocol has raised concerns regarding the secondary focus on victims. This concern is evidenced in a number of ways. First, the Trafficking Protocol is based on an assumed link between transnational organised crime (TOC), human trafficking and the trafficking in commodities such as drugs and weapons.[2] As a result of the TOC focus, it is argued, the Trafficking Protocol prioritises *crime management* through border security, criminal law, prosecution and punishment of traffickers as the required response to address and eliminate human trafficking (Lee 2011; Milivojevic and Pickering 2013; Segrave et al. 2009). The Trafficking Protocol places emphasis upon combating TOC via 'more [focus] on the criminal networks and less on their victims' (Oberholer 2003, p. 196). This is evident, for example, in Article 5 of the Protocol, which requires state parties to adopt measures to criminalise trafficking and bring to justice those who perform, participate in or organise trafficking offences. In relation to victims, the provisions pertaining to providing assistance and support (including protecting victims' privacy and identity as well as providing information, legal assistance, appropriate housing, counselling, medical and psychological assistance, employment and educational opportunities) are recommended in 'appropriate cases' and 'to [the] extent possible under...domestic law' (Article 6.1). Countries of destination are urged to 'consider' adopting mechanisms that will allow victims to remain in their countries either temporarily or permanently in 'appropriate cases' (Article 7), whereas countries of origin should facilitate return of their citizens or residents 'without undue or unreasonable delay' whereby it is 'preferable' for returns to be voluntary (Article 8.2). As Sullivan (2003, p. 84) has noted, the language the Trafficking Protocol adopts in relation to victims is 'hedged with minimalism and ambiguity'. In comparison, the requirements pertaining to creating legal mechanisms and enforcing them are direct and a require-ment of all signatories (Segrave and Milivojevic 2010). As Milivojevic and Pickering (2013, p. 594) put it, 'although it was claimed that "[t]he fact that trafficking is formally integrated into the sphere of the combat of transnational organised crime does not mean that it has nothing more to do with human rights" (Chew 2005, p. 75), the shift towards the punitive, law and order-driven state intervention [has been] stri-dent and largely unchallenged'. Within this context, measures aimed at supporting victims remain optional and ambiguous, thus framing the victim of trafficking as a secondary concern to criminal justice meas-ures that increasingly require border regulatory measures to identify and intercept transnational organised crime practices.

Independent of the developments in the United Nations in 2000, the United States adopted its own international agenda for addressing human trafficking via the *Victims of Trafficking and Violence Protection Act of 2000*, or the Trafficking Victims Protection Act (TVPA). Unlike the Trafficking Protocol, this mechanism created an international moni-toring body as a central component of its counter-trafficking strategy. Establishing itself as the 'global sheriff' on efforts to address and erad-icate trafficking (Chuang 2006) the US created the Office to Monitor and Combat People Trafficking (OMCPT), which was tasked with under-taking an annual review of selected nations' counter-trafficking efforts across the globe that is published in the Trafficking in Persons Report (hereinafter TIP report; see USDOS 2013 for latest report). Part of this review process involves ranking countries according to the implemen-tation of their counter-trafficking responses (based on a three-tiered ranking system, ranging from Tier 1 to Tier 3,[3] USDOS 2014, p. 43). The process of reporting and ranking reveals the US government's priorities in addressing human trafficking.

With the TIP report process, assessment has largely focused on the development and implementation of domestic and cross-border crim-inal justice efforts, particularly law enforcement outcomes (number of victims identified and number of successful prosecutions) as indicators of 'successful' counter-trafficking initiatives (Gallagher 2011; Segrave and Milivojevic 2010). While adopted by the United States, rather than by the international community, there is no doubt that the TIP report has significant influence on national responses to human trafficking. The TIP report has been identified as a diplomatic tool that has achieved – via pressure and coercion – a global uptake of counter-trafficking strat-egies that are focused on achieving and maintaining a high ranking within the report (Chuang 2006; Pickering 2011; Skinner 2008). The TIP report has influenced both wealthy and less wealthy nations counter-trafficking responses via strategies that include diplomatic and financial pressure related to the threat of sanctions for less wealthy nations reliant on US financial support (Milivojevic and Segrave 2012). Importantly, and similarly to the Trafficking Protocol, the TIP report places emphasis on the importance of victim-centred policy responses based on the assumption that greater provisions of welfare and trauma support to (primarily) women will enhance the potential for victims to become 'good' witnesses and ensure successful prosecutions (USDOS 2007, p. 37). The approach embodied within the TIP report remains invested in the 'ideal victim' narrative, where the individual (most often a woman or child) is traumatised by the trafficking experience. Both the broader media and celebrities alike (Winter and Castillo 2011) reinforced the importance of counter-trafficking strategies encouraged by the TIP report and other key international documents that focus on 'rescuing' and trauma-healing, with an emphasis on successful prosecution as the ultimate restoration of order and the realisation of justice (Segrave et al. 2009). There is limited discussion in the dominant public or policy discourse of long-term migration status and the journeys of those who are repatriated to their country of origin following their identification as victims (Segrave et al. 2009). Thus again, it is largely criminal justice measures that are the indicators of successful counter-trafficking strategies.

Both frameworks[4] are driven primarily by criminal justice concerns and priorities, such that the status of victims has historically been a secondary concern. While the TIP report has been the subject of criticism by numerous academics (Chuang 2006; DeStefano 2007; Potocky 2010; Segrave et al. 2009), it continues to play a substantial influential role in national counter-trafficking campaigns. The UN operates less successfully as an enforcement mechanism to ensure the Trafficking Protocol is upheld, but the definition and response is consistently referenced by regional and national responses to human trafficking (Milivojevic and Segrave 2012). What is absent from the two-response mechanisms is an understanding of human trafficking that readily locates the exploitation of transnational migrants within the context of globalising processes and regulatory practices. A more nuanced understanding of human trafficking that goes beyond the traditional focus on transnational crime actors and innocent, deceived and passive victims (often juxtaposed with Nils Christie's (1986) 'ideal offenders') creates a platform from which we interrogate current responses to victims of trafficking and the inherent problems associated with assumptions regarding victim experiences and appropriate responses to victims.

Globalisation, border control and mobility: interrogating the privilege of border control

A significant area of emerging critique of human trafficking and other related issues (e.g. refugee policies and people smuggling policies) within the field of critical criminology is analysis focused on the interrogation of state practices driven by border control priorities (Aas 2008; Lee 2011; Pickering and Weber 2006, 2013; Wonders 2006). This work has outlined the ways in which broader developments associated with globalisation have given rise to increased (yet at the same time limited) mobility and border crossing internationally and domestically. As a consequence, nations are consistently responding to this increased mobility through the implementation of stricter border control regimes that target specific groups of non-citizens whose cross-border migration is discouraged and/or disallowed, creating what Bauman (1998) calls a 'hierarchy of mobility'. From this perspective, human trafficking and migration may be recognised and seen as closely connected (Aradau 2008, p. 21). That is, in a context where the primary concern of states is the breaching of immigration controls and the protection of their borders, transnational migrants (particularly women) from the Global South (in particular) are more vulnerable to situations of exploitation related to irregular cross-border migration that may include human trafficking (Aradau 2008; Anderson and Davidson 2006; Jordan 2002).

Within this field some critiques have offered gendered accounts of these practices. Pickering (2011) and Segrave et al. (2009), for example, critically examine the ways in which sex and gender fundamentally shape women's experiences of border crossing and exclusionary practices, arguing that the policing of sex trafficking is a practice that is first and foremost concerned with the breach of the border and is increasingly policed *within* countries and on those who work within the sex industry. By policing trafficking in such a way, the impact of border regulation in relation to the following issues is not examined: limited opportunities to migration, the push towards irregular migration opportunities and the subsequent disempowerment for those working in countries of destination without the right to work. So too, narratives of extreme victimisation and exploitation remain the 'real' face of human trafficking, and national responses to victimisation are driven by assumptions of the needs of those who experience extreme sexual exploitation. There is an opportunity for this analysis of gendered border control to be taken further in relation to the response to human trafficking, particularly the boundaries of what is appropriate support to be provided for victims, through drawing upon critical feminist research around victimisation more generally.

Gender and victimisation: interrogating recognition and response

Feminist critiques of the increased recognition and status of victims and the consequences of government reforms for women, as explored by Bumiller (2008) and others (Cook and Jones 2007; Larcombe 2002; Randall 2010; Stanko 1994; Stevenson 2000) provide a critical platform from which to examine responses to victims of trafficking and the implementation of support within the landscape of human trafficking. Bumiller's (2009) critique of criminal justice reforms in particular reveals how commonplace practices of responding to the victimisation of women may promote problematic forms of state control over the disrupted lives of victims. That is, strategies employed to help victims are focused on individualistic forms of problem solving rather than seeking a more comprehensive understanding of victimisation (Bumiller 2009, p. xiv). As we attend to the individual victim, Bumiller (2009) argues, we may also be ensuring that the broader social and structural context remains unexamined, as does the role of the State in ensuring that narratives of victimisation remain limited to trauma-focused accounts. In addition, Walklate (2011) has argued that studies of criminal victimisation need to shift focus to include the notion of resilience, something often missing in (and which increasingly limits) the vulnerability/trauma-driven 'politics of pity' (Aradau 2004) that dominates contemporary counter-trafficking narratives. Within human trafficking scholarship, there remains limited analysis of the ways in which contemporary responses to victims may be counterproductive and/or may be reproducing assumptions about victimisation that have little relevance to the lived experience of migrant women who have been exploited.

A key component of the feminist critique of the focus on victims concerns the co-option of victimisation within a 'medical model' (Best 1999, p. 124), whereby the language of illness/symptom/diagnosis/treatment has been widely adopted among 'helping professionals' who have become a large part of the victim support infrastructure. According to this model, responses to victimisation through medical services (such as medical examinations, counselling, clinical psychology and the services of licensed clinical social workers) are viewed as important aspects of victim support for victims who have experienced sexual abuse, rape, violence and trauma (Best 1999; Maier 2008; Wolhuter et al. 2009). Responding to the victimisation of women and their experiences of violence within a medical framework has also been linked to criminal justice outcomes that rely upon the collection of evidence of trauma, such that the purpose is to verify that victimisation has taken place (Foley 2002). The medicalisation of victimisation is thus seen as an essential part of the criminal justice narrative (Foley 2002). The medical model of victim support involves 'patching', 'treating' and 'retraining' women in a 'one size fits all approach' that does not acknowledge the conditions that cause and condone the victimisation of women and does not consider the complex realities and diverse experiences inherent to women's lives (Bumiller 2009; DeKeseredy 2011; Foley 2002). Bumiller (2009) has argued that this model has resulted in women's voices and experiences remaining under strict regimes of control (see also Hague and Mullender 2006), whereby the state has responded to women's accounts of harm and exploitation by implementing crime control strategies in the guise of victim support services that aim to 'protect vulnerable' women (Bumiller 2009, p. 96). From this account, victim support services can be seen in some instances to disempower women by acting as interventions designed to assist women to 'recover' while dismissing women's accounts, for example, of the failures of institutions such as the criminal justice system to respond adequately to their experiences and/ or the ability of institutions to silence women's more complex accounts of victimisation (Noweir 2013). The recent events involving the exposure of the internationally renowned Cambodian counter-trafficking campaigner Somaly Mam saw one of the celebrated 'champions' of the global counter-trafficking movement as well as victims of trafficking she assisted completely discredited (Buncombe 2014). This devastating revelation of false claims to victimisation and questioning of the utilisation of donated funds also both brought to the fore the eagerness with which the international community embraced linear, trauma-driven narratives of human trafficking and confirmed that these 'ideal victims' of trafficking are hard, if not indeed impossible, to find. The realities of victimisation tend to be less palatable and less easily identifiable, and consequently, they tend not to encourage large-scale eliciting of sympathy, because of the intersection of citizenship status, labour law breaches, ethnicity and gender.

The emerging critique of victim support is indicative of a new wave of emerging feminist critique that sparks a concern to interrogate how we define and limit victim experiences *through* providing support and assistance. This work, together with the analysis of border control priorities outlined earlier, offers an important platform from which to examine responses to victims of human trafficking and to, therefore, expand the victimological interrogation of international responses to harm.

Foundations of analysis: case studies

The three case studies examined here were chosen partly for pragmatic reasons (the authors' previous research into human trafficking and responses to victimisation have focused on these three nations) but also because together they offer insight into diverse locations. We are interested in the ways in which these nations have developed victim support provisions within their counter-trafficking policies. Before we begin the analysis of victim provisions, we outline the major components of their counter-trafficking strategies, the recent data on human trafficking in these locations and the support provisions offered to victims who have been officially identified as potential victim of trafficking.

A: Australia

Australia is recognised as primarily a destination country for women subjected to sexual servitude (sex trafficking) and, to an increasing extent, for women and men subjected to forced labour and exploitation (USDOS 2013). As an island nation that is not easily accessible, Australia does not experience the significant numbers of regular and irregular migrants crossing borders as do other nations in the region or internationally. Nonetheless while human trafficking is not a high-volume crime concern for Australia, it is a nation that has prioritised human trafficking since 2003 as a national concern, and it is a nation that has held a Tier 1 ranking within the US Trafficking in Person's report (hereinafter TIP report) since the TIP report first included Australia (USDOS 2007–2013), indicating that the government of Australia 'fully complies with the minimum standards for the elimination of trafficking' (USDOS 2013, p. 78).

Australia first responded to human trafficking in 2003 with the introduction of the *Commonwealth Action Plan to Eradicate Trafficking in Persons*. The background to the implementation of this response has been discussed elsewhere (Burn and Simmons 2006; McSherry 2007; Norberry 2004–2005), but it is worth noting here that it was considered to be diplomatic pressure rather than evidence of large numbers of cases of human trafficking that led to the introduction of a national counter-trafficking strategy. The policy has been amended since its introduction; however, changes have been minimal, and the focus of the policy remains on four key elements: prevention; detection and investigation; criminal prosecution; and victim support and rehabilitation (Australian Government 2009; David 2008; Phillips 2008).

The current counter-trafficking legislation in Australia includes *the Criminal Code Amendment (Trafficking in Persons) Act 2005*, which contains the general criminalisation requirements against the offence under Australian law to bring it in line with the *United Nations Trafficking in Persons Protocol*. In 2013 the *Crimes Legislation Amendment (Slavery, Slavery-like conditions and People Trafficking) Act 2013* was passed, containing a number of new laws expanding and separating out trafficking-related offences from sexual exploitation to include the identification of trafficked persons in other industry sectors. Specific trafficking offences for the purpose of forced labour, forced marriage, harbouring a person for the purposes of furthering the trafficking offence, for organ removal and aggravated debt bondage have now been included under Australian counter-trafficking law (TC Bernie School of Law [no date a]; Australian Government 2013b). At the same time, the Australian Government passed the *Crimes Legislation Amendment (Law Enforcement Integrity, Vulnerable Witness Protection and Other Measures) Act 2013*, which provides protections for vulnerable witnesses giving evidence in Commonwealth criminal proceedings and applies to victims of human trafficking and slavery. Such protections include testifying in court through closed circuit television, video link or video recording; limitations on contact with the defendant and/or the public; access to a support person while giving evidence; and identity protection from the media (Australian Government 2013b).

While Australia has a relatively comprehensive legislative response to trafficking in persons, victim protection and support provisions outside of the criminal justice process are not legislated. Instead, victim protection and support policy is incorporated within the Australian Government's Anti-People Trafficking Strategy, developed in 2003 and funded with more than $100 million (AUD) to date (TC Beirne School of Law [no date a]; Australian Government 2013b). There are two components to support provisions: welfare-related support and migration-related provisions.[5]

The Australian Red Cross[6] has been the contracted provider of the Support for Victims of People Trafficking Program victim support since March 2009. This program provides victims in cases referred to the Australian Federal Police (AFP) with welfare-oriented support and some legal assistance for up to 45 days, as part of the 'intensive victim support', and ongoing support to those whose cases are pursued via further investigation and prosecution beyond the first 45 days. This intensive period of support gives victims access to secure accommodation and a living allowance and monies for the purchase of essentials, such as clothing and toiletries, access to health care including counselling, access to interpreters and access to legal services (Australian Government 2012,

p. 31). The migration-related provisions of this support pertain generally to restrictions. The victim support provisions are connected to a system of victim-related visas for non-citizens who require visas to remain in Australia during the investigation (including those who held an irregular status at the time of initial contact with authorities). A person referred to the AFP is granted a Bridging F Visa (BFV) which allows them to lawfully remain in Australia for up to 45 days and receive the short-term 'intensive victim support' package (Australian Government 2012, p. 28). During this time they are not allowed to work.

After the initial 45-day period, victims of trafficking may be eligible for ongoing support on the condition that the AFP believes the person has been trafficked and where that person is willing to cooperate with the AFP in their investigation (Australian Red Cross [no date]). A second BFV may be granted for an additional 45 days on a case-by-case basis if the person expresses a willingness to assist with the investigation but is not ready to do so within the first 45 days (due to mental health, medical or other valid reasons). Where a person agrees to assist and cooperate with the investigation and through the criminal justice process towards a prosecution, they may be granted a Criminal Justice Stay (CJS) visa. This visa was not created specifically for trafficked persons, but it has been issued to provide support to non-citizen victims of crime who are involved in the criminal justice process. Those who hold a CJS visa have very different conditions to those remaining in Australia on a BFV. A CJS visa allows an individual to work, access Medicare, apply for Centrelink income support and receive the other components of welfare and trauma support under the Justice Support Stream of the Support Program. Criminal Justice Stay visas will be cancelled at the conclusion of the prosecution case as required under S162 of the Migration Act 1958. Unless the trafficked person has been granted a Witness Protection (Trafficking) (Permanent) visa or a Protection visa, they will be repatriated from Australia at this stage (TC Beirne School of Law [no date b]).

In order to qualify for a Witness Protection (Trafficking) (Permanent) visa, the trafficked person needs to be able to demonstrate that they have made a significant contribution to the prosecution case and that they will be in danger if returned to their home country. Changes to visas in 2009 mean that all trafficking victims who qualify for witness protection are immediately eligible for a permanent Australian visa. Conditions and rights entitlements of this permanent visa include full work rights, eligibility for Medicare as well as income support and access to the Justice Support Stream of the Support Program (TC Beirne School of Law [no date b]). It is important to note that at no stage of victim support provisions is there any specific or formal process in place to support victims such that they can recover unpaid wages or compensation. The pursuit of wages is a civil law, workplace relations matter that is separate to the pursuit of criminal charges. In regard to the payment of unpaid wages to victims of trafficking, there is one known investigation in Australia leading to an Indian restaurant owner being charged with a trafficking offence for the exploitation of an Indian worker, Mr R, in his restaurant. Although the restaurant owner was found not guilty of trafficking in persons, Mr R was awarded 40 days of unpaid wages[7] under the provisions of the *Workplace Relations Act 1966 (Cwlth) s 719*.

To date, the number of potential victims estimated to be in Australia, the number of cases referred by Department of Immigration and Border Protection (DIBP) to the AFP for investigation and the number of victims who are assisted by the government indicate that a relatively small proportion of cases are identified and followed through the criminal justice process. For example, in the 2012–2013 reporting period, 52 referrals were made to the AFP, of which 29 were investigated (AFP 2013, p. 71). Since January 2004 there has been a lot of 17 convictions on human trafficking or slavery-related charges, notwithstanding amendments to legislation over this period of time (ICHTS 2013, p. 20). Outside of official process data on victims identified, the numbers vary: groups such as Project Respect, an Australian non-government organisation (NGO) that is committed to helping women exit the sex industry, estimates that 1000 women are trafficked into Australia each year and under contract at any one time paying off a debt (Project Respect 2004), while the sex worker advocate group the Scarlet Alliance suggests the figure of ten victims of sex trafficking annually is more accurate (Scarlet Alliance 2003).

The Department of Immigration and Border Protection, formerly the Department of Immigration and Citizenship (DIAC) are the primary source of referral to the AFP of potential victims. Referrals from DIBP account for just over 60 per cent of referrals; however, as the numbers above indicated, not all of these access victim support and/or are subject to further investigation (Australian National Audit Office 2009, p. 58; Segrave and Milivojevic 2010). In the DIAC's most recent annual report (2012–2013), it reported that in this reporting year 18 persons were granted Witness Protection (Trafficking) (Permanent) visas, with 12 such visas granted to suspected victims of trafficking and six granted to immediate family members of the victims (Department of Immigration and Citizenship 2013, p. 169). In the most recent report from the Interdepartmental Committee on Human Trafficking and Slavery (formerly the Australian

Government Anti-People Trafficking Interdepartmental Committee), it reported that between 2012 and 2013 a total of 21 persons accessed the Victim Support Program,[8] of which 12 (57 per cent) were victims of trafficking for the purpose of sexual exploitation and 16 persons were victims of trafficking for non-sexual exploitation (ICHTS 2013, p. 38). Prior to the annual reporting on victim support access, the 2004–2011 data indicated that 184[9] victims over the seven-year period had accessed assistance through the Office for Women's Support for Trafficked Persons (STP) Program funded by the Australian Government. This is compared to 305 investigations into trafficking-related offences conducted by the AFP in the same timeframe (of which 13 people have been convicted for people trafficking-related offences from January 2004 to June 2011) (Larsen and Renshaw 2012, p. 2). The data on victim support access, however, is not indicative of the total number of potential victims identified annually, as some victims may receive support over more than one financial year (Australian Government 2012, p. 35). Since 2005 the number of clients on the Victims of Trafficking Support Program at any one time from 2005 to 2012 has ranged from 41 to 83. (Australian Government 2013b, p. 3; Australian Government 2012, p. 35). Some of these clients have been on the support program for more than one year and/or over reporting periods. However, in terms of new clients accessing the victim support program, the numbers reported above for the 2012–2013 period are reflective of previous years: in 2009–2010, 24 new trafficked victims were supported by the Program; 29 in 2010–2011; 9 in 2011–2012; and 21 in 2012–2013. (Australian Government 2011, 2012, 2013a, 2013b). This data tells us that there is a consistently low number of victims being identified, compared to estimates regarding the potential number of victims and that only a small proportion are accessing ongoing support and assistance and/or are involved in cases that progress through to prosecution. Critically, the support provisions have been the subject of no public analysis in relation to the extent to which they meet the needs of victims (Noweir 2013).

B: Thailand

Unlike Australia, Thailand, as a nation with land borders and surrounded by less wealthy nations, is a source, destination and transit country for human trafficking (USDOS 2013). Its counter-trafficking efforts have been recognised by the TIP report as improving but requiring improvement. From 2009 Thailand has consistently ranked as a Tier 2 country, reflecting an assessment that the Government of Thailand 'does not fully comply with the minimum standards for the elimination of trafficking' and that the 'government has not shown sufficient evidence of increasing efforts to address human trafficking' (USDOS 2013, p. 359).

However, unlike the Australian and United Kingdom context, policy engagement with human trafficking in Thailand has a long history, dating back to 1928 (Skrobanek et al. 1997, p. 27). The contemporary engagement began in 1997 with the creation of the *Measures in Prevention and Suppression of Trafficking in Women and Children Act (B.E. 2540* 1997). This legislation was exclusively focused on the trafficking of women and increased the punitive sanctions attached to offences both pertaining to direct involvement in the trafficking of persons and conspiring to engage in trafficking-related offences (Pollock 2007). The influence of international pressures and US-led criticism of the government's exclusive focus on the trafficking of women and children saw the introduction of a more comprehensive legislative framework implemented in 2008: the *Anti-trafficking in Persons Act (B.E. 2551* 2008).

In this Act, it is legislated that victims of trafficking have the right to protection and support (Association of Southeast Asian Nations [ASEAN] 2011). Provisions of protection and support for trafficked persons contained within the Act include food, shelter, medical treatment physical and mental rehabilitation, education, training, legal aid, return to country of origin and compensation (Section 33). Further, this Act stipulates that a fund be established to support the prevention and suppression of human trafficking as well as to finance protection and assistance to trafficked victims (Section 42) (see also United Nations Office on Drugs and Crime UNODC 2012). There are special provisions concerning the protection of victim-witnesses who agree to testify (Section 36). The extent to which these provisions are enacted and accessed is difficult to assess as there is no publically available data regarding implementation of these support provisions. What is known is that the main provision of victims support for non-citizens includes their detention in women and children centres that are focused on providing them with food, shelter, education and support until the criminal justice process has concluded (Segrave et al. 2009). In the *Anti-trafficking in Persons Act (B.E. 2551* 2008), Section 33 contains provisions to regularise the visa status of trafficking victims who may need to remain in Thailand either for medical purposes or to participate in legal proceedings:

> For the purpose of taking proceedings against the offender under this Act, or providing medical treatment, rehabilitation for the trafficked person, or claiming for compensation of the trafficked person, the competent official may assist the trafficked person to get a permission

to stay in the Kingdom temporarily and be temporarily allowed to work in accordance with the law. In so doing, the humanitarian reason shall be taken into account. (ASEAN2011, p. 21)

Recent data published by the US Department of State suggests that the majority of trafficking victims identified within Thailand are migrants from neighbouring countries who are coerced, or defrauded into labour or commercial sexual exploitation or children placed in the sex trade; conservative estimates put this population in the tens of thousands of victims (USDOS 2013). It has also been suggested that a significant portion of labour trafficking victims within Thailand are exploited in commercial fishing, fishing-related industries, low-end garment production, factories and domestic work, and some are forced to beg on the streets (USDOS 2013). However, despite the claims of high number of victimisation, the numbers identified by authorities are not much greater than the corresponding numbers in Australia. In 2009 the Royal Thai Police identified 145 victims, and in 2010 it identified 122 victims (UNODC 2012, pp. 52–53). Of the 122 victims identified in 2010, UNODC provides a breakdown of trafficking types: 46 persons were identified as being trafficked into situations of forced labour, 73 persons were trafficked into sexual exploitation and 3 persons were trafficked for the purpose of forced begging (UNODC 2012, p. 53). Of those that receive support, the majority are women and children. The UNODC reported that in 2011 and 2012, 112 victims of trafficking received assistance and support from the Ministry of Social Development and Human Security (MSDHS) (UNODC 2012).

C: United Kingdom

Similarly to Australia, Britain is primarily a country of destination for victims of trafficking, but its proximity to other nations is reflected in the much higher estimates and recorded figures (USDOS 2013). In 2013 the United Kingdom Human Trafficking Centre (UKHTC), under the Serious and Organised Crime Agency (SOCA) reported 2,255 potential victims of trafficking encountered in 2012 by 17 UK police forces. This is an increase of 178 persons to the number encountered in 2011 (SOCA 2013). Of the 2,255 potential victims, 35 per cent were identified as victims of sexual exploitation and 23 per cent were identified as victims of labour exploitation. The United Kingdom has consistently been assessed by the United States as a Tier 1 country, with the most recent US Department of State report indicating that the 'government has improved its identification of trafficking victims ... and increased the number of trafficking victims who received access to care and support' (USDOS 2013, p. 378).

UK legislation to prevent and combat trafficking in persons is currently not contained within any one Act. In August 2013, the UK Government announced that it would introduce a Modern Slavery Bill to consolidate offences related to slavery under one act. Following the issue of a report on pre-legislative scrutiny by the Joint Select Committee on Modern Slavery and the Government's subsequent response to this report, the Bill has just been introduced to the House of Commons on 10 June 2014 (www.parliament.uk [no date]) for its first reading. Currently, British trafficking in persons legislation is presented under sections 57–60 of the Sexual Offences Act 2003, covering trafficking for the purpose of sexual exploitation; Section 4 of the *Asylum and Immigration (Treatment of Claimants) Act* 2004 for non-sexual exploitation trafficking in persons offences; and Section 71 of the *Coroners and Justice Act* 2009, which criminalises the holding of another person in slavery or servitude or criminalises requiring another person to perform force or compulsory labour without the need to prove trafficking (HM Government 2012).

As in the Australian context, there are no specific legislative provisions for the protection and support of trafficked victims identified in the United Kingdom. Victim protection and support policy lies outside of the legislative realm and is largely conditional on the trafficked person's cooperation in the criminal justice process. Victim protection and support policy has recently been reinforced and strengthened under the UK Government's Human Trafficking Strategy (2011). Current victim identification and support practices, including the National Referral Mechanism, has been influenced by the United Kingdom's obligations under the Council of Europe Convention on Action against Trafficking in Human Beings (signed in 2007, entry into force in April 2009) and outlined under the national strategy (HM Government 2011, pp. 912; Lipscombe and Beard 2014).

In contrast to its earlier plan, the government's most recent human trafficking strategy focuses on four key areas: improved victim care arrangements (through the implementation of the Victim Support Program), an enhanced ability to act early before the harm has reached the United Kingdom, smarter multi-agency action at the border and better coordination of law enforcement efforts within the United Kingdom (HM Government 2011, p. 7). It is evident from this strategy that while victims are in one of four priority areas, this is overshadowed by the remaining three, which are all focused on law enforcement and border security. Within the United Kingdom, potential victims of trafficking access support via the Anti-Human Trafficking Victim Support Program when a designated 'first responder'[10] refers a suspected victim of trafficking to a Competent Authority (CA) (specifically The UK Human Trafficking Centre and the Home Office Immigration and Visas), whose role is to determine whether there is a legally substantiated case of human trafficking (SOCA 2012). While this is being determined, the victim is referred to the Salvation Army's Victim Support program. Under this program they have access to protection and support services for up to 45 days while the initial investigation is undertaken to determine if they are likely to be a victim of trafficking. The decision of the CA regarding whether there is a case is also a determinant of whether a potential victim will be granted victim status and receive government-funded support beyond the 45-day program. Under the program potential victims of trafficking have access to a range of support services, including secure accommodation, legal advice, health care, counselling and educational opportunities.

If a person is determined by the CA to be, or likely to be, a victim of trafficking, it is the victim's decision whether they remain in the United Kingdom to cooperate with the police investigation and criminal justice process concerning their case. If a trafficked victim agrees to cooperate, they may be granted discretionary leave (DL) to remain in the United Kingdom for a period of up to one year. Those persons on DL are entitled to access public funds and are entitled to work (Gov.uk [no date]). This one year period may be extended on a case-by-case basis if need be, to a maximum of 30 months. In exceptional circumstances, subsequent periods of DL can be granted. When a person has been on DL for a period of 30 months, they are eligible to apply for permanent settlement. The DL period can be used to lodge an asylum application, and if it is refused, the DL period allows for enough time to lodge an appeal on a negative decision.

If a trafficked victim chooses not to cooperate in the investigation and prosecution stage, they have two options to consider, depending on whether they wish to remain in the United Kingdom or they wish to return home. If they wish to return home voluntarily, assistance and support is available through the government (Home Office Assisted Voluntary Return of Irregular Migrants – AVRIM) and NGOs. Alternatively, where a trafficked person does not wish to return home, DL to remain may also be considered by the Home Office whereby the outcome of this consideration will be dependent on the victim's personal circumstances (National Crime Agency [no date]).

Interrogating the parameters of victim support for victims of human trafficking

What is evident across the three nations is the consistency of core components of victim support, both in terms of the *provision* of support and the *prioritisation* of victim support in relation to criminal justice priorities/ measures. We elaborate on three key issues in order to explore the implications of current responses to human trafficking and the recognition of trafficking victims. Specifically, we examine the role of gatekeepers in the provision of access, in the emphasis on welfare and trauma-focused support provisions and in the end of support with the assumption of the return to the victims' country of origin. We bring these concerns together in this discussion to highlight key points for consideration of the implications of current responses and to highlight the important intervention that critical feminist examination of victim and border-related policy responses offers to challenge the status quo.

The first concern pertains to recognising victims of trafficking. Research by Noweir (2013) and Segrave et al. (2009, 2010) reveals that gendered narratives of victimisation in all three case study countries, Australia, Thailand and the UK, prevail in the processes involved in identifying victims. Authorities (police and immigration) are predominantly responsible for identifying victims of trafficking in the first instance (Segrave et al. 2009; Segrave and Milivojevic 2011). In all three nations it is *only* those who are identified by authorities as potential victims whose cases require further investigation and who are able to access victim support. This differs from other forms of victim support in the community, such as support for victims of sexual assault or intimate partner violence, where there are support services in place funded by governments that are not provided on the basis of progress of the case through the criminal justice system.[11] Why does it matter that authorities act as gatekeepers to victim support? There are a number of implications to consider including how decision-making processes are scrutinised. The available evidence suggests that assumptions regarding how victims behave, what they look like, and so on influence decision-making processes. For example, in Australia, Segrave et al.'s work revealed that while the focus was on South East Asian women as victims, some participants involved in immigration and policing work had little sympathy for 'unhappy sex workers' whom they believed were not being exploited but were simply dissatisfied with the pay or other work conditions (Segrave et al. 2009; see also Pickering and Ham 2014). This highlights the importance of carefully examining how narratives of victimisation also intersect with narratives of gender, race and appropriate femininity, an examination that connects to more recent work such as Pickering and Ham's (2014; see also Ham et al. 2013) recent work interrogating the decisions at the airport made by officials. They found that Asian women arriving at Australian airports are the subject of targeted suspicion that they may be potential sex workers and/or victims of sex trafficking, a suspicion that leads to interrogation of their reasons for travel and their luggage – suspicions which are reinforced by assumptions made about the type of underwear they have packed in their luggage (Pickering and Ham 2014). It is clear that gendered and racialised narratives of victimisation include expectations of victim behaviour, ranging from assumptions made regarding what they wear (or pack to wear). Not only is how we understand victims relevant to the decisions made by authorities in identifying potential victims; how we understand them also informs the response package.

The second concern is the provision of support services available to victims, specifically what is provided and what is not. As outlined in relation to Australia, the United Kingdom and Thailand, the provision of support services in each country largely reflects support services based on trauma. In each country the services provided are intended to assist victims of trafficking based on therapeutic models, aimed at treating 'broken' and 'injured patients' who can and will be treated and healed via a myriad of medical and psychological interventions. Specifically they all focus on counselling, retraining, medical care and legal support to pursue criminal cases. Such provisions frame experiences of victimisation within a medical and clinical lens that assumes that trauma and victimisation are key concerns for *all* victims of trafficking. It is also critical to attend to what is outside the framework of support. The right to work differs across the three nations: in the United Kingdom victims have the right to work; in Australia it is only following an investigation and the move to a Criminal Justice Stay visa that victims can work (which means up to 45 days of a welfare based income); and in Thailand there is no formal support of work outside shelters. Access to remuneration and/or compensation is also not clearly provided and varies across the three nations.

In Australia, while trafficking laws have been strengthened with the passing of the *Crimes Legislation Amendment (Slavery, Slavery-like Conditions and People Trafficking) Act 2013*, there is no corresponding Commonwealth compensation scheme for victims of trafficking. Statutory victim compensation schemes are established across each of the eight states and territories of Australia; however, they do not reflect the Commonwealth jurisdiction and therefore often fail to provide appropriate compensation to victims of a Commonwealth offence such as trafficking. Two recent Federal Parliamentary Inquiries[12] forwarded recommendations to the government to establish a federal compensation scheme for victims of trafficking (Anti-Slavery Australia 2013). In Thailand, sections 34 and 35 of the *Anti-trafficking in Persons Act (B.E. 2551* 2008) contain provisions in regard to compensation for trafficked persons who agree to cooperate with criminal proceedings:

> Section 34: For the benefit of the assistance to a trafficked person, the inquiry official or public prosecutor shall, in the first chance, inform the trafficked person his right to compensation for damages resulting from the commission of trafficking in persons and the right to the provisions of legal aid.

> Section 35: In case where the trafficked person has the right to compensation for damages as a result of the commission of trafficking in persons and express his intention to claim compensation thereof, the Public Prosecutor, to the extent as informed by the Permanent Secretary for Social Development and Human Security or any person designated by him, shall, on behalf of the trafficked person, claim for compensation thereof. (ASEAN 2011, p. 24)

In the United Kingdom, victims of trafficking can access the Criminal Injuries Compensation Scheme, which is a broader compensation scheme designed to compensate victims of violent crime in the United Kingdom. However the Criminal Injuries Compensation Authority makes is clear that being a victim of human trafficking does not necessarily mean that an applicant will be eligible for compensation under the Scheme. In order to qualify, an applicant must have suffered a personal injury which was sustained in the United Kingdom and have been identified as a victim of trafficking by the Competent Authority under the National Referral Mechanism (Criminal Injuries and Compensation Authority 2014; Ministry of Justice 2012). The Home Office has most recently reported that compensation and reparation orders for victims of trafficking in persons are included in the Modern Slavery Bill that was published and introduced to Parliament on 10 June 2014. The Bill contains a new reparation order to encourage the courts to compensate victims where assets are confiscated from perpetrators (Parliament UK 2014).

Bumiller's (2009) concern that support services focused on healing and treating women through the implementation of a range of medical and psychological interventions reinforce simplistic and individualistic narratives of victimisation is clearly applicable here. The absence of clear mechanisms that emphasise unpaid labour suggests the reliance on emotive assumptions about victims' needs that rely on gendered stereotypes that look to passive, vulnerable women (Surtees 2005, p. 16). We argue, as have others (Demleitner 2001, p. 259), that not only do many victims of trafficking (women and men alike) *not* fit this stereotypical image; even those who do are unlikely to benefit from support that provides almost exclusively welfare and trauma support provisions and remains without any support that recognises the loss of wages and income. Thus, across very different national contexts, the impact of an international framework that buys into a limited concern for and response to victim experiences is reflected in the implementation of counter-trafficking efforts.

The final concern is to examine the termination of support. In some jurisdictions this is more evident or overt in policy than in others, but what is clear is that long-term victim support is not available beyond criminal justice processes, and it is definitely not available to those whose cases do not flow through the criminal justice system. It is assumed that all 'trauma-focused' support ends as individuals either receive a long-term visa or are repatriated. Despite the reliance on the narrative of trauma, there is no articulation of when support may end and why it is ended at particular points in time. Victims are required to return home (regardless of their desire – we are not arguing that all victims do not wish to return home) at the completion of their involvement with the criminal justice system unless they are eligible for another visa. This requirement highlights the interconnection between victim narratives and border priorities, and it reveals the role of citizenship in underpinning the limits of national responses across all three nations.

Conclusion

This chapter sought to identify emerging criminological and victimological areas of scholarship and to bring them together in an analysis of responses to victims of human trafficking. We have examined the interplay between national and international responses to human trafficking to identify that there is a consistency regarding the understanding of, response to and prioritisation of victimisation. While there have been a range of local contextual factors that have influenced the specific development of counter-trafficking efforts in Thailand, Australia and the United Kingdom, generally speaking all three nations have policies in place that emphasise criminal justice efforts to interrupt trafficking-related exploitation, in which victims are assumed to need extensive welfare and psychological and physical support. This chapter intended to expand the critical gendered account offered by Bumiller (2009) and others (Segrave et al. 2009; Segrave and Milivojevic 2010) regarding the implications of victim support provision that are framed as 'responsive' to victim's needs, which understand victimisation as an individualised experiences that require medical and psychological intervention. While the provision of services may be celebrated as a recognition of gendered forms of harm and exploitation (in relation to sexual assault and intimate partner violence, for example) they also can serve to silence accounts of institutional harm and of social control and can fail to offer a platform from which to interrogate the broader social, political, economic and institutional processes that give rise to harm.

From the process of identifying victims to the delimiting of what provisions are appropriate for victims, we can recognise that agency to trafficked persons is denied and the economic reasons driving many to choose to leave their homes is ignored. As a result, these policy efforts effectively transform victims into 'mere objects of interventions by others' (Buckland 2008, p. 42). In part, this resonates with Bumiller's (2009) argument as we see the reinforcement of assumptions that human trafficking victimisation is a trauma-based experience, within which victims have no avenue to assert themselves and/or utilise their agency. We argue that citizenship adds a further element to the restrictions on victim recognition and the parameters of support, in part driven by the inherent mistrust of non-citizens (and fear that individuals will abuse the system). Restrictions surrounding victim recognition and provision of support is evident from the decision regarding whether an individual may be a victim of trafficking, to the inclusions and exclusions of victim support, to the assumption that victims will return home. We witness in national contexts the assertion of state control upon non-citizens, be they victims or offenders, in ways that demonstrate how national priorities pertaining to border control supersede the rhetoric of state concerns to respond to human trafficking. The result of this – to extend Bumiller's (2009) analysis – is the failure to recognise how national and international responses to migration, border control and security – including responses to human trafficking – may exacerbate the vulnerability of non-citizens in individual nation-states.

Notes

1. As one of the authors (Segrave 2007; Segrave et al. 2009) and others (Farrell et al. 2010; Hoyle et al. 2009; Pickering 2011) have noted, not *all* victims of trafficking come to the attention of authorities and potentially many of those who come into contact with authorities are not recognised as victims because of their irregular migration status, whereby they are treated as illegal non-citizens and deported. This process of identification is complex, and a full interrogation is beyond the scope of this chapter, but it has been examined elsewhere (Noweir 2013; Segrave et al. 2009).
2. For extensive debate on this, see Segrave et al. (2009, pp. 10–16).
3. Definitions of the Tier rankings are as follows: Tier 1 'Countries whose governments fully comply with the TVPA's minimum standards for the elimination of trafficking'; Tier 2 'Countries whose governments do not fully comply with the TVPA's minimum standards but are making significant efforts to bring themselves into compliance with those standards'; Tier 2 Watch list 'Countries whose governments do not fully comply with the TVPA's minimum standards, but are making significant efforts to bring themselves into compliance with those standards, and for which: (a) the absolute number of victims of severe forms of trafficking is very significant or is significantly increasing; (b) there is a failure to provide evidence of increasing efforts to combat severe forms of trafficking in persons from the previous year, including increased investigations, prosecution, and convictions of trafficking crimes, increased assistance to victims, and decreasing evidence of complicity in severe forms of trafficking by government officials; or (c) the determination that a country is making significant efforts to bring itself into compliance with minimum standards was based on commitments by the country to take additional steps over the next year'; Tier 3 'Countries whose governments do not fully comply with the TVPA's minimum standards and are not making significant efforts to do so.' (USDOS 2014, p. 43).
4. There are important regional mechanisms also in place; however, detailed examination of these mechanisms is beyond the scope of this chapter. The approach adopted by the United Nations has been echoed in efforts adopted within regional mechanisms such as the OSCE Action Plan to Combat Trafficking in Human Beings (2003), the Council of Europe's Convention on Action Against Trafficking in Human Beings (2005) and ASEAN's Declaration against Trafficking in Persons, especially Women and Children (2004). These instruments have reflected components of the Trafficking Protocol with some evidence of greater concern or and recognition of victims in some cases. For example, the COE's Convention on Action against Trafficking ('the Convention') which came into force in February 2008 established minimum standards of protection for victims and a specific monitoring mechanism for state parties' compliance with the Convention. While still focused on law enforcement outcomes, the Convention adopted a more tangible human rights framework than the Trafficking Protocol via specifying nation- states' responsibilities in relation to upholding victims' rights play equally important role in anti-trafficking strategies (see Segrave and Milivojevic 2012). ASEAN's Declaration, on the other hand, outlined key measures aimed at ensuring cross-border law enforcement cooperation and the protection and support of victims when returned to their country of origin (Pollock 2007, p. 180).

5. These provisions are available to all potential victims, but the stipulations specified for accessing visas and the requirement of repatriation apply to only those who did not have a valid visa at the time they were identified by authorities and/or those whose visa expired during this process.
6. In March 2009, the Red Cross was contracted to deliver the Support for Trafficked People Program and the contract has been extended to 2015 (Australian Government 2012, p. 35).
7. The case of *R v Yogalingham Rasalingam (2007)* was the first case in Australia where the accused was charged with trafficking offences under Division 271 of the Criminal Code (Cth). While Mr Rasalingam was found not guilty of the trafficking offence, the victim, Mr R, who had worked in Mr Rasalingam's Indian restaurant for a period of 40 days, from 9 a.m. until midnight between June and July of 2006 without payment, received unpaid wages of AUD $11,560.31 following the commencement of an investigation by a workplace inspector. This same investigation resulted in the successful application of civil penalty provisions against the business of Mr Rasalingam for a sum of AUD $18,200, see Schloenhardt and Curley [no date]..
8. This refers to new clients rather than to clients referred onto the support program in previous reporting periods.
9. Of the 184 victims supported, 149 were identified as female victims of trafficking for the purpose of sexual exploitation with 19 males referred to the STP identified as victims of trafficking for purposes of non-sexual exploitation in various labour industries. Four minors aged between 15 and 17 years identified as trafficked into Australia accessed the STP within the 2004–2011 time period, although the type of trafficking they experienced is not reported (Larsen et al. 2012, pp. xi and 16). It is not clear what type of trafficking (sexual or non-sexual) or gender the outstanding 12 persons who accessed the STP at this time were.
10. First responders currently include the Serious Organised Crime Unit or the UKHTC, Local Authorities, UKBA, Poppy Project, TARA Project (Scotland), Migrant Helpline, Medaline Trust, Kalayaan, Salvation Army, Gangmasters Licensing Authority, UK Police Forces, Local Authority Children's Services, Barnardo's, Northern Ireland DHSS, Northern Island Public Safety and Unseen (SOCA, 2012).
11. For example, in Victoria, Australia, all victims of crimes have access to counselling and other support services, and it is possible to access support for violent crime without reporting to the police. See https://www.vocat.vic.gov.au/financial-assistance-available/counselling-expenses/urgent-counselling.
12. 2012 Senate Legal and Constitutional Affairs Committee *Inquiry into the Crimes Legislation Amendment (Slavery, Slavery-like conditions and People Trafficking) Bill* and 2013 Human Rights Sub-Committee of the Joint Standing Committee on Foreign Affairs, Defence and Trade *Inquiry into Slavery, Slavery-like Conditions and People Trafficking.*

References

Aas, K.F. 2008. *Globalization and Crime*. London: Sage Publications Ltd.

Aas, K. and Bosworth, M. eds. 2013. *The Borders of Punishment: Migration, Citizenship and Social Exclusion*. Oxford: Oxford University Press.

Anderson, B. and O'Connell Davidson, J. 2006. The trouble with trafficking. In: Van Den Anker, C. and Doomernik, J. eds. *Trafficking and Women's Rights*. Basingstoke: Palgrave Macmillan, pp. 11–26.

Andrijasevic, R. 2010. *Migration, Agency and Citizenship in Sex Trafficking*. Basingstoke: Palgrave Macmillan.

Anti-Slavery Australia, 2013. *Compensation for victims of trafficking: Fact sheet*. http://www.antislavery.org.au/images/stories/9_-_Compensation_for_vicitms_of_human_trafficking.pdf [Accessed: 18 June 2014].

Aradau, C. 2004. The Perverse Politics of Four-Letter Words: Risk and Pity in the Securitisation of Human Trafficking. *Millennium: Journal of International Studies* 33(2), pp. 251–277.

Aradau, C. 2008. *Rethinking Trafficking in Women: Politics out of Security*. Basingstoke: Palgrave Macmillan.

Association of Southeast Asian Nations (ASEAN). 2011. *Progress Report on Criminal Justice Responses to Trafficking in Persons in the ASEAN Region*. Bangkok. July 2012, http://www.ungift.org/doc/knowledgehub/resource-centre/ASEAN_Progress_Report_TIP.pdf [Accessed: 18 June 2014].

Australian Federal Police (AFP) 2013. *Annual Report 2012–2013*. Canberra: AFP.

Australian Government. 2009. Australian Government Anti-People Trafficking Strategy June 2009, Australian Government Factsheet.

Australian Government. 2011. Trafficking in Persons: The Australian Government's Response 1 July 2010–2030 June 2011. Anti-People Trafficking Interdepartmental Committee.

Australian Government. 2012. Trafficking in Persons: The Australian Government's Response 1 July 2011–2030 June 2012. Anti-People Trafficking Interdepartmental Committee.

Australian Government. 2013a. Australian Government Strategy to Combat Human Trafficking and Slavery Whole-of-Government Performance Management Reporting, 1 July–31 December 2012. Attorney General's Department. http://www.ag.gov.au/CrimeAndCorruption/HumanTrafficking/Documents/Trafficking_PerformanceManagementFramework_JulytoDecember2013_NarrativeforPublicRelease.pdf [Accessed: 18 June 2014].

Australian Government. 2013b. Australian Government Strategy to Combat Human Trafficking and Slavery Whole-of-Government Performance Management Reporting, 1 January–30 June 2013. Attorney General's Department. PDF: http://www.ag.gov.au/CrimeAndCorruption/HumanTrafficking/Documents/AusGovAntiPeopleTraffickingStrategy1Janto30Jun12.pdf [Accessed: 18 June 2014].

Australian National Audit Office. 2009. Management of the Australian Government's Action Plan to Eradicate Trafficking in Persons. Attorney General's Department, Department of Immigration and Citizenship, Australian Federal Police, Department of Families, Housing, Community Services and Indigenous Affairs. PDF: http://www.anao.gov.au/uploads/documents/2008-09_Audit_Report_30.pdf

Australian Red Cross. [No date]. Support for People Who have been Trafficked to Australia. PDF: http://www.redcross.org.au/files/ARC_Trafficking-_English.pdf

Bauman, Z. 1998. *Globalization: The Human Consequences*, New York: Polity Press.

Best, J. 1999. Victimization and the victim industry. *Society* 34(4), pp. 9–17.

Bumiller, K. 2009. *In an Abusive State: How Neoliberalism Appropriated the Feminist Movement against Sexual Violence.* Durham, NC: Duke University Press.

Buckland, B.S. 2008. More than Just Victims: The Truth about Human Trafficking. *Public Policy Research* 15(1), pp. 42–47.

Buncombe, A. 2014. Cambodian Anti-trafficking Campaigner Somaly Mam Exposed as Fraud, The Independent, 29 May. http://www.independent.co.uk/news/world/asia/cambodian-antitrafficking-campaigner-somaly-mam-exposed-as-fraud-9454475.html [Accessed: 13 June 2014].

Burn, J. and Simmons, F. 2006. Trafficking and Slavery in Australia: An Evaluation of Victim Support Strategies. *Asian and Pacific Migration Journal* 15(4), pp. 553–571.

Chew, L. 2005. Reflection by an Anti-trafficking Activist. In: Kempadoo, K. ed. *Trafficking and Prostitution Reconsidered: New Perspective on Migration, Sex Work and Human Rights.* Boulder, CO: Paradigm Publishers.

Christie, N. 1986. The Ideal Victim. In: Fattah, E. ed. *From Crime Policy to Victim Policy: Reorienting the Justice System.* New York: St Martin's Press.

Chuang, J. 2006. The US as Global Sheriff: Using Unilateral Sanctions to Combat Human Trafficking. *Michigan Journal of International Law* 27(2), pp. 441–493.

Cook, K. and Jones, H. 2007. Surviving Victimhood: The Impact of Feminist Campaigns. In: Walklate, S. ed. *Handbook of Victims and Victimology.* Cullompton: Willan.

Criminal Injuries and Compensation Authority 2014. *Victims of Human Trafficking and the Criminal Injuries Compensation Scheme.* 4 March 2014. https://www.gov.uk/government/publications/victims-of-human-trafficking-and-the-criminal-injuries-compensation-scheme [Accessed: 18 June 2014].

David, F. 2008. *Trafficking of Women for Sexual Exploitation.* Canberra, Australian Institute of Criminology, Research and Public Policy Series, No. 95.

DeKeseredy, W.S. 2011. *Violence against Women: Myths, Facts, Controversies.* Toronto: University of Toronto Press.

Demleitner, N.V. 2001. The Law at a Crossroads: The Construction of Migrant Women Trafficked into Prostitution. In: Kyle, D. and Koslowski, R. eds. *Global Human Smuggling: Comparative Perspectives.* Baltimore, MD: The John Hopkins University Press, pp. 257–293.

Department of Immigration and Citizenship. 2013. *Annual Report 2012–2013.* Canberra: Australian Government.

DeStefano, A.M. 2007. *The War on Human Trafficking: US Policy Assessed.* Piscataway, NJ: Rutgers University Press.

Doezema, J. 2000. Loose Women or Lost Women? The Re-emergence of the Myth of 'White Slavery' in Contemporary Discourses of Trafficking in Women. *Gender Issues* 18(1), pp. 23–50.

Doezema, J. 2002. Who Gets to Choose? Coercion, Consent, and the UN Trafficking Protocol. *Gender & Development* 10(1), pp. 20–27.

Farrell, A., McDevitt, J. and Fahy, S. 2010. Where are all the Victims? *Criminology and Public Policy* 9(2), pp. 201–233.

Foley, M. 2002. Who is in Control?: Changing Responses to Women Who have been Raped and Sexually Abused. In: Hester, M., Katie, L. and Radford, J. eds. *Women, Violence and Male Power.* Buckingham: Open University Press, pp. 166–175.

Gallagher, A. 2011. Improving the Effectiveness of the International Law on Human Trafficking: A Vision for the Future of the US Trafficking in Persons Report. *Human Rights Review* 12(3), pp. 381–400.

Gov.uk. [no date]. *Granting Discretionary Leave*. https://www.gov.uk/government/uploads/system/uploads/attachment_data/file/312346/discretionaryleave.pdf [Accessed: 13 June 2014].

Hague, G. and Mullender, A. 2006. Who Listens? The Voices of Domestic Violence Survivors in Service Provisions in the UK. *Violence Against Women* 12(6), pp. 568–587.

Ham, J., Segrave, M. and Pickering, S. 2013. In the Eyes of the Beholder: Border Enforcement, Suspect Travellers and Trafficking Victims. *Anti-Trafficking Review* 2, pp. 51–66.

HM Government 2011. *Human Trafficking: The Government's Strategy*. https://www.gov.uk/government/uploads/system/uploads/attachment_data/file/97845/human-trafficking-strategy.pdf [Accessed: 16 June 2014].

HM Government 2012. *Report on the Internal Review of Human Trafficking Legislation*. https://www.gov.uk/government/uploads/system/uploads/attachment_data/file/97846/human-trafficking-legislation.pdf [Accessed: 16 June 2014].

Hoyle, C., Bosworth, M. and Dempsey, M. 2011. Labelling the Victims of Sex Trafficking: Exploring the Borderland between Rhetoric and Reality. *Social and Legal Studies* 20(3), pp. 313–329.

Interdepartmental Committee on Human Trafficking and Slavery (ICHTS). 2013. *Trafficking In Persons: The Australian Government Response*, 1 July 2012– 30 June 2013. Canberra: Attorney-General's Department. http://www.ag.gov.au/CrimeAndCorruption/HumanTrafficking/Pages/Australiasresponsetohumantrafficking.aspx [Accessed: 4 September 2014].

Jordan, A. 2002. Human Rights or Wrongs? The Struggle for a Rights-based Response to Trafficking in Human Beings. In: Masika, R. ed. *Gender, Trafficking and Slavery*. Oxford: Oxfam, pp. 28–37.

Kempadoo, K. 2005. From Moral Panic to Global Justice: Changing Perspectives on Trafficking. In: Kempadoo, K., Sanghera, J. and Pattanaik, B. eds. *Trafficking and Prostitution Reconsidered: New Perspectives on Migration, Sex Work and Human Rights*. Boulder, CO: Paradigm Publishers, pp. vii–xxxiv.

Krieg, S. 2009. Trafficking in Human Beings: The EU Approach between Border Control, Law Enforcement and Human Rights. *European Law Journal* 15(6), pp. 775–790.

Larcombe, W. 2002. The 'Ideal Victim' v Successful Rape Complaints: Not What You Might Expect. *Feminist Legal Studies* 10(2), pp.131–148.

Larsen, J.J. and Renshaw, L. 2012. *People Trafficking In Australia*. Canberra: Australian Institute of Criminology, Trends and Issues in Crime and Criminal Justice, No. 441.

Larsen, et al. 2012. *Trafficking in Persons Monitoring Report: January 2009–June 2011*. Australian Institute of Criminology, Monitoring Reports Series, No. 19. http://www.aic.gov.au/documents/C/5/B/%7bC5B4F700-79D2-495E-9B04-CC5447EF7AD0%7dmr19_003.pdf [Accessed: 17 June 2014].

Lee, M. 2011. *Trafficking and Global Crime Control*. London: Sage.

Lipscombe, S. and Beard, J. 2014. *Human Trafficking: UK Responses*. House of Commons Library, 13 January 2014, SN/HA/4324. file:///C:/Users/powellr/Downloads/sn04324.pdf [Accessed: 16 June 2014].

Victimisation, Citizenship and Gender   81

Maier, S.L. 2008. 'I Have Heard Horrible Stories...': Rape Victim Advocates' Perceptions of the Revictimization of Rape Victims by the Police and Medical System. *Violence Against Women* 14(7), pp. 786–808.

McSherry, B. 2007. Trafficking in Persons: A Critical Analysis of the New Criminal Code Offences. *Current Issues in Criminal Justice* 18(3), pp. 385–398.

Milivojevic, S. and Pickering, S. 2013. Trafficking in People, 20 Years On: Sex, Migration and Crime in the Global Anti-Trafficking Discourse and the Rise of the 'Global Trafficking Complex'. *Current Issues in Criminal Justice* 25(2), pp. 585–604.

Milivojevic, S. and Segrave M. 2012. Evaluating Responses to Human Trafficking: A Review of International, Regional and National Counter-Trafficking Mechanisms. In: J. Winterdyk, Perrin, B. and Reichel, P. eds. *Human Trafficking: Exploring the International Nature, Concerns, and Complexities.* Boca Raton, FL: Taylor and Francis, pp. 233–264.

Ministry of Justice 2012. Reform of the Criminal Injuries Compensation Scheme. July 2012. https://consult.justice.gov.uk/digital-communications/victims-witnesses/results/eia-criminal-injuries-comp-scheme.pdf [Accessed: 18 June 2014].

National Crime Agency. [No date]. *National Referral Mechanism.* http://www.nationalcrimeagency.gov.uk/about-us/what-we-do/specialist-capabilities/uk-human-trafficking-centre/national-referral-mechanism [Accessed: 18 June 2014].

Norberry, J. 2004–2005. *Criminal Code Amendment (Trafficking in Persons Offences) Bill 2004.* Parliament of Australia, Department of Parliamentary Services, Bills Digest No. 96. http://www.aph.gov.au/binaries/library/pubs/bd/2004-05/05bd096.pdf [Accessed: 13 June 2014].

Noweir, M. 2013. *Supporting Victims of Human Trafficking: Examining the Design and Implementation of Victim Support within Australia and the UK.* Master's Thesis. Monash University, Australia.

Oberholer, R. 2003. To Counter Effectively Organized Crime Involvement in Irregular Migration, People Smuggling and Human Trafficking from the East: Europe's Challenges Today. In: Nevala, S. and Aromaa, K. eds. *Organized Crime, Trafficking, Drugs: Selected Papers Presented at the Annual Conference of the European Society of Criminology.* Helsinki, Finland: United Nations European Institute for Crime Prevention and Control (HEUNI).

O'Brien, E. 2013. Ideal Victim in Trafficking Awareness Campaigns. In: Carrington, K., Ball, M., O'Biren, E. and Tauri, J. eds. *Crime, Justice and Social Democracy: International Perspectives.* Basingstoke and New York: Palgrave Macmillan, pp. 315–326.

O'Connell Davidson, J. 2010. New Slavery, Old Binaries: Human Trafficking and the Borders of 'Freedom'. *Global Networks* 10(2), pp. 244–261.

Parliament UK 2014. *Modern Slavery Bill 2014–2015.* PDF: http://www.publications.parliament.uk/pa/bills/cbill/2014-2015/0008/15008.pdf [Accessed: 4 September 2014].

Phillips. J. 2008. *People Trafficking: An Update on Australia's Response.* Parliament of Australia, Department of Parliamentary Services, Research Paper, 22 August 2008, No. 5. PDF: http://www.aph.gov.au/binaries/library/pubs/rp/2008-09/09rp05.pdf

Pickering, S. 2011. *Women, Borders and Violence: Current Issues on Asylum, Forced Migration, and Trafficking.* New York: Springer.

Pickering, S. and Ham, J. 2014. Hot pants at the Border: Sorting Sex Work from Trafficking. *British Journal of Criminology* 54(1), pp. 2–19.

Pickering, S. and Weber, L. 2006. Borders, Mobility and Technologies of Control. In: Pickering S. and Weber, L. eds. *Borders, Mobility and Technologies of Control.* Dordrecht: Springer, pp. 1–19.

Pollock, J. 2007. Thailand. In: Global Alliance Against Traffic in Women (GAATW) eds. *Collateral Damage: The Impact of Anti-trafficking Measures on Human Rights around the World.* Bangkok: GAATW.

Potocky, M. 2010. The Travesty of Human Trafficking: A Decade of Failed US Policy. *Social Work* 55(4), pp. 372–375.

Project Respect 2004. *One Victims of Trafficking is Too Many: Counting the Human Cost of Trafficking.* Melbourne: Project Respects.

Randall, M. 2010. Sexual Assault Law, Credibility, and 'Ideal Victims': Consent, Resistance and Victim Blaming. *Canadian Journal of Women and the Law* 22(2), pp. 397–433.

Saunders, P. and Soderlund, G. 2003. Threat or Opportunity? Sexuality, Gender and the Ebb and Flow of Trafficking as Discourse. *Canadian Woman Studies* 22(3–4), pp. 16–24.

Scarlet Alliance, 2003. *Submission to: Parliamentary Joint Committee on the Australian Crime Commission Inquiry into Trafficking in Women – Sexual Servitude September 2003.* PDF: http://www.scarletalliance.org.au/library/traff_sub03 [Accessed: 25 July 2015].

Schloenhardt, A. and Curley, C. [no date]. *Case Report (Criminal): R v Yogalingham Rasalingam.* Human Trafficking Working Group, TC Beirne School of Law, University of Queensland. http://www.law.uq.edu.au/documents/humantraffic/case-reports/trafficking-offences/rasalingam.pdf [Accessed: 17 June 2014].

Segrave, M. 2007. *Restoring Order: Statecraft, the Border and Sex Trafficking.* PhD Dissertation. Monash University, Australia.

Segrave, M. ed. 2013. *Human Trafficking.* Farnham: Ashgate.

Segrave, M. and Milivojevic, S. 2010. Auditing the Australian Response to Human Trafficking. *Current Issues in Criminal Justice* 22(1), pp. 63–81.

Segrave, M., Milivojevic, S. and Pickering, S. 2009. *Sex Trafficking: International Context and Response.* Cullompton: Willan.

Serious Organised Crime Agency (SOCA) 2012. *National Referral Mechanism Statistics – July to September 2011.* Serious Organised Crime Agency, UK.

Serious Organised Crime Agency (SOCA) 2013 *Intelligence Assessment. UKHTC: A Strategic Assessment on the Nature and Scale of Human Trafficking in 2012.* August 2013. Serious Organised Crime Agency UK.

Simeunovic-Patic, B. 2005. Protection, Assistance and Support of Trafficked Persons: Current Responses. In: Bjerkan, L. ed. *A Life on One's Own: Rehabilitation of Victims of Trafficking for Sexual Exploitation.* Oslo: Fafo, pp. 23–68.

Skinner, E.B. 2008. *A Crime so Monstrous: Face to Face with Modern Day Slavery.* New York: Free Press.

Skrobanek, S. Boonpakdi, N. Janthakeero, C. 1997. *The Traffic in Women: Human Realities of the International Sex Trade.* London: Zed Books.

Spencer, J. and Broad, R. 2012. The 'Groundhog Day' of the Human Trafficking for Sexual Exploitation Debate: New Directions in Criminological Understanding. *European Journal on Criminal Policy and Research* 18(1), pp. 269–281.

Stanko, E.A. 1994. Dancing with Denial: Researching Women and Questioning Men. In: Maynard, M. and Purvis, J. eds. *Researching Women's Lives from a Feminist Perspective*. Oxon, UK: Taylor & Francis, pp. 93–105.

Stevenson, K. 2000. Unequivocal Victims: The Historical Roots of the Mystification on the Female Complainant in Rape Cases. *Feminist Legal Studies* 8(3), pp. 343–366.

Sullivan, B. 2003. Trafficking in Women: Feminism and New International Law. *International Feminist Journal of Politics* 5(1), pp. 67–91.

Surtees R. 2005. *Second Annual Report on Victims of Trafficking in South Eastern Europe*. Geneva: International Organisation for Migration.

TC Beirne School of Law, Human Trafficking Working Group. [No date a]. *Australia's Policies on Trafficking in Person*. http://www.law.uq.edu.au/ht-policies [Accessed: 18 June 2014].

TC Beirne School of Law, Human Trafficking Working Group. [No date b]. *Visas for Trafficking Victims in Australia*. http://www.law.uq.edu.au/ht-visas [Accessed: 18 June 2014].

United Nations Office on Drugs and Crime (UNODC) 2012. *Global Report on Trafficking in Persons*, United Nations Office on Drugs and Crime, Vienna. http://www.unodc.org/documents/data-and-analysis/glotip/Trafficking_in_Persons_2012_web.pdf [Accessed: 13 June 2014].

US Department of State 2007. *Trafficking in Persons Report*. Washington, DC: US Department of State.

US Department of State 2011. *Trafficking in Persons Report*. Washington, DC: US Department of State.

US Department of State 2013. *Trafficking in Persons Report*. Washington, DC: US Department of State.

US Department of State 2014. *Four 'Ps': Prevention, Protection, Prosecution, Partnerships*. http://www.state.gov/j/tip/4p/ [Accessed: 13 June 2014].

Walklate, S. 2011. Reframing Criminal Victimization: Finding a Place for Vulnerability and Resilience. *Theoretical Criminology* 15(2), pp. 179–194.

Weitzer, R. and Ditmore, M. 2010. Sex Trafficking: Facts and Fictions. In: Weitzer, R. ed. *Sex for Sale: Prostitution, Pornography and the Sex Industry*. London: Routledge.

Winter, K. and Castillo, D. 2011. Imperious Freedom: The Tangled Narrative of Anti-Human Trafficking Discourse. *Left History* 15(2), pp. 63–82.

Wolhuter, L., Olley, N. and Denham, D. 2009. *Victimology: Victimisation and Victims' Rights*. Milton Park: Routledge Cavendish.

Wonders, N. 2006. Global Flows, Semi-Permeable Borders and New Channels of Inequality. In: Pickering, S. and Weber, L. eds. *Borders, Mobility and Technologies of Control*. Dordrecht: Springer, pp. 63–86.

4

Justice for Rape Victims? The Spirit May Sound Willing, but the Flesh Remains Weak

Jan Jordan

Growing recognition of rape victims

There has been growing recognition in recent years of the ways in which being a victim of sexual violence is synonymous with experiencing multiple forms of victimisation and re-victimisation. International research has identifiedvarious ways rape victims have felt re-traumatised by their contact with the various agencies of the criminal justice system, as well as in their own informal networks, by the media and potentially by any persons responding to their assertion that they have been raped (Ahrens 2006; Campbell and Raja 1999; Gregory and Lees 1999; Kitzinger 2009; Temkin and Krahé 2008; Taslitz 1999). Police services around the world have been criticised for failing to believe and investigate fully the allegations made by rape complainants (Du Mont et al. 2003; Jordan 2004; Kelly 2002, 2008; Lonsway 2010; O'Keeffe et al. 2009; Stanko and Williams 2009), and numerous writers researching rape victims' experiences in court have dubbed it the 'second rape' (Doyle and Barbato 1999; Koss 2000; Madigan and Gamble 1991; Martin and Powell 1994; Orth 2002).

In recent years internationally, feminist advocates and rape support groups have challenged state responses to rape, resulting in significant changes being made to law, policy, training and practice. These developments have occurred within the wider context of the victims' rights movement, as governments around the world have sought to find ways of enabling the justice system to be more aware and cognisant of victims' needs. The enormity of these shifts should not be underestimated, reflecting as they do a move away from criminal offenders' being the central and dominant focus towards a more victim-centred approach. Indeed such a shift has had implications within academia also, as victimology has developed and become recognised as a legitimate field of research and inquiry (Walklate 2007).

Many countries have introduced victims' rights charters and other measures intended to protect victims' interests. These have enshrined in law that victims can expect, for example, to be treated with compassion, to be kept informed about case progress and to be supported during justice system processes. Victims of the most serious violent offences have sometimes been accorded further recognition through specific clauses or policy statements introduced to underline the importance of ensuring the victims of these crimes are treated sensitively and offered additional information and services.

Outside of the state sector, key changes have also occurred within professional and non-governmental organisations. In New Zealand, for instance, criticism of the inhumane, even barbaric, way that forensic medical examinations of rape victims could be conducted prompted women doctors to establish their own training and organisation (Young 1983). Known as Doctors for Sexual Abuse Care, this group sought to ensure that in as many areas of the country as possible victims could be examined by a specially trained woman doctor, yielding vastly improved accounts of how this potentially invasive procedure was experienced (Jordan 2001). From the 1970s onwards rape crisis agencies were established by feminists in many nations to provide rape victims with support and counselling, and as recognition of the impact of rape trauma has grown, their role and importance has increasingly been underlined (Ahrens 2006; Campbell 2002; Cook and Jones 2007; Kingi and Jordan 2009). Despite this, most such agencies today remain grossly underfunded and are often reliant on the work of volunteers to deliver services (Maier 2011; Ullman and Townsend 2007). This represents a curious contradiction in that although state rhetoric regarding the importance of meeting victims' needs is now routine, it has not been accompanied by increased funding for those providing the specialised services and victim support now recognised as central to their recovery. The salience of this observation, initially noted many years ago, remains evident in 2014:

> by individualizing the experience of victimisation, and reducing it to a list of what 'you can expect' from criminal justice agencies, it distracts attention from the possibility that there might be structural problems underlying crime and criminal victimisation and that collective action might be an effective method of response. (Williams 1999, p. 394)

On the one hand, then, we can identify an array of measures and services declaring their intention to treat victims of rape with respect and compassion and to ensure their needs are met. On paper the various charters, policies, pamphlets for victims and so forth look positive and supportive. The 'victims matter' rhetoric reassures casual onlookers that the agencies serving victims are dedicated to victims' well-being, so much so that assertions have been made that the state has become excessively oriented towards victim, using popular notions of victims' rights as a legitimating factor for increased punitiveness as part of the 'war on crime' (Dubber 2002).

On the other hand, a different story emerges in the form of extensive criticisms' suggesting that the many promises made to victims are, at best, delivered selectively. Police policy implementation, for example, may still often be dependent on individual officer discretion, effectively producing a lottery system in which victims/survivors may or may not receive informed and sensitive treatment (Cook 2011; Jordan 2001, 2011; Stern 2010). Furthermore, a recurring pattern has emerged of reviews and reforms, followed by further reviews and reforms, each time effectively signalling that change is easier to achieve through rhetoric and on paper than it is in day-to-day practice and decision making (Brown 2011; Jordan 2011).

This chapter aims to navigate a path between these two positions in order to reflect why, despite the significant advances made, rape remains one of the lowest reported crimes with the highest attrition rates. It begins by analysing a recent high-profile rape case in New Zealand and the mixed police and public reactions to it, using this as a platform from which to launch into critical examination of how, in both local and international contexts, police and societal attitudes to rape remain fundamentally little changed despite the plethora of reviews, recommendations and reforms repeatedly being enacted.

Background

In common with many countries, New Zealand has a history of police scandals relating to inadequate and inappropriate behaviours and responses to rape victims. In the 21st century the most significant of these was the uncovering of historic rapes of young women perpetrated by serving police officers during the 1980s. These involved multiple complainants, yet few dared report in the climate of the time, and they could encounter the police code of silence if they did. It took approximately 20 years before details of these crimes went public, which was enabled by the courage of one woman, Louise Nicholas, who from age 13 has been subjected to multiple rapes by police, including group rapes. She was supported by other brave complainants, her family, a tenacious journalist, and some dedicated police officers (Nicholas 2007). The outcomes included a large-scale police investigation of multiple historic rape complaints, the conviction and imprisonment of several former police officers, and the prosecution and trial of one of the highest-ranked officers in the land, who, though subsequently acquitted, was widely believed to have been guilty of the charges brought against him. The government responded by establishing the Commission of Inquiry into police conduct surrounding rape and sexual violence offences (Bazley 2007). The latter was concerned not only with the historic cases but also with how to improve current police sexual assault investigations and conduct towards women more widely, including within police ranks (Rowe 2009).

The Commission's findings included identification of a 'culture of scepticism' that could negatively influence police responses to rape complainants. It also noted the widespread discretion held by district commanders throughout the country and observed that

> Policies and directives are issued to districts without any obvious mechanisms for ensuring that they are understood and consistently followed by front-line staff. (Bazley 2007, p. 8)

Thus, despite a 1998 policy stipulating that detectives interviewing rape complainants should have completed a specialist adult sexual assault investigation course, nearly ten years on many had not yet undertaken such training. Sixty recommendations were made, with one of the first acted upon being the adoption of a code of conduct to guide police behaviour, given that none had existed previously (Bazley 2007).

In the years since then, the organisation's performance has been regularly reviewed to assess the extent of its compliance to these recommendations, with the progress cards typically suggesting some lag and dragging of the police heels. The third and most recent report noted that

> Although sexual assault crimes are a relatively small proportion of all crimes, ensuring that they are properly investigated and that members of the Police are not perpetrators of them are especially important for trust and confidence in the Police. (Office of the Auditor General 2012, p. 4)

Despite concerns over the seemingly slow pace of change, some positive indicators were noted. These included an increase in the number of police districts with dedicated adult sexual assault teams to five, the formation of a training review group and plans to introduce an early intervention system nationwide to alert police to conduct by officers that could potentially lead to more serious forms of inappropriate behaviour. Reduced length catch-up courses meant that by 2013 most detectives had received the mandated adult sexual assault specialist training; police morale was recovering; and general levels of public confidence appeared high in the police. Raised expectations and a degree of complacency meant many were surprised when in September 2013 a district commander was pressured to apologise after describing a ten-year-old rape victim as a 'willing' participant in sex in a letter to the accused's wife (Dougan 2013). The commissioner of police stated at the time that, while this was a 'disappointing comment' from a senior officer, he did not consider that it signified a need for a cultural shift within New Zealand Police (Television New Zealand 2013). Two months later another case rocketed to prominence.

Case study: Auckland's online 'rape club'

Day One: In November 2013 a news story broke about a group of young men, calling themselves the 'Roast Busters', who had been boasting on Facebook about how successful they were at getting young women drunk before raping them (Rutherford 2013). Not only did these lads appear to feel no remorse, but also they chose to name and shame the girls online as well. The young men involved were typically 16–18; the girls they targeted were as young as 13 and 14.

The case came to public attention only when a television station reported on 4 November 2013 that it had, for some time, been investigating the group's activities (Rutherford 2013). Appearing first as an item on national news, the piece included comments from two of the young men involved boasting about their conquests and saying they were keen to recruit more boys to join them.

Also interviewed, anonymously, was a young woman who described being under 16 when three of this group raped her, an experience she struggled to remember clearly given that she kept blacking out from excess alcohol. A senior police detective was interviewed who acknowledged police had known of the group's activities since 2011 (Dudding 2013). He maintained that no intervention was possible, because their online posts were morally objectionable but not criminal, prompting

TV3 to point out that when they contacted Facebook about the site's contents, it was taken down within two hours. When challenged why no action had been taken against these boys, the assurance was given by the district communications manager that

> A full and thorough investigation has been conducted but in the absence of significant evidence, such as formal statements, there is not enough evidence to prosecute the alleged offenders. (Leask 2013)

Later that day the local detective inspector also confirmed no further action was possible, because none of the girls had made formal statements to police. He urged: "It takes one girl to be brave enough to do that. ... Without actual evidence my hands are tied" (Rutherford 2013).

Day Two: The following day, as increasingly senior officers up the police hierarchy were brought in, the local district commander rejected any suggestions that the investigation had stalled because a police officer's son was involved (Leask 2013). The son of a Hollywood actor, now living in West Auckland, was also implicated in the club's activities, and public debate over the case intensified. The Commissioner of Police repeated the admonition voiced by previous senior officers proclaiming nothing further could be done until a formal complaint was made. He also implored any girls victimised by the group to be "brave" and come forward.

Day Three: Next day a teenage girl appeared on national television alleging that she was raped by members of the rape group when she was 13, told her parents and went to the police with them to lodge a complaint. She made a formal, video-recorded statement but said this experience caused her further shame when police asked her about the clothes she was wearing that night and suggested she use dolls to act out what happened (New Zealand Herald, 2013). No charges were laid, and she believed that if the police had acted then, other girls would not have suffered the same experience. Within little over an hour the district commander released a statement confirming that it now appeared a formal complaint had in fact been received by police in December 2011.

Day Four: The story changed again early morning when police released a statement clarifying that a total of four complaints had been received from teenage girls, aged 13–15. Three approached police in 2011, of whom one proceeded to make a formal complaint with a recorded statement. A fourth girl spoke with police in late 2012 about the same rape group. One of the girls described how during an interview with the police she felt she was made to believe she had consented to the sex and had heard nothing further from them – until yesterday.

The minister of police summoned the commissioner of police, who reassured this fourth girl that there had been a full and thorough investigation into the formal complaint made. Both agreed they were 'disappointed' that neither had been appraised that such a complaint had been made until yesterday and that they had each learned more about the case from the media than from their own staff.

This revelation and mounting public pressure resulted in the minister of police's referring the case for investigation by the Independent Police Conduct Authority, an investigation still ongoing at the time of writing (April 2014).

The case of the 'Roast Busters' dominated national media for more than a week, with radio, television and Internet sites all reflecting strong and often opposing viewpoints. One vociferously asserted perspective levelled criticism at the young girls who were raped. They were blamed for hanging out with these guys, for drinking alcohol, and for dressing suggestively (Fairfax News 2013). Two radio talk show hosts provoked outrage from many quarters for the way they spoke to a girl, 'Amy', who called in saying she had been raped as a 14-year-old by members of the rape club. The pair's questions focused on Amy's behaviour, including asking what she had been drinking and wearing and how old she was when she lost her virginity. Sufficient levels of public outrage were expressed that several large companies pulled their advertising from the show and the hosts were pressured to apologise and take time off the air (Herald on Sunday, 2013).

The radio show hosts and other commentators asserted that the girls sought out the young men involved and that the sex was consensual, ignoring the fact that under New Zealand law it is a crime to have sexual intercourse with anyone under 16 years of age, whether supposedly consensual or not (NZ Crimes Amendment Act (2005) Part 7, section 134). It is also a crime to proceed with sexual intercourse with someone too intoxicated to be able to provide consent (ibid., section 128A), another factor widely overlooked.

Comments now shifted in some quarters to blame the parents of these girls for not being aware of where their daughters were and how much they were drinking (Irvine 2013).

A parent should know, for example, where their 13-year-old daughter is. Not in the kind of place where they're getting munted with a bunch of older boys. (Sunday Star Times 2013, p. 15)

With the blame game now in full swing, others criticised the police for failing to act and once again being in the spotlight for appearing not to take rape complaints seriously and for not believing the complainants (MacLennan 2013).

Under such pressure, the commissioner of police conceded that possibly the police should have made public earlier their knowledge of the group's activities. Somewhat defensively, he added:

> But we had the best intentions at heart, to have victims come to us so that we could progress matters. We're actually in the business of helping victims like this. (Television New Zealand 2013)

A spokesperson apologised to the girl concerned, and to the public, over the apparent police confusion as to whether she had made a formal complaint.

One observable difference between the responses to the 2013 cases and those identified in the 2007 Commission of Inquiry was that more questions were asked regarding the behaviour of the males involved. Initially, there were knee-jerk responses calling for revenge and vigilante actions against the boys. Young women quickly responded by taking to Facebook themselves, starting postings calling for support and justice for the victims as well as for a stance to be taken against rape culture in New Zealand (McCracken and Leask 2013. Indeed, some commentators loudly pronounced this case useful as a tool to encourage wider discussions in New Zealand society regarding prevailing notions of masculinity and sexual norms, particularly when alcohol is involved.

In this particular case we can see a microcosm of the issues and attitudes identifiable in many different nations and contexts, all of which operate as barriers to improving rape victims' experiences in the justice system. Four of these are briefly canvassed below, drawing on further details from the case involving boys from the 'rape club'.

Firstly, it puts beneath the spotlight a range of issues raised in international research, suggesting that victims of sexual violence still struggle to have their allegations believed. Secondly, it illustrates how even if believed, victims of rape risk being blamed for inviting their own victimisation. Both these observations suggest that, despite 40 years of consciousness-raising efforts to challenge rape myths and promote women's sexual equality, deep schisms of misogyny continue to run through our social fabric. Thirdly, some of the attitudes expressed reflected ongoing beliefs in male sexual entitlement, demanding closer scrutiny of dominant constructs of masculinity. Related to this are attitudes towards alcohol and its role in sexual offending. Lastly, this case also reveals that despite repeated admonitions to police to improve their conduct of rape and sexual assault investigations, there is still no guarantee that reported cases will proceed far in the criminal justice system. Each of these points is now briefly canvassed.

Questions of victim credibility

The teenage girls victimised in this case faced accusations from some quarters that they had fabricated their accounts. Inferences were made suggesting their allegations should perhaps best be dismissed as incidents of 'regretful sex'. One article, for example, began by asserting that

> A secondary school counsellor told the Bay of Plenty Times Weekend that some students were getting so drunk they were waking up to discover they had had sex with no memory of it, or deeply regretting their decision to have sex while their inhibitions were lowered by alcohol. (Irvine 2013, 7)

Typical of such accounts was the omission of any reference to the choices made by boys to sexually exploit girls who were made vulnerable by alcohol or how their actions contributed to the girls' drunken states.

Doubting women's words when they allege rape is one of the oldest and most enduring defences available. The spectre of false accusations has a rich history, dating far back into antiquity (Jordan 2004). Depicting women as malicious liars saw devices such as the scold's bridle invented and more recently contributed to criminologists such as Otto Pollak (1950) advocating that women were biologically predisposed to lying, deception and concealment. Research on false rape complaints in the United States, the United Kingdom, Canada and New Zealand suggests many police continue to subscribe to the view that women often lie about rape, ignoring the fact that men who rape are prolific liars and deniers of their sexual offending (Jordan 2004; Kelly 2010; Lonsway 2010). This belief has been referred to in a range of international contexts as evidence of a 'culture of scepticism' infusing police ranks (Bazley 2007; Jordan 2004; Kelly 2010; Stern 2010). The associated dangers are well recognised:

> The underlying skepticism that sexual assault survivors face when they disclose may be the single most damaging factor in our societal response. It may also be the most powerful tool in the arsenal of rapists because it allows them to commit their crimes with impunity. (Lonsway 2010, p. 1367)

Many of the factors interpreted by police as denting a complainant's credibility can, if viewed through a different lens, instead denote vulnerability. While police may express concerns that drunk teenage girls will invent rape stories to excuse sexual liaisons later regretted, plying inexperienced drinkers with alcohol can also be viewed as a centuries-old method used by men to obtain sex or, expressed more directly, to use alcohol to perpetrate drug-rape.

Questions of victim culpability

Many comments made about the 'Roast Busters' case focused heavily on the nature and behaviour of the girls who were making the allegations. Questions were raised regarding their morality and choice of clothing, and they were blamed for going out and seeking the company of these young men. Some commentators, rather than criticising the ways the boys used alcohol, said the girls needed not to drink so much since surely they knew what would happen.

Fortunately, however, at least some voices expressed alternative views, such as the following:

> To describe the activities of the Auckland teenagers who allegedly had group sex with drunk underage girls and then bragged about it online as 'mischief' is to perpetuate the myth that the victims of sexual assault are to blame for what befalls them. (Dominion Post 2013, 10)

This attitude reflects a perception of women still as sexual gatekeepers, asserting it is the females' responsibility to ensure she is not easily rapeable since the male has such little control over his libido. The paradox of modern man sits here – a rational and powerful entity right up to the moment when his easily stimulated penis takes charge, at which point he can but follow where it leads. In the 21st century it is still up to girls and women to refrain from drinking, flirting or engaging in other behaviours viewed as equally culpable.

How rape victims are perceived has been the subject of many surveys of attitudes and public opinion. A salutary finding from the more recent of these suggests that despite many campaigns aimed at increasing awareness, attitudes towards victims remain steadfastly uninformed and judgemental. A survey conducted in 2005, for instance, found strongly judgemental attitudes expressed towards victims if they were wearing sexy clothing or were drunk at the time of the rape (Amnesty International 2005; Walklate 2008). In a similar vein, a more recent survey in London found nearly two-thirds of the sample believed victims should accept responsibility if they had been drinking to excess or had blacked out before the rape (The Havens 2010, cited in Horvath et al. 2011).

A more recent overview conducted within the United States suggested that, while there may have been some reduction in victim-blaming attitudes towards rape victims, nevertheless these continue to remain problematic and contribute to the ongoing cultural (mis)conceptions of rape (McMahon 2011). Similarly, an American study conducted specifically to ascertain shifts in police officers' adherence to rape myths found that, despite some positive changes, significant numbers still held attitudes endorsing traditional rape myths (Page 2010).

One of the most pervasive forms of assigning culpability to a rape victim comes from the victim. The tendency for those victimised by rape to engage in highly critical self-blaming has been widely noted (Ahrens 2006; Gavey 2005), an attribute affecting the extent to which women will define themselves as legitimate victims and linked to their reporting behaviour (Sable et al. 2006). Extensive social conditioning suggests that a woman victim views herself as culpable in some way since she also has been raised in an environment saturated with the 'she was asking for it' myth. This helps to explain the lack of formal complaints made against the Auckland rape club boys.

Perceptions of masculinity and male sexual entitlement

Discussion regarding the behaviour of the young men reflected a spectrum of views, ranging from 'boys will be boys' through to condemnation of their predatory behaviour. With a certain naiveté some commentators suggested it was a relief that these offenders had been stopped in their tracks, as if to imply that they were the only ones engaging in such behaviour and that girls are now safe. Others, more realistically, saw this as an opportunity to reflect on the values still informing 21st-century masculinity (Hager 2013). Concern that this rape club represented the tip of the iceberg of male sexual proprietariness prompted a few commentators to call for deeper scrutiny of the messages given regarding normative masculinity (Gaayathri 2013).

Statements made by the boys themselves suggested they viewed sexual conquest as an essential feature of heteronormative masculinity. One claimed:

My first actual roast for the Roast Busters was bad, It was fun, I felt like the man. (Rutherford 2013)

Another member of this 'club' insisted the girls knew what these guys were like yet gravitated towards them like sexual magnets. He said:

> A true roast is where you know you are going there intentionally to roast this female. We don't choose a roast, the roast chooses us. We have girls hitting us up to "hang out with us'. They know what we're like; they know what they're in for. (Rutherford 2013)

When asked online to repeat a saying he liked to make, he replied:

> Go ahead: call the cops. ... They can't un-rape you. (Rose 2013)

They were less forthright regarding the volume of alcohol they felt necessary to give the girls to ensure their 'participation'. Evidence from elsewhere suggests some men may encourage heavy drinking by women and may view intoxication in women as signifying sexual availability (Horvath and Brown 2007).

Rather than being the extreme aberrations many commentators portrayed, these boys' attitudes reflect more widely held rape-supportive norms and behaviours. In reviewing youth studies conducted in the United States, Britain and New Zealand, Michael Flood and Bob Pease concluded that

> For many boys and girls, sexual harassment is pervasive, male aggression is normalized, there is constant pressure among boys to behave in sexually aggressive ways, girls are routinely objectified, a sexual double standard polices girls' sexual and intimate involvements, and girls are compelled to accommodate male needs and desires in negotiating their sexual relations. (2009, p. 129)

The attitudes expressed regarding masculinity reflect our societal ambivalence regarding what it means to be a man. Despite some calls to challenge a traditional macho image, there has been no lessening of the idolisation of physically strong and tough male super-heroes.

Role of police as gatekeepers to the justice system

Comments made by top-ranking police in the rape club case revealed little comprehension regarding why the girls victimised might be reluctant to approach police and have justifiable anxieties about doing so.

The one girl 'brave' enough to make a formal complaint felt blamed by the police, while a lack of action against the boys appeared more supportive of their behaviour than of hers. More generally, the knowledge that the police had been aware of the boys' predatory behaviour against underage girls for two years provoked high public criticism, as the following comment reflects:

> It is the actions of the police in this case that worries me. They need to take a long hard look at how they treat those reporting sexual assaults. It's not good enough to say, after declaring no victims have come forward, 'sorry, that's not quite correct, four girls did speak with us but we didn't have enough evidence to go on'. What do they want? To be there on the spot when the girls are getting raped. (The Daily Post 2013, p. 9)

This case revealed the major attrition point in the justice system – the police investigations stage. Most rapes and sexual assaults are not reported to the police, but for the approximately 10% that are, how the police respond is the key determinant of case outcomes. International research identifies this as the most critical factor contributing to the gap – or as Liz Kelly termed it, 'the chasm' – between the numbers reporting rape and the few cases advancing to prosecution of an offender (Kelly et al. 2005; Lea et al. 2003; Munro and Kelly 2009). The chances of a conviction resulting from prosecution are even more remote, typically constituting between 5 percent and 15 percent of all reported rapes (Daly and Bouhours 2010; Temkin and Krahé 2008).

Recognition of the extent to which the police serve as gatekeepers to the criminal justice system highlights the powerful position they occupy in relation to victims as well as offenders. While many studies have focused on abuses of police powers in relation to persons identified as likely criminal offenders, comparatively fewer have applied this lens to their actions with respect to crime victims. How the police respond to victims is vital on many levels, with one of the most significant being in terms of the validation role they can play. What many victims of rape assert is that what they most want from the police is to be believed and to have their experience and feelings validated – in other words, to hear these powerful arbiters of 'truth' attest that what the offender did was wrong. While the critical function played by police as gatekeepers to the criminal justice system remains evident (Jordan 2004; Stanko and Williams 2009; Taylor and Gassner 2010), this constitutes one of the most strategic areas in which to invest energy and resources.

International parallels

Strong opinions were expressed regarding the police response, or lack thereof, in the 'Roast Busters' case. This event could be viewed, in many ways, as a public relations disaster for the police. As detailed earlier, there was the initial declaration by the commissioner that the police's hands were tied given that no formal complaint had been made, followed within 24 hours by an embarrassing turnaround when it emerged that at least one girl had made such a complaint two years earlier. It emerged that four girls had reported these same boys, but investigations did not proceed, and presumably their reports were not linked. Despite the behaviour of these young men being known about for two years there was no obvious intervention by the police – the young men were left free to continue both their activities as well as their Facebook bragging of their sexual conquests. Nor were steps taken to alert the community of the risks or to support those victimised. At the time of writing many are struggling to understand why, after considering the case for nearly a year, the police announced in October 2014 that there would be no prosecution action taken against any of the boys involved (Steward 2014). The police report on this case suggests that, despite five formal complaints and evidence suggesting sexual offending occurred against 25 additional girls, the case did not pass the evidentiary threshold required for prosecution action to proceed (New Zealand Police 2014). Such a conclusion must indicate, at least in part, their appraisal that any potential jury would be unlikely to view these girls as credible and legitimate victims and perceive the boys as sexual offenders.

While similar cases and responses are observable in many international contexts, cultural differences are evident also. Although the legacy of patriarchy is almost universal, its particular manifestations reflect the varying historical, religious, social and political factors that help to shape national identities. This is evident, for example, in the way in which women are blamed for inviting and inciting rape in many societies, while how they specifically do so varies, as will the consequences. New Zealand has a relatively recent colonial history within which sex ratio imbalances existed initially and forms of hegemonic masculinity developed, emphasising toughness, a rugged independence and hard work followed by equally hard drinking and hard playing (Phillips 1987). Beer was the breast milk during European settlement, with a heavy drinking culture persisting into the 21st century. Youth culture is today still characterised by heavy drinking, physical bravado and beliefs in male dominance and sexual entitlement – all factors associated with high rates of sexual violence (Flood and Pease 2009). They are also factors closely associated with the cultural beliefs and lifestyles of the police service, at least until recently. While police management strive to improve gender imbalances and adherence to codes of conduct, cultural legacies remain imprinted within institutional norms and practices.

The 'Roast Busters' case is but the latest in a series of apparent police failures to act that have resulted in increased harm to victims. As well as the rapes of Louise Nicholas and other women mentioned earlier in this chapter, the New Zealand Police have been recently criticised over their failure to believe a woman raped by Malcolm Rewa in 1987, effectively allowing him to go on to attack at least 26 other women and thus become one of the country's most predatory serial rapists (Jordan 2008; Taylor 2013).

There is nothing unique about the New Zealand Police. The criticisms made against it strongly echo voices expressed internationally regarding perceived police mishandling of local cases. In England, for example, much public agitation emerged following the revelation that the police had failed to act on women's allegations of rape made against cabbie John Worboys. After he was arrested as 'one of the most prolific serial sex attackers in British criminal history' (Addley and Laville 2009), believed responsible for committing more than 100 drug-assisted rapes in total, two victims complained about the actions of the Metropolitan Police when they tried to report rapes committed by him (Laville and Dodd 2010). The Independent Police Complaints Commission (IPCC) upheld the women's complaints against five officers, including among their findings both 'individual and systemic' failings, including serious errors of judgement and evidence that police had 'adopted a mindset of believing Worboys and not the victim' (ibid.). Had the police not 'missed crucial investigative opportunities', Worboys would probably have been in custody earlier and many of his later victims spared. The IPCC, however, did not recommend disciplinary action against the officers involved, provoking anger and dismay from victims and victims' advocates. In February 2014 a ruling found that the Metropolitan Police's failure to conduct an adequate investigation of the women's complaints constituted a violation of their human rights, leaving the women now eligible to claim compensation (Bindel 2014).

There is also nothing unique about the boys who prided themselves as the Roast Busters. Their attitudes and behaviours are unfortunately mirrored in the actions and attitudes of young men the world over, as exemplified in a recent US case. In Ohio, in 2012 a 16-year-old female high school student, incapacitated by alcohol, was subjected to repeated sexual assaults perpetrated by football players from the same school. Two of the young men subjected her to forced digital penetration of the vagina and other sexual assaults while their mates filmed and photographed the incidents. Their actions that night were subsequently publicised through various forms of social media. Facebook coverage revealed the young men's jocular attitude as they undressed and violated her, yet there were many in their local town of Steubenville who were outraged, not at the boys' behaviour but at the girl whose allegations portrayed the community and two of its star football players in such a negative light (Macur and Schweber 2012). While groups of boys have used alcohol as a tool in sexual exploitation for centuries, what these recent cases alert us to is the added dimension of increased humiliation via social media devices.

Further international parallels exist. The police responses often reflected stereotypically attitudes towards women and sex, attitudes redolent with stereotypical assumptions and victim blaming. The agency entrusted with enabling rape victims to access justice is itself imbued with similar characteristics to those held by men who rape, including a tendency to exhibit elements of both machismo and misogyny, as well as to objectify and sexualise women's bodies. The police, despite extensive efforts to recruit more women, remain a predominantly male-dominated organisation difficult for women to advance within (Brown and Heidensohn 2000).

Such criticisms of systemic failures are not intended to detract from the efforts of those dedicated individual police officers who strive to serve rape victims well. It is encouraging that improved training programmes mean there are probably more such aware and committed officers and detectives within the organisation. However, while senior managers in police organisations may voice their support for various reform initiatives, it is unrealistic to expect a new training imperative or policy directive to change the social attitudes of a lifetime throughout the force. An enhanced focus on structural and systemic failures helps us to understand why the myriad reviews and reform packages are not producing the expected changes. As a US law professor observed, 'Patriarchal rape tales will not give up the ghost easily' (Taslitz 1999, p. 42), and the historical legacy and structural features within police organisations contribute to their being among the most haunted. The surprise is not that the police scandals keep happening; it is that most of them still manage to fly beneath the media's radar. It is a scandal every time a victim of rape is blamed or disbelieved, every time her trauma is dismissed as mere regret or attention seeking. For certain groups of vulnerable victims, including women with intellectual or psychiatric disabilities, there is such little chance of their cases receiving serious police investigation that professor Betsy Stanko, an academic conducting research with the London Metropolitan Police, recently proclaimed that the rape of such women has effectively been decriminalised (Newman 2014a).

Conclusion

There are breezes of change blowing, but the winds blow selectively in that we are a long way from the day when all rape victims will be viewed and treated equally. Victims who conform more closely to so-called real rape stereotypes are still those most likely to be believed and responded to sensitively and positively by police (Brown and Horvath 2009; Jordan 2004; Kelly et al. 2005; Temkin and Krahé 2008). They stand the greatest chance of their cases being investigated fully, even if few proceed to trial. As one English commentator observed recently,

> police know that jurors are reluctant to convict unless there is CCTV footage of a woman being dragged into a hedge by a masked, armed man who is shouting, 'I am going to rape you', and even then he would probably convincingly argue that it was a 'sex game' gone wrong. (Bindel 2014)

The fact that rapes perpetrated by strangers are rare occurrences, and most women are raped by men they already know, defies news and popular media's ongoing depiction of 'every woman's worst nightmare' being the stranger rape scenario. Women raped by current and former partners not only make up one of the largest categories of rape victims but are also just as, often more, traumatised given the added betrayals of trust involved (Bennice and Resick 2003; Bergen 2006). Today it remains difficult to easily determine who the victim is when popular images of real victimhood continue to reflect outmoded stereotypes and sexist, often misogynist, attitudes.

The case study and material presented here give us both cause for concern as well as grounds for hope. On one level, it is reprehensible that after 40 years of advocating for victims' rights and introducing rafts of measures aimed ostensibly at ensuring these are met, there is still so much more that needs to happen to transform these from rhetoric to reality. Such apparent tardiness is not, however, incomprehensible. Framing victims' needs as consumer rights through charters and the like enables an individualised focus to be sustained while structural and systemic issues remain hidden (Williams 1999). Thus despite all the declared changes in recent years, rape remains both the lowest reported crime and the offence with the highest attrition rates (Daly and Bouhours 2010; Kelly et al. 2005). Even more concerning are revelations such as those in the United Kingdom indicating that since 2011 the number of rape cases referred to prosecutors for charging has in fact fallen by more than a third – the chances of a conviction resulting from prosecution are becoming increasingly remote (Newman 2014a). The director of public prosecutions noted 'worrying variations' in how rape cases were dealt with nationwide:

> There is best practice out there. It's just that not everyone is doing it.
> (Alison Saunders, DPP, cited in Newman 2014b)

So where is the hope? It is evident in the persistence and resilience of feminist groups and rape support agencies' tireless commitment to continue advocacy work despite the state's equally persistent refusal to adequately fund the very services identified as a fundamental right. A further welcome sign lies in the ways in which scandalous rape cases may be more likely now to receive condemnation from a range of quarters, not only from feminist critics. Also impressive is the capacity of those victimised by rape to continue to find ways to resist victim identity and embrace the dual identities of victim and survivor.

Finally, despite the criticisms levelled here, grounds for hope exist when we see individuals within police and other justice agencies who are committed to delivering optimal services to those victimised by sexual violence. Through their efforts, it is encouraging to see some victims receiving the support they need to access justice – a major concern, however, remains with the continuing lack of consistency. This translates into reporting rape being akin to taking a ticket in a lottery – some days you might win, be believed, be supported and be respected; other days you will not. Despite all the reviews and recommendations, it is impossible to guarantee that every woman who reports a rape will consistently receive the service victims' charters proclaim she is entitled to receive. Her access to justice as a victim cannot be assured until that vision is realised.

Overall, this chapter has argued that there has been a considerable body of state rhetoric in recent years, suggesting a willingness to improve services to victims and enhance criminal justice options. Accordingly, in many countries we find growing evidence of victims' rights charters, policies aimed at improved service delivery, increased accountability mechanisms and a never-ending cascade of reviews and commissions of inquiry, each producing its own lists of recommendations. All of this noise is politically useful in giving the impression that the state is willing to make the substantive changes required to serve victims well. However, the body of attitudes still entrenched in patriarchal rape myths, and evidenced when scandals erupt, shows that even though the spirit sounds willing, the flesh remains profoundly weak.

References

Addley, E. and Laville, S. 2009. John Worboys: Polite in Court, A sexual Predator in his London Cab. *The Guardian*, 13 March 2009.

Ahrens, C.E. 2006. Being Silenced: The Impact of Negative Social Reactions on the Disclosure of Rape. *American Journal of Community Psychology* 38(3–4), pp. 263–274.

Amnesty International. 2005. *Sexual Assault Research: Summary Report*. London: Prepared by ICM for Amnesty International UK.

Bazley, Dame M. 2007. *Report of the Commission of Inquiry into Police Conduct, Volume 1*. Wellington: Commission of Inquiry into Police Conduct.

Bennice, J.A. and Resick, P.A. 2003. Marital Rape: History, Research, and Practice. *Trauma, Violence, and Abuse* 4(3), pp. 228–246.

Bergen, R.K. 2006. *Marital Rape: New Research and Directions*. VAWNET Applied Research Forum, National Online Resource Center on Violence Against Women.

Bindel, J. 2014. Will the John Worboys Case Force the Police to Take Rape Seriously? *The Guardian*, 28 February 2014.

Brown, J. 2011. We Mind and We Care but Have Things Changed? Assessment of Progress in the Reporting, Investigating and Prosecution of Alleged Rape Offences. *Journal of Sexual Aggression* 17 (3), pp. 263–272.

Brown, J. and Heidensohn, F. 2000. *Gender and Policing: Comparative Perspectives*. Basingstoke: Palgrave Macmillan.

Brown, J. and Horvath, M. 2009. Do You Believe Her and is it Real Rape? In: Horvath, M. and Brown, J. eds. *Rape: Challenging Contemporary Thinking*. Cullompton: Willan Publishing, pp. 325–342.

Campbell, R. and Raja, S. 1999. Secondary Victimization of Rape Victims: Insights from Mental Health Professionals Who Treat Survivors of Violence. *Violence and Victims* 14(3), pp. 261–275.

Campbell, R. 2002. Emotionally Involved: The Impact of Researching Rape. New York: Routledge.

Cook, K. 2011. Rape Investigation and Prosecution: Stuck in the Mud? *Journal of Sexual Aggression* 17 (3), pp. 250–262.

Cook, K and Jones, H. 2007. Surviving Victimhood: The Impact of Feminist Campaigns. In: Walklate, S. (ed.) *Handbook of Victims and Victimology*. Devon: Willan, pp. 125–145.

Daly, K. and Bouhours, B. 2010. Rape and Attrition in the Legal Process: A Comparative Analysis of Five Countries. In: Tonry, M. ed. *Crime and Justice: An Annual Review of Research (39)*. Chicago: University of Chicago Press, pp. 485–565.

Dominion Post. 2013. Busting the Myth Around Sex Abuse. *Dominion Post*, 14 November 2013, p. 10.

Dougan, P. 2013. Cop: Raped 10-year-old 'Willing'. *New Zealand Herald,* 28 September 2013.

Doyle, S. and Barbato, C. 1999. Justice Delayed is Justice Denied: The Experiences of Women in Court as Victims of Sexual Assault. In: Breckenridge, J. and Laing, L. eds. *Challenging Silence: Innovative Responses to Sexual and Domestic Violence.* Sydney: Allen and Unwin, pp. 47–68.

Du Mont, J., Miller, K. and Myhr, T.L. 2003. The Role of 'Real Rape' and 'Real Victim' Stereotypes in the Police Reporting Practices of Sexually Assaulted Women. *Violence Against Women* 9(4), pp. 466–486.

Dubber, M.D. 2002. *Victims in the War on Crime: The Use and Abuse of Victims' Rights.* New York: New York University Press.

Dudding, A. 2013. Dark Underbelly of Society Raises Potent Ghosts. *Sunday Star Times,* 10 November 2013, p. A10.

Fairfax News. 2013. Expert Appointed to Head Roast Busters Probe. 11 November 2013. http://www.stuff.co.nz/national/9386579/Expert-appointed-to-head-Roast-Busters-probe

Flood, M., and Pease, B. 2009. Factors Influencing Attitudes to Violence Against Women." *Trauma, Violence and Abuse* 10 (2), pp. 125–142.

Gaayathri. 2013. Roast Busters and Rape Culture. Posted 9 November 2013. https://ahumanstory.wordpress.com/2013/11/09/roast-busters-and-rape-culture/

Gavey, N. 2005. *Just Sex? The Cultural Scaffolding of Rape.* Hove: Routledge.

Gregory, J. and Lees, S. 1999. *Policing Sexual Assault.* London: Routledge.

Hager, M. 2013. Rape is Never Okay: The Roastbusters Disgrace. Posted 4 November 2013. http://mandyhager.blogspot.co.nz/2013/11/rape-is-never-okay-roastbusters-disgrace.html

Herald on Sunday. 2013. Victims Face Lack of Respect. *Herald on Sunday,* 10 November 2013, p. A.40.

Horvath, M. and Brown, J. 2007. Alcohol as Drug of Choice: Is Drug Assisted Rape a Misnomer? *Psychology, Crime & Law* 13(5), pp. 417–429.

Horvath, M.A.H., Tong, S. and Williams, E. 2011. Critical Issues in Rape Investigation: An Overview of Reform in England and Wales. *The Journal of Criminal Justice Research* 1 (2), pp. 1–18.

Irvine, E. 2013. Unsupervised Teen Drinking Prompts Fears 'Roast Busters' Scenario could Happen Here. *Bay of Plenty Times,* 16 November 2013, p. A.7.

Jordan, J. 2001. Worlds Apart? Women, Rape and the Reporting Process. *British Journal of Criminology* 41(4), pp. 679–706.

Jordan, J. 2004. *The Word of a Woman? Police, Rape and Belief.* Houndmills, Basingstoke: Palgrave Macmillan.

Jordan, J. 2008. *Serial Survivors: Women's Narratives of Surviving Rape.* Sydney: The Federation Press.

Jordan J. 2011. Here We Go Round the Review-Go-Round: Rape Investigation and Prosecution – Are Things Getting Worse not Better? *Journal of Sexual Aggression* 17(3), pp. 234–249.

Kelly, L. 2002. *A Research Review on the Reporting, Investigation and Prosecution of Rape Cases.* London: Her Majesty's Crown Prosecution Service Inspectorate.

Kelly, L. 2008. Contradictions and Paradoxes: International Patterns of, and Responses to, Reported Rape Cases. In: Letherby, G., Williams, K., Birch, P. and Cain, M. eds. *Sex as Crime?* Cullompton: Willan Publishing, pp. 253–279.

Kelly, L. 2010. The Incredible Words of Women: False Allegations in European Rape Research. *Violence against Women* 16 (12), pp. 1345–1355.

Kelly, L., Lovett, J. and Regan, L. 2005. *A Gap or a Chasm? Attrition in Reported Rape Cases.* Home Office Research Study 293. London: Home Office Research, Development and Statistics Directorate.

Kingi, V., and Jordan, J., (2009) *Responding to Sexual Violence: Pathways to Recovery.* Wellington: Ministry of Women's Affairs.

Kitzinger, J. 2009. Rape in the Media. In: Horvath, M. and Brown, J. eds. *Rape: Challenging Contemporary Thinking.* Cullompton: Willan Publishing, pp. 74–98.

Koss, M. P. (2000). Blame, Shame and Community. *American Psychologist,* 55(11): 1332–43.

Laville, S. and Dodd, V. 2010. Police Errors Left Rapist John Worboys Free to Strike – But no Officers Face Sack. *The Guardian,* 20 January 2010.

Lea, S., Lanvers, U. and Shaw, S. 2003. Attrition in Rape Cases: Developing a Profile and Identifying Relevant Factors. *British Journal of Criminology* 43(3), pp. 583–599.

Leask, A. 2013. Roast Busters Scandal: Teen Left School after Incident at Party. *New Zealand Herald,* 8 November 2013.

Lonsway, K. 2010. Trying to Move the Elephant in the Living Room: Responding to the Challenge of False Rape Reports. *Violence Against Women* 16 (12), pp. 1356–1371.

MacLennan, C. 2013. Police Force Fails NZ's Women ... Again. *New Zealand Herald,* 8 November 2013.

Macur, J. and Schweber, N. 2012. Rape Case Unfolds on Web and Splits City. *The New York Times,* 16 December 2013.

Madigan, L. and Gamble, N. C. (1991). *The Second Rape: Society's Continued Betrayal of the Victim.* New York: Lexington Books.

Maier, S. I. (2011). Rape Crisis Centers and Programs: Doing Amazing, Wonderful Things on Peanuts. *Women and Criminal Justice,* 21 (2): 141–169.

Martin, P. and Powell, R. 1994. Accounting for the 'Second Assault': Legal Organizations Framing of Rape Victims. *Law and Social Inquiry* 19(4), pp. 853–890.

McCracken, H. and Leask, A. 2013. Roast Busters: Girls Hit Back with Online Campaigns. *New Zealand Herald,* 9 November 2013.

McMahon, S. October, 2011. Changing Perceptions of Sexual Violence Over Time. Harrisburg: National Online Resource Center on Violence Against Women. http://www.ncdsv.org/images/Vawnet_ChangingPerceptionsOfSexualViolence OverTime_10-2011.pdf

Munro, V.E. and Kelly, L. 2009. A Vicious Cycle? Attrition and Conviction Patterns in Contemporary Rape Cases in England and Wales. In: Horvath, M. and Brown, J. eds. *Rape: Challenging Contemporary Thinking.* Cullompton: Willan Publishing, pp. 281–300.

New Zealand Herald. 2013. Roast Busters: Victim Made Complaint to Police Two Years Ago. *New Zealand Herald,* 6 November 2013.

New Zealand Police. 2014. *Investigation Overview – Operation Clover.* Wellington: New Zealand Police, 28 October 2014.

Newman, M. 2014a. Rape has been 'Decriminalised' for the most Vulnerable says Senior Met Adviser. *The Bureau of Investigative Journalism.* 28 February 2014.

http://www.thebureauinvestigates.com/2014/02/28/rape-has-been-decrimi-nalised-for-the-most-vulnerable-says-senior-met-adviser/
Newman, M. 2014b. Rape Convictions at Four Year Low Despite Attempts to bring more Cases to Court. *The Bureau of Investigative Journalism.* 2 May 2014. http://www.thebureauinvestigates.com/2014/05/02/rape-convictions-at-four-year-low-despite-attempts-to-bring-more-cases-to-court/
Nicholas, L. 2007. *Louise Nicholas: My Story.* Auckland: Random House.
Office of the Auditor General. 2012. *Response of the New Zealand Police to the Commission of Inquiry into Police Conduct: Third Monitoring Report.* Wellington: Office of the Auditor General.
O'Keeffe, S., Brown, J. and Lyons, E. 2009. Seeking Proof or Truth: Naturalistic Decision Making by Police Officers when Considering Rape Allegations. In: Horvath, M. and Brown, J. eds. *Rape: Challenging Contemporary Thinking.* Cullompton: Willan Publishing, pp. 229–254.
Orth, U. 2002. Secondary Victimization of Crime Victims by Criminal Proceedings. *Social Justice Research* 15(4), pp. 313–325.
Page, A.D. 2010. True Colors: Police Officers and Rape Myth Acceptance. *Feminist Criminology* 5(4), pp. 315–334.
Phillips, J. 1987. *A Man's Country? A History.* Auckland: Penguin Books.
Pollak, O. 1950. *The Criminality of Women.* Baltimore, MD: University of Pennsylvania Press.
Rose, D. 2013. Roast Buster Accused Bragged about Group Sex. http://www.stuff.co.nz/national/crime/9364531/Roast-Buster-accused-bragged-about-group-sex
Rowe, M. 2009. Notes on a Scandal: The Official Enquiry into Deviance and Corruption in the New Zealand Police. *The Australian and New Zealand Journal of Criminology* 42(1), pp. 123–158.
Rutherford, K. 2013. Facebook Teen Sex Shaming Exposed. http://www.3news.co.nz/Facebook-teen-sex-shaming-exposed/tabid/423/articleID/319919/Default.aspx#ixzz2xtCfzi00
Sable, M.R., Danis, F., Mauzy, D.L. and Gallagher, S.K. 2006. Barriers to Reporting Sexual Assault for Women and Men: Perspectives of College Students. *Journal of American College Health* 55(3), pp. 157–162.
Stanko, B. and Williams, E. 2009. Reviewing Rape and Rape Allegations in London: What are the Vulnerabilities of the Victims Who Report to the Police? In: Horvath, M. and Brown, J. eds. *Rape: Challenging Contemporary Thinking.* Cullompton: Willan, pp. 207–225.
Stern, Baroness V. 2010. *Stern Review of Rape Reporting in England and Wales.* London: Home Office.
Sunday Star Times. 2013. Saga of sex, lies and stereotyping. *Sunday Star Times,* 10 November 2013, p. 15.
Steward, I. 2014. No Charge for Roast Busters. *The Press,* 30 October 2014, p. 2.
Taslitz, A.E. 1999. *Rape and the Culture of the Courtroom.* New York: New York University Press.
Taylor, P. 2013. Police Failed to Check Rapist's Alibi. *New Zealand Herald,* 22 August 2013, p. A10.
Taylor, S.C., and Gassner, L. 2010. Stemming the Flow: Challenges for Police Adult Sexual Assault with Regard to Attrition Rates and Under-reporting of Sexual Offences. *Police Practice and Research: An International Journal* 11(3), pp. 240–255.

Television New Zealand. 2013. *Q+A*, Series 2013, Episode 36. http://tvnz.co.nz/q-and-a/s2013-ep36-video-5705782

Temkin, J. and Krahé, B. 2008. *Sexual Assault and the Justice Gap: A Question of Attitude.* Oxford: Hart Publishing.

The Daily Post. 2013. Rape: Time for the Police to Step Aside. *The Daily Post*, 12 November 2013, p. 9.

Ullman, S. and Townsend, S. M. (2007). Barriers to Working with Sexual Assault Survivors: A Qualitative Study of Rape Crisis Center Workers. *Violence Against Women*, 13: 412–443.

Walklate, S. (ed.) 2007. *Handbook of Victims and Victimology.* Devon: Willan.

Walklate, S. 2008. What is to be Done about Violence against Women? Gender, Violence, Cosmopolitanism and the Law. *British Journal of Criminology*, 48(1), pp. 39–54.

Williams, B. 1999. The Victim's Charter: Citizens as Consumers of Criminal Justice Services. *The Howard Journal* 38(4), pp. 384–396.

Young, W. 1983. *Rape Study: A Discussion of Law and Practice.* Volume I. Wellington: Institute of Criminology and Department of Justice.

5
Competing Conceptions of Victims of Domestic Violence within Legal Processes

Julie Stubbs and Jane Wangmann

It is well established that victims of crime are often measured against an idealised standard of victimhood, typically to the detriment of those who are seen to depart in significant ways from notions of the ideal. However, as Paul Rock noted (2002, p. 17), we need to give more attention to the ways in which various framing discourses are deployed and give shape to our understandings of victimisation. There is 'interpretative work done at every level in bringing the categories victim and offender into play' (Rock 2002, p. 21). Laws and legal practices are significant in how matters are framed and in constituting the subjects and objects of law. In this chapter we examine this further by reference to the multiple and competing conceptions of the victim of domestic violence that emerge in different domains of legal practice. We focus on victims of domestic violence who as mother are more likely to be subjected to particular scrutiny and to competing, and often conflicting, requirements and obligations (Douglas and Walsh 2010; Hester 2010; Jaffe et al. 2003; Kaye et al. 2003).

We move from law as a single entity to examine multiple sites in which women victims seek a response to the gendered harm of domestic violence. How do women make sense of the differing constructs and demands placed upon them by these different and often competing discourses presented by each area of law? In so doing we are not suggesting that there is, or should be, some 'static or singular' identity for women victims of domestic violence (Comack and Brickey 2007, p. 26); rather, we recognise that there is a 'diversity of subject positions' within and across these legal domains (Comack and Brickey 2007, p. 26). Positioning women's lives 'at the centre' rather than in terms of legal categories (Graycar and Morgan 2002, p. 1) allows us to focus on the ways in which the same harms and the same parties are subject to different questions, legal requirements, positioning and constructions. At the same time, it is difficult to find a way to effectively discuss these constructions and their contradictions without also deploying legal categories. This presents a continuing limitation on how to speak about domestic violence within the language of law. Like Hester (2011), we examine three particular legal sites that demonstrate that the battered woman of legal discourse is subject to multiple renderings that reconfigure, reinterpret and revalue her experiences in different legal domains: (1) child protection, (2) family law and (3) criminal law and civil protection order proceedings.. Further complexity is added to these multiple conflicting (legal) renderings through the recognition of the ways in which women experiencing domestic violence are also socially located (in terms of race, age, disability, culture, sexuality, poverty and immigration status) (Laing 2013). In this chapter we raise particular concerns about the experiences of Indigenous women victims of domestic violence in their engagement with, or absence from, these legal domains. Not only do discourses and practices within these different domains reshape a woman's experiences of violence, but they also demand that she 'perform her self' differently in different forums to gain entitlement to legal redress intended to secure safety for herself and her children (Merry 2003).

Why focus on law?

For some time critical feminist scholars have problematised the emphasis on law as a way of dealing with violence against women. Diane Martin (1998), Laureen Snider (1998) and others cautioned against feminist engagement with criminal law on the basis that it empowers the state and not women. We have also seen the negative consequences of criminalisation strategies, such as zero tolerance policing and mandatory arrest in the increased arrest of women victims of domestic violence, and an apparent net widening in which minor offences by juveniles within families are becoming criminalised, resulting in more young people being brought within the criminal justice system (on the growth in arrest of girls related to domestic violence assault, see contributors to Zahn 2009 on the United States and Holmes 2010 on New South Wales (NSW)). Bumiller (2008) and Richie (2012) each offer a compelling analysis of how progressive feminist programmes for dealing with violence against women have been re-shaped and appropriated within neoliberal and neoconservative political contexts in ways that have done more to promote criminalisation than women's autonomy and freedom. Law and law reform are unlikely to be adequate and sufficient means by which to bring about genuine social change which will ameliorate violence against women. However, law remains a means and a context that many women engage with, whether through choice, however constrained that might be, or compulsion. While it is necessary and desirable to consider alternative modes of responding to violence against women and to advocate strategies to enhance women's safe and fair engagement in public and private domains, it remains important to challenge law and legal practice. The feminist project to transform law and legal practice in this area is an ongoing one, albeit one which faces enormous challenges.

The battered woman of legal discourse

Scholars working in the area of violence against women have long recognised that law is constitutive; for instance, it is gendered and gendering. Carol Smart's (1992) article, *The Woman of Legal Discourse*, made a significant and enduring contribution to the development of feminist theory and praxis, in particular in identifying how law functions 'as a process of *producing* fixed gender identities rather than simply as the application of law to previously gendered subjects' (Smart 1992, p. 34);[1] '[w]oman is a gendered subject position which legal discourse brings into being' (Smart 1992, p. 34). Kathy Daly (1994) extended the analysis to law as raced and constitutive of race – which Smart recognised in her article but did not develop. Theoretical work on the intersection of categories of social relations (Crenshaw 1991) and the performance of identity (Butler 1990), are now well established in critical race theory, feminist legal theory and some forms of criminology (Daly and Stephens 1995), and they have been used to analyse violence against women (Cunneen and Stubbs 2004; Mason 2002; Sokoloff and Dupont 2005; Stubbs and Tolmie 1995).

One focus of work using this approach has been on identifying the gendered and racialised assumptions inherent in allegedly neutral constructs such as the 'reasonable man' or the 'ordinary person'. Legal discourse not only draws on gendered and racialised assumptions about 'the battered woman' (Allard 1991; Crenshaw 1991; Stubbs and Tolmie 1995) or 'the rape victim' but actively constructs them (Merry 1995; Nicolson 2000), particularly through valuing and endorsing some forms of femininity and devaluing others.

For instance, Sally Engle Merry has written on how gender identities are produced through law and legal practice:

> the court offers a form of interpretive talk. ... [T]his is authoritative talk legitimated by the state and backed by penalties and disciplinary systems ... how domestic violence cases are handled, what is said, and what the parties hear about gender relations can play a part in redefining gender identities and contesting implicit ideas of gender inequality. (Merry 1995, p. 52)

However, legal discourse offers many women false hopes:

> By endowing women with autonomous selves who can choose to stay or leave a violent man, but by failing to provide economic means to leave such men, the discourse of the courts reconstructs women who fail to leave as undeserving of help. (Merry 1995, p. 49)

Thus, women who are victims of domestic violence who turn to law 'encounter conditional help' (Merry 2003, p. 353) in accordance with whether they are considered to be deserving or undeserving, innocent or complicit (Bumiller 1990; Stanko 2000). While the standards against which they are judged are not fixed, 'the changing cultural construction of the good victim defines the privileged subject of legal assistance and excludes others as unworthy of help' (Merry 2003, p. 355). Binary oppositions such as those of 'innocent' victims and 'wicked' offenders are entrenched in adversarial legal practice, political discourse and media accounts (Rock 2002, p. 15), and they disadvantage many battered women, especially those who fight back, have a criminal history, abuse alcohol or other drugs or are seen as less than ideal parents. Feminist scholars have also drawn attention to the limitations of other binaries such as victim/agent (Maher 1997; Miller 2005). For battered women, '[v]ictimization and agency are false dichotomies; both fail to take account of women's daily experiences of oppression, struggle, and resistance within ongoing relationships' (Schneider 1992, p. 549; Mahoney 1991).

In Australia, Aboriginal women experience high levels of violence (Memmott et al. 2006) but are unlikely to be 'privileged subjects of legal assistance'. Indeed, Aboriginal women have been found to be the most disadvantaged group in Australia in terms of access to justice (HREOC 2004, p. 184). Research about the legal needs of Indigenous peoples and the provision of legal aid has tended to focus almost entirely on the criminal justice system, with very little attention paid to Indigenous peoples' needs in relation to civil law, including family law and child protection matters (areas where Indigenous women's needs predominate) (Cunneen and Schwartz 2009a). Importantly, Cunneen and Schwartz draw connections between the lack of engagement with civil law and the risk of engagement with the criminal law system (Cunneen and Schwartz 2009b). The position of Aboriginal women with respect to the law's response to domestic violence further emphasises the need to be attentive not only to gender and race but also to the colonial context which frames and underpins legal and policy responses. As Kyllie Cripps has argued, responding effectively to family violence[2] in Indigenous communities requires attention to two groups of factors. The first concerns factors associated with colonisation (i.e. dispossession and forced relocation and historical practices and policies such as removal of children), and the second concerns the continuing marginalisation, disadvantage and discrimination faced by Indigenous peoples in Australia (as cited in Murray and Powell 2011, p. 63).

While engaging with law may be used as a strategy by some victims to seek to redefine gender identity, for instance, through asserting their autonomy from the abuser and to seek validation (Merry 2003), dominant legal narratives of domestic violence have often resulted in women not recognising themselves in the account that is told (Mahoney 1991). In part, this is because legal narratives are constructions which cannot ever hope to capture the complexities, nuances and ambiguities of women's lives. The cases of domestic violence most likely to gain coverage in the media are those which are most extreme or unusual (Minow 1990). For instance, the small number of cases in which women kill an abuser attract a disproportionate amount of public attention. Both legal narratives (Schneider 2000) and media accounts commonly depict violence against women in an individualised way, with an incident-based focus which gives little acknowledgement to the wider context of the offence (Morgan and Politoff 2012, p. 32).

Over recent decades both adversarial criminal justice and other initiatives such as restorative justice have sought to recognise victims' needs and to integrate victim participation within legal processes, for instance, by giving victims 'a voice', acknowledging the harm they have suffered, treating them with fairness and respect and offering the chance for an apology (Strang and Sherman 2003). However, some scholars have noted the individualising effect of such developments: 'recounting one experience of victimisation reinforces the victim experience as an individual harm' (Goodey 2000, p. 23) and 'serves to make the victim experience apolitical' (Goodey 2000, p. 22; Stubbs 2002). Similarly, Sandra Walklate (2006) has noted that positivist victimology and some restorative justice scholarship tends to hold an undifferentiated view of the crime victim, which suggests that victims are 'just like us', masks patterns in victimisation and offending and reduces the relationship of crime to marginalisation and subordination. These features are at odds with progressive feminist scholarship, which seeks to situate violence against women with reference to the subordination of women; viewing violence against women through an individuated lens is indeed depoliticising and consistent with the appropriation of feminist concerns to other political agendas, including responsibilising of both victims and offenders in ways described by commentators on late modern penality (Bumiller 2008).

Legal discourse about domestic violence also interacts with wider cultural understandings, both reflecting and reinforcing stereotypical views of violence against women (Bumiller 1990; Maguigan 1995). For instance, it is now well recognised that feminist self-defence work which sought to challenge myths about domestic violence through the introduction of evidence of the 'battered woman syndrome' too often has been counter-productive when legal discourse has rewritten stories of women's resilience to conform to cultural stereotypes of pathology, incapacity or lack of reason (Allard 1991; Comack 1987; Schneider 1986, 1992). Indigenous women and others who do not meet stereotypes of '*the* battered woman' typically have not benefited from attempts to extend legal defences to battered women (Douglas 2012; Stubbs and Tolmie 1995, 1999).

Merry (2003, p. 353) has argued that victims of violence involved in legal processes need to 'perform a self' that 'conform[s] to the law's definitions of rational and autonomous reactions to violence' and thus demonstrate that they are 'entitled' to help. For instance, a woman is commonly required to be 'the rational person who follows through, leaves the batterer, cooperates with prosecuting the case, and does not provoke violence, take drugs or drink, or abuse children' (Merry 2003, p. 353). However, not only do different domains of legal practice use different ways of framing domestic violence and give different emphasis to the facts and circumstances of individual cases, but they also constitute ideas about the 'entitled victim' specific to their domain of practice which impose performative requirements on victims. For the victim of domestic violence caught up in multiple domains of legal practice, and especially mothers, this often imposes competing requirements on victims whereby performing in a way necessary to be deemed 'entitled' in one domain may undermine their entitlement in another legal domain. The remainder of this chapter examines this issue more fully.

Multiple legal domains, competing professional discourses and inconsistent demands

Australia's constitutional arrangements and forms of legal ordering have created a complex network of courts and processes to be negotiated by women dealing with domestic violence and parenting issues following separation. Where there are child protection issues, the complexities are compounded. The pursuit of legal responses to domestic violence necessitates not only women's 'stradd[ling] the constitutional division of power' (ALRC and NSWLRC 2010, para [2.69]) but also their straddling an array of judicial settings (magistrates' courts, district and county courts, supreme courts, tribunals, family courts and children's courts) and a variety of non-judicial dispute resolution processes (such as family dispute resolution). As such, women commonly find themselves dealing with more than one court, in different jurisdictions with different rules, different procedures and a critically different focus. Significantly, women are often navigating these disparate systems simultaneously (Laing 2013, p. 51). The various legal settings offer ambiguous and ambivalent messages about domestic violence. The women are subject to competing professional discourses and demands upon them which may be inconsistent and irreconcilable (Douglas and Walsh 2010; Hester 2010).

The recent work of the ALRC and NSWLRC did much to expose and discuss this fragmented legal landscape for women and children in Australia. The terms of reference for this inquiry included family law, criminal law, civil protection orders, victim's compensation, child protection legislation and rules of evidence (ALRC and NSWLRC 2010). A subsequent ALRC inquiry addressed the way in which domestic violence emerges and is responded to in federal laws, such as social security, child support and family assistance, employment, superannuation and migration (ALRC 2012).

One of the key recommendations of this inquiry (ALRC and NSWLRC 2010) was the development of a common interpretative framework to apply across these legal domains. This was in recognition of the different legal definitions applicable across legal domains and jurisdictions, as well as the different definitions adopted by 'disciplines other than law' such as 'social sciences, health and welfare providers' – hence the 'desirability of attaining a common understanding of what constitutes family violence across family violence legislation' (ALRC and NSWLRC 2010, para [5.2–5.3]). As a result, the Commissions recommended an interpretive framework which acknowledges the context in which acts of family violence take place (i.e. behaviour that 'coerces or controls' a person or 'causes' that person to be 'fearful'). This is accompanied by a non-exhaustive list of the types of acts and behaviours that might fall within the purview of this definitional framework (Recommendation 5–1).[3]

Such a common interpretative framework is an important measure to address the fragmentation that not only results from the Australian federal system but is also inherent in law's doctrinal categories. We argue, however, that even if a common definitional framework were implemented across the Australian jurisdictions and legal domains, women's experience of legal responses to address domestic violence would remain conflictual and confused because the 'victim' is conceptualised and constructed differently for the purposes of each legal domain.

Higgins and Kaspiew (2011) have examined similar concerns in relation to parents who raise allegations of child abuse. Agencies thatsuch parents come into contact with differ in their focus, and as a result parents face an array of different questions: Are they a protective parent (child protection)? Does the behaviour that is of concern meet the statutory threshold for intervention (child protection)? Are they an adequate parent with capacity to ensure the child is safe (children's court)? Do they maintain and encourage ongoing parental relationships with the child following separation (family law)? Is the child safe in a particular household unsupervised (family law)? Is there a need to supervise the time a child spends with a parent (family law)? Is the act defined as a crime and is there sufficient evidence to support a successful prosecution (criminal law)? (Higgins and Kaspiew 2011, p. 7). This array of questions positions the parent in starkly different and often contradictory ways. Furthermore, many of these questions have quite a different tenor when gender and race are considered. Statistics indicate that the vast majority of parents subjected to these questions are women and that Indigenous families and women frequently face more scrutiny and intervention than non-Indigenous women do (Nixon and Cripps 2013). The history of state intervention, especially the removal of children from Indigenous families as part of the 'Stolen Generations' (HREOC 1997), and Aboriginal deaths in custody have left enduring legacies, which means that some Indigenous women are unwilling to engage with law when they suffer violence from their partners.

Hester (2011) characterises the inconsistent and irreconcilable legal responses to women's and children's needs for safety from domestic violence as arising from different 'planetary' regimes. She describes a 'three-planet model' composed of

- the 'domestic violence planet' – that is, criminal law and civil protection orders and associated support structures and agencies directed towards this legal conception of domestic violence;
- the 'child protection planet' – that is, the various state child protection regimes directed towards ensuring child safety;
- the 'child contact planet' – that is, the family law system, in which continuing parental relationships with children post-separation tend to be emphasised.

The ALRC and NSWLR similarly referred to these areas of law as separate 'silos' (2010, p. 52). In this chapter we build on Hester's work in the context of the Australian legal response to domestic violence.

Criminal law and quasi-criminal protection orders

One of the key ways in which domestic violence is addressed in Australia (and other jurisdictions) is through the criminal justice system. The message that 'domestic violence is a crime' has been an integral feature of the initial work of the women's movement to highlight violence in the home, and it remains a critical message even as the need for integration with services other than law are emphasised. One notable characteristic of the Australian approach to domestic violence is the strong focus on protection orders (Hunter 2008, p. 5); these are commonly described as quasi-criminal in that the order itself is based on the civil standard, but the breach constitutes a crime. Some commentators have argued that protection orders are 'trumping' the operation of the criminal law (Douglas and Godden 2002). Criminal law and civil protection orders should not be seen as alternative responses; rather, both are required to provide different and potentially complementary responses to the harm of domestic violence. In this section, we explore the problems created for women through the criminal law's focus on incidents, the relegation of women to the role of witness and the dominant characterisation of women in this sphere as passive victims rather than as agents in proceedings or as active victims who may also respond with violence. Many of these concerns extend to civil protection orders.

Despite the long-standing emphasis on criminal law as a response to domestic violence, there has been sustained criticism of that response. One of the key critiques has been the fact that it relies on an incident-based account of violence. Norrie (2001, p. 224) has described the 'psychological individualism' of the criminal law as shaping how evidence is received at every stage of the criminal justice process. This reinforces the tendency for an incident-driven account of domestic violence to prevail (Stubbs and Tolmie 2005, p. 197). Other criticisms have centred on its tendency to focus on physical harms (although in the last decade this has been redressed somewhat through the creation of the offences of stalking and intimidation in many jurisdictions and, in some jurisdictions, the creation of offences of economic abuse and emotional abuse[4]), the high burden of proof, a punishment focus rather than future protection, rules of evidence and other matters (Buzawa and Buzawa 2002; Hunter 2008, p. 1; Schneider 2000, especially ch. 7; Tuerkheimer, 2004, pp. 971–974). The development of protection order regimes in Australia, as elsewhere, was seen as directly responding to these criticisms (ALRC and NSWLRC 2010, para [4.6]; Hunter 2008, p. 1); as having the potential to prevent future harm arising from domestic violence and to be tailored to the needs of each victim; and thus acting as an important adjunct to the criminal law. However, questions remain about the extent to which the protection order system has retained an emphasis on incidents, and particularly on acts of physical violence (Wangmann 2012).

While there has been some progress within aspects of criminal law to define domestic violence within a contextual rather than an incident-based framework (e.g. in Victoria, there has been legislative endorsement of the admissibility of social framework evidence in family violence related homicide cases[5]), in the various Australian legislative schemes for civil protection orders (Wangmann 2012) and in family law[6] – the legal process necessitates incidents as the way in which the narrative about violence can be conveyed in a manner understood by law. Mahoney has argued

This [the focus on incidents and the number of incidents] makes it possible to bring a woman and her history into court with objective indicia of her status as a battered woman. (Mahoney 1991, p. 28)

At the same time, the focus on incidents allows the perpetrator of violence to explain his behaviour as 'isolated', not as a pattern of behaviour, where '[t]he decontextualized examination of disaggregated incidents can leave a case in shreds' (Hunter 2008, p. 41). As Evan Stark has effectively argued, the focus on acts of violence, rather than on the context in which such acts are perpetrated, has meant that the various services, particularly law, has failed to adequately define or respond to the harm of domestic violence (2007).

Criminal law tends to emphasise incidents of violence (rather than their pattern and cumulative effect); it also focuses on individuals, primarily the defendant (unlike other areas of law discussed in this chapter where the perpetrator may be absent or barely recognised). As Hester has argued, on the criminal law this 'planet' it is the male perpetrator (has he committed a criminal offence? what punishment should be imposed?) and the female victim (as a witness and as a person requiring the protection of a civil protection order) that are the foci (2011, p. 841) – 'children are not so prominent' (2011, p. 842). This can adversely affect both women who are mothers, where the interconnected nature of the parental relationship cannot be separated (Mahoney 1991, p. 19) and women who experience gender-based harms such as domestic violence (where the harm might also affect other family members, friends or new partners). Furthermore, the focus on the individual tends to deny, or play out in a particular way with, other integral characteristics such as race, culture, socioeconomic status and sexuality.

The emphasis on incidents as the defining criterion for domestic violence has also led women who retaliate to or defend themselves against the violence that they experience to be liable to be charged with a domestic violence offence or have a civil protection order sought against them. Women who are defendants in domestic violence criminal proceedings or civil protection order proceedings do not comply with the stereotype of a 'deserving' victim (Fitzroy 2001, p. 11), clearly disrupting the victim–offender binary. They are seen to have performed contrary to the narrative of domestic violence that is expected and understood within criminal law and civil protection order schemes (and arguably other legal domains). While research indicates that women actively respond to the violence that they experience in multiple, strategic ways (Campbell et al. 1998; Dutton 1993; Littleton 1989), this is not widely recognised in popular conceptions of 'a victim of domestic violence', which tend to continue to position victims as passive, submissive, downtrodden and unable to 'leave', yet these conceptions, conversely, also expect separation – an action of considerable agency.

Protection order schemes are predicated on the need to protect – the victim requires the protection of an order. As Durfee (2010, p. 243) has argued, this tends to emphasise 'powerlessness and ... helplessness' rather than strength or agency. This presents a paradox for women seeking a protection order: they must have sufficient agency to seek an order, but at the same time,

> To be considered legitimate victims of domestic violence, petitioners must be seen as powerless, fearful, unable to resist their abusers, and helpless enough to merit legal intervention. Women who are not passive, helpless, and/or fearful are not considered 'legitimate' victims and their motivations for filing a protection order are questioned.

> Yet, these same characteristics that legitimate a woman's claim to the status of victim can also be used to discredit her claims entirely. Victims must also be seen as agents of active (albeit unsuccessful) resistance. Victims who do not leave their abusers are often portrayed as masochistic, pathological, and/or mentally ill. (Durfee 2010, pp. 244–245)

Within the criminal and civil protection order discourse, a woman's credibility is likely to be called into question if she failed to 'leave' or create sufficient distance and separation between herself and her violent partner (Harrison 2008, p. 395). The heightened attention to questions of 'leaving', or not, is at odds with the extensive literature demonstrating that women face many obstacles in trying to end a violent relationship, that some women leave only to be forced to return and that leaving may not be safe or effective in ending domestic violence (Buel 2003; Mahoney 1991; Stark 2007). In the past decade, scholars and activists have highlighted the role that coercive control plays in entrapping women in violent relationships (Ptacek 1999; Stark 2007). However, with rare exceptions, the criminal law continues to emphasise discrete incidents of largely physical violence, and not coercive control, which means that the risks faced by many women victims of domestic violence are not well understood in the criminal justice system.

Over the last decade, pro-arrest or mandatory arrest and prosecution policies have been introduced in many jurisdictions, especially in North America. While Australia has tended not to adopt an approach of mandatory arrests, favouring instead a pro-arrest and or pro-prosecution approach (Hunter 2008, p. 5), there are some mandatory aspects within the quasi-criminal domestic violence protection order schemes.[7] The mandatory policies characteristic of the North American response have attracted considerable debate among feminist advocates (Bumiller 2008; Richie 2012; Schneider 2000, p. 184) and continue to be controversial. While such approaches may assist women who do not want the burden of deciding whether or not a perpetrator faces criminal consequences, they also limit women's autonomy and decision making when women engage with the criminal justice system. What should be done to assist women who are reluctant to engage with the criminal justice system in the prosecution of their current or former partner? These policies may be particularly fraught for (some) racialised women (Richie 2012). For instance, Indigenous women in Australia may have little faith in the criminal justice system, born out of their historical experience of both the under-policing of crimes against Indigenous people and the over-policing of offences by Indigenous people, which resulting in very high incarceration rates and deaths in custody for them (Cunneen 2001; Nancarrow 2006).

In recent years greater attention has been focused on the increasing number of women defendants in domestic violence matters (NSW Legislative Council 2012; WLS 2014) amid concerns that many of these women are also victims of domestic violence undeservedly affected by pro-arrest policies. These cases highlight additional concerns, such as how to assist police and courts to fairly appraise a victim who fights back (in circumstances not defined by the narrow concept of self-defence) and to identify who is a genuine victim deserving of protection.

A further concern about criminal justice discourse and practice concerning domestic violence is that sexual violence is commonly absent from other legal domains that address domestic violence. It would appear that there remains a bifurcation of responses to sexual violence and other acts/behaviours that form intimate partner violence (IPV) (i.e. physical violence, verbal abuse and property damage). While sexual violence is explicitly included within definitions of domestic violence in legislation and policy statements in Australia, it is rarely acknowledged in legal narratives or practice concerning domestic violence, with sexual assault and domestic violence commonly treated as distinct, rather than over-lapping, areas of policy and practice. Intimate partner sexual violence remains seen as primarily the province of criminal law and is not raised to any great extent in protection order proceedings or in family law matters (Durfee 2010, p. 243; Moloney et al. 2007, p. 69; Wangmann 2010, p. 958). There are numerous reasons why sexual violence may not be raised within other legal settings, but this must raise questions about the extent to which women are likely to be adequately served by legal responses that have a partial and or distorted understanding of the violence that they face.

Family law

Family violence in the form of IPV and in the form of child abuse has long been recognised in Australia, and elsewhere, as a central concern of the family law system (Brown et al. 2001). Over the last two decades, there have been a number of progressive developments (in court decisions, legislative amendments and policy change), but tensions remain, and some of the reforms adopted have failed to translate in practice. So, despite progressive change, there is continued – and at times intense – criticism. For example, reforms introduced in 2006 stipulated the need to balance two primary considerations in determining the best interests of the child when making a parenting order – 'the benefit to the child of having a meaningful relationship with both...parents' and the 'need to protect the child' from harm, including family violence. These provisions came to be seen in direct conflict with each other (Kaspiew et al. 2009, pp. 347–350). Other changes made in 2006 required (as one of the additional considerations going to the best interests of the child) that a parent demonstrate a willingness to facilitate relationships with the other parent (this was known as the 'friendly parent criterion') and provided that a costs order could be made by the court where an allegation or denial of family violence was found to be false. Together these provisions were seen to silence women's allegations about domestic violence, particularly where they lacked independent evidence to support their allegations.

These provisions were highly criticised and were ultimately repealed or amended by the *Family Law (Family Violence and Other Measures) Act 2011* (Cth). The friendly parent criterion and the costs provisions were removed entirely, and it was made clear that greater weight is to be accorded to the 'need to protect' consideration. This is an important amendment – however, we suggest that there will remain tensions for mothers who are unable to present sufficient evidence to satisfy the court that the violence 'counts' when making future parenting orders. Violence 'counts in those cases where it is presented as a "disqualifying factor"' by meeting 'a stringent standard in relation to severity and the availability of evidential support', compared to those cases where the violence alleged is 'contextual' because it is 'less severe' and there is no evidence beyond that of the woman and her former partner (Kaspiew 2005, pp. 122–123). Furthermore, despite these recent amendments, the Australian family law regime stays firmly within a pro-contact culture which, like other jurisdictions such as the United Kingdom, has 'embraced a construction of child welfare that places co-operative parenting and contact with the non-residential parent at the centre of children's well-being' (Kaganas and Sclater 2004, p. 3).

Such legislative changes are welcome and important; however, they do not address the ways in which mothers experiencing family violence face markedly different demands within family law compared with the public law domains of criminal law, civil protection orders and child protection. In family law the emphasis is on continuing the relationships between children and their parents following the parent's separation. In this domain parents are expected to agree on arrangements for their children with a focus on future parenting (and not with a view on past parenting practices) (see also Hester 2011, p. 846; Rathus 2007). This *expectation* of a continuing relationship between the former intimate partners as they parent their child(ren), stands in contrast to the domains of child protection, criminal law and civil protection where while separation from a violent partner is not necessarily required, it is emphasised. In this context scholars have highlighted the ways in which certain stereotypes of women have become prominent in this arena. Helen Rhoades (2002), for example, has noted the rise of the 'no contact' mother, who unreasonably seeks to obstruct contact; this image persists despite being at odds with the findings of research. Within a similar character framework, Lesley Laing (2013, p. 52) has noted the extent to which women are accused of seeking civil protection orders, not for their protection from domestic violence but rather to gain a 'tactical' advantage to limit or prevent fathers spending time with children post-separation.

Recognition of the impact of separation on children and their continuing needs to maintain relationships with their parents – and the ongoing nature of being a parent – also has a particular impact on the way in which a mother who raises allegations of IPV and/or child abuse is constructed. While the spousal relationship between the parents can be 'dissolved', parenting is seen as indissoluble (Parkinson 2011, p. 12). Here the father is highly visible (unlike in criminal law or child protection), not as a perpetrator of violence but 'primarily as a father' (Hester 2011, p. 849). Several scholars have found that notwithstanding being a perpetrator of family violence, a father may be constructed as a 'good enough father' (Douglas and Walsh 2010, p. 494; Hester 2011, p. 849; Murray and Powell 2011, p. 92) for the purposes of a parenting order, while as parents mothers are subject to far more scrutiny than fathers are, both within family law and child protection settings (discussed below).

This continuing nature of parental relationships in family law has multiple effects on mothers who experience family violence. For instance, an assumption that spending time with a parent is inherently good for a child leaves a mother who opposes a continuing relationship, or seeks to restrict how that relationship will take place, open to the allegation that she is unreasonable. A mother in this situation may be characterised as either 'implacably hostile' or 'appropriately protective' depending upon the nature of the evidence that she can raise to support her allegations and the views of the various professionals (family dispute resolution practitioners, family consultants, lawyers and judges) about the extent to which the violence is relevant to the question of ongoing contact with the parent whom the child does not live with most of the time.[8] This was explicit within the now removed 'friendly parent' criterion, but it is arguable that it continues to shape decisions about shared parental responsibility, equal time or substantial and 'significant time'. How is it possible for mothers to articulate their reluctance about an ongoing relationship with the violent parent? How can a mother effectively explain this reluctance without being seen as raising notions of fault and blame and as being focused on the past rather than the future?

The future focus of parenting orders also means that orders agreed to or made by a court may downplay the risks of further violence that mothers face at times of handing over a child(ren) to a violent former partner. Parenting orders may nominate 'safe' changeover locations or provide that parenting time is to be supervised by others. However, as Hester has argued, 'the primary concern in the family courts is in getting women to overcome their fears of further abuse from ex-partners, rather than challenging the violence of men' (Hester 2011, p. 849). This is not to say that such measures are not important or are not valued by women, as the contact a father has with children post-separation has been documented in many studies as a continuing site for abuse and harassment (Coy et al. 2012; Kaye et al. 2003; Laing 2013; Radford and Hester 2006).

In addition to assumptions about the benefits of ongoing relationships between parents and their children, the Australian family law system continues to be framed by the discourses of no-fault and a more amicable divorce system (Rhoades et al. 2010), and this affects the way in which violence can be raised, valued and heard. There is a continuing resonance of these discourses in the language of mutuality that imbues cases that involve domestic violence. While there has been welcome progress in the recognition and prominence placed on family violence in parenting matters, family violence cannot be heard and taken into account within family law when evidence is not available (Moloney et al. 2007) or not well understood. Given the private nature of family violence, there may be a lack of evidence to support claims (or denials), and women may not have reported the violence (Hester 2011, p. 848), or the violence may not be seen as 'violence that counts' (see Kaspiew 2005).

For Indigenous women, it is not only that their claims about violence are not heard within the family law system but also that they themselves are largely absent (Cunneen and Schwartz 2009a). This arises from factors such as: a lack of knowledge within some Indigenous communities about the family law system and its relevance to separating families; questions about whether it takes account of different models of families and parenting as practised within Indigenous communities; and the absence of legal aid or advice about this area of law. Since 2006 there has been increasing awareness of the need to do more to enable access to the family law system for Indigenous families (Family Law Council 2012), with specific recognition of different kinship structures and the importance of children's connections with culture included in the legislation.[9] These developments and initiatives are welcome – our point here is that the lack of access to the family law system impacts the extent to which Indigenous women are assisted in dealing with violence when they have children, and instead the focus tends to be on child protection interventions rather than on family law, which may lead to potentially negative consequences for Indigenous women. In this way legal responses for Indigenous women have remained centred on criminal law and child protection – these two areas of the law in particular have been associated with the experience of colonisation and continuing disadvantage and discrimination.

Child protection

Mothers experiencing domestic violence often encounter the child protection system regarding concerns for their child's safety. The intervention of the child protection system is in terms not only of direct abuse and neglect of the child but also concern the harm suffered by children living in a household in which violence takes place. In this legal arena the focus is on the child and the child's safety and protection – the woman appears in the guise of mother/parent (Douglas and Walsh 2010; Murray and Powell 2011). Women whose children are the subject of child protection proceedings are more likely to be positioned as responsible for the ongoing care of children when there has been domestic violence by the father, and thus, the key question that they face is their capacity (or failure) to protect to protect the child. This may be a difficult position for women victims of domestic violence to navigate as they struggle to protect themselves and to identify the safe options for themselves and their child(ren) (Hester 2011, p. 843).

The particular position of women in the child protection arena takes a sharper focus when we appreciate the relative absence of questions about the violent father, in contrast to the family law arena where the father is very much present and emphasised, whether he is violent or not (Murray and Powell 2011, p. 88). Overall, mothers tend to be scrutinised far more in this legal domain than the perpetrator father (Douglas and Walsh 2010, p. 493). Furthermore, the gender neutrality of much of the legislation and policy in this area (Murray and Powell 2011) embeds the invisibility of who is doing what to whom – and hence, it is another reason why mothers may experience particular limitations of their capacity to care for their children and themselves.

The child protection domain is the jurisdiction of the states and territories in Australia, and as noted earlier, this adds to the fragmentation for mothers and children experiencing domestic violence who seek assistance from law(s). Each state has its own child protection legislative regime – clearly, the focus is on the child, and particularly the 'child in need of protection'. Invariably across all jurisdictions, intervention is based on concern that the child may be at risk of harm.[10] As in many other jurisdictions (Hester 2011, p. 843), the last two decades has seen increased recognition of the impact of domestic violence on children as a child protection concern (Murray and Powell 2011). In a number of Australian jurisdictions, domestic violence has been included as a form of child abuse in policies mandating that specified professionals report abuse to child protection authorities (Nixon and Cripps 2013; Wood 2008). How provisions mandating notification operate has been questioned, particularly in relation to Indigenous women where there is concern that, rather than such provisions' enhancing safety for children, Aboriginal women will be dissuaded from seeking help regarding domestic violence for fear of being reported to a child protection agency and hence risk their children being removed (Nixon and Cripps 2013). In Australia the child protection system has historically been more interventionist in the lives of Aboriginal and Torres Strait Islander families, leaving a legacy of the Stolen Generations and the continuing high rate of removal of children from Indigenous parents. In addition to (and because of) this important, continuing historical context of colonisation, Nixon and Cripps (2013, p. 170) emphasise that Aboriginal women and children 'may be even more detrimentally impacted', given the high rates of violence within communities, the chronicity of that violence, its often public nature, over-policing and the already pervasive levels of contact with child protection services. Perhaps more so than any other group of women in Australia, Indigenous women experience the child protection system and criminal legal system as negative and highly punitive.

In families in which there has been domestic violence, child protection agencies often 'encourage' women to seek a civil protection order which excludes the father from the home, thus providing protection to the mother and child(ren).[11] Thus, 'separation [is seen] ... as the favoured approach' despite what is known about separation's being a particularly dangerous time for women escaping domestic violence (Hester 2011, p. 843). Even if women do 'leave' their violent partner, the violence may not stop, and they may be further scrutinised concerning their capacity to care for their children post-separation – for instance, in terms of accommodation, financial capacity and their own mental health (Murray and Powell 2011). Mothers engaging with the child protection system frequently fear the removal of their children because of their 'failure' to protect their child (Douglas and Walsh 2010, p. 489). Their capacity to 'protect' the child – rather than their own need for protection – is the subject of most scrutiny, and yet they may both be at risk due of domestic violence.

As noted by Douglas and Walsh, nonviolent mothers are positioned by many child protection workers as being 'responsible for ending the violence' by leaving or ending the relationship (2010, p. 490). The violent parent is largely absent from the question of 'responsibility'. Mothers 'walk a tightrope' (Wilcox 2000, as cited in Douglas and Walsh 2010) in that if they admit they need assistance, they may jeopardise the perception they can care for their children. Child protection discourses simultaneously construct mothers 'as oppressed by men, as responsible for child protection, and as making choices about their children's care. These discourses sit uneasily together' (Scourfield 2001, as cited in Douglas and Walsh 2010, p. 503).

Concluding comments

Examining the different ways in which mothers experiencing domestic violence are framed, and the competing performative requirements that they face across legal domains, challenges conventional understandings of crime victims in several ways. First, it demonstrates that singular, undifferentiated conceptions of crime victims are flawed both conceptually and for policy purposes. It draws our attention to the more complex and nuanced work required to bring about progressive reforms to legal practices. While refining legal rules continues to be important, it is unlikely to be sufficient to ensure that victims of domestic violence receive the best possible outcome. One common response to the fragmentation and dissonance across the systems has been the notion of integration. However, integration alone, particularly if viewed as merely the facilitation of movement from one legal domain to another, will not address the competing ways in which victims of domestic violence are required to perform in order to gain the attention (or, perhaps in some instances, inattention) of the law; rather, we need to ask questions about the way in which the law itself constructs women victims of domestic violence in ways that work against integration. Since the law and legal actors do not just respond to some prefigured construct of a victim but actively constitute what it means to be a victim deserving of a legal response, the understanding of domestic violence that they bring to bear in this work is crucial. Making transparent the conflicting constructions and competing demands faced by mothers who are also victims of domestic violence may be a necessary first step in beginning to bring about cultural change across the legal system in support of giving meaning to the aspirations of a common interpretative framework.

Notes

We would like to thank Scarlet Wilcock for her research assistance.

1. Note, though, Smart's concern not to treat law as singular or to privilege it; see also Smart 1989.
2. 'Family violence' is the preferred term used by Indigenous communities to describe a wide range of forms of violence that take place within the familial setting and that have wide ranging familial impacts. It is, however, also a contested term as it is seen to obfuscate the gendered nature of violence within Aboriginal communities: see discussion in Murray and Powell 2011, pp. 60–62.
3. A definition based on this recommendation was inserted in the Family Law Act by the *Family Law Legislation Amendment (Family Violence and Other Measures) Act 2011* (Cth). Within NSW, many of the elements recommended by the ALRC and NSWLRC have been adopted in working towards a 'shared policy definition' of domestic and family violence which also recognises the diversity of victims who are subject to domestic violence; the particular legislative responses in NSW recognise a very broad definition of relationships: NSW Government 2014, pp. 11–12.
4. For example, see *Family Violence Act 2004* (Tas) s 8 and s 9.
5. *Crimes Act 1958* (Vic), s 9AH.
6. See, for example the definition of family violence introduced into the *Family Law Act 1975* (Cth) by the *Family Law Legislation Amendment (Family Violence and Other Measures) Act 2011* (Cth).
7. See for example *Crimes (Domestic and Personal Violence) Act 2007* (NSW) s 27 and s 49.
8. Since 2006 the *Family Law Act 1975* (Cth) refers to which the child lives and with whom the child spends time (previous terminology had been residence and contact from 1995; and yet more previous terminology had been custody and access from 1975).

9. See *Family Law Act 1975* (Cth) s 60B(3), s 60CC(3)(h), and s 61F.
10. See, for example Douglas and Walsh's discussion of the child protection legislative regime in Queensland (2010, p. 491).
11. It is interesting to note that this practice has been shared across jurisdictions: in the United Kingdom, see Hester 2011, p. 843.

References

Allard, S. 1991. Rethinking Battered Woman Syndrome: A Black Feminist Perspective. *UCLA Women's Law Journal* 1(1), pp. 191–207.

ALRC (Australian Law Reform Commission). 2012. *Family Violence and Commonwealth Laws – Improving Legal Frameworks.* ALRC Report 117. Sydney: ALRC.

ALRC and NSWLRC (Australian Law Reform Commission & the New South Wales Law Reform Commission), 2010. *Family Violence – A National Legal Response.* Final Report, ALRC Report 114, NSWLRC Report 128 Sydney: ALRC.

Brown, T., Sheehan, R., Frederico, M. and Hewitt, L. 2001. *Resolving Family Violence to Children: The Evaluation of Project Magellan, a Pilot Project for Managing Family Court Residence and Contact Disputes when Allegations of Child Abuse have been made.* Family Violence and Family Court Research Program, Melbourne: Monash University.

Buel, S. 2003. Effective Assistance of Counsel for Battered Women Defendants: A Normative Construct. *Harvard Women's Law Journal* 26, pp. 217–350.

Bumiller, K. 1990. Fallen Angels: The Representation of Violence against Women in Legal Culture. *International Journal of the Sociology of Law* 18(2), pp. 125–142.

Bumiller, K. 2008. *In an Abusive State: How Neoliberalism Appropriated the Feminist Movement against Sexual Violence.* Durham, NC: Duke University Press.

Butler, J. 1990. *Gender Trouble: Feminism and the Subversion of Identity.* New York: Routledge.

Buzawa, E.S. and Buzawa, C.G. 2002. *Domestic Violence: The Criminal Justice Response.* 3rd ed. Thousand Oaks, CA: Sage.

Campbell, J., Rose, L., Kub, J. and Nedd, D. 1998. Voices of Strength and Resistance: A Contextual and Longitudinal Analysis of Women's Responses to Battering. *Journal of Interpersonal Violence* 13(6), pp. 743–762.

Comack, E. 1987. Women Defendants and the 'Battered Wife Syndrome': A Plea for the Sociological Imagination. *Crown Counsel Review* 5(11), pp. 6–10.

Comack, E. and Brickey, S. 2007. Constituting the Violence of Criminalized Women. *Canadian Journal of Criminology and Criminal Justice* 49(1), pp. 1–36.

Coy, M., Perks, K., Scott, E. and Tweedale, R. 2012. *Picking up the Pieces: Domestic Violence and Child Contact.* Rights of Women and CWASU. London: Rights of Women.

Crenshaw, K. 1991. Mapping the Margins: Identity Politics, Intersectionality, and Violence against Women. *Stanford Law Review* 43(6), pp. 1243–1299.

Cunneen, C. 2001. *Conflict, Politics and Crime: Aboriginal Communities and the Police.* Sydney: Allen & Unwin.

Cunneen, C. and Schwartz, M. 2009a. Civil and Family Law Needs of Indigenous People in New South Wales: The Priority Areas. *University of New South Wales Law Journal* 32(3), pp. 725–745.

Cunneen, C. and Schwartz, M. 2009b. From Crisis to Crime: The Escalation of Civil and Family Law Issues to Criminal Matters in Aboriginal Communities in NSW. *Indigenous Law Bulletin* 7(15), pp. 18–21.

Cunneen, C. and Stubbs, J. 2004. Cultural Criminology: Engaging with Race, Gender and Post-colonial Identities. In: Ferrell, J., Hayward, K., Morrison, W. and Presdee, M. eds. *Cultural Criminology Unleashed*. London: Glasshouse Press, pp. 97–108.

Daly, K. 1994. Criminal Law and Justice System Practices as Racist, White and Racialized. *Washington and Lee Law Review* 51(2), pp. 431–464.

Daly, K. and Stephens, D. 1995. The Dark Figure of Criminology: Towards a Black and Multi-ethnic Feminist Agenda for Theory and Research. In: Rafter, N.H. and Heidensohn, F. eds. *International Feminist Perspectives in Criminology*. Buckingham: Open University Press, pp. 189–215.

Douglas, H. 2012. A Consideration of the Merits of Specialized Homicide Offences and Defences for Battered Women. *Australian and New Zealand Journal of Criminology* 45(3), pp. 367–382.

Douglas, H. and Godden, L. 2002. *The Decriminalisation of Domestic Violence*. Brisbane: Griffith University.

Douglas, H. and Walsh, T. 2010. Mothers, Domestic Violence and Child Protection: Toward Collaboration and Engagement. *Violence Against Women* 16(5), pp. 537–542.

Durfee, A. 2010. The Gendered Paradox of Victimization and Agency in Protection Order Filings. In: Garcia, V. and Clifford, J. eds. *Female Victims of Crime: Reality Reconsidered*. Upper Saddle River, NJ: Prentice Hall, pp. 243–258.

Dutton, M.A. 1993. Understanding Women's Responses to Domestic Violence: A Redefinition of Battered Women Syndrome. *Hofstra Law Review* 21(4), pp. 1191–1242.

Family Law Council (2012), *Improving the Family Law System for Aboriginal and Torres Strait Islander Clients*. Barton, ACT: Commonwealth of Australia.

Fitzroy, L. 2001. Violent Women: Questions for Feminist Theory, Practice and Policy. *Critical Social Policy* 21(1), pp. 7–34.

Goodey, J. 2000. An Overview of Key Themes. In: Crawford, A. and Goodey, J. eds. *Integrating a Victim Perspective within Criminal Justice*. Dartmouth: Ashgate, pp. 13–34.

Graycar, R. and Morgan, J. 2002. *The Hidden Gender of Law*. 2nd ed. Leichhardt: Federation Press.

Harrison, C. 2008. Implacably Hostile or Appropriately Protective?: Women Managing Child Contact in the Context of Domestic Violence. *Violence Against Women* 14(4), pp. 381–405.

Hester, M. 2010. Commentary on 'Mothers, Domestic Violence, and Child Protection,' by Heather Douglas and Tamara Walsh. *Violence Against Women* 16(5), pp. 516–523.

Hester, M. 2011. The Three Planet Model: Towards an Understanding of Contradictions in Approaches to Women and Children's Safety in Contexts of Domestic Violence. *British Journal of Social Work* 41(5), pp. 837–853.

Higgins, D. and Kaspiew, R. 2011. Child Protection and Family Law...Joining the Dots. *National Child Protection Clearinghouse Issues No.34*, 34.

Holmes, J. 2010. Female Offending: Has there been an Increase? *Crime and Justice Statistics Bureau Brief*, issue paper no. 46. Sydney: NSW Bureau of Crime Statistics and Research.

HREOC (Human Rights & Equal Opportunity Commission) 1997. *Bringing them Home: Report of the National Inquiry into the Separation of Aboriginal and Torres Strait Islander Children from their Families.* Sydney: HREOC.

HREOC (Human Rights & Equal Opportunity Commission) 2004. Aboriginal & Torres Strait Islander Social Justice Commissioner. *Social Justice Report 2003.* Sydney: HREOC. https://www.humanrights.gov.au/our-work/aboriginal-and-torres-strait-islander-social-justice/publications/social-justice-report-10 [Accessed 9 March 2015].

Hunter, R. 2008. *Domestic Violence Law Reform and Women's Experience in Court: The Implementation of Feminist Reforms in Civil Proceedings.* Amhurst, NY: Cambria Press.

Jaffe, P. Crooks, C. and Poisson, S. 2003. Common Misconceptions in Addressing Domestic Violence in Child Custody Disputes. *Juvenile and Family Court Journal* 54(4), pp. 57–68.

Kaganas, F. and Sclater, S.D. 2004. Contact Disputes: Narrative Constructions of "Good" Parents. *Feminist Legal Studies* 12(1), pp. 1–27.

Kaspiew, R. 2005. Violence in Contested Children's Cases: An Empirical Exploration. *Australian Journal of Family Law* 19(2), pp. 112–143.

Kaspiew, R., Gray, M., Weston, R., Moloney, L. Hand, K. and Qu, L. 2009. *Evaluation of the 2006 Family Law Reforms.* Melbourne: Australian Institute of Family Studies.

Kaye, M., Stubbs J. and Tolmie J. 2003. Domestic Violence, Separation and Parenting: Negotiating Safety Using Legal Processes. *Current Issues in Criminal Justice* 15(2), pp. 73–94.

Laing, L. 2013. *'It's Like this Maze you have to make your Way Through': Women's Experiences of Seeking a Domestic Violence Protection order in NSW.* Sydney: Faculty of Education and Social Work, University of Sydney.

Littleton, C. 1989. Women's Experiences and the Problem Of transition: Perspectives on Male Battering of Women. *University of Chicago Legal Forum* 1989, pp. 23–58.

Maguigan, H. 1995. Cultural Evidence and Male Violence: Are Feminist and Multiculturalist Reformers on a Collision Course in Criminal Courts? *New York Law Review* 70(1), pp. 36–99.

Maher, L. 1997. *Sexed Work: Gender, Race and Resistance in a Brooklyn Drug Market.* Oxford: Clarendon Press.

Mahoney, R. 1991. Legal Images of Battered Women: Redefining the Issue of Separation. *Michigan Law Review* 90(1), pp. 1–94.

Martin, D.L. 1998. Retribution Revisited: A Reconsideration of Feminist Criminal Law Reform Strategies. *Osgoode Hall Law Journal* 36(1), pp. 151–188.

Mason, G. 2002. *The Spectacle of Violence: Homophobia, Gender, and Knowledge.* New York: Routledge.

Memmott, P., Chambers, C., Go-Sam, C. and Thomson, L. 2006. Good Practice in Indigenous Family Violence Prevention – Designing and Evaluating Successful Programs. Issues Paper: 11. Sydney: Australian Domestic & Family Violence Clearinghouse. http://www.austdvclearinghouse.unsw.edu.au/Word%20Files/Issues_Paper_11.doc [Accessed: 9 March 2015].

Merry, S.E. 1995. Gender Violence and Legally Engendered Selves. *Identities* 2(1–2), pp. 49–73.

Merry, S.E. 2003. Rights Talk and the Experience of Law: Implementing Women's Human Rights to Protection from Violence. *Human Rights Quarterly* 25(2), pp. 343–381.

Miller, S. 2005. *Victims as Offenders: The Paradox of Women's Violence in Relationships.* New Brunswick, NJ: Rutgers University Press.

Minow, M. 1990. Words and the Door to the Land of Change: Law, Language, and Family Violence. *Vanderbilt Law Review* 43(6), pp. 1665–1699.

Moloney, L., Smyth, B. and Weston, R. 2007. *Allegations of Family Violence and Child Abuse in Family Law Children's Proceedings: A Pre-reform Exploratory Study.* Research Report No. 15, Australian Institute of Family Studies, Melbourne.

Morgan, J and Politoff, V. 2012. *Victorian Print Media Coverage of Violence Against Women: A longitudinal Study.* VicHealth and the University of Melbourne. http://www.vichealth.vic.gov.au/Publications/Freedom-from-violence/Victorian-print-media-coverage-of-violence-against-women.aspx [Accessed: 9 March 2015].

Murray, S. and Powell, A. 2011. *Domestic Violence: Australian Public Policy.* North Melbourne: Australian Scholarly Press.

Nancarrow, H. 2006. In Search of Justice for Domestic and Family Violence: Indigenous and Non-Indigenous Australian Women's Perspectives. *Theoretical Criminology* 10(1), pp. 87–106.

New South Wales Government 2014. *It Stops Here: Standing Together to end Domestic and family Violence in NSW – The NSW Government's Domestic and Family Violence Framework for Reform.* Sydney: New South Wales Government.

NSW Legislative Council, Standing Committee on Social Issues Parliament of NSW. 2012. *Domestic Violence Trends and Issues in NSW Inquiry.* Sydney: NSW Parliament.

Nicolson, D. 2000. Criminal Law and Feminism. In: Bibbings, L. and Nicolson, D. eds. *Feminist Perspectives on Criminal Law.* London: Cavendish Publishing, pp. 1–28.

Nixon, K. and Cripps, K. 2013. Child Protection and Indigenous Intimate Partner Violence: Whose Failure to Protect? In: Strega, S. Krane, J. Lapierre, S. Richardson, C. and Carlton, R. eds. *Failure to Protect: Moving Beyond Gendered Responses.* Halifax, NS: Fernwood Publishing, pp. 166–188.

Norrie, A. 2001. *Crime, Reason and History: A Critical Introduction to Criminal Law.* 2nd ed. London: Butterworths.

Parkinson, P. 2011. *Family Law and the Indissolubility of Parenthood.* New York: Cambridge University Press.

Ptacek, J. 1999. *Battered Women in the Courtroom: The Power if Judicial Responses.* Boston, MA: Northeastern University Press.

Radford, L. and Hester, M. 2006. *Mothering through Domestic Violence.* London: Jessica Kingsley Publishers.

Rathus, Z. 2007. Shifting the Gaze: Will Past Violence be Silenced by a Further Shift of the Gaze to the Future under the New Family Law System? *Australian Journal of Family Law* 21(1), pp. 87–112.

Rhoades, H. 2002. The 'No Contact Mother': Reconstructions of Motherhood in the Era of the 'New Father'. *International Journal of Law, Policy and the Family* 16(1), pp. 71–94.

Rhoades, H., Frew, C. and Swain, S. 2010. Recognition of Violence in the Family Law System: A Long Journey. *Australian Journal of Family Law* 24(3), pp. 296–312.

Richie, B. 2012. *Arrested Justice: Black Women, Violence, and America's Prison Nation.* New York: New York University Press.

Rock, P. 2002. On Becoming a Victim. In: Hoyle C. and Young, R. eds. *New Visions of Crime Victims.* Oxford: Hart Publishing, pp. 1–22.

Schneider, E. 1986. Describing and Changing: Women's Self-defense Work and the Problem of Expert Testimony on Battering. *Women's Rights Law Reporter* 9(3–4), pp. 195–222.

Schneider, E. 1992. Particularity and Generality: Challenges of Feminist Theory and Practice in Work on Woman-Abuse. *New York University Law Review* 67(3), pp. 520–568.

Schneider, E. 2000. *Battered Women and Feminist Lawmaking.* New Haven, CT: Yale University Press.

Smart, C. 1989. *Feminism and the Power of Law.* London: Routledge.

Smart, C. 1992. The Woman of Legal Discourse. *Social and Legal Change* 1(1), pp. 29–44.

Snider, L. 1998. Toward Safer Societies: Punishment, Masculinities and Violence against Women. *British Journal of Criminology* 38(1), pp. 1–39.

Sokoloff, N. and Dupont, I. 2005. Domestic Violence at the Intersections of Race, Class, and Gender – Challenges and Contributions to Understanding Violence against Marginalized Women in Diverse Communities. *Violence Against Women* 11(1), pp. 38–64.

Stanko, E. 2000. *The Good the Bad and the Vulnerable: Fearing Victims and Victims' Fears.* London: Sage.

Stark, S. 2007. *Coercive Control: How Men Entrap Women in Personal Life.* Oxford: Oxford University Press.

Strang, H. and Sherman, L. 2003. Repairing the Harm: Victims and Restorative Justice. *Utah Law Review* 2003(1), pp. 15–42.

Stubbs, J. 2002. Domestic Violence and Women's Safety: Feminist Challenges to Restorative Justice. In: Strang, H. and Braithwaite, J. eds. *Restorative Justice and Family Violence.* Melbourne: Cambridge University Press, pp. 42–61.

Stubbs, J. and Tolmie, J. 1995. Gender, Race and the Battered Woman Syndrome: An Australian Case Study. *Canadian Journal of Women and the Law* 8(1), pp. 122–158.

Stubbs, J. and Tolmie, J. 1999. Falling Short of the Challenge? A Comparative Assessment of the Australian Use of Expert Evidence on the Battered Woman Syndrome. *Melbourne University Law Review* 23(3), pp. 709–748.

Stubbs, J. and Tolmie, J. 2005. Defending Battered Women on Charges of Homicide: The Structural and Systemic Versus the Personal and Particular. In: Chan, W. et al. eds. *Women, Mental Disorder and the Law.* London: Glasshouse Press, pp. 191–210.

Tuerkheimer, D. 2004. Recognizing and Remedying the Harm of Battering: A Call to Criminalize Domestic Violence. *Journal of Criminal Law and Criminology* 94(4), pp. 959–1031.

Walklate, S. 2006. Changing Boundaries of the 'Victim' in Restorative Justice: So Who is the Victim Now? In: Sullivan, D. and Tifft, L. eds. *Handbook of Restorative Justice: A Global Perspective.* Milton Park: Routledge, pp. 273–285.

Wangmann, J. 2010. Gender and Intimate Partner Violence: A Case Study from NSW. *University of New South Wales Law Journal* 33(3), pp. 945–969.

Wangmann, J. 2012. Incidents versus Context: How Does the NSW Protection Order System Understand Intimate Partner Violence? *Sydney Law Review* 34(4), pp. 695–719.

WLS (Women's Legal Services NSW) 2014. *Women Defendants to AVOs: What is their Experience of the justice system?* Sydney: WLS NSW.

Wood, J. (The Hon.) 2008. *Report of the* Special *Commission of Inquiry into Child Protection Services in NSW*. Volume 1. Sydney: NSW Government.

Zahn, M. ed. 2009. *The Delinquent Girl*. Philadelphia, PA: Temple University Press.

6
Care Bears and Crime-Fighters: Police Operational Styles and Victims of Crime

Dean Wilson and Marie Segrave

> So you go through the Academy and you learn all this good stuff and then you come out here and work with a senior constable who's burnt out, who thinks the job has gone...and there's nothing in it for him. So you're working with a whole range of different people – you don't get to pick who you work with – so some of it might rub off on you, especially if you're trying to be mentored by them, trying to pick up what works and what doesn't, and sometimes you get called a 'Care Bear' if you get too overindulgent in trying to help people. *Regional station, snr. sgt, 25 years with Victoria Police*

Over the last two decades victims' rights and victims' needs have gained traction as a key concern for policing agencies internationally (Hoyle and Young 2003). A range of developments have seen a shift in police protocols regarding their interactions with victims of crime – often based on research with victims and/or successful advocacy by victims' rights organisations. These shifts range from expanding the curriculum of police recruit training (to include more detailed recognition of victims of crime) to increasing contact protocols with victims during the course of investigations and to the development of systems of referral to connect victims of crime with support services provided by agencies in the broader community.

Such shifts have frequently been underpinned by the idea that successful interactions with victims of crime will increase trust in the police and by implication enhance police legitimacy. The degree to which this is in fact the case is a matter of debate (Skogan 2006a; Bradford et al. 2009; Elliott et al. 2011; Jackson et al. 2013). Nevertheless, whether such interactions are assessed as *asymmetrical* (Skogan 2006a) or *symmetrical* (Myhill and

Bradford 2011), this chapter adopts a different perspective by examining the importance of police culture in the formation of 'bedside manner'. Skogan provides a pithy summation of the importance of this for police interactions with victims of crime, noting that

> Police are judged by what physicians might call their 'bedside manner'. Factors like how willing they are to listen to people's stories and show concern for their plight are very important, as are their politeness, helpfulness and fairness. (2006, p. 104)

The interviews (n=111) analysed in the present discussion were conducted over the course of a larger project funded by the Australia Research Council, and they examined the interface between Victoria Police and victims of crime (for a more detailed overview of the broader project, see Segrave and Wilson 2011). Following an initial pilot survey (n=76), semi-structured interviews were conducted with police officers drawn from nineteen different stations across the State of Victoria, Australia. The interviews were conducted in five urban (city) stations, six outer urban (suburban) stations, four major regional stations (regional cities with a population greater than 200,000) and five regional and remote stations (Segrave and Wilson 2011). The interviews discussed here were conducted with general duties officers. This is significant as general duties officers' experiences with, and definitions of, 'victims of crime' differ significantly from the more protracted and intense interactions of some specialist areas, such as homicide and major road crash investigation (Colvin and Wilson 2009a, 2009b).

The design and aims of this study focused on the views and experiences relayed by operational police officers. A limitation of this approach is the emphasis upon language rather than observable action. As Waddington (1999) has argued, the relationship between values expressed 'back stage' in the canteen do not automatically translate into and fashion interactions with members of the public. While a fine-grained ethnographic study of policing might reveal more about the synergy between discursively expressed values and actions on the ground, we draw on Reiner's summation: while we accept that the association between ideas and action is far from linear, 'this does not mean that people's perspectives – complex, ambivalent and fluid as they may be – bear *no* relation to their practices' (2010, p. 115). Moreover, in such a sizeable and diverse policing organisation, semi-structured qualitative interviews were a research tool broad enough to interrogate complexity and difference while being deep enough to probe the 'common sense' assumptions of police officers – what Chan (1997, 2003), drawing on Bourdieu (1990), refers to as the 'habitus' of policing.

The data analysis suggested that three consistent operational styles were adopted by participants which framed their interactions with victims of crime. We have termed these three working dispositions 'social workers', 'pragmatists' and 'crime-fighters'. While we have used slightly different terms, these categorisations broadly equate to Reiner's (1978) classic designations of 'social worker', 'professional' and 'new centurion'. The terminology has been updated to reflect the terminology utilised and approach applied by serving police members who participated in this study. In a large and diverse institution such as Victoria Police, operational styles in relation to victims of crime were mediated by a range of factors of which geographic location was particularly important, as was the degree of attachment to the local community. In the discussion that follows, we commence by examining victim-related training before outlining the dominant operational styles that were evident in the analysis. This is followed by an exploration of the key factors that influence and mediate policing styles.

Victoria Police and victims of crime

Australian police forces are organised on state or territory wide basis, with Victoria Police consisting of approximately 120,000 members distributed across a jurisdiction of 91,749 square miles (Victoria Police 2011, p. 59). The research presented here was conducted during a period when the Victoria Police were increasingly compelled via legislative instruments to provide a proscribed base level of services to victims of crime. In Victoria, the primary piece of legislation impacting police interactions with victims of crime is the *Victims' Charter Act 2006*. Similar charters are common across the US, the UK, Europe, Canada, New Zealand and Australia, and they are used as a mechanism for setting minimum standards for the treatment of victims and witnesses (Booth and Carrington 2007). Many victims charters – including that of Victoria – are not legally binding, and they have consequently been critiqued for setting only minimal standards that are largely unenforceable and afford victims negligible substantive rights (Booth and Carrington 2007; Hoyle and Zedner 2007). The *Victims' Charter Act*

2006 lays out the contemporary understanding of the needs and rights of victims of crime, recognising

> that all persons adversely affected by crime, regardless of whether they report the offence, should be treated with respect by all investigatory agencies ... and should be offered information to enable them to access appropriate services to help with the recovery process. (Victims' Charter Act: s. 4b)

The Charter outlines the rights of victims and the obligations of criminal justice services (including police, courts, corrections and victims services) (Victims' Charter Act: ss. 6–8).

For Victoria Police, the key obligations stipulated by the Charter include treating victims fairly; providing information regarding rights and the contact details of relevant support services (including counselling and compensation); taking care of victims' property if it is required as evidence and returning it once it is no longer needed; and providing updates on the progress of the victim's case, including whether a charge has been lain and the process in court to follow (such as providing details on bail processes). The Charter also includes a requirement that investigatory agencies, such as Victoria Police, take into account the diverse needs of persons based upon race, gender, culture, sexual orientation, disability, religion and age (Victims' Charter Act: s. 6.2). Additionally, it emphasises the importance of providing persons adversely affected by a crime (adopting a broad definition of 'victims of crime' that includes witnesses and secondary victims) with the necessary information regarding available victim support services in a 'clear, timely and consistent' manner (Victims' Charter Act: s. 7a).

Since the implementation of the Charter in 2006, Victoria Police have developed and put into effect various policies and practices designed to fulfil the obligations of the Charter. This commitment was embodied in *The Way Ahead Victoria Police Strategic Plan 2008–2013*[1] *(2007)*, which promised the development of training programs to educate police members about their responsibilities under the Charter and the introduction of a range of protocols and processes for victim interaction (primarily related to computerised notification systems). While the Charter arguably lacks legal teeth, our experience within the organisation during the period it was implemented suggested that it did exert some influence in terms of fashioning a general milieu – at least among 'management cops' (Reuss-Ianni and Ianni 1983) – that prioritised victims of crime to an unprecedented extent. It is against such a policy backdrop that this research was conducted (Segrave and Wilson 2011).

'Police culture' and victims of crime

Any discussion of police perceptions of their role in relation to victims of crime is inseparable from the issue of how police work is perceived generally within a broader 'police culture'. The literature on 'police culture' is vast, and the topic stimulates extensive and heated debate, particularly in relation to the question of the potential for cultural change within police organisations (Chan 1996, 2003; O'Neill et al. 2008; Reiner 2010; Loftus 2009, 2010). However, there are enduring characteristics of police cultures across jurisdictions that are pertinent to this analysis. In a recent ethnographic study of policing in northern England, Loftus noted that 'detection and catching [of] offenders was elevated as the core justification for policing... [while] in contrast responsibilities such as completing paperwork and attending incidents which involved a service element were not considered authentic policing experiences' (Loftus 2009, pp. 91–92). Importantly, this perception remained unchanged among police in Loftus's study, despite emerging from a police organisation that had undergone significant cultural change in terms of policy and composition (Loftus 2009). It has been argued that the ramifications of this 'action-oriented' police perspective can be significant for police–victim encounters. For example, Mawby suggests that

> It seems that the nature of policework, and particularly the way police interpret their jobs and the aspects of their work they value, may mean that victim-oriented work is accorded less priority than crime-fighting, in much the same way that community policing is commonly undervalued. (2007, p. 215)

Our initial explorations into this question indicated that role perceptions within Victoria Police were considerably more nuanced and less overwhelmingly action-oriented than Mawby (2007) suggests. An initial pilot survey was conducted which included the open-ended question: 'What is the police role in victim support?' While the survey generated only 76 responses from across Victoria Police,[2] it enabled some initial indicative trends and themes to inform the development of the major qualitative study that forms the basis of this analysis (involving semi-structured interviews with over 200 active Victoria Police members across the state). When asked to provide an open-ended qualitative response of their perception of the police role in dealing with victims of crime, respondents engaged functional terms such as 'providing support', 'being honest' and 'keeping victims informed' to describe this aspect of their work. Nevertheless, there were clearly some respondents who viewed dealing with victims of crime as a distraction from 'real' police work. For example, one respondent specified that the role of the police was 'to make sure criminal matters are investigated and suspects taken to court, full stop', while another commented, 'we have enough to do without ensuring victims' needs are met'. Additionally, 53 per cent of respondents reported that dealing with victims' needs 'impeded regular police duties' (Colvin and Wilson 2009c).

While this initial data was too statistically thin to permit generalisation, it signposted the disparate viewpoints regarding the importance of victims of crime among general duties police officers. Subsequently participants' subjective assessments of the police role in relation to victims of crime – and the rationales underpinning these assessments – constituted an important focus of inquiry within the interview process. In addition, we found it important to broach the question of training and its impact as training and education are so frequently advanced as 'one of the keys to changing police attitudes to victims' and the most obvious antidote whenever problematic practices surface within police organisations (Williams 1999, p. 105). We therefore examine recollections and perceptions of two forms of training currently in operation at Victoria Police that constitute formal and informal modes of learning: first, the training provided within the Police Academy during the first five months of entering the police force and, second, on-the-job learning of probationary constables placed with mentors. Through examining the operational styles of policing adopted by general duties police officers and the ways in which attitudes and practices have been fashioned via formal and informal training, we gain some insight into the formation of organisational styles that in turn shape police perceptions of victims of crime.

Learning about victims: academy training for new recruits

We begin, as all our participants began, with the formal training received by recruits at the Police Academy. At the outset it is important to note that our sample of participants had been serving police officers for varying lengths of time: while the average was 14 years, the range was two months to 39 years (Segrave and Wilson 2011, p. 83). Just over half the participants interviewed had been serving ten years or less and of these, 12 were a year or less out of police academy training. This length of time is important when considering discussions of all forms of training, but it has implications for consideration of academy training in terms of the *type* of recruit training participants had received in the academy (sessions on victims experiences are relatively new to Academy training) and the *time* that had passed since they had received this training. This was reflected in the level of recall of recruit training. It was the small numbers of probationary constables (n=12) who had recently experienced training who generally recalled participation in specific victim-awareness training. For example,

> There definitely were avenues and different sorts of modules that were made up for victims of crime. I've got to say it wasn't touched on heavily, just because there is so much procedure and policy that you've got to learn in such a short timeframe, but they do definitely make sure they touch base on just how to deal with them and always ensure that...if [possible]...one member is speaking to the victim [while another] member is speaking to the offender and you try and make sure that there is always the appropriate level of care for both. *Urban station, Prob. Const., five months with Victoria Police*

> They do...a session on it [victims of crime], there is a lecture on it...and it was actually quite good....They tell you how to deal with it. *Urban station, Prob. Const., six months with Victoria Police*

However, as these quotations reveal, even months out of the Academy, the specific curriculum details of victim-awareness training were not readily recalled by participants. Officers who had passed through the Academy only a few years previously also remembered only the most basic information imparted in their training:

> There was a bit of training in relation to [victims]....I think the Victim's Charter Guide was going to be introduced. They were telling us it would be introduced in the next couple of years or so, so there was a bit of training from...what I remember. *Urban station, const., three years with Victoria Police*

> I can't remember anything, which would lead me to think that very little is taught in relation to dealing with victims. I think from memory the only sort of training they gave you in relation to victims was death messages and dealing with getting death messages to family members. *Urban station, snr. const., six years with Victoria Police*

The recollection and subsequent mobilisation of knowledge imparted during Academy training was seen to be impeded by the sheer volume of information contained in the Academy curriculum, both in relation to victims and more generally:

> Look, you're getting fed a lot of information all at once when you're at the Academy so...you learn so much and then you're just thrown into the deep end – bang you're a policeman now. I probably had a small understanding of what was required. Until you come out and you're actually dealing with it every day, then you sort of familiarise yourself with what's going on. *Urban station, const., three years with Victoria Police*

These findings support the extant research on the impacts of police education. Bradley (2010, p. 101) has observed that pre-operational training generally fails 'to have much impact upon the competence and conduct of new police practitioners'. What was repeatedly emphasised during interviews was the perceived gulf between the 'theory' training experienced in the Academy and the 'reality' of policing experienced in operational police stations. For example, one senior constable suggested that the Academy is 'la-la land', arguing that 'nothing prepares you for what you're going to face – nothing.' (*Regional station, snr. const., nine years with Victoria Police*). The perception of a clear-cut rupture between classroom theory and street reality was time and again highlighted by participants, and it found expression in the recurrent telling by police officers of the story of their first 'death knock'.

The 'death knock' is a confronting aspect of the police role where police have to inform a member of the public that their family member has died. The performance of 'death knocks' was frequently described as one of the most agonising policing tasks for which it was difficult, if not impossible, to prepare. While some participants recalled a session at the Academy on how to prepare to undertake a death knock, others (generally participants who had been with Victoria Police for over ten years) recalled no formal training. Consistently, regardless of how long participants had been operational police, the death knock was utilised as a discursive device to demonstrate the limits of formal pre-operational training:

> Nothing will prepare you for telling someone that their loved one has passed away, especially when it's unexpected. [It's] very emotional. But as for how much they can teach in the Academy, I reckon it is

sufficient [what they teach] because you only learn so much in a classroom, and that's where a good mentor comes into it. *Regional station, const., four years with Victoria Police*

I wasn't well enough trained to provide advice...we didn't have ...enough knowledge of the process of grief. *Remote station, snr. const., 24 years with Victoria Police*

The influence of Academy training on operational styles seems to be limited, given the very small number of participants who recalled any aspects of their training at all. Moreover, its relevance once in the field was viewed by many officers as negligible, and the strong and consistent narratives of the first death knock discursively underscored what many saw as the impossibility of classroom learning being able to prepare them for the raw realities of active policing. In direct contrast to this was the uniformity with which participants referred to and recalled what they learned when they 'hit the ground' as probationary officers, and it is to that that we now turn.

Learning the art of policing: informal mentoring in operational duties

Previous research has found that efforts to inculcate desired behaviours and attitudes in the Academy can rapidly unravel once recruits enter the field and are absorbed into the workaday realities of the organisational culture (Haarr 2001; Chan 2003). In relation to preparation for how to work with victims of crime, the learning in the Academy was not recognised by police as having a significant impact – it was in the field that the 'real' learning was felt to occur. The indicative statement that 'you only learn so much in a classroom, and that's where a good mentor comes into it' (*Regional station, const., four years with Victoria Police*), resonated throughout the interviews and is again evident in the following comment:

> the majority of it is just on-the-job training; the quality of your training is going to come down to the quality of the people you work with, and the care factor of the people you work with, and that varies from station to station. *Outer urban station, snr const., 18 years with Victoria Police*

Participants consistently referred to the significant influence of mentors on how probationary and early career police developed their operational style – both generally and in relation to their work with victims of crime. That the training and socialisation of police officers once they enter the field is of crucial importance is a well-researched subject (Van Maanen 1973; Fielding 1988; Chan 2003). Chan, for example, has identified that while new recruits may have the crime-fighting approach to policing challenged at the Academy, not long after graduation they 'started to repeat the mantra' that academy training was '"warm and fuzzy stuff" and quite irrelevant to real policing' (2003, p. 315). Similarly, Haarr's (2001) study of training police in community and problem-solving approaches found that the positive enthusiasm of new recruits sharply dissipated after 16 months in the field among mentors cynical about the value and utility of new approaches to policing.

The development of fundamental assumptions about what constitutes 'real' policing that emerge post-Academy are intertwined with conceptions of police work as action-oriented, rooted in the use of force and privileging physicality. Thus, understandings of 'real' policing as synonymous with crook-catching and crime-fighting both reinforce and express the oft-noted 'masculine ethos' of policing (Heidenshon 1992; Fielding 1994; Brown and Heidenshon 2000; Herbert 2001; Westmarland 2008; Reiner 2010) which, despite transformations in recruitment and training in recent decades, has remained remarkably persistent across organised police forces internationally (Brown 2008). One consequence of what some scholars have termed the 'cult of masculinity' (Smith and Gray 1985) in policing is that interacting with members of the public (be they victims or offenders) in a fashion likely to earn the moniker 'care bear' becomes both devalued and feminised within an occupational culture that holds action, toughness and physicality in highest esteem. This tension was encapsulated in the words of one female senior sergeant:

> I think that masculinity has got something to do with it too. Men seem to think it's weak to spend five minutes talking to someone that you've dealt with a few times that keeps on being drunk. They tend to think it's weak to show that you think that what they've done is understandable to the point where they had a reason. They seem to think [about] it like that. *Regional station, snr. sgt, 25 years with Victoria Police*

Such observations may appear to offer a bleak picture of the potential for police–victim interactions, and it is here that some important caveats and engagements with notions of 'police culture' are necessary. First, there is an acknowledged problem with assuming that the dominant street-cop culture is in fact the *only* strand of police culture (Foster 2003; Westmarland 2008). Research for our own larger project revealed that specific specialist units were considerably more 'victim-centred' in their approach. In contrast to the findings of some earlier studies (Stenross and Kleinman 1989), homicide detectives often had extended and involved contact with victims (Colvin and Wilson 2009b). Additionally, in the face of the apparently crushing weight of police occupational culture, it is important to remember, as Chan suggests, that 'police officers, working within the structural conditions of policing, play an active role in developing, reinforcing, and/or transforming cultural knowledge. They are not passive carries of police culture' (2003, p. 28). Thus, the post-academy experience was far more nuanced than simply the transmission of an action-oriented, masculinised notion of policing that devalued other tasks. In many cases the recollections of those mentored also reveal them questioning, contesting and negotiating the values and norms of their mentors. Moreover, mentors themselves communicated a multitude of subtle variants that diverged from the core narrative of physicality, action and machismo.

Building upon this discussion of where knowledge and learning about the police role in relation to victims occurs, we now turn to an examination of police participants' attempts to delimit where policing begins and ends in relation to working with victims of crime. This is the basis from which we can then assess the three dominant operational styles of policing – social workers, pragmatists and crime-fighters – and how these styles frame victim-police interactions and police perceptions of their responsibility towards victims.

Drawing the line: police work and victims of crime

A significant component of this study was dedicated to mapping perceptions and attitudes within Victoria Police of police obligations towards victims of crime, in an era of increased attention to, and accountability for, police–victim interactions. We wanted to know more than simply whether police followed victim-oriented protocols; we also endeavoured to interrogate the occupational milieu within which such protocols and procedures are implemented. In order to examine these, we explored the breadth of victimisation and victims of crime that general duties police deal with; indeed, participants consistently reminded interviewers that 'victims of crime' covers a broad area of authority. As one senior inspector commented when discussing operational practices with victims of crime in his regional town, 'victims are a big part of the job, and it's a really varied part of the job' (*Major regional station, inspector, 28 years with Victoria Police*).

When discussing the degree of involvement with victims of crime, participant responses were contingent upon a number of factors, which were in turn victim dependent (e.g. the level of contact individual victims seek and the type of victimisation experienced), officer-dependent (e.g. judgements made regarding the legitimacy of 'victim' status and the disposition of the individual officer) and organisation and context dependant (e.g. time and resources available generally and at the time police are responding). Of interest here is the organisational imprecision expressed by participants. Despite broad claims regarding victim-focused reforms across Victoria Police, the realities for day-to-day police working across the State in diverse stations is that they can encounter significant breadth in relation to victims and victims needs, and this interaction is mediated by multiple pressures on police, including pressures to attend call-outs and respond immediately to emergency situations. As a consequence some officers tended to be uncertain as to where and how to set the limits of their interactions with and obligations to victims of crime:

> It's a fine line. How far do we go? We could maintain contact over an extended period of time... [but] once it goes to court [do we] forget about them ...? Do we not have a six-month follow-up after the court date? I mean, where do we draw the line? *Outer urban station, snr. const., 26 years with Victoria Police*

As this excerpt from a senior police officer with many years of operational experience demonstrates, clarifying the role police should take in responding to victims of crime is exceedingly complex for policing agencies and for officers. On one level, there are the provisions of the *Victims' Charter* and internal policies and procedures aimed at imposing broad service standards on police members.[3] These are rhetorical commitments that Victoria Police works towards, albeit without any tangible consequences should the agency fall short of the mark. However, operational police are required to have knowledge of these commitments, and officers must meet obligations regarding recording victim interaction, linking victims to support services and communicating investigation developments and outcomes to victims. On another level, we can examine how police perceive working with victims of crime in relation to other policing tasks, particularly in terms of identifying operational priorities. Our identification of different policing styles in relation to victims largely emerged from how this aspect of police work was prioritised in relation to other policing tasks. The interviews revealed that there was confusion and negotiation of managing top-down administrative burdens with the immediacy of everyday policing in drawing a line that indicates where police work begins and ends in relation to victims of crime.

The attitudes and operational styles of police came to the fore in their explanations and descriptions of their response to, and treatment of, victims of crime within this context. Recourse to stereotypical conceptions both of what police work was considered to be and, importantly, of what it was not was often drawn upon to justify where police work ends, as the following two comments illustrate:

> I think we do look after them, but at some stage you have to let them go. I mean...police [are] not counsellors, so you can't be going on [communicating] two years later with the victims. *Outer urban station, snr. const., 20 years with Victoria Police*

> I mean the victim only wants to do so much: express what has happened and make a report, make a statement, that's virtually the police's role, there's not much else you can do. We're not equipped to do anything else. You're not a counsellor. *Urban station, snr. const., eight years with Victoria Police*

The distinction between 'counsellors' and police used above was repeatedly mobilised to demarcate the obligations of police to victims of crime. This conception aligns with the observations of Herbert (2001), who compared police occupational conceptions of the work of crime-fighting in relation to community policing, whereby 'hard' policing (crime-fighting) is at one end of the spectrum and 'counselling' or 'social work' is at the other (devalued) end.

In drawing such a boundary, officers defaulted to procedural certainties to make sense of a panoply of interactions with the public that were often shambolic and ill-defined. For some officers, the solution to the dilemma of ill-defined obligations (questions such as, "when do we stop informing them?") is to adopt a minimalist approach, while others in our study differentiated themselves from a policing approach that failed to take into consideration the specific experience of victims and to respond accordingly to their needs in the course of undertaking an investigation. This finding embodies the tensions between competing visions of the police role that are embedded within policing culture. It is clear from this research and previous research that police occupational cultures are not monolithic, and numerous studies have developed typologies of police orientations and styles (Reiner 2010). For the purposes of the present study, we examine three broad categories of disposition towards work with victims of crime: 'social workers', 'pragmatists' and 'crime-fighters'. These differentiating terms perform as ideal types. Rather than labelling individual officers, they delineate broad organisational norms and are expressive rather than descriptive.

Social workers

Some participants emphasised the 'service workers" view of police and their role in relation to dealing with victims, echoing the stipulations of the *Victims' Charter* that require police to provide victims with respectful treatment and regular information on the progress and outcome of their cases. This description fits broadly within the community policing model which, while interpreted and applied in a variety of ways, –established a more expansive framework than the crime-control focus of the modern tradition of policing (Fleming and O'Reilly 2008; Brogden and Nijhar 2005; Fielding 1995; Skogan 2006b). Many participants referred to the broader service role of police by identifying the range of roles police perform. Exemplary here was one participant's comment:

> You join the job to put on many different hats. One time you have to be a marriage counsellor. ... [S]ometimes you have to be a babysitter. Another time you have to be the bloke who's putting handcuffs on someone because they've ... committed an offence. *Urban station, const., one year with Victoria Police*

Within this context of service provision, a handful of participants viewed victims as the primary responsibility of police:

> [O]bviously we have a huge duty of care ... probably 100 per cent duty of care in relation to victims. *Outer urban station, snr. sgt., 25 years with Victoria Police*

> We have a duty to obviously keep them up to date, ensure that if they require counselling, if they require assistance in court, if they require any other needs, that they're taken care of. Every victim should be treated obviously as best that we can. *Outer urban station, snr. const., ten years with Victoria Police*

> Basically we're there to provide support [and] knowledge for the victim. They've come to us for a reason, they've been a victim of a

crime, so it's our job to support them and do as much as we can for them. *Regional station, snr. const., four years with Victoria Police*

These participants applied an understanding of police 'duty' that is expansive, embracing the recognition that good working relationships with victims is helpful to police and to the community. While few police officers specifically identified victim support as a primary function of policing, a significant minority of participants, ranging from senior and long-serving police to junior and recent recruits, embraced an overall service-provision approach to policing as opposed to a reactive crime response model. Critically, these attitudes and interpretations of the role as a broad one fed into perceptions of the protocols and strategies currently in place on providing support to victims:

> [Police should go] at least to a point where you know [the victim is] getting the assistance that they require. So they may not have the ability or the means to get assistance, but if you can put something into place, it might just be a phone call and pass on a phone number, and then you just follow it up to see that they've been contacted. ... Obviously there's limits to how far you need to go, but with certain circumstances sometimes it's as little as a phone call, and it just makes a huge difference to that person ... even if it's just ten to 15 minutes listening to what they've got to say, and that's all they needed: just someone to listen ... and they're satisfied with that. *Outer urban station, const., two years with Victoria Police*

More commonly, however, police emphasised the importance of working professionally with victims in order to maintain a level of service that would ensure that victims of crime would cooperate with police both immediately and in the future. The underlying rationale behind this position is offender focused (rather than victim focused), wherein officers view victims as witnesses who are integral to securing prosecution, and victim satisfaction is an important component of securing traditional police targets.

Pragmatists

There are compelling practical reasons why victims of crime are important to police. As numerous studies have found, these reasons include the likelihood that victims provide leads to offenders and assist as witnesses in prosecutions but also, and more broadly, that securing the general cooperation and trust of the public, including victims, helps to ensure they will act as sources of information on crimes and cases (Mawby 2007; Coupe and Griffiths 1999). These pragmatic concerns are not lost on many front-line police, who are aware that appropriate interactions with victims of crime are likely to prove invaluable in the detection and prosecution of offenders. One officer noted that

> if we want [victims'] assistance to help us to do our job, we've got to give them the assistance in return; it's a two-way street. We don't get anything if we don't give them something as well. *Regional station, snr. const., seven years with Victoria Police*

Such instrumental motivations are not necessarily problematic if victims of crime are treated respectfully and kept informed as a result. Indeed, instrumental considerations can easily coexist with a victim-oriented style. A crime investigation unit officer, for example, expressed both a pragmatic rationale for fostering the trust of victims in the criminal justice system subsequent to a police encounter and a genuine concern for the distress of individual victims:

> Every victim should be treated obviously as best that we can because...this might sound a bit sucky, but if it was your family member, you would want them treated exactly the same. Nothing would piss a policeman off more than to know that someone hadn't treated their family member how they think they should be treated. And they're potential jurors at the end of the day as well. *Outer urban station, snr. const., ten years with Victoria Police*

The pragmatic approach was the second most consistently adopted approach of police when describing their role. Potentially, as noted at the outset, there may be a mismatch between the discursive recognition of victims' needs and the importance of attending to victims of crime compared to the day-to-day policing practices of participants. Nonetheless, it points to pragmatic priorities as having the potential to be the framework through which to foster support and adoption of shifts in policing practice.

Crime-fighters

A significant proportion of participants argued that while victims do comprise a major component of their encounters with the public, their focus was generally not on victims of crime. From this perspective crime and its prevention is the demarcation of police work:

> Our primary role is ... to protect the public, keeping the streets safe. ... [T]hat's what we're there to do. We're there to prevent crimes. *Outer urban station, snr. const., eight years with Victoria Police*

Indeed, a number of participants observed that while police experience interactions with victims of crime on a daily basis, it is rare for the topic of conversation among police officers to be victims and/or the provision of victim services. This observation is significant in terms of how a 'police culture' is formed in practice. Shearing and Ericson (1991) have suggested that 'police stories' constitute an important repertoire, or 'cultural tool kit' (p. 506), with which police can organise and regularise diverse and random interactions they encounter. This finding has implications for developing training that translates into the day-to-day application of policing, as opposed to training that is 'required' for police to complete but which is seen as divorced from the reality of what police do and what police talk about. It also has implications for the implementation of the various victim-oriented processes required by agencies such as Victoria Police, including increased interaction with victims and the recording of every interaction with victims over the course of the investigation. The shift to move policing agencies towards being more victim-oriented via creating administrative accountability processes for operational police can in fact further entrench the crime-fighting mentality and the rejection of the 'social work' requirements of attending to victims as this senior officer's comments demonstrate:

> Where do we draw the line between what we are as police officers and [what] they want us to be – [which is] social workers? Whose responsibility is that? I'm here to investigate a crime. I'm here to see well if someone has committed that crime, identify the person, charge them and put them before a magistrate. Where does it come in now that I suddenly have to be a social worker and I have to liaise with this victim and refer them to that person and ring them up a week later and see what they've done next? It's just increasing the workload of general duties members or any member. *Outer urban station, snr. const., 26 years with Victoria Police*

In addition, despite requiring police to increase their interactions with victims, the majority of the 'crime-fighter' operational police made it clear that not only is victim support not their role, it is also something for which they are ill-equipped in terms of training and expertise:

> I always look [at it this way:] my job is to investigate what happened and charge the people with the offence. I'm not a community worker or a counsellor or anything, and I don't have the training for it either. *Urban station, const., two years with Victoria Police*

Some participants ardently dismissed any organisational emphasis on victims as either undermining a focus on 'real police work' or as an unsustainable expansion of the policing area of authority that would untenably intensify already demanding workloads. Participants who were 'crime-fighters' repeatedly asserted that victims were a low priority in contrast to the 'real' police work of catching offenders. As the following officer commented, dealing with victims was

> important, but it comes secondary to actual investigation of the crime itself. I mean, I guess it depends on what unit [or] ... area you work in, but it's secondary to the actual physical work that you have to go out and do yourself because [the investigation is] ... what takes up most of your time, and that's where you're catching your offenders. *Urban station, const., three years with Victoria Police.*

In this way the hierarchy of policing priorities was clearly articulated. In viewing victims as a secondary concern, participants were very clear that their responsibility to victims must be limited:

> I don't think we should be responsible for ... ensuring that the victim gets the counselling they need to get, or has access to those sorts of things. At the end of the day, we're here to catch crooks and put them before the court. *Outer urban station, snr. const., nine years with Victoria Police*

Overall, the majority of police interviewed defined their role according to a crime-fighting mandate – a perspective that appears to be largely learned and reinforced when police move from the Academy to the station, despite finding that police are called upon for a diverse range of tasks on a daily basis. Nevertheless, the extent to which police identified with the crime-fighting, social worker or pragmatist operational styles was also contingent upon a range of other factors that we shall now explore.

Location, resources and time

The three typologies of operational dispositions towards dealing with victims of crime outlined above (social worker, pragmatist and crime-fighter) are developed through two broad factors: location, both in terms of geographical station and particular unit within the organisation, and resourcing, both with regard to perceptions of workload and the perceived level of organisational support available to facilitate working with victims. Each of these is discussed in turn below.

Location

A unique contribution of this study is the breadth of stations across the state included. Geography has implications for police–victim interactions in a range of ways, including the resources at a given station, the dominant type of crime police are responding to and the role of police within the broader community. Comparing policing experiences in the urban (city) stations to that of regional stations, the volume of crime can differ (though this may be the type of crime rather than the general volume of crime because some major regional stations have significantly high workloads), but so too, critically, can the anonymity of police. A major difference was identified in the nature of interactions with victims of crime between urban and rural stations. Broadly speaking, policing in smaller regional and rural communities enabled more intense and ongoing relationships with victims of crime than was feasible in urban stations, in part due to busy routines but more often reported as resulting from the smaller population and the decreased anonymity of police when off duty and out in the community. In smaller stations, where a small number of police dealt with a clearly defined community through extensive contact, police members felt more responsible for ensuring that community members are satisfied with the service provided. This was a point frequently made by officers (the majority of participants) who had experience of both urban and rural contexts, as the following examples make clear:

> And I suppose in terms of the country, again, because people know who you are, there's more – I don't know whether it's accountability but maybe it is to a point because you know that you're going to see them. There's only ten coppers and whatever in the town, so you know that you might see them down at the supermarket with your wife or whatever, so you've got to do the right thing by them, not that you wouldn't anyway, but it just sort of reinforces it. *Outer urban station, snr. const., 12 years with Victoria Police*

Knowing a few of my friends who are out at small stations, they're more personal with the people than what we are here because we just have a high volume of people coming through whereas they get a chance, and more time, to actually speak with people, whereas we're always on the go here so we don't [get that chance]. *Outer urban station, snr. const., 28 years with Victoria Police*

Generally the difference in location highlighted most by police participants was this regional/city divide, as all police in regional locations had some experience in city stations and/or another station prior to the one in which they were located at the time of interview. It was consistently perceived that those in regional locations had more time to deal with victims of crime in an appropriate and satisfactory manner, in contrast to the experience of working within the busy metropolitan stations, where the work pressures were seen to be higher and the community more anonymous. As one officer noted:

[I] noticed ... that you're anonymous in the city, so where you move from job to job you do have contact [with victims], but you tend to think, 'I will never see this person again', whereas in the country you know the person's father, you know the kid; whoever you deal with may be on the same football team; your son goes to school with [them]; everything is connected. *Regional station, snr. sgt., 25 years with Victoria Police*

The more victim-oriented approach adopted by police in smaller regional and rural stations reflects the importance placed on securing the cooperation of the community for the effectiveness of local policing. As one officer from a rural station remarked,

It's not that you take the confrontational approach in the city, but you're a lot more aware that in the country you're part of the community in that you've got to have the support of them to do your job simply because, looking after number one, backup [is] half an hour away. So you learn to communicate pretty well. *Outer urban station, snr. const., 12 years with Victoria Police*

A number of police reflected on their experiences in different stations and the corresponding shift in their attitude towards and treatment of victims. Participants who had moved from inner-city suburbs to outer-city suburbs, and those who had moved from a city to a regional station, identified a shift in their perceived role and their approach; however, this was also noticeable for participants who had moved stations within the city. This officer's experience in moving from the Central Business District (CBD) to an inner suburban station in the city encapsulated these differences:

> Come night-time, working in the city, you're basically a glorified security guard just trying [to stop] drunken brawl after drunken brawl you attend. But here ... you're dealing with people on a more personal level, whether that be your victims or your offenders, because although the residential area within the city is expanding, most of your offenders and victims are transients. They come from other areas. So they'd be in and out. I've been working in [this inner-city suburb] where generally the offenders and the victims reside in the area. You're dealing with them more on a personal level. So you're seeing the same faces around. You know who's who.... There are segments of the community ... you deal with more ... often. And then they know you. *Urban station, snr. const., five years with Victoria Police*

Differences between stations were found to be due to both geographical and socioeconomic factors. As this officer's remarks reflect, there are sometimes stark differences between suburban stations even when they are adjacent, based purely upon socioeconomic contrasts:

> In [one bay-side suburb] a lot of it is public relations type [policing], keeping the public happy; it's more proactive rather than active policing. Whereas here we mostly just respond to calls that come through triple zero because we're busier. *Urban station, snr. const., 11 years with Victoria Police*

Discussion of the role of police and the pressures placed on them in different stations and regions often facilitated discussion of how police manage their priorities in relation to meeting victims' needs and fulfilling their broader obligations within the context what the overwhelming majority perceived as resource constraints.

Time and resources

In almost every interview, participants – regardless of the operational style they described – asserted that the potential to fulfil a victim-oriented role was seriously curtailed by competing workplace demands and limited resources, and many felt that the frenetic pace of station activity precluded providing a desirable quality of service. The following comments from officers are exemplary here:

> [Y]ou're in here, and you're interviewing someone for an offence, and you've got ten jobs on your plate out on the road, and D24 are ringing you, 'How long are you going to be?' ... [I]n a perfect world, if you live in an area where it's quite safe ... you can take your time and do everything. But unfortunately ... it's natural to not put in much time and effort or be able to respond to people as you would like to. *Outer urban station, snr. const., five years with Victoria Police*

> As much as you try to give 100 per cent, you don't have the time to do it all, because while you're in here doing paperwork for the victim that's been ... robbed, hurt, whatever ... you've got the board constantly ringing on the phone saying, 'How long are you guys going to be?' *Outer urban station, snr. const., five years with Victoria Police*

> Like we go to a job for say, cold burglary, which is very low priority because the offenders have left and we just need to take reports. This person's just had their – their personal space has been violated. Someone that they don't know has gone through all their stuff, and all that. We've got jobs piling up on our plate; we need to come get [the] ... details. Sometimes we don't have the time to try to comfort them, explain to them the process and whatnot. ... We definitely try to, and it's always in the back of your mind, but sometimes we just can't. *Urban station, const., two years with Victoria Police*

These discussions were often punctuated by lists of what resources that particular station required – another van, more staff, and so on. For some participants this was a reality of the job, but it was one that did not impact on their view of police work, while for others it reflected a tension between what they would ideally do for victims and what they actually did as a result of work pressure:

> it's all based on time [and] resources ... We've only got enough time to Band-Aid every single situation we go to ... I hated the job for the first year ... because I come from nursing where I was helping everybody and now I've come to this job where every situation you go into, every home you go into, you just go, 'what can I do so this doesn't come back to bite me on the arse, or you don't call back again tonight?' That's all we're doing really. Are we really helping anybody? *Outer urban station, const., two years with Victoria Police*

These findings are important opportunities for policing agencies to consider how change can be managed in practice. In addition, the reality of 24/7 police work creates further barriers to managing interactions with victims, including maintaining regular contact in the face of fragmented work schedules:

> Look, I worked the morning shift today, I'm off tomorrow and then I start night shift for a week, have big changeovers, then I go on holidays. So basically, if I get a file today there's no way I can follow it up in the next four, five weeks. *Outer urban station, const., one year with Victoria Police*

> It's often quite hard because if you haven't got an offender and you're trying to do an investigation, it takes time because you're doing shift work and you might be on a night shift when you get an assault. And you can't follow up with witnesses or anything for another week or two, and if they're ringing every second day wanting to know what's happening, and you keep going, 'well, I can't do anything, I'm on night shift', because you don't want to be going around to people's houses at three a.m. and getting them to sign a statement or whatever. *Urban station, snr. const., five years in Victoria Police*

It is worth examining the claim that police have neither the time nor the resources to deal with victims of crime in more detail, with reference to research in this area. At the outset, it must be stated that this is a perennial claim of front-line police identified in studies of policing across the Anglo-American world. Nevertheless, the idea that police are continually rushing from incident to incident is not borne out by empirical research into police activity. While there are times (weekend evenings, for example) and places (such as inner cities) where police may be in constant demand, this is the exception rather than the norm. Thus, David Bayley's overview of extant research led to the conclusion that 'rigorous studies of workloads tend to show that patrol officers have a considerable amount of uncommitted time' (1994, p. 43; for a meta-analysis of studies in this area, see Brodeur 2010, pp. 150–161). Therefore it is worth questioning why the assertion that limited time and resources prohibit more comprehensive encounters with victims of crime is so persistently made. On this question, Bayley offers some pertinent observations:

> Most jobs are boring in part, but few people define their work in terms of those periods. Police officers, who are active, gung-ho people,

naturally dwell on the purposeful, adventuresome side of their job. They tend to magnify the time spent actually 'fighting crime'. It is hard for them to admit that they often simply drive around. Moreover, because their work is sometimes dangerous, it is easy for them to confuse the fatefulness of what they do with busyness (1994, p. 43).

Participants were adamant that they worked under considerable time pressures, and at times they no doubt do. It is also apparent that, in terms of maintaining contact with victims of crime, the rotations of shift work construct a tangible obstacle to continuity and the appropriate timing of communication with victims. Nevertheless, the comments of the participants revealed much about the way police work and how they prioritise competing demands, to reveal a slightly different picture. Underpinning many of the interviews was a particular view of dealing with victims of crime: that it would be possible, and good, to spend more time with victims of crime *if there were absolutely nothing else to do*. This relates to the question of police perceptions of their role in relation to victims of crime. Ensuring that victims of crime have more satisfactory encounters with police is inextricably linked to cultural transformation within police organisations. The central barrier to such transformation is the tenacity of the crime-fighting operational style, which studies continue to reveal is a remarkably constant aspect of police culture and one that is extremely resistant to change (Loftus 2009).

Conclusion

It is worth in conclusion to reflect on some of the central findings of our research and some of the challenges – and opportunities – they suggest. The organisation at the centre of our study, Victoria Police, was one endeavouring to improve police–victim interactions, and our project was one element of this larger aspiration. Taken at face value, some of our findings would be depressingly familiar to police scholars: much of the potential benefit of academy training evaporates quickly in the station house; there is a strident strand of machismo action-orientation within general policing (or 'street cop') culture that tends to lump dealing with victims into a 'rubbish' box, along with other service-oriented tasks; and many police – rightly or wrongly – feel too stretched and are consequently disinclined to embrace additional tasks that raise the attendant spectre of yet more paperwork and emails.

But there are grounds for optimism too. The orientation of machismo and action is there and is dominant – but it is not all pervasive. There are many general duties officers who go well beyond the basic requirements of policy in their interactions with victims. Both the 'social workers' and 'pragmatists' placed a high value on their interactions with victims of crime, and these officers already are, or will become in the future, mentors themselves. Moreover, location was a crucially important variable in our study, with officers in smaller regional locations with close connections to the community seeing police–victim interactions as an integral element of building trust in those communities. It would seem, also, that that most disputed notion of 'police culture' is both the problem and the solution. How to harness its more positive aspects and give some of the 'care bears' more traction remains the challenge.

Notes

Research for this chapter was funded by Australia Research Council Linkage Project Grant LP0775304 'The police role in victim and witness support: researching a best practice model'. The authors would also like to acknowledge the invaluable assistance of Anika Dell, Emma Colvin and Kate Fitz-Gibbon in the research for this chapter and the wider project.

1. This strategic plan was relevant at the time the research was conducted and formed the overarching Victoria Police framework. It was replaced by the 2012–2015 *Victoria Police Blueprint*, which reaffirmed the commitment to 'develop a victim-centric service delivery strategy, expanding on the success of the Victims' Charter' (Victoria Police 2011, p. 5).
2. Specifically, 76 Victoria Police personnel completed a pilot online survey. The majority of respondents were male (75 per cent) and primarily held the rank of constable (60 per cent). A quarter of respondents were sergeants, and just over ten per cent were ranked inspector or above. Both the mean and median age of the respondents was 40 years old. Just over 50 per cent of respondents were based in metropolitan Melbourne, whereas 40 per cent were based in a regional or rural area. The primary responsibilities of the respondents was varied: approximately 30 per cent involved in specialist crime units, 43 per cent engaged in general duties and the remainder involved in other duties, including traffic.
3. The *Victims' Charter Act* (2006) sets out expectations for the treatment of victims –, that is, courtesy, respect and dignity by police and other key agencies.

References

Bayley, D. 1994. *Police for the Future*. New York: Oxford University Press.
Booth, T. and Carrington, K. 2007. A comparative analysis of the victim policies across the Anglo-speaking world. In: Walklate, S. (ed.) *Handbook of Victims and Victimology*. Cullompton: Willan, pp. 380–415.

Bourdieu, P. 1990. *In Other Words: Essays Toward a Reflexive Sociology.* Cambridge: Polity Press.

Bradford, B., Jackson, J. and Stanko, E. 2009. Contact and Confidence: Revisiting the Impact of Police Encounters with the Police. *Policing & Society* 19(1), pp. 20–46.

Bradley, D. 2009. Education and Training. In: Wakefield, A. and Fleming, J. (eds) *The Sage Dictionary of Policing.* London: Sage, pp. 100–102.

Brogden, M. and Nijhar, P. 2005. *Community Policing: National and International Models and Approaches.* Cullompton: Willan.

Brown, J. and Heidensohn, F. 2000. *Gender and Policing.* Basingstoke: Palgrave.

Brown, J. 2008. From Cult of Masculinity to Smart Macho: Gender Perspectives on Police Occupational Culture. In: O'Neill, M., Marks, M. and Singh, A.-M. (eds) *Police Occupational Culture: New Debates and Directions.* Bingley: Emerald, pp. 205–226.

Brodeur, J. 2010. *The Policing Web.* Oxford: Oxford University Press.

Chan, J. 1997. *Changing Police Culture: Policing in a Multicultural Society.* Cambridge: Cambridge University Press.

Chan, J. 2003. *Fair Cop: Learning the Art of Policing.* Toronto: University of Toronto Press.

Colvin, E. and Wilson, D. 2009a. *Major Collisions Investigation Group: Victim Support Issues Paper.* Unpublished Research Report. Melbourne: Monash University.

Colvin, E. and Wilson, D. 2009b. *Homicide Division: Victim Support Issues Paper.* Unpublished Research Report. Melbourne: Monash University.

Colvin, E. and Wilson, D. 2009c. *Results and Analysis of Pilot Survey on Police Perceptions of Victims of Crime.* Unpublished Research Report. Melbourne: Monash University.

Coupe, T., and Griffiths, M. 1999. The Influence of Police Actions on Victim Satisfaction in Burglary Investigations. *International Journal of the Sociology of the Law* 27(4), pp. 413–431.

Elliott, I., Thomas, S., Ogloff, M. and James, R. 2011. Procedural Justice in Contacts with the Police: Testing a Relational Model of Authority in a Mixed Methods Study. *Psychology, Public Police and Law* 17(4), pp. 592–610.

Fielding, N. 1988. *Joining Forces: Police Training, Socialisation and Occupational Competence.* London: Routledge.

Fielding, N. 1994. Cop Canteen Culture. In: Newburn, T. and Stanko, E. (eds) *Just Boys Doing Business? Men, Masculinities and Crime.* London: Routledge, pp. 46–63.

Fielding, N. 1995. *Community Policing.* Oxford: Clarendon Press.

Fleming, J. and O'Reilly, J. 2008. In Search of a Process: Community Policing in Australia. In: Williamson, T. (ed.) *The Handbook of Knowledge Based Policing: Current Conceptions and Future Directions.* Chichester: Wiley-Blackwell, pp. 139–156.

Foster, J. 2003. Police Cultures. In: Newburn, T. (ed.) *Handbook of Policing.* Cullompton: Willan, pp. 196–227.

Haarr, R. 2001. The Making of a Community Policing Officer: The Impact of Basic Training and Occupational Socialization on Police Recruits. *Police Quarterly* 4(4), pp. 402–433.

Heidensohn, F. 1992. *Women in Control? The Role of Women in Law Enforcement.* Oxford: Clarendon Press.

Herbert, S. 2001. 'Hard Charger' or 'Station Queen'? Policing and the Masculinist State. *Gender, Place and Culture* 8(1), pp. 55–71.

Hoyle, C. and Young, R. 2003. Restorative Justice, Victims and the Police. In: Newburn, T. (ed.) *Handbook of Policing.* Willan: Cullompton. pp. 680–706.

Hoyle, C. and Zedner, L. 2007. Victims, Victimization and Criminal Justice. In: Maguire, M., Morgan, R. and Reiner, R. (eds) *The Oxford Handbook of Criminology.* 4th ed. Oxford: Oxford University Press, pp. 461–495.

Jackson, J., Bradford, B., Stanko, B. and Hohl, K. 2013. *Just Authority?: Trust in the police in England and Wales.* Abingdon: Routledge.

Reuss-Ianni, E. and Ianni, R. 1983. Street Cops and Management Cops: The Two Cultures of Policing. In: Punch, M. (ed.) *Control in the Police Organization.* Cambridge, MA: MIT Press, pp. 251–274.

Loftus, B. 2009. *Police Culture in a Changing World.* Oxford: Oxford University Press.

Loftus, B. 2010. Police Occupational Culture: Classic Themes; Altered Times. *Policing & Society* 20(1), pp. 1–20.

Mawby, R.I. 2007. Public Sector Services and the Victim of Crime. In: Walklate, S. (ed.) *Handbook of Victims and Victimology.* Cullompton, Willan, pp. 209–239.

Myhill, A. and Bradford, B. 2012. Can Police Enhance Public Cooperation by Improving Quality of Service? Results from Two Surveys in England and Wales. *Policing and Society,* 22(4), pp. 397–425.

O'Neill, M., Marks, M. and Singh, A.-M. (eds) 2008. *Police Occupational Culture: New Debates and Directions.* Bingley: Emerald.

Reiner, R. 1978. *The Blue Coated Worker.* Cambridge: Cambridge University Press.

Reiner, R. 2010. *The Politics of the Police.* 4th ed. Oxford: Oxford University Press.

Segrave, M. and Wilson, D. 2011. *The Station Study Report: Victoria Police and Victims of Crime, Police Perspectives and Experiences from across Victoria.* Melbourne: Monash University.

Shearing, C. and Ericson, R. 1991. Culture as Figurative Action. *British Journal of Sociology* 42(4), pp. 481–506.

Sims, L. and Myhill, A. 2001. *Policing and the Public: Findings from the 2000 British Crime Survey.* London: Home Office.

Skogan, W. 2006a. Asymmetry in the Impact of Encounters with the Police. *Policing & Society* 16(2), pp. 99–126.

Skogan, W. 2006b. *Police and Community in Chicago.* New York: Oxford University Press.

Smith, D. and Gray, J. 1985. *The Police and People in London.* Aldershot: Gower.

Stenross, B. and Kleinman, S. 1989. The Highs and Lows of Emotional Labour: Detectives' Encounters with Criminals and Victims. *Journal of Contemporary Ethnography* 17(4), pp. 435–452.

Van Maanen, J. 1973. Observations on the Making of Policemen. *Human Organizations* 32(4), pp. 407–418.

Victoria Police 2007. *The Way Ahead: Strategic Plan 2008–2013.* Melbourne: Victoria Police.

Victoria Police 2011. *Victoria Police Blueprint: 2012–2015.* Melbourne: Victoria Police.

Victoria Police 2011. *Annual Report 2010–2011*. Melbourne: Victoria Police.

Waddington, P. 1999. Police (Canteen) Sub-Culture: An Appreciation. *British Journal of Criminology* 39(2), pp. 286–308.

Westmarland, L. 2008. Police Cultures. In: Newburn, T. (ed.) *Handbook of Policing*. 2nd ed. Cullompton: Willan, pp. 253–280.

Williams, B. 1999. *Working with Victims of Crime: Policies, Politics and Practice*. London, Jessica Kingsley.

7
Victim Impact Statements, Sentencing and Contemporary Standards of Fairness in the Courtroom

Tracey Booth

The participation of crime victims in sentencing proceedings through victim impact statements (VIS) is a prominent and contentious feature of criminal justice policy in most common law jurisdictions where the legal proceedings are of an adversarial nature.[1] While of course no one is 'anti-victim', incorporating a subjective victim voice in the legal proceedings, particularly through VIS read aloud to the court by victims (oral VIS), has proved controversial for many commentators and legal practitioners (Ashworth 1993; Bandes 1996; Booth 2007a, 2012; Edwards 2004; Erez 2000; Erez et al. 2014; Hall 1991; Henderson 1985; Hoyle et al. 1998; Kirchengast 2010; Logan 2008; Rock 2010; Sanders et al. 2001; Sarat 1997).

It seems obvious that incorporating victims and their oral statements in the sentencing process will be challenging for sentencing judges trained in adversarial traditions in common law jurisdictions. Victims are both physically and practically excluded from the adversarial sentencing hearing. Only the prosecution and the defendant are parties to the legal proceedings and party status gives these participants power to identify the issues, present the evidence, test the evidence and make submissions as to penalty. An independent and impartial judge manages the proceedings and determines the penalty. Victims are not parties; they are not represented; they are confined to the rear of the courtroom in the public gallery as bystanders; and they have no power in the sentencing hearing.

Legislation has introduced VIS to this established model, and their role is far from clear. The functions of VIS are generally articulated in instrumental and/or expressive terms (Cassell 2009; Erez, 2004; Garland 2001; NSW LRC 1996; Roberts and Manikis 2010). From an instrumental perspective, VIS are said to be useful sentencing tools that provide information to assist judges to formulate more proportionate and accurate sentences. But many commentators are concerned that using the highly subjective and emotional VIS for this purpose could be inconsistent with the legal goals of sentencing and the values of objectivity and formality that underpin law and the legal proceedings (Ashworth 1993; Booth 2007a; Henderson 1985).

In addition or alternatively, the role of VIS is said to be expressive or communicative. Through VIS victims can recount their experiences and express their feelings about the crime to the court, the offender and the wider community (Cassell 2009; Roberts and Erez 2004, 2011; Szmania and Gracyalny 2006). According to Erez (2004), the expressive function of VIS is designed to redress the exclusion and marginalisation of victims in the sentencing hearing as well as improve their courtroom experiences. Opponents argue that the inclusion of VIS in the proceedings, especially oral VIS, is likely to generate inappropriate emotional displays, embarrassment and confrontation in legal proceedings; present an onerous management task for the sentencing judge; and be detrimental to the offender's entitlement to a fair hearing and the integrity of the proceedings more generally (Abromovsky 1992; Arrigo and Williams 2003; Bandes 1996, 2009; Gewitz 1996; Rock 2010; Sarat 1997; Schuster and Propen 2010).

Shifts in community sensibilities, however, have generated changes to community standards and expectations of fairness in the courtroom (Spigelman 2004; *R v Dietrich* (1992) 177 CLR 292). Shapland argues that failure to accommodate the interests and concerns of victims in a manner that maintains public confidence in the administration of justice can threaten the integrity of the legal proceedings (Shapland 2010; see also Garkawe 1994; Shapland and Hall 2010). A significant factor said to be undermining public confidence in the current criminal justice system is the poor treatment of victims and their exclusion from criminal justice processes (Shapland and Hall 2010, p. 188). In the context of sentencing, poor treatment of victims could compromise the legitimacy of the process and generate public disorder (Shapland 2010, p. 365). Research indicates that the way victims are treated in the courtroom and especially their experience of presenting their VIS to the court has a significant bearing on the perceived fairness of the proceedings and victim satisfaction with the VIS more generally (Meredith and Paquette 2001; Rock 2010; Victim Support Agency 2009).

The Victorian case of *Borthwick* (2010) VSC 613 illustrates these tensions (ABC Radio National 2011; Booth 2011; Iaria 2010). Borthwick was convicted of manslaughter. At the sentencing hearing, the defence objected to VIS submitted by members of the deceased's family on the basis that much of the content was highly prejudicial, inflammatory and inadmissible. According to media reports, the court then spent some 90 minutes reviewing these objections, editing and deleting 'inadmissible' material in the VIS in open court. The family victims silent during this process were furious and distressed when they were given amended versions of their statements to read to the court. The deceased's sister tore her VIS in two and 'stormed out of the courtroom in tears' (Iara 2010); later, family members gave extensive media interviews describing their distress and anger at the perceived unfairness of their treatment in the courtroom (ABC Radio National 2011; Booth 2011).

Garland argues that VIS have led us into 'unfamiliar territory where the ideological grounds are far from clear and the old assumptions an unreliable guide' and our sense of how things work needs to be clarified (2001, pp. 4–5). In this chapter, I draw from my recent study of victim participation in the sentencing of homicide offenders in the New South Wales (NSW) Supreme Court (Booth 2012) to consider how sentencing judges in common law jurisdictions can respond to victims' interests in the courtroom in a manner designed to enhance the fairness of the proceedings for victims while not jeopardising the offender's entitlement to a fair hearing. This chapter is divided into three parts. Part I provides an overview of the task of the sentencing judge in a contemporary context. It will outline shifts in approaches to judging from the traditional legalistic model to emerging restorative and therapeutic approaches. The requirement of fairness is a core component of contemporary criminal justice, and this part will also explore what contemporary standards of fairness require in relation to the treatment of victims in the courtroom. Analysis of key findings of my study is the subject of part II and provides the foundation for the proposals put forward in the next section. In part III, I suggest ways in which sentencing judges in common law jurisdictions can enhance the treatment of victims in courtroom processes associated with oral VIS. These suggestions are designed to create more sensitive space in which victims present their statements as well as promote a more inclusive approach to managing victims' participation.

Part I: Judging in the contemporary context

Approaches to judging

Judges are responsible for upholding public confidence in the administration of justice and are charged with conducting a fair hearing from
the perspective of not only the parties involved but also the wider
community (Spigelman 2004). Common law principles and ethical
guidelines guide judicial conduct (Roach Anleu and Mack 2005). In
accordance with adversarial traditions, courtroom interaction in superior courts has been structured by formality, rituals, technical legal rules
and the concepts of rationality and reason (McBarnett 1981; Tait 2001).
'Courts experience constant transformation', however, and as a consequence, the administration of justice 'at any given historical moment'
is 'dependent on the societal context' (Jeffries 2002, p. 1; see also Doak
2008; Kirchengast 2011). So as to maintain public confidence in the
administration of justice, it is important that courts sustain connection
with social change and societal expectations. In response to widespread
dissatisfaction with the justice system, recent changes in approaches to
'law and lawyering' (Daicoff 2006, p. 1) have been well documented,
and according to Freiberg, depicting our current justice system as 'adversarial' is 'becoming less accurate descriptively and less desirable norma-
tively' (Freiberg 2007, p. 207).

During the last two to three decades, shifts to more therapeutic and
restorative approaches to the law and its institutions have emerged
(Daicoff 2006; King et al. 2009). Therapeutic justice is not so much a
theory as a perspective or lens through which to observe the operation
and impact of the law (King 2003; King et al. 2009; Wexler and Winick
1996). Broadly, a therapeutic approach is one that is concerned with the
impact of laws, legal procedures, legal actors and legal institutions on
the physical and psychological well-being of those who are involved in
legal processes. Related research has generally focused on improving the
operation of the law and the legal environment to maximise the law's
therapeutic value and generate law reform (Goldberg 2005; King et al.
2009; Wexler and Winick 1996). Although much of the work in this
area has revolved around the impact of the law on the well-being of the
defendant in the context of problem-solving courts or tribunals and/
or dealing with the causes of crime (Goldberg 2005), the core values of
therapeutic justice – voice, validation, respect and self-determination –
are universal to all who are affected by the law, including victims (King
2008).

Therapeutic justice has had a significant impact on the judicial land-scape. A therapeutic approach to judging does not require judges to act as therapists; rather, it requires judges to be aware of and to seek to reduce the potential anti-therapeutic or detrimental effects of legal proceedings on participants. Canadian Judge Susan Goldberg argues that following such an approach, judges are interested rather than dispassionate; engage in open communication where stories are heard rather than limit communication; engage in direct dialogue with parties rather than through the lawyers; are perceptive rather than impervious to emotional nuances; and conduct proceedings with less emphasis on formality and more focus on the concept of 'inclusiveness' (Goldberg 2005, p. 4). As such, 'though it is not social work, therapeutic judging requires a greater commitment of emotional energy than traditional judging' (Frieberg 2007, p. 217). While it is said that this shift to a more therapeutic approach has led judges to consider how they can better treat those in the courtroom 'with courtesy, respect and dignity' (King 2003, p. 172) some judges and legal practitioners are cautious about the inherent challenge to the traditional passive role of the judge in the courtroom and concerned about the lack of appropriate training (Frieberg 2007, p. 217).

Restorative justice also has had a significant impact on law and legal processes. While a precise definition of restorative justice is elusive (Stang and Braithwaite 2001, p. 2), for the purposes of this research it is conceived broadly in terms of process, values, aims and outcomes – an umbrella under which a variety of practices and processes sit (Braithwaite and Strang 2001; Dignan 2007; Hoyle 2010; Shapland et al. 2006; Strang 2002; Walklate 2007;). The essence of restorative justice is the recognition that the key stakeholders in a criminal matter are the offender, the victim and the community. A restorative justice initiative focuses on healing and responsibility in the aftermath of the offence. Restorative values include fairness, restoration/healing, inclusivity, collaboration, respect, dignity, support, safety, democracy, empowerment, account-ability, responsibility and reparation (Dignan 2007; Hoyle 2010; Strang 2002). In the context of the sentencing hearing, VIS reflect restorative values and aims.

Alongside these reflective changes to 'law and lawyering', more prosaic considerations of managerial justice and the impact of consumerism have transformed the justice system into a 'service to be measured and consumed' (Ryan 2003, p. 131). In such a 'market-driven' atmosphere, Jeffries argues that the public has been able to make 'increasing demands of the court' and that the role of the court is 'being increasingly judged in terms of service quality and its responsiveness to the news and expectations of those involved in the proceedings as well as the wider community' (Jeffries 2002, p. 9–10). Consequently, courts have been obliged to address consumer needs, and as a result, better court buildings have been built, facilities have improved, more information has been made available to court users and training has been provided for front-line staff (Jeffries 2002, p. 10).

The degree to which these shifts have been embraced in the judging landscape varies, but at the very least, such changes in thinking have led to a greater awareness of the impact of law and legal processes on all who become involved in the courtroom processes (King 2003, 2008).

The requirement of fairness

Much of the reform of substantive criminal laws and procedure over the past 150 years has been a function of the elevation of 'fairness' as a core principle of the modern criminal trial and a reflection of its dynamic nature (Spigelman 2004). In the criminal justice context, issues of fairness have generally been addressed in terms of the defendant's entitlements and a fundamental element of our current criminal justice system is 'that a person should not be convicted of an offence save after a fair trial according to law' (Gaudron J in *Dietrich* (1992) 177 CLR 292, 362). With regard to sentencing, particular legal principles have emerged to protect the interests of the offender during the hearing, including entitlements to legal representation, to address the court, to challenge the case against him/her, to be sentenced justly and according to law and to be judged by an independent and impartial tribunal (Edwards 2009, p. 299). Together with these specific safeguards, there is also a more general requirement that the sentencing hearing be conducted according to the 'requirement of fairness'.

The trial is a dynamic institution of social power that is adaptive to changing social needs and conditions (Doak 2008; Kirchengast 2011). Consequently, laws and court procedures adapt to and reflect changing community standards and contemporary expectations of fairness (Spigelman 2004; *R v Dietrich* (1992) 177 CLR 292). Legislative changes to established sentencing practices through the introduction of VIS, particularly oral VIS, reflect such changing sensibilities and expectations of victim involvement in sentencing processes. As originally instituted, VIS were written statements submitted to the sentencing court thereby allowing victims to express their feelings to the sentencing judge; in most jurisdictions, these statements were not read aloud to the court. In the last decade, however, several common law legislatures – including jurisdictions in Australia, New Zealand, the United Kingdom and Canada – have extended victims' entitlements to allow victims, or their representatives, to read their statements aloud to the court. Through reading aloud such oral VIS, victims are made visible in the sentencing hearing, and they have the opportunity to communicate to not only the judge but also the offender and the wider community.

Garkawe argues that in exercising their legal entitlement to submit VIS, victims have acquired interests in the proceedings that could be 'substantially affected' by the handling of their statements in the court-room (1994, p. 603). Media reports of angry, distressed victims who perceive unfair treatment and re-victimisation by the law and its agents in the courtroom such as occurred in *Borthwick* are the stuff of political nightmare.

Victim participation through VIS is novel in the modern sentencing hearing, and a major concern is that being responsive to the interests of victims in the sentencing hearing will occur at the expense of the offender's entitlements. Particularly problematic from the offender's perspective is the threat to the impartiality of the sentencing judge, the questionable probative value of VIS that contain material prejudicial or inflammatory to the interests of the offender and the practical difficul-ties inherent in challenging VIS (Bandes 1996; Edwards 2009; Logan 2008).

Thus, an issue for contemporary sentencing judges is to determine how to be responsive to contemporary standards of fairness in relation to the interests of the victim without detracting from the offender's entitlements. Drawing from the findings of my study discussed further in the next section, it is argued that 'procedural justice' provides the key. Essentially, procedural justice is about fairness, and research has shown that participants in decision-making processes are more affected by the quality of procedures by which decisions are made than by the outcomes (Lind and Tyler 1988; Mack and Roach Anleu 2010; Tyler 2003). The procedural fairness of a given decision-making process can be assessed according to both the quality of the decision-making proce-dure and the quality of the interpersonal treatment during that proce-dure (Tyler 2003). A fair decision-making procedure involves the use of objective information; consistent, neutral decision making; and provi-sion for those involved to present their case – that is, to have a voice in the hearing (Tyler 2003, p. 298). The quality of interpersonal treatment reflects a person's standing and status, and it is measured according to the degree to which people are treated with dignity and respect as well as the extent to which their rights and concerns are acknowledged (Tyler 2003, p. 298).

Lind and Tyler argue that the opportunity to speak and put forward one's views is a significant feature of the fairness of the decision-making procedure. Having an opportunity to submit a VIS in the sentencing hearing and thus be heard as to how they have been affected by the crime can be regarded as 'a potent factor in the experience of procedural justice' (Lind and Tyler 1988, p. 101). Nonetheless, while a legislative right to submit a VIS might create an image of a procedurally fair process, it is contended that the treatment of the victim in the courtroom is also crucial to that victim's assessment of the fairness of the procedure and also to that victim's experience of fairness in the legal proceedings (Wemmers 1998, p. 74). Fair procedures can indicate respect and value for the victims, whereas unfair procedures indicate marginalisation or exclusion from the hearing (Murphy and Tyler 2008, p. 653). Recent research has indicated that perceptions of procedural injustice can lead a person to experience negative emotions and affect the degree to which they comply with the decisions and directions of the court (Murphy and Tyler 2008).

Part II: The study

My study was designed to explore the participation of a discrete group of crime victims – the family of the deceased victim, or 'family victims' – in the sentencing of homicide (murder or manslaughter) offenders in the NSW Supreme Court. Like other common law jurisdictions, family victims in NSW are entitled under legislation (the *Crimes (Sentencing Procedure) Act 1999* (NSW) (*CSPA*)) to submit a written VIS to the sentencing hearing and also read their statements aloud to the sentencing court. There is no prescribed VIS form and no agency designated to prepare VIS on behalf of the deceased's family. Section 26 of the *CSPA* limits the content of the statement to the impact of the deceased's death on the family. In contrast to other common law jurisdictions, however, when sentencing homicide offenders (Kirchengast 2011; Roberts and Manikis 2010), although a NSW sentencing court *must* receive a VIS properly submitted by a family victim, the court *must not* take account of that VIS in the determination of penalty 'unless it considers it appropriate to do so'.[2] The NSW Supreme Court has taken the view that it is not appropriate to take account of VIS from family victims, because the resulting penalty might reflect not the culpability of the offender but instead the value and worthiness of the deceased person. The more valuable and worthy the deceased, the greater the impact of the death on the deceased's family, the greater the harm caused by the offence and the greater the penalty imposed; such a result would be inconsistent with fairness and equality before the law (*R v Previtera* (1997) 94 A Crim R 76).

A key purpose of this study was to produce a rich and rounded picture of victim participation in the sentencing of homicide offenders and, in doing so, investigate the presentation of VIS in the courtroom. Data was gathered through the observation of 18 sentencing hearings of homicide offenders in the NSW Supreme Court and semi-structured interviews with 14 family victims; a grounded theory model using a constant, comparative approach was adopted as a basis for analysis of this data (Charmaz 2006). To further enrich the picture of what was 'told' in the VIS and the 'telling' of those statements in the courtroom, I analysed the content and performance of 24 VIS read aloud using narrative analysis techniques (Gubrium and Hostein 2009; Reissman 2008). The aim of this analysis was to gain greater insight into the presentation of oral VIS and explore in detail the 'ritual' and impact of the performance in the courtroom with particular reference to interactional ground rules and behaviour norms.

The hearings were observed in the NSW Supreme Court between July 2007 and December 2008. Of the 18 hearings, seven offenders had been convicted of murder, ten offenders had been convicted of manslaughter and one offender had been convicted of being an accessory after the fact to murder. A total of 38 VIS were received by the courts in these hearings, 30 of which were read aloud. The remaining VIS were submitted in writing only in six matters; in three of those cases, the judge took the time to read the written VIS while sitting on the bench, whereas in the remaining matters, the VIS were put to one side with the rest of the written material that had been tendered presumably to be read later when the judge was off the bench. Observations were recorded in field notes and transcribed within a few hours of the hearing. These notes were supplemented with digital copies of the transcripts of 16 of the 18 hearings and 24 of the 30 VIS read aloud in those hearings.

Fourteen family victims from 14 discrete cases were interviewed between April 2007 and October 2008. Twelve of the 14 interview participants were recruited through the Homicide Victims Support Group (HVSG). The NSW Police and HVSG have a memorandum of understanding whereby, in the case of homicide, the deceased's family members are put in touch with the HVSG and provided with support and assistance as required. Although there is bias inherent in becoming a member of a victim support group, given the memorandum of understanding with the NSW police, the HVSG was the first port of call for most family victims in NSW, and it maintains a large membership, with whom it keeps in regular contact. Furthermore, in at least six cases observed, the families were supported by counsellors from the HVSG. Thus, a recruitment strategy through the HVSG promised to reach a wide range of family victims. Of the remaining two participants, one contacted me after reading my article about family victim participation in the sentencing process published in the *NSW Law Society Journal* (Booth 2007b), and the other was recruited through another victim support group, namely Homicide Survivors Support after Murder.

An important caveat is that, as a small in-depth study of victim participation in homicide sentencing in the NSW Supreme Court, the extent to which the results can be considered to be of more general application is limited. The study, however, is not intended to be representative of victim participation in the sentencing of homicide offenders more generally; rather, it is designed to illuminate the nature and dynamics of participation of family victims in select sentencing hearings. The findings from this group of victims nevertheless highlight issues that are relevant to sentencing in all common law jurisdictions.

Findings and analysis

Important findings related to the impact of oral VIS on legal proceedings and the manner in which the court responded to the interests of victims in particular situations. In light of the concerns outlined above, perhaps the most striking finding was that although the subjective and emotional nature of the VIS and the distress and/or anger expressed by victims as they read their statements undoubtedly increased the emotional tension in the courtrooms, the hearings were not disrupted (Booth 2012), even in two matters where the defence successfully objected to VIS. Indeed, all but one hearing proceeded with dignity and formality. In this exceptional matter, brothers of the deceased cried and raised their voices at times as they read their VIS. Later, when they were seated in the public gallery, two of the brothers shouted at the offender several times as he was giving evidence, and they were ejected from the courtroom by police officers. This 'flooding out' of emotions by the family victims did create a disturbance, but the judge maintained control, and the proceedings continued in an orderly manner. While many victims did express anger towards the offender and the crime as well as legal constraints on what could be said in their statements, no victims were observed to express anger at their treatment in the legal proceedings, nor am I aware of evidence of later complaints to the media.

As I have argued elsewhere (Booth 2012) family victims were 'cooled out' by various processes before, during and after the hearing so as to manage and contain the emotional tension in the courtroom as well as help victims present their VIS. Before the hearing, the prosecution prepared victims for the sentencing hearing and worked with them to ensure that the VIS complied with legal requirements so as to prevent or reduce the rejection of VIS in the courtroom. Under NSW law, VIS should not contain 'offensive, threatening, intimidating or harassing' material (reg 10(6) *Crimes (Sentencing Procedure) Regulation 2010*), and the content of the statements is limited to the impact of the deceased's death on the deceased's family. During the hearing, aside from two cases discussed further below, there was no legal debate regarding the admissibility of the VIS; judges also afforded victims dignity and respect as they presented their statements through a range of strategies, including demonstrations of empathy and providing explanations of various stages of the process. After the hearing, judges used their sentencing judgments to comment on the VIS, thereby acknowledging and validating the experiences of family victims.

The events in *Borthwick* provide an example of what might occur if victims are not successfully 'cooled out'. In that case, the prosecution had not 'vetted' the VIS before the hearing and the statements tendered in court contained inadmissible material that included highly prejudicial allegations that the offender had engaged in criminal conduct with which he had not been charged. During later interviews, the family victims said that they did not know that the offender could object to their VIS and/or that the court could reject or amend their statements. Furthermore, at no stage did the judge explain what was happening to their statements (Booth 2011).

Given the perceived disjuncture between the legal process and family victims, the sentencing hearing is a setting in which cooling-out processes can assist victims to cope with their distress, defuse or reduce victims' anger and/or resentment and help them exercise their entitlement to present their VIS (Booth 2012). Negative emotions associated with grief, disappointment and resentment could 'flood out', impede the orderly process of the legal proceedings, threaten the dignity and fairness of the hearing and undermine public confidence in the administration of criminal justice. An important component of the management of victim participation in the hearings observed was the quality of the interpersonal treatment of victims by many of the sentencing judges that revealed sensitivity to particular interests and concerns of the victims, a feature lacking in *Borthwick* (Booth 2012). Particular features of this treatment will be discussed further in making recommendations in the next section.

The observation fieldwork also raised issues associated with the integration of victims and the VIS in the sentencing hearing more generally. Joh's description of VIS as 'occupying a strange and awkward presence in a sentencing proceeding' (2000, p. 37) seemed especially apt as 'space' for victims in the process – whether it be the place from where they read their statements or the stage in the hearing where the statements were presented – was marked by some ambiguity (Edwards 2004). An important task for the sentencing judge is to ensure that victims have appropriate 'space' in which to exercise their entitlement to subject VIS, but in the hearings observed, there appeared to be no designated place in the courtroom from which a family victim was to read their statement and judicial practices varied. Most victims read their statements from a seated position, but in that case where there was some disturbance described above, the victims were made to stand beside the bar table to read their VIS to the court.

Victim participation in the hearings was kept quite separate from the remainder of the proceedings. VIS were dealt with first before moving to the substantive issues regarding sentence. The content of the statements was unrelated to matters that were discussed otherwise during the proceedings and, in most cases, were not referred to again in the hearing. It was my impression that the court, in dealing with VIS first, endeavoured to get the VIS 'out of the way' so that the real legal business of the hearing could proceed. In fact, on most occasions, immediately after the victim had finished reading his or her statement and often even before the victim had resumed his or her seat in the public gallery, the court continued with the hearing straightaway. Another striking feature was that despite the evident distress of other people in the public gallery, on almost all occasions no time was provided for those distressed to regroup and recover their composure.

In the following part, I suggest modifications to processes in the courtroom that could enhance the fairness of the proceedings from the perspective of the victim without detracting from the offender's entitlements or the integrity of the hearing more generally.

Part III: Recommendations

The inclusion of victims and their VIS in sentencing modifies the adversarial sentencing hearing and reflects shifts in community sensibilities and expectations of fairness in legal proceedings. Fairness to victims in this context, however, is more than the entitlement to submit a VIS; fairness involves meeting a range of procedural conditions, including being treated with dignity; kept informed and consulted where appropriate; and being engaged as a participant with due recognition by the court.

If a victim elects to submit a VIS, the task of the judge is to provide the

> forum in which [they] can make a public statement in words of their own choosing, in order to have the emotional catharsis of ensuring that their grief and loss have not been either ignored altogether, or expressed in what they see as an inadequate way. (Sully J in *R v FD; R v JD* (2006) 160 A Crim R 392414)

Creating such a forum represents a therapeutic shift for the sentencing judge, although judges are not required to act as therapists; the law is not designed to assist victims to achieve particular emotional states. Rather, a therapeutic approach in this context is one that requires a judge to be aware of and be responsive to the potential anti-therapeutic effects of legal processes on victims in the courtroom. The aim of the recommendations below is two-fold: to heighten judicial awareness of the potential anti-therapeutic effects of particular processes on victims' experiences presenting their VIS and to enhance dignity and respect afforded to victims in the courtroom more generally. Not only will victims' experiences of procedural justice be improved, but conflict and tension arising from victim participation could be reduced.

The recommendations that follow are categorised under two broad headings. The first, integrating oral VIS in the hearing, relates to issues of space and time. 'Space' refers to the position from which the victim reads their statement and also support that might be provided to the victim to enable them to use this space. The issue of 'time' refers to the period allocated to VIS in the hearing. The second category, dealing with challenges to VIS considers issues relating to objections and amendment of VIS by the court.

Integrating oral victim impact statements in the proceedings

Two significant aspects of space are relevant to the interests of the victim – the place in the courtroom from which victims read their statement and protections and/or support provided to victims to help them take advantage of their entitlement. As already noted, my study found that there was no designated space in the courtroom from which the family victim was to read his or her statement. Most victims were directed to read their VIS to the court from a seated position in either the witness box or the jury space; from either position they could look out into the court and the public gallery, access water and tissues as needed and be moderately comfortable while they read their statement. In two matters, however, the judge directed the victims to stand near the bar table facing the judge; these victims stood with their backs to the public gallery (and other family members and/or supporters), without access to support such as water and/or tissues and no place to lay their statements. The presentation of their VIS in these circumstances was clearly difficult for these two victims.

The provision of a comfortable space for victims in the body of the court as they read their statements does not detract from the offender's entitlement to a fair hearing. Victims should be given the option to be seated while they read their respective statements to the court. Not surprisingly, in the matters observed most victims cried as they spoke, used tissues and drank water. For those victims who stood while they read their statements, it was difficult for them to hold their statements steady and also wipe their tears or access water. Given the nature of a VIS, being forced to stand makes a difficult task that much more arduous and adds an unnecessary burden onto the victim.

Another issue for the judge to consider in choosing the appropriate space is whether that position enables victims to look out into the courtroom. An important feature of a VIS is said to be its potential communicative capacity (Erez and Roberts 2004, 2010). Through their statements, victims have the opportunity to talk about their experiences and speak to the judge, the court, the offender and/or the wider community if they wish (Erez and Roberts 2004, 2010; Szmania and Gracyalny 2006). It is important that judges respond to victims' interest in fairness in the proceedings from victims by establishing a space for victims that could enhance the communicative capacities of VIS.

Sentencing courts could also consider whether in the circumstances it is appropriate to make special arrangements to assist the victim in present his or her statement. In one hearing observed, a family victim tried to walk in front of the bar table to reach the witness box in order to read her statement. It seemed that she took this route in order to avoid walking close to the offender in the dock. Rules of procedure dictate, however, that no one walks in front of the bar table while the court is in session. Court officers practically tackled her to avoid such a breach of protocol, and she was then forced to walk behind and close to the offender. In these circumstances, a more sensitive response to the interests of the victim would have been to allow her give the offender a wider berth and walk in front of the bar table.

Indeed, it is not difficult to envisage other situations such as sexual assault matters where a victim might need added support so that he or she can exercise their entitlement to read their statement aloud to the court. In those circumstances the court could consider making special arrangements to provide assistance. Legislation in most Australian jurisdictions now allows eligible victims to read their VIS to the court from another place via some form of audio-visual link. For instance, section 30A(3) of the NSW *CSPA* provides:

> If the proceedings for the offence concerned are proceedings in which the victim to who the victim impact statement relates is entitled to give evidence by means of closed-circuit television arrangements, the victim is also entitled to read out the statement in accordance with those closed-circuit television arrangements.

Legislation in Victoria[3] and Queensland[4] has gone further, and both jurisdictions set out alternative arrangements to support victims to read their statements aloud to the court. These arrangements include

- obscuring the victim's view of the offender. The Victorian legislation suggests that screens could be used so that the person reading the victim impact statement is out of the offender's direct line of vision;
- allowing a support person to stand beside the victim while that victim reads their statement to the court;
- closing the court or restricting those who can be present in the courtroom while the statement is being read;
- requiring the lawyers not to robe.

An application for such alternative arrangements could come from the victim and/or prosecution or simply on the motion of the court. There is no reason to suppose that such alternative arrangements could detract from the offender's entitlement to a fair hearing. The offender could still challenge the VIS if appropriate, and subject to the law, victims could be cross-examined on their statement.

With regard to time there are two aspects worth noting – the time allocated to presentation of VIS and the court's 'attention span'. Alongside reflective shifts in approaches to legal processes, more prosaic considerations of managerial justice have made increasing demands on the court in terms of efficiency and courts are under pressure to deal with matters as rapidly as possible. An important and positive feature of the hearings observed was that though several VIS were lengthy, or presentations were delayed by the victim's distress, no family victims were hurried to finish reading their statements. On one occasion, due to the victim's distress as he read his statement, the judge adjourned the matter briefly to enable the distressed family victim to recover his composure, though this was unusual. While the presentation of oral VIS might take some time, it is important that victims are not restricted in the time available to them.

A less positive feature of the hearings observed was the court's short 'time span' allocated to VIS. Oral VIS differ from other oral testimony in that victims do not present their statements in the traditional question and answer format. Instead, victims read their written statements aloud to the court in an uninterrupted narrative or monologue. Not surprisingly, many family victims exhibited distress – shedding tears, holding their VIS with trembling hands and speaking with quavering voices. As already noted in the hearings observed, immediately after the VIS were completed, the court continued with other business, often even before the family victim had resumed his or her seat in the public gallery and certainly without any respite for those family victims who were distressed after the VIS were read. It is important that courts recognise the inclusion of the victims in the hearings by affording them dignity and respect. Thus, a more appropriate response would be to give the victims time to resume their place in the public gallery and perhaps even adjourn the matter for a short period to allow the victim and their family to regain composure.

Dealing with challenges to VIS

It is evident that legal challenges to VIS have the potential to be stressful for victims. In *Borthwick* the victims were frustrated and angered not only because sections of their VIS were changed but also because they felt that they were not treated fairly in the process (ABC Radio *Law Report* 2011; Booth 2011). In particular, the victims complained:

- The defence did not explain the substance of their objections or articulate which were the offending sections of the statements.
- The sentencing judge did not explain to the victims what was happening to their VIS.
- The court spent 90 minutes reviewing and editing their statements, but the victims were not consulted during this process.
- They were then given the edited versions of their statements and told that was the only version that they could read to the court.

- No explanation in relation to what was deleted or the final edited versions was forthcoming from the court to the victims.

The victims were both physically and practically excluded from the process of dealing with their VIS. Following widespread media attention, the Victorian Supreme Court reviewed the handling of VIS in the sentencing court and a new practice direction commenced in May 2011. The aim of this direction is to prepare future victims for potential objections, but given the nature of the complaints of the deceased's family in *Borthwick*, it is striking that the practice direction does not address the other issues raised, particularly the treatment of the victims in the courtroom.

Objections to VIS were made in two hearings observed and dealt with in a manner that was inclusive of the interests and concerns of the victims. In the first matter, the primary objection related to whether the victims were eligible to submit VIS under the legislation; in the second matter, objections were concerned with the admissibility of some of the content of the statements. In both cases (as in *Borthwick*), neither the defence nor the judge explained the nature of the objections to the court. However, after upholding the objection (and unlike *Borthwick*) the sentencing judges took time to explain the ruling. In the first matter, the VIS were rejected in their entirety because the offence was not one where the victims were eligible under the law to submit a VIS. The judge did not simply reject the VIS and move on to the next issue, however. Instead, he took time to explain his ruling because he said he wanted to ensure that the deceased's 'family understood' that they were prevented from submitting their VIS 'because of the law and not because of anything they have written'. This judge did not speak to the victims directly, but in addressing the court generally, the victims would hear this explanation in the public gallery; it was evident that the judge intended the victims to hear and understand his explanation.

The second matter was a high-profile case, and the very small courtroom was crowded with friends and supporters of the offender as well as journalists. In similar fashion to *Borthwick*, the defence submitted the VIS to the court with the offending sections highlighted; the editing process involved only the judge and the lawyers. There was certainly potential for the family victims to have been humiliated and angered at the public rejection of their personal statements and could have generated similar tension and conflict as occurred in *Borthwick*. The judge did not consult with the victims during the editing process, but once he finished, he did explain the law and his reasoning clearly and at length to the court. Of particular note was the fact that he emphasised that the decision to delete sections of the VIS was neither personal nor reflective on the victims. The judge said to the first victim, 'It's not a subjective criticism of you Ms [x], but it's a matter we must do according to law and according to the regulations in respect of victim impact statements'. He also sought to reassure the victims when they read their statements. When the first victim came forward to read her VIS, the judge addressed her directly and told her that the opportunity to read her VIS 'was not wasted' because being unable to read the highlighted sections 'wouldn't matter very much to the impact of what you say'.

Certainly with regard to the content of the statements, the interests of the offender and the victims conflicted. On the one hand, the victims wanted their statements to remain unchanged, as a personal expression of their thoughts and feelings; on the other hand, the offenders wanted to exclude inadmissible material that might be prejudicial and adversely impact the penalty imposed. According to the rules of fairness, the offender is entitled to challenge irrelevant or prejudicial matters that might be included in VIS, and if successful, that material will be excluded.

However, it is argued that because victims are entitled to submit a VIS and this entitlement will be affected by objections, victims have an interest in being afforded dignity and respect in the process (Booth 2011, 2012; Garkawe 1994). And the court can be responsive to that interest without derogating from the offenders' entitlement to a fair hearing. Perhaps most importantly, there is no need for the court to conduct proceedings as if the victims are not present. I am not suggesting that the court should consult with victims in relation to the appropriateness of or ruling on defence objections. That enquiry is about the law, and victims are not parties to the hearing. Nonetheless, the sentencing judges should anticipate victims' grief, disappointment and resentment and respond sensitively to victims' interests. Such a response could be for the judge to explain:

- the nature of the offender's objections;
- the reason for the court's ruling;
- the ways in which the VIS have been amended.

As in the second matter described above, the judge could also speak reassuringly to the victims when they come to read their amended statements to the court.

Consistent with adversarial traditions, the judge does not have to provide this explanation by speaking to victims directly (though arguably this would not interfere with the judge's neutrality). Instead as was the case in matters I observed, judicial comments regarding the VIS and the law can be directed to the court more generally with the knowledge that the victims in the public gallery will be able to hear the remarks. This would demonstrate awareness of as well as respect and sensitivity for the interests of the victims, and it would not interfere with the defendant's entitlements – indeed, the interests of the defendant and the court are enhanced if emotional tension and conflict is reduced in the hearing.

Conclusion

The inclusion of victims and their VIS in the adversarial sentencing hearing reflects contemporary community sensibilities and expectations of fairness. A significant role of VIS in sentencing is to give victims a degree of status and 'voice' in the proceedings. Poor treatment of victims in this context, such as arguably occurred in *Borthwick*, has the potential to compromise the integrity of the law and its institutions and generate public disquiet.

Such victim participation is unprecedented in the modern sentencing hearing, however, and is indeed 'unfamiliar territory' (Garland 2001, p. 5) for sentencing judges. The requirement of fairness essential to legal proceedings has traditionally centred on the provision of a fair trial for the parties involved and a plethora of legal rules have developed to protect the defendant's entitlements in particular. Opponents of VIS argue that giving victims an interest in the hearing through the submission of VIS has the potential to derogate from the fairness of the hearing. But as it has been argued in this chapter, fairness to victims need not override existing protections and actually might enhance the fairness of the proceedings more generally.

Fairness to victims in the sentencing hearing is not satisfied simply by entitling the victim to read his or her VIS to the court. The court must also ensure that victims experience procedural justice in the process, which in this context is a function of the quality of the interpersonal treatment meted out to victims. Drawing from the findings of my qualitative study of victim participation in the sentencing of homicide offenders in NSW, this chapter has made recommendations in order to assist sentencing courts in common law jurisdictions to provide appropriate space and support for victims in the hearing as they present their VIS and also to be responsive to victims' interests in the course of challenges to VIS. The old assumption that victims can be ignored during the proceedings is no longer appropriate; instead, sentencing judges must be alert to potentially anti-therapeutic effects of legal process on victims and ensure that victims are afforded dignity and respect.

Notes

1. Typically, VIS provide details of the harm suffered by the victim as a result of the offence.
2. Italics have been added. Section 28(4)(b) *Crimes (Sentencing Procedure) Act 1999* (NSW).
3. Section 8R *Sentencing Act 1991* (Vic).
4. Section 15B *Victims of Crime Assistance Act 2009* (QLD).

References

Arrigo, B. and Williams, C. 2003. Victim Vices, Victim Voices and Impact Statements: On the Place of Emotion and the Role of Restorative Justice in Capital Sentencing. *Crime and Delinquency* 49(4), pp. 603–626.

Ashworth, A. 1993. Victim Impact Statements and Sentencing. *Criminal Law Review*, pp. 498–509.

Bandes, S. 1996. Empathy, Narrative and Victim Impact Statements. *University of Chicago Law Review* 63(2), pp. 361–412.

Booth, T. 2007a. Penalty, Harm and the Community: What Role now for Victim Impact Statements in Sentencing Homicide Offenders in NSW? *University of New South Wales Law Journal* 30(3), pp. 664–685.

Booth, T. 2007b. The Contentious Role of Victim Impact Statements in Sentencing Homicide Offenders in NSW. *Law Society Journal* 45(10), pp. 68–71.

Booth, T. 2011. Crime Victims and Sentencing: Reflections on *Borthwick*. *Alternative Law Journal* 36(4), pp. 236–239.

Booth, T. 2012. 'Cooling Out' Victims of Crime: Managing Victim Participation in the Sentencing Process in a Superior Sentencing Court. *Australian and New Zealand Journal of Criminology* 45(2), pp. 214–230.

Cassell, P. 2009. In Defense of Victim Impact Statements. *Ohio State Journal of Criminal Law* 6(2), pp. 611–648.

Chalmers, J., Duff, P. and Leverick, F. 2007. Victim Impact Statements: Can Work, Do Work (For Those Who Bother to Make Them). *Criminal Law Review*, pp. 360–379.

Charmaz, K. 2006. *Constructing Grounded Theory: A Practical Guide through Qualitative Analysis*. Thousand Oaks, CA: Sage.

Daicoff, S. 2006. Law as a Healing Profession: The 'Comprehensive Law Movement'. *Pepperdine Dispute Resolution Law Journal* 6(1), pp. 1–61.

Doak, J. 2008. *Victims' Rights, Human Rights and Criminal Justice: Reconceiving the Role of Third Parties*. Oxford: Hart Publishing.

Edwards, I. 2004. An Ambiguous Participant: The Crime Victim and Criminal Justice Decision Making. *British Journal of Criminology* 44(6), pp. 967–982.

Edwards, I. 2009. The Evidential Quality of Victim Personal Statements and Family Impact Statements. *International Journal of Evidence and Proof* 13(4), pp. 293–320.

Erez, E. 2000. Integrating a Victim Perspective in Criminal Justice through Victim Impact Statements. In Crawford, A and Goodey, J. eds. *Integrating a Victim Perspective within Criminal Justice*. Aldershot, Hants, Great Britain: Ashgate.

Erez, E. 2004. Victim Voice, Impact Statements and Sentencing: Integrating Restorative Justice and Therapeutic Jurisprudence Principles in Adversarial Proceedings. *Criminal Law Bulletin* 40, pp. 483–500.

Freiberg, A. 2007. Non-Adversarial Approaches to Criminal Justice. *Journal of Judicial Administration* 16(4), pp. 205–222.

Garkawe, S. 1994. The Role of the Victim during Criminal Court Proceedings. *University of New South Wales Law Journal* 17(2), pp. 595–616.

Garland, D. 2001. *The Culture of Control: Crime and Social Order in Contemporary Society*. Oxford: Oxford University Press.

Goffman, E. 1952. On Cooling the Mark Out: Some Aspects of Adaption to Failure. *Psychiatry: Journal of Interpersonal Relations* 15, pp. 451–463.

Goldberg, S. 2005. *Judging for the 21st Century; A Problem-solving Approach*. Ottawa: National Judicial Institute.

Gubrium, J. and Holstein, J. 2009. *Analyzing Narrative Reality*. Los Angeles, CA: Sage.

Henderson, L. 1985. The Wrongs of Victim's Rights. *Stanford Law Review* 37(4), pp. 937–1021.

Hoyle, C. 2010. The Case for Restorative Justice. In: Cunneen, C. and Hoyle, C. *Debating Restorative Justice*. Oxford: Hart Publishing.

Iaria, M. 2010. Judge Flags New Victim Statement Policy. *The Age*, 21 September 2010.

Jeffries, S. 2002. *Transforming the Criminal Courts: Politics, Managerialism, Consumerism, Therapeutic Jurisprudence and Change*. Canberra: Australian Institute of Criminology.

Joh, E.E. 2000. Narrating Pain: The Problem with Victim Impact Statements. *Southern California Interdisciplinary Law Journal* 10(1), pp. 17–37.

King, M. 2003. Applying Therapeutic Jurisprudence from the Bench. *Alternative Law Journal* 28(4), pp. 172–175.

King, M. 2008. Restorative Justice, Therapeutic Jurisprudence and the Rise of Emotionally Intelligent Justice. *University of Melbourne law Review* 32(3), pp. 1096–1126.

Kirchengast, T. 2010. *The Criminal Trial in Law and Discourse*. Basingstoke: Palgrave MacMillan.

Lind, E. and Tyler, T. 1988. *The Social Psychology of Procedural Justice*. New York: Plenum Press.

Logan, W. 2008. Confronting Evil: Victims' Rights in an Age of Terror. *The Georgetown Law Journal* 96(3), pp. 721–776.

McBarnet, D. 1981. *Conviction: Law, The State and the Construction of Justice*. London: Macmillan Press Ltd.

Meredith, C. and Paquette, C. 2001. *Victims of Crime Research Series: Summary Report on Victim Impact Statement focus groups*. Ottawa: Policy Centre for Victim Issues, Department of Justice Canada.

New South Wales Law Reform Commission. 1996. *Sentencing*. Sydney: New South Wales Law Reform Commission.

Roach Anleu, S. and Mack, K. 2005. Magistrates' Everyday Work and Emotional Labour. *Journal of Law and Society* 32(4), pp. 590–614.

Roberts, J.V. and Erez, E. 2004. Communication in Sentencing: Exploring the Expressive Function of Victim Impact Statements. *International Review of Victimology* 10(3), pp. 223–244.

Roberts, J.V. and Erez, E. 2010. Communication at Sentencing: The Expressive Function of Victim Impact Statements. In: Bottoms, A. and Roberts, J.V. eds. *Hearing the Victim: Adversarial Justice, Crime Victims and the State*. Cullompton: Willan.

Roberts, J.V. and Manikis, M. 2011. *Victim Personal Statements: A Review of Empirical Research*. London: Commissioner for Victims and Witnesses in England and Wales.

Rock, P. 2010. Hearing Victims of Crime: The Delivery of Impact Statements as Ritual Behaviour in Four London Trials for Murder and Manslaughter. In: Bottoms, A. and Roberts, J.V. eds. *Hearing the Victim: Adversarial Justice, Crime Victims and the State*. Cullompton: Willan.

Ryan, M. 2003. *Penal Policy and Political Culture in England and Wales*. Winchester: Waterside Press.

Sarrat, A. 1997. Vengeance, Victims and the Identities of Law. *Social and Legal Studies* 6(2), pp. 163–189.

Shapland, J. 2010. Victims and Criminal Justice in Europe. In: Shoham, S. Knepper, P. and Kett, M. eds. *International Handbook of Victimology*. Boca Raton, FL: CRC Press.

Shapland, J. et al. 2006. Situating Restorative Justice within Criminal Justice. *Theoretical Criminology* 10(4), pp. 505–532.

Shapland, J. and Hall, M. 2010. Victims at Court: Necessary Accessories or Principal Players at Centre Stage? In: Bottoms, A. and Roberts, J.V. eds. *Hearing the Victim: Adversarial Justice, Crime Victims and the State*. Cullompton: Willan, pp. 163–188.

Schuster, M. and Propen, A. 2008. Making Academic Work Advocacy Work: Technologies of Power in the Public Arena. *Journal of Business and Technical Education* 22(3), pp. 229–329.

Schuster, M. and Propen, A. 2010. Degrees of Emotion: Judicial Responses to Victim Impact Statements. *Law, Culture and the Humanities* 6(1), pp. 75–104.

Spigelman, Hon J CJ. 2004. The Truth can Cost too Much: The Principle of a Fair Trial. *Australian Law Journal* 78(1), pp. 29–49.

Strang, H. 2002. *Repair or Revenge: Victims and Restorative Justice*. Oxford: Clarendon Press.

Szmania, S.J. and Gracyalny, M.L. 2006. Addressing the Court, the Offender and the Community: A Communication Analysis of Victim Impact Statements in a Non-capital Hearing. *International Review of Victimology* 13(3), pp. 231–250.

Tait, D. 2001. Popular Sovereignty and the Justice Process: Towards a Comparative Methodology for Observing Courtroom Rituals. *Contemporary Justice Review* 4(2), pp. 201–218.

Tyler, T. 1988. What is Procedural Justice? Criteria used by Citizens to Assess the Fairness of Legal Procedures. *Law and Society Review* 22(1), pp. 103–136.

Tyler, T. 2003. Procedural Justice, Legitimacy and the Effective Rule of Law. *Crime and Justice* 30(1), pp. 283–357.

Walklate, S. 2007. *Imagining the Victim of Crime*. Milton Keynes: Open University Press.

Wemmers, J. 1998. Procedural Justice and Dutch Victim Policy. *Law and Policy* 20(1), pp. 57–76.

Wexler, D. and Winick, B. 1996. *Law in a Therapeutic Key: Developments in Therapeutic Jurisprudence*. Durham, NC: Carolina Academic Press.

Winnick, B. 2008–2009. Therapeutic Jurisprudence: Perspectives on Dealing with Victims of Crime. *Nova Law Review* 33(3), pp. 535–543.

8
Satisfied? Exploring Victims' Justice Judgments

Robyn Holder

It is remarkable that, with nearly 50 years of research on the experiences of victims of crime with criminal justice systems across common law countries, including Australia, there is enduring attachment to the use of 'satisfaction' as a measure – because the term can hide as much as it reveals. While useful for policy purposes, it tells us little of the detail that persons are being asked to assess, is vague on context, ignores motivations and expectations and fixes identity and place. Moreover, it deftly sidesteps the more fundamental critique that persons, as victims, make of the system – that is, the absence of justice itself. This chapter takes satisfaction seriously and looks to unpack the judgements about justice that lie behind it.

Although satisfaction has been used to quantify assessments of a whole host of environments and interactions from health systems to commercial retail and to democracy itself, there is a paucity of critical analysis on what the term might mean and, consequently, its import. The satisfaction measure is commonly viewed as arising from a deep and wide shift towards marketisation in many areas of public life that took place since the 1980s in liberal democracies around the globe. It is perhaps not unrelated that, over this time, public policy commentators – political and academic – noticed and expressed concern about the disenchantment with and disengagement of citizens from the public sphere (Norris 1999; Pattie et al. 2004). More broadly then, satisfaction joins with related measures such as confidence and support to chart plummeting ratings of many public institutions.

In this chapter, satisfaction is taken as a starting point from which to explore perspectives on justice and to leverage understanding of what might be at stake in victim ratings of the public institutions of justice. It does so through an exploratory study involving a small group of men and women who were victims of violence. Interviewed three times during the course of their journey through the criminal justice process in a large Australian city, the reflections of these men and women showed context-specific evaluation. They addressed a number of dimensions that they drew upon different conceptions of justice; and also spoke of different recipients to which the good of justice was directed. These comprise *value* underpinnings to satisfaction. The chapter considers the submerged theoretical and ideological assumptions behind satisfaction as a measure of citizen interactions with and assessments of authority.

Measuring what?

Reviews of the satisfaction measure across different domains have been unanimous in critiquing its conceptual murkiness and imprecision. Significant questions persist about what actually is being measured, the relevance of antecedent factors and expectations, differing emphases on outcome and process and the weighting given to affective and cognitive influences. In the transactional world of consumption, satisfaction has been posed as a response that pertains to a particular focus and at a moment in time (Giese and Cote 2000, p. 4). In service areas such as health, research has attempted to disentangle satisfaction as a quality measure, as something related to effectiveness or to expectation and/ or as a relational assessment (Williams et al. 1998). It has been criticised as a 'seriously flawed' term (Gill and White 2009, p. 8) and for being 'under-theorized' (Aspinal et al. 2003, p. 324). Satisfaction has been linked to developments in thinking of persons as consumers or clients, to a desire for greater participation by service users and as a means of 'institutional validation' (Williams et al. 1998, p. 1352). More recently, the perceived value of a service (McDougall and Levesque 2000) and the justice components of satisfaction (Laxminarayan et al. 2013; Martínez-Tur et al. 2006) have been examined.

Whether using public satisfaction with, support for, attitudes about or confidence and trust, criminal justice research has wrestled with similar complexities. These have identified not only contextual differences to assessments (Indermaur and Roberts 2009) but also differences dependent on direct or indirect experience with the entities (Van de Walle 2009), and whether or not the experience being assessed is citizen-initiated (Skogan 2005). Furthermore, how interaction with justice authorities is experienced is recognised as crucial (Bradford et al. 2009; Tyler and Huo 2002). Studies suggest that these assessments are deeply embedded within pre-existing beliefs about the law (Murphy and Cherney 2012) and within the values and morals of community life (Jackson and Sunshine 2007). Similar challenges have confronted research examining public attitudes to other government authorities. These have considered whether public attitudes are diffuse or specific, single or multi-dimensional, socio-cultural or performance-based (Easton 1975; Norris 1999) – as well as related to institutional structure; available information; the nature of the entity (Kelleher and Wolak 2007); and the importance of time, place and public discourse (Van de Walle et al. 2008).

This brief summary of individual and group evaluations, whether in private or public domains, reveals similarities as well as differences. Of special interest is the convergence of attention on the values underpinning evaluations. From this perspective, satisfaction becomes something of a torch that can shine light on matters of deeper importance to persons.

Participants in justice

With this in mind, the research discussed in this chapter used 'more individualized, more qualitative and more in-depth methods' to analyse experience of and attitudes towards criminal justice (Van de Walle 2009, p. 395). The methodology is discussed more fully elsewhere (Holder 2013). In brief, a combination of interview and survey methods with a longitudinal prospective panel of adult victims of violence aimed to explore justice – the concept and the institutions – as multi-faceted phenomena. Working prospectively with individuals as they look ahead to the criminal justice process helps to mitigate the constraints of the single retrospective survey and to illuminate contextualised construction of meaning (Charmaz 2006). Participants were interviewed at three stages (using a combination of semi-structured and quantitative questions at each time): the first occasion was after police had charged an accused person with an offence and prior to a court hearing; the second was after the finalisation of the matter at court; and the third was 6–8 months after court finalisation. However, attrition is a problem in longitudinal research (Ruspini 1999). In commencing with 33 people at the first interview, there were 26 at the second and 19 at the third and final interview.

The panel comprised 27 adult women victims of domestic assault and six adult men who were victims of non-domestic assault. All of the perpetrators in these incidents were male. The participants were recruited over a period of 11 months during 2009 to 2010. They agreed to be involved in the research following an invitation issued by relevant victim support service with whom they were in contact. As a self-selecting sample, there is no claim to representativeness. The participants formed a cohort panel based on selection criteria. They were not a cohort in commencing and finishing in the criminal justice process at the same time or as recipients of the same 'treatment'. Rather, their common attribute was their shared experience of participation in the standard and routinised procedure of criminal case processing.

For any lay person, criminal justice is at once simple and complex. It was certainly outside the familiar for most of the research participants. The system comprises a series of locations and moments spread over time in which victims interact with various professionals representing state entities of police, prosecution and courts. These are at once single encounters, and they are also representative of a whole system. The different exchanges can be experienced positively or negatively; one exchange may cancel out the benefits of an earlier positive one or redeem the overall engagement. The different moments also present possibilities for participants to grow their thinking about what was happening and why. But together these features complicate understanding what is being evaluated by individuals. Therefore, a longitudinal engagement through this process is a method that allows an *unfolding* of motivation, expectation, assessment and reflection.

The satisfaction measure used was a simple one. At different points in the research the participants were asked, 'generally speaking, how satisfied were you with the [police or prosecution or the court or justice system overall] handling of your case?' The question at each stage thus provided some comparative assessment across the entities. More importantly, it acted as a rough dependent variable to facilitate analysis of justice judgements. The idea of justice was the deductive value assumed to lie beneath – but which idea of justice?

Theorising on justice judgements

In exploring ideas of justice, two dominant paradigms are useful– one focuses on distributive or outcome justice, and the other on procedural justice. Within each are embedded a number of distinguishing features. Distributive justice argues that people in conflict will agree that a settlement is fair and just using different criteria of deservingness, equity, need or merit (Adams 1965; Blau 1964; Deutsch 1985; Hatfield et al. 1978; Homans 1961). The first two criteria are commonly referenced in assessments about the fairness of criminal justice. In distributive justice theory, people are said to prioritise what they 'get' of a valued resource. A just process thereby becomes something that maximises a just outcome to the individual and their group (Thibaut and Walker 1975). This mode of thinking assumes that humans are selfish beings who rationally calculate the costs and benefits of attaining their goals.

The second paradigm of procedural justice assumes humans to be primarily relational in their concerns. Procedural justice attends to 'people's need for status, standing, and belonging' as being key drivers in justice judgements (Skitka et al. 2011, p. 101). It cares less about the steps that maximise gain and more about how the processes demonstrate value to the group (Lind and Tyler 1988; Tyler 1989) and which ones validate social identity (Tyler and Blader 2003). The fairness of the procedures used by the decision maker and the fairness with which they treat the person(s) subject to the decision are central concerns in procedural justice.

There has been some tendency to pose these two theoretical approaches as conflicting or in tension. More recently, however, the strong and interactive relationship between assessments of the outcome and of procedural aspects in overall justice judgements has been acknowledged (Brockner and Wiesenfeld 1996; Folger 1986; Hauenstein et al. 2001). Some contemporary theorists go further by posing distributive and procedural justice as dimensions of an integrated, normative conception of justice (Colquitt et al. 2005; Folger and Cropanzano 2001; Lind 2001; Van den Bos et al. 1997). Therefore, rather than ascribe 'single motives or simple frames' at singular moments to human behaviour, people are understood to be 'both flexible and complex' in their thinking about justice (Skitka et al. 2011, p. 28). Notwithstanding the evolution of academic thinking, and because of popular belief that victims of crime seek personal goals above all else in justice, the different orientations of these two approaches were used in this research to sketch the contours to victims' thinking over time.

Considering victim experiences with justice

The overall background to this discussion is, of course, pervasive public disquiet about the operation of criminal justice. A 2007 survey of over 8,000 Australians revealed that, while nearly three quarters (70 per cent) have confidence in criminal courts' regard for defendants' rights, only 47 per cent think similarly with regard to victims' rights, and just over half (52 per cent) think that courts deal with matters fairly (Indermaur and Roberts 2009, p. 3). In Australia, as elsewhere in the common law world, the experiences of ordinary people – in all their diversity and as victimised by a range of personal and property crimes – with the institutions of justice have been found almost universally wanting.[1]

These experiences are often telescoped to certain stock reductions: either that dissatisfaction with justice is about its outcomes, most notably sentence leniency; and/or that dissatisfaction with justice is about how as victims they were treated, most notably by exclusion and discourtesy. Very few studies go behind these narrow and particularised assessments of dissatisfaction. Most are also limited by the singular, retrospective capture of experience at one point in time. Since the 1990s, exceptions have focused on restorative justice and on victims' roles and perspectives within its diverse applications (Weitekamp and Kerner 2002; Zehr 1990). Although immensely influential, this work has been constrained by its focus on the beginning or end of the criminal justice process – that is, on restorative justice as a diversion from the court or in the sentencing process (Strang 2002; Wemmers and Cyr 2006). More recent research has sought to examine victims' experiences through a procedural justice lens (Wemmers 2013).

Notwithstanding these debates, there remains, within the body of scholarship that deals with victims and justice, a notable consistency to the core criticisms offered and consistency to the critique irrespective of offence type or victim type.[2] These centre on[3]

- victims' sense of alienation and exclusion from all aspects of the justice process;
- the experience of routine discourtesy and disrespect;
- the absence of information and the withholding of information;
- the lack of support, assistance and advocacy;
- disquiet as to the thorough, unbiased and timely performance of justice as it functions from investigation to prosecution, adjudication and sentence management;
- the perception that process efficiencies trump the proper administration of justice, especially with regard to charge negotiation;
- inappropriate or inadequate decision-making, especially with regard to sentencing;
- the failure to hear from or involve victims adequately or at all;
- a perception that, while defendants have rights and representation, victims have neither.

These elements informed the design of the participant surveys and inter-view questions for the three occasions in the current study. To what extent were people given the opportunity to express their views, and were these considered? Did they understand and agree with decisions reached? Were people treated with respect and provided with information? These ques-tions cohere with victim interests in recognition and respect and with inclusion and participation, and they drew heavily from procedural and distributive justice literature. The research did not use existing validated instruments to measure these dimensions.[4] Decisions were made both to draw variables from existing surveys[5] and to use questions designed specifically for the research population and setting. The choice of vari-ables was judged in relation to their relevance to the literature.

As a crude comparative measure, satisfaction with the various justice entities in this study affirmed previous research (Figure 8.1). Only the results from those 19 people who completed all three interviews are shown.[6]

There was a significant difference between overall satisfaction with police and overall satisfaction with regard to prosecution, the court and the justice system. The differences between prosecution, the court and justice overall, however, is not significant.[7] In essence, the participants in this study were very satisfied with police intervention, but afterwards, their satisfaction with other agencies and with the justice system overall fell and did not recover.

What might account for these shifts in opinion and assessment by victims? Given that victims commonly initiate the contact with police,

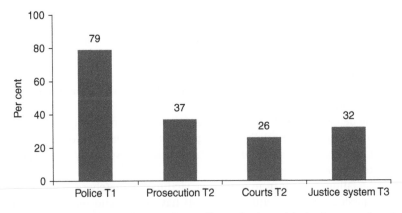

Figure 8.1 Percentage of victims' overall satisfaction with justice agencies at Time 1, Time 2 and Time 3 (N = 19)

part of the explanation relates to these encounters' being citizen-initiated.[8] Members of the public who have sought engagement with law enforcement place a stronger emphasis on performance as opposed to procedural fairness (Hinds and Murphy 2007; Murphy 2009; Wells 2007). That is, the authority is being invited to do or to perform a function unique to it. The immediacy of the problem faced by the individual, the availability and salience of police and the perceived and actual effectiveness of police are important criteria to those seeking help. Further, public trust in police is separate from and considerably higher than trust in law courts for Australia as a whole.[9] Clearly, citizens view police as a distinct emergency or help agency.

But what of the other institutions of the justice system proper – prosecution and courts? These are viewed in a different light to law enforcement but give rise to questions about the components and contexts of the different justice judgements. While their transient status as victim or witness is crucial, people as victims are also citizens who draw on wider ideas in the community about criminal justice. Acknowledgement of victims as people with different identities and interests additional and prior to their victimisation is not a new insight (Walklate 2007). However, its import is under-examined and returns us again to the nature of measurement.

Measuring experiences of justice

Beyond satisfaction, four conceptually coherent and meaningful scaled measures were derived from the quantitative data and used as repeat measures for engagements with police, prosecution and the court.[10] These were outcome acceptance, quality of interpersonal treatment, influential voice and respect for offender rights (Table 8.1). Scales help focus attention and create some coherence to data,[11] but their main function in this study was to leverage exploration of the commentary victims gave about what was happening.

The scales can be taken to represent dimensions of people's experiences of justice. At the first interview in relation to the experience with police, *outcome acceptance* was strong and can be described as a quasi-distributive measure. The scale incorporates items measuring victims' sense of the fairness of the decision of the authority as well as their perspective that the decision was expected. The items describing *interpersonal treatment*, such as respect and dignity, are commonly found in the procedural justice literature. However, the *quality* of that treatment is emphasised with the inclusion of items that acknowledge aspects of the person's status. At the

Table 8.1 Individual survey items used to construct the justice assessment scales

Scale	Variables
Outcome acceptance	I agree with decision I accept decision I received an honest explanation for decision I understand decision The decision was fair The decision was expected
Quality of interpersonal treatment	I was treated with respect I was treated with dignity Fair treatment of me Respect my rights Were helpful I was treated as victim
Influential voice	There was opportunity to express my views I was able to influence the decision My views were considered before decision I received the decision I deserved The decision was what I wanted
Respect offender rights	Treated the violent person with respect Respect offender rights

police intervention this cluster of items was less strong than the outcome acceptance scale. The items to do with voice in the third scale are also found in procedural justice studies. The scale is described as *influential voice* because of the way in which the expressive and participatory items cohered with assessments on the outcome decision – it was an outcome the victim deserved and an outcome the victim wanted. The fourth scale, *respect offender rights*, may seem unusual. Concern for the treatment and rights of the offender is not generally asked about in victim studies.[12] In this study, however, all victims identified offender-related objectives in describing their motivations for legal intervention. Therefore, this particular measure of *respect offender rights* is not so surprising and suggests that victims' goals are not as exclusively private and personal as has been argued.[13] Although these latter two scales were not as strong as the first two, their importance emerged more powerfully in participant narratives, so they have been retained.[14]

The mean of each of the scales (using only those cases who completed a first and second interview, N = 26) allows comparison of interactions across the measures. These show the different views and experiences that people have of police, prosecution and the court (see Figure 8.2).

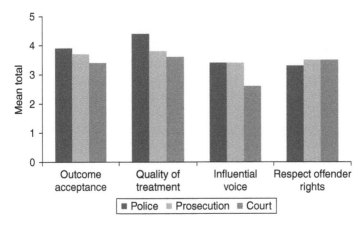

Figure 8.2 Victims' assessments of police, prosecution and courts at Time 1 and Time 2 (Scale mean: 1 = Strongly disagree; 5 = Strongly agree) (N = 26)

People made strong and positive assessments of the quality of inter-personal treatment they received from police. This was significantly different from the assessments made of the quality of interpersonal treatment experienced prosecution and from the court. The difference between prosecution and the court on the quality of their interpersonal treatment of the victim was not significant. People had a negative assessment of the strength of their *influential voice* with regard to the court. The assessment was significantly lower than those for police and prosecution. The difference between police and prosecution, however, was not significant. Finally, there was no statistical significance in assessments of police, prosecution and the court with regard to the scales measuring victims' assessed *outcome acceptance* or victims' perspectives on justice entities' *respect for offender rights*.

Correlations with satisfaction

To summarise thus far, victims' satisfaction with police at their first interview was high, but at their second and third interviews, satisfaction with prosecution, the court and with justice overall fell to approximately a third. Four dimensions to victims' justice judgements were identified. While outcome acceptance was strong for victims across all justice entities, it was in the quality of interpersonal treatment and victims' influential voice with regard to prosecution and to the court where significant differences were found.

With all of the justice entities – police, prosecution and the court – the quality of interpersonal treatment correlated in a strong and significant manner to satisfaction with each entity, especially prosecution. The same was found with the correlation between outcome acceptance and satisfaction. For the victims' influential voice scale, this was found to correlate in a strong and significant measure with satisfaction with prosecution and with the court. Of interest was the strength of the relationships between the scales. With regard to all three justice entities, the stronger the influential voice, the more accepting are victims of outcomes reached by each agency.

At this point, it is clear that victims' evaluations differentiate between the different justice entities that they encounter. It is also clear that different dimensions comprise these assessments, and these dimensions are weighted differently by victims when reflecting on the agencies of police, prosecution and the court. Thus, similar concepts in different contexts inform satisfaction differently. Together, the dimensions of the quality of interpersonal treatment, outcome acceptance, the influential voice and respect for the offenders' rights constitute an integrated justice judgement (see Figure 8.3).

Discursive underpinnings of justice judgements

Identifying and quantifying the underlying dimensions of the experiences of victims with different justice agencies creates only a surface

Figure 8.3   Integrated components to victims' justice judgements

picture. If justice judgements are based on several criteria, then the discursive underpinnings further reveal them as layered, nuanced and contingent. The rest of this chapter uses victims' narratives to flesh out their multi-dimensional judgements about justice.

The quality of interpersonal treatment

The importance of interpersonal treatment of citizens by authorities has a long research history. That people are treated with respect and dignity and that the authority is fair and unbiased[15] in its treatment of citizens have been shown as important to people in a range of settings (Dai et al. 2011; Elliot et al. 2012; Murphy 2009).

While the quality of interpersonal treatment was important, the actual experience was very different with regard to police and the other justice entities. On a single measure of whether the treatment of the person by the relevant entity was fair, 96 per cent agreed or strongly agreed it was so with police but only 58 per cent with regard to prosecution and 62 per cent with regard to the court. The literature highlights different reasons why these issues about fairness and treatment are important and the manner in which fair processes generate fair outcomes (MacCoun 2005; Thibaut and Walker 1975), and it has emphasised the 'effects of values associated with group membership' and the ways in which group procedures work (Lind and Tyler 1988, p. 231). Overall, the fair, respectful and unbiased treatment of individuals by authorities is emphasised as generating cooperation and compliance (Tyler 1990/2006; Tyler and Lind 1992).

The emphasis on compliance may not be as relevant for victims of violence when they are initiators of contact with authorities as it is for encounters with members of the public that are initiated by authorities (Murphy 2009). However, the issue of cooperation is clearly relevant, especially at the decision-making stage of prosecution. At their second interview, just over a third (27 per cent) of the participants[16] indicated that they asked prosecution not to proceed, and all of these were domestic assault victims. Four domestic assault victims were unsure of or cautious about their willingness to cooperate with prosecution (15 per cent). Nonetheless, a significant majority (69 per cent) of all the participants said that they did want all or some of the charges prosecuted. Only four of the domestic assault victims expressed a definite preference against prosecution.[17] Finally, two people – both of whom were domestic assault victims – said that they also asked the court to drop the charges in relation to the incident.

Compliance and cooperation reflects a state-centric perspective on the relationship between citizens and authorities, however. A citizen-

centric perspective, on the other hand, invites a different consideration of a different set of issues. One possibility is simply that the victim
values customer service and feels valued 'as a person' (Elliot et al. 2012,
p. 444). Another is that the quality of treatment carries a social and
political message and is related to a person's citizen-status vis-à-vis the
state (Duff 2010). The narratives of participants in this study incorporated both perspectives and revealed four themes embracing recognition
of standing, equality of treatment, information as both reciprocity and
recognition and interaction as a demonstration of respect.

Recognition of standing

Among the participants, standing emerged as a deep and robust conception that was more than a legal construct. This included being valued
as a person where the incident and matter was taken seriously as well as
the victim taken seriously. Police, said Karla,[18] 'never made me feel like
a stupid woman'. Yet the nuances and differing qualities to the experience of interpersonal treatment signalled more than a service-based
assessment.

Recognition appeared to connote a reflection of the person's particular
status. For some, such as Janelle, this was positive. She said that authorities 'treated me like a normal person, not sorry for me or anything – like
I had a right to be there'. Others, such as Edward, reflected negatively.
He was offended that he was treated like 'just another one'.

The connection between respect and recognition of one's standing
was particularly acute for people whose relationship with authorities was unstable. For Deanna, born outside Australia, the experience
initially 'won my confidence in the justice system. At first I was para-
noid because I am not a citizen, and [I wondered,] would they be biased.
I thought they were fair.' Indeed, she went on to say, 'the law applies
to everyone in the community'. Birgit, whose life history involved care
arrangements with welfare authorities as well as prior offending, nonetheless felt that her positive treatment indicated that 'it matters what
happened to me'.

Respectful recognition also went directly to a perspective on the
specificity of individual standing. Xenia, for example, said, 'it's about
me, not them [the authorities]'. At her final interview she went further
by saying, 'no one cares what I want. They are only after what they
want... who's interest is the law in?' For some, this sense of their unique
role expanded to claims for particular advocacy or representation.[19] 'I
needed someone just for me', was Ursula's comment.

Equality of treatment

Others drew strong connections between recognition and respect, and their perception of equal treatment. David, who had a prior history of nonviolent offending, felt he was not treated of equal worth to others in the community. At his second interview, he described how he had wanted to change his life but 'felt discriminated against'. It was, he said, 'a waste of time and effort. ... We all waited around; I gave evidence, but they brought up my old mental health history and that I wasn't a competent witness'. David reckoned, 'because I was an ex-offender, live in public housing and am a young man, there was no effort in it.' He felt that the system had been fairer to him as an accused than when he was a victim. At his third interview, David again emphasised how it was 'much harder as a victim. I guarantee you that'. He understood that it was not possible to 'be completely fair to everyone' but that getting 'torn to pieces' on the witness stand was 'ridiculous'.

Equitable treatment also encompassed the offender and was chiefly commented upon as a positive. While the items measuring respect for the rights of the offender did cluster in the analysis, the scale did not correlate strongly with overall satisfaction or indeed with any other factors. Nonetheless, the majority strongly agreed that prosecution and the courts treated the violent person with respect and with respect for his rights. Zola strongly agreed, at her second interview after the case had finalised, that justice had been done. She was asked why she thought this, and she said that 'the fact that they're all neutral – prosecutors and judges – and they respected both our rights. They didn't eliminate his rights to help me. In that way, justice was fair.' However, when asked about fairness to themselves as victims, the assessment reversed. Over half (58 per cent) agreed or strongly agreed that prosecution treated them fairly, and 62 per cent felt this with regard to the court.

Information as reciprocity and recognition

Respectful treatment was also more than equality, fairness and standing. People saw respect discharged practically in part through the provision of information. However, the provision of information by authorities was differentiated. A majority (77 per cent) of people agreed or strongly agreed that police gave them information useful to help them deal with the problem, and 81 per cent agreed or strongly agreed that police gave them information about victim services. However, comparable figures for prosecution were 35 per cent and 50 per cent.

A similar experience was evident in responses to the question whether people strongly agreed or agreed that they were kept informed about what was happening to the case. Edward commented negatively on 'the lack of information'. He said, 'it was frustrating. You just didn't know even how to chase the case, chase the police officer. It's all just difficult really. I had to do the chasing.'

For many, the case status updates, information about their rights and responsibilities, and the sources of support offered and given pointed to their unique importance in a very particular space. Charlie's comment that 'they made time to see me and tell me' signalled to him that he was important enough for authorities to do so. Deanna received a different message about her importance. She said she 'was never even sent a subpoena' and 'felt like a ball being tossed about'. Both men and women commented that, without the victim advocates,[20] they might never have known what was going on.

Interaction as demonstrations of respect

To the absence of information was added the absence of interaction with authorities. The provision of information indicated the possibility of dialogue – 'the ability to participate in a face-to-face way' as Karla put it. But without the interaction, it was 'like I wasn't relevant to anything'.

When interaction did take place, people noted its quality in both positive and negative terms. Polly felt she was made to 'feel like a child who didn't know what was good for me'. For her, the interactions were occasions of disrespect. She recounted the prosecuting official saying to her, 'there are women like you all the time and we just carry on'. She said, 'I didn't like he said I had to do this and I had to do that'. Charlie, on the other hand, said that even though 'justice might not have been served on the perpetrator... I was certainly included, and the positive was that I felt I was treated as a member of the community. The circumstances of the incident could have been swept away. They followed it as much as they could.'

If interaction signalled something important about the particular status and standing of the person, it also marked something of the citizen's wider interests. Nada's concluding comments in her final interview emphasised that 'part of justice is seeing the effort for justice they put in and the impact of that'. Her reflection says something of her interest in observing the normative and actual performance of public institutions charged with very particular responsibilities.

Outcome acceptance

The composite scale measuring outcome acceptance was a strong across the justice entities. As a single item, acceptance of the decisions of authorities was also very high. Eighty fiveper cent agreed or strongly agreed that they accepted the decision of police and of the court, and 92 per cent agreed or strongly agreed that they accepted the prosecution decision. However, whereas the majority felt that the decision that police (81 per cent) and prosecution (85 per cent) made was fair, only 69 per cent felt this with regard to the court. A similar proportion agreed with the court's decision. Only with the prosecution did a majority of people (69 per cent) indicate that the decision made by the agency was what they wanted. With both police and the court, a smaller and similar proportion (46 per cent) indicated that the decision arrived at by these entities was what they wanted.

Clearly, the very idea of 'outcome acceptance' holds considerable nuance in the differing settings of police, prosecution and the court. People's reflections at their second and third interviews after the case had finalised at the court offered different angles to their assessment of the outcomes. These were about:

- What the offender 'got' and the impact on him;
- What the victim 'got' and the meaning of this to them, and
- The normative and governance implications of the outcome to the victim.

Thinking on offender-related outcomes

The clustering of comments about the outcomes the violent person received comprised the largest component of reflection for the study participants. These grouped around two key areas: the nature and appropriateness of the sentence; and the perceived or desired impact of the various decisions on the violent person.

Comments on the nature and appropriateness of the sentence were both positive and negative. Birgit was pleased that the court did not 'just let him out on bail', and she said that 'the time inside [prison] is good'. She said, 'I'm thinking the judge looked back over our history and the previous bail and stuff and the judge thought "right, you're not getting this"'. She did, however, think that eight months of custody was 'too long' and that it 'should maybe be four months'. Also commenting on the time her ex-partner spent on remand, Holly felt that it was an 'opportunity to detox and that's been good for him'.

Others commented about the simple fact of the decision arrived at. Yvette felt the dismissal of the case against her husband was 'the right decision'. Karla thought the plea of guilty by her husband meant 'it is an ownership of his actions rather than it being forced upon him'. For Svetlana, 'he did what he did and got something for it'. Bailey said that the conviction meant 'something happened; ... there was an outcome'. Similarly, Deanna said, 'I'm very glad he's convicted'. To her, it was modest indication that justice was done, but it was also 'a personal victory'.

Janelle, on the other hand, felt that the 12-month good behaviour bond for her ex-partner was 'a crock'. She said, 'I would have preferred weekend detention or lock-up. He's gotten away with so much – for example, his past driving offences. I feel he's gotten away with it and won't learn anything from it.'

Her comment went to the perceived or desired impact of the various decisions on the offender. As another strong aspect, impact obviously also bled into reflection on the appropriateness of the outcome and carried an interest in efficacy. Typically, the observations revolved around the violent person's having an opportunity to reflect. For Svetlana, 'he needs the supervision to see what he's done'. Zola was unhappy with the sentence arrived at by the court, but she also said that 'it has made him stop and think'. At Finoula's final interview, she reflected that the outcome had 'planted a seed in [my partner's] mind not to do this to anyone else. I hope he's learned from it, but I don't think so.'

The process for Holly had been long drawn out and she expressed dissatisfaction with the outcome. She said 'I want punishment to fit the crime. Two years is massive. If they really did give a crap about rehabilitation for him then the outcome of going to gaol isn't right.' Finn also felt that the good behaviour bond ordered by the court against the young offender in his case wasn't appropriate. He said it was not 'something he has to deal with'. He said that 'it's finished and all over in the eyes of the court', but the young person 'needs to face the fact if he is going to keep being a criminal. Or is he going to do something different?' At his final interview, Finn also positioned his comments in a wider frame of reference. 'If you're hungry and steal a chocolate bar, you're likely to get worse [than for violence]', he said. 'Stealing is bad, but it isn't life threatening or hurting.'

Thinking on victim-related outcomes

The participants commented about what they as victims 'got' (or did not get) through the outcomes and about the meaning these carried for them. At their first interview, there was a strong emphasis from all victims on stopping the violence as an initiating motivation. Many of the domestic assault victims, therefore, made later remarks on the implications of the court outcome for their safety. Olivia felt that the outcome had stopped some of 'the extreme stuff'. However, she said that 'while it recognised what he'd done and was a kind of win ... I still sleep with [my daughter] with the phone and the keys and with the door locked.' On the other hand, for Genevieve the conviction made her 'feel safer'. Emphasising the wider implications of safety, Birgit felt that the custodial sentence given to her ex-partner gave her and their son some 'time out for us'.

Others' comments reflected on how the outcome missed connecting with what they as victims wanted. Although Karla said that the system 'protected me from verbal bullying and assault', she also wanted something more. She thought that the non-recorded conviction of her husband was expected 'but probably not what I hoped for'. Instead she 'would have liked and still would like a true recognition of the pain and angst he caused me through the experience'. Edward felt that justice had been done to the offender, but not towards himself. He said, 'the costs [of my injury] are significant – thousands of dollars. I was in the wrong place, now I'm out of pocket.' While the court made a reparation order in his favour, he was left to chase payment himself.

Thinking on normative and governance outcomes

Other comments were emblematic of a normative theme to people's reflections about the outcome. Karla felt the outcome was 'the right thing'. Lorraine felt that the good behaviour bond told her ex-partner that 'he couldn't do it'. Teresa said something similar in commenting that 'the thing I most wanted was that he be shown what he did was wrong. That he was convicted and sentenced told him that.'

Charlie had cause to reflect on the normative meaning of outcome when the case involving him as a victim was dismissed. He said he was 'not too fussed' about its dismissal by prosecution. Nonetheless, at his final interview, he did not agree that justice had been done, 'because I think there needed to be consequences on his actions'.

The normative meaning of the outcome overlapped with people's thoughts about the wider context and governance implications of what had transpired. Bailey felt that the outcome 'was "fit" for the actual incident'. He approved that, while his case 'was reasonably minor ... it was noted and went through a due process'. At his final interview, he went further by commenting,

I think the outcome was appropriate to what happened. It wasn't that serious so didn't need a heavy-handed response. I imagine it's the same as others like it. I don't think he was mistreated, and I wasn't underdone. He got his punishment, and I didn't require any reparation.

Comments such as these focus attention on the private and public frames that people apply in their thinking. Deanna reiterated that 'the law applies to everyone in the community'. At her final interview, Finoula said that her ex-partner 'can't just go bashing people because he thinks he can. It's about consequences to actions. The justice system is there to remind people of this.'

These comments direct attention away from wants and desires and towards 'ought' (Skitka 2009, p. 102) – that is, towards the wide civic implications of justice. It was particularly relevant when victims felt the harm or wrong was intentional and undeserved. People's interests were composite and looked towards different objects.

Influential voice

The idea of 'voice' is central to procedural justice studies (Folger 1977; Thibaut and Walker 1975; Van den Bos et al. 1996). In studies on victims of crime, voice has been explored in a number of ways: as contributing to higher confidence levels (Bradford 2011), in regulating anti-social behaviour (Bright and Bakalis 2003), in mediation (Wemmers and Cyr 2006) and in victim impact statements (Cassell 2009. A key question in this literature is whether voice is passive or expressive or whether it is designed to influence (Roberts and Erez 2004). However, over the course of the three interviews, multiple different meanings emerged out of the notion of 'having a say' in relation to all three justice agencies – police, prosecution and the court.

Phrases such as 'involvement', 'being able to talk' and 'being consulted' were frequent. However, these simple phrases hid more nuanced interests that:

- were about the uniqueness of being known and 'knowing';
- were demonstrations of respect and recognition;
- were constitutive of a dialogue between themselves and justice officials;
- went to a perception that decision-making itself was full and 'proper';
- saw the giving and receiving of information as a powerful transaction (as well as being powerful in itself).

The idea of knowing and being known expressed the sense that people knew something that was useful and particular: their views were important and their experience valuable. Finn said, 'I've heard from people around here that he's a little bastard. He's been able to shrug and walk out.' About her ex-partner, Birgit said, 'We should have a say – we know the violent person better than the judge'.

More importantly, 'knowing something' was 'being known' and affirmed the centrality of their real lives. 'This is someone's life they're dealing with', said Roslyn. There was a sense that their centre of gravity was being pulled somewhere else – '[It's] about me, not them. It was weird', said Xenia – and that expressing opinions and wants refocused back on their known and lived reality – the 'real world', not the institutional world. Embedded within this was an assertion of one's dignity: '[they] kept me up-to-date. It really helped', said Svetlana.

Having one's voice heard and understood was, unsurprisingly, experienced as a demonstration of respect and recognition. Deanna said that she was 'kept in the dark about the changes and updates, like I did not have a right to know.' Said Finn:

> I don't expect them to be over for a cup of tea every day, but contact [me] once every so often and to know what is happening with dates and things and what is the case made up of. I really didn't know. I kept the [police] card for ages, but there was no point. I don't think they really care that much.

Critically, victims perceived their own voice as not echoing in the dark but as constituting dialogue with officials. At her first interview, Roslyn expected 'to be asked questions about what [I] wanted in the future'. At her final interview, Olivia said she would have 'liked more input, to be more involved and get more information'. Dialogue was not undirected communication but went to understanding and 'answers' (Charlie). Said Teresa, 'I was never contacted by the prosecution or the court. I would have liked them to contact me. The [support agency] gave information, but if I had questions, I don't know if they would have been able to answer. For example, I asked why he had not entered a plea and the [support agency] couldn't tell me. I would have thought the [prosecution] could tell me why.'

Having dialogue also went to the 'properness' of decision making.[21] Nada said that 'the magistrate needs to hear from the victim to make a proper decision. There is a lot lost between what happens and reading something off a paper.' Properness was about the decision maker being fully informed: 'It shouldn't be done in isolation' said Roslyn. 'There should be an interview of sorts.' Hearing the whole story also meant that the decision maker would see the 'many shades of grey' said Teresa; it would mean that 'everything' would be 'taken into account and...the best interests of everyone thought about' was Xenia's comment.

Remarks about the communicative effect of voice acknowledged the power of information. 'If you know something then you don't feel further victimised', said Roslyn. But Karla worried, 'who tells you about the process?' Edward also commented that he 'needed lots of information and had to ask all over the place'. These reflections also marked a shift from the subject 'victim' back towards the more critically informed citizen. Said Winona, 'I think it would be good to get more technical info about what happens in the justice system and a bit more detail on my case and why'. Wanting to be and perform as a respected victim-citizen underlay Polly's statement that, 'I don't know what the procedures are or what is expected of me. I would expect someone to let me know.'

The complexity inherent in voice has been simplified to just its expressive nature (Roberts and Erez 2004). As expression within the criminal justice system, the victim's voice is characterised as subjective (Edwards 2004, p. 976), designed to emote and, in consequence, to have therapeutic benefits (Erez et al. 2011).[22] The diverse meanings highlighted here point to something different; that is, they point to people's recognition of the unique character of the decision-making spaces with which they are engaged – spaces that have functions that address a convergence of different concerns for victims, offenders and communities. Victims feel they can, or even should, contribute to consideration of these concerns.

For the participants, the variables on voice clustered with their preferred decision or outcome. There was an interest in a voice that *influences*. Moreover, even when the strength of their influential voice was assessed as moderate to low, it bore a strong relationship with peoples' overall satisfaction with each of the justice institutions.

Concluding discussion

The nuance revealed by observation and reflection shows the importance of the specificity of context to procedural and distributive justice judgements. Satisfaction as a measure could not get to this. It performed a useful function in providing a snapshot of victim assessments – across the totality of their involvement – of police, prosecution and the courts and of the justice system overall.

Getting at the contingent nature of justice, however, required 'real world justice research' (Skitka 2009, p. 107). Doing this uncovered dimensions to victim evaluations: outcome acceptance, the quality of interpersonal treatment, influential voice and respect for offenders' rights. These dimensions fluctuate in importance, but all are present in assessments about the three justice agencies. While the elements can be distinguished, they are clearly not separate. Rather, they form dimensions of an integrated conception of justice that is supple in the real world setting of criminal justice. Neither do they require fixing to any single understanding of human behaviour.

However, as measures that are derivative of distributive and procedural justice theories, these too were insufficient to capture the complexity of contextualised thinking. A number of themes were found layered in victims' reflections, and they are summarised below (Table 8.2). The dimension respecting offenders' rights is not listed separately. Victims threaded concern for this issue through the dominant dimensions as issues of equality of treatment, knowing something of the offender, the appropriateness of the outcome and fairness.

Participant narration showed that the nuances embedded in these dimensions of justice were highly contextualised and particularised. The emphases placed on the quality of their interpersonal treatment embraced recognition of their unique standing and circumstances,

Table 8.2 Themes underlying victims' distributive and procedural justice evaluations

Quality of interpersonal treatment	Outcome acceptance	Influential voice
Recognition of standing	Relationship to offender-related concerns	Uniqueness of being known and 'knowing'
Equality of treatment	Relationship to victim-related concerns	Demonstrations of respect and recognition
Information as reciprocity and recognition	Normative and governance concerns	Constitutive of a dialogue with justice officials
Interaction as respect		Connection with 'properness' of decision making
		Giving and receiving information as a powerful transaction

as well as respect for their personhood. Respect and recognition were demonstrated through the manner in which information was or was not provided to people by authorities. People experienced information both as a power resource and as reciprocity. They also understood interaction with authorities as dialogue. An expectation for fairness in criminal justice was articulated in perspectives on equitable and fair treatment for themselves as well as for the violent person.

Justice as the attainment of outcome was experienced in a number of ways. The reflections people offered went to a trilogy of interests. The good of justice was hoped to flow to the victim, the offender and the community. At the same time, outcome reflections sharpened to focus primarily on the nature, appropriateness and impact of the sentence on the violent person and the consequence to themselves as a victim and a person. There was also reflection on the extent to which the outcome calibrated with the normative and governance functions of justice. Perhaps inevitably, the resolutions people actually experienced were partial and incomplete (Sen 2009).

The importance of *voice* is related to not just its expressive nature but also a sense that the outcome arrived at is acceptable and fair. People understood themselves as 'knowers' who added to the quality and meaningfulness of decision making. To be heard was to be recognised as someone with distinctive and important insight into particular circumstances that carried more general import. The interest victims might have that their voice is influential or directing of the decision maker is generally disavowed in the criminal justice sphere. Moreover, institutional efforts to become 'customer friendly' miss the mark. As Ursula said, 'they all listen, but you are no further ahead'. Common perceptions of voice as simply expressive perhaps need to be rethought.

Pinning justice to its distributive or its procedural effects in a dynamic setting is also woefully inadequate. In human hands, justice was conceptualised as a vibrant experience and relevant to a set of external and internal standards. It was not static, nor did it adhere to one object. It spoke to differing interests that victims brought to the doors of criminal justice. Justice was both attenuated and animated through a series of interactions with different decision makers. Each interaction provided opportunities for ideas about justice to be articulated, to be made transparent and to be enacted. Many of these opportunities were badly handled by authorities and consequently were lost. Also lost was understanding that victims' interests in different ideas of justice went way beyond the calculation of satisfaction.

Notes

I am grateful to Professor Peter Grabosky, Professor Julie Stubbs and Associate Professor Kristina Murphy for their always helpful comments.

1. See, for example, with regard to Australia (Cook et al. 1999), the United Kingdom (Hall 2009; Walklate 1989; Maguire and Ponting 1988), the United States (Davies et al. 2007) and Canada (Roach 1999).
2. For seminal texts on the experience of domestic violence victims, see Buzawa and Buzawa (2003), Temkin and Krahé (2008) on sexual assault, Morgan and Zedner (1992) on child victims, Maguire and Bennett (1982) on residential burglary and Rock (1998) on homicide.
3. For discussion of these experiences in the Australian Capital Territory (ACT) where this research took place, see Holder (2008).
4. See, for example, Reisig et al. (2007) for tests into the reliability and validity of composite measures used in procedural justice studies.
5. Survey questions were drawn from Braithwaite (March 2001) and Murphy et al. (2010a, b).
6. People were asked to rank their response on a five-point Likert scale where 1 = extremely dissatisfied and 5 = extremely satisfied. Answers were reverse coded from the original. Because the overall satisfaction measure was asked in relation to different entities, it does not generate direct comparisons. However, it does provide a means to reflect different interactions at different times.
7. A one-way repeated measures ANOVA (analysis of variance) was conducted on the mean scores to determine if there was statistical significance on the overall satisfaction scores with regard to the different agencies at Time 1, Time 2 and Time 3. An examination of the pairwise comparisons was done to reveal significances.
8. Different types of research have generated differing results. Some earlier US research noted a more positive orientation of victims towards police than towards prosecutors, judges and other justice personnel (Forst and Hernon 1985; Kelly 1984). However, other survey and population-based studies reveal a different picture. Shapland et al. (1985), for example, show that victim satisfaction with police diminishes over time. The British Crime Survey showed that victim/witnesses were more likely to be satisfied 'with other parts of the criminal justice system' than their 'dealings with police'. But the analysis also showed that people who had been victims of crime or witnesses in the past 12 months were less likely than were non-victims to express confidence in the criminal justice system (Smith 2010, pp. 2 and 10). The Australian Social Attitudes Survey (AuSSA) showed that people who had contact with courts in the previous 12 months (i.e. all the respondents undifferentiated between victims and non-victims in their contact with the courts) had higher levels of confidence and were less likely to support harsher sentencing (Roberts and Indermaur 2009, p. 18).
9. In Valerie Braithwaite's Australian DemGov dataset, 35 per cent of people expressed 'a lot' of trust and 45 per cent 'a fair bit' of trust in police. For law courts the percentages were 9 per cent and 39 per cent. In a Canadian study, Lynne Roberts suggests that the differences may be due to the crime control mandate of police more closely aligning with public priority and perception and less with the due process model of criminal courts (Roberts 2007).

10. Given the small numbers, the data was somewhat cautiously assessed as suitable for factor analysis using a number of different tests. Principal components analysis (PCA) generated seven components with eigenvalues exceeding 1 (Pallant 2011, p. 181). Sampling adequacy usually rests on the number of cases. However, the ratio of participants to items is also relevant (Nunnally 1978; Tabachnick and Fidell 2005). In this study, the ratio varied between 33:1 (Time 1) and 18:1 (Time 3). Furthermore, while the Kaiser-Meyer-Olkin (KMO) measure failed, Bartlett's Test was significant.

11. Clustering several variables suggests measurement of similar dimensions in the data. These clustered variables are grouped into scales, which lent greater parsimony and coherence to analysis and interpretation (Pallant 2011, p. 182). Although this process helped to pinpoint what is meaningful or trivial about the data, caution was exercised over assumptions that factor analysis represents 'real-world dimensions' (Field 2000, p. 428). In addition, because of the small sample size, a conservative factor loading of 0.5 was used for interpretation purposes (Field 2005, p. 452). These features necessitated choice of non-parametric tests in analysing the data, specifically Spearman's correlation coefficient two-tailed. The reliability score for each scale was high, notwithstanding that it is common to have low scores on scales with fewer than ten items (Pallant 2011, p. 97).

12. The study by Wemmers and Cyr (2004) illuminating victim concerns for young offenders stands outside this claim. Restorative justice researchers have generally noticed victim concerns for the rehabilitation of offenders, especially young offenders.

13. For example, see Matravers (2010).

14. For a further check on the robustness of all the scales, a second factor analysis was done only using the items that had initially clustered. These factored into the same four clusters.

15. These are among other key procedural features such as voice, accuracy and neutrality. See Thibaut and Walker (1975) and Leventhal (1980). And see Tyler (2006/1990).

16. At the Time 2 interviews, N = 26.

17. That is, 15 per cent of the total sample at Time 2 (N = 26) or 19 per cent of the domestic assault group (N = 21).

18. All names used for the participants in this chapter are pseudonyms.

19. For discussion on the issue of victim representation, see, for example, McGlynn and Munro (2010) on victims of sexual assault, and for victims more generally, see Davis and Mulford (2008).

20. In this instance, the advocates were staff from a community-based domestic violence advocacy service and from a government victim support agency.

21. In the procedural justice literature, this notion is usually categorised as 'accuracy'. That is, a perspective that the decision maker is accurate in the decision informs the justice assessment. In this study, the idea of the decision being made 'properly' was based on whether the decision maker considered all relevant evidence. The idea was therefore connected to the influential voice of the victim. If the victim had not been heard and understood, then the decision was not fully 'proper'.

22. Discussing international criminal responses to mass atrocities, Eric Stover also comments on the tendency to 'valorise "therapeutic value"' to victims who are testifying (Stover 2011, p. 131).

References

Adams, J.S. 1965. Inequity in Social Exchange. *Advances in Experimental Social Psychology* 2, pp. 267–299.

Aspinal, F., Addington-Hall, J., Hughes, R. and Higginson, I. 2003. Using Satisfaction to Measure the Quality of Palliative Care: A Review of the Literature. *Journal of Advanced Nursing* 42(4), pp. 324–339.

Blau, P. 1964. Justice in Social Exchange. *Sociological Inquiry* 34(2), pp. 193–206.

Bradford, B. 2011. Voice, Neutrality and Respect: Use of Victim Support Services, Procedural Fairness and Confidence in the Criminal Justice System. *Criminology and Criminal Justice* 11(4), pp. 345–366.

Bradford, B., Jackson, J. and Stanko, E. 2009. Contact and Confidence: Revisiting the Impact of Public Encounters with Police. *Policing and Society* 19(1), pp. 20–46.

Braithwaite, V. 2001. *The Community Hopes, Fears and Actions Survey: Goals and Measures*. Working Paper No. 2. Centre for Tax System Integrity. Canberra: The Australian National University.

Bright, S. and Bakalis, C. 2003. Anti-Social Behaviour: Local Authority Responsibility and the Voice of the Victim. *The Cambridge Law Journal* 62(2), pp. 305–334.

Brockner, J. and Wiesenfeld, B. 1996. An Integrative Framework for Explaining Reactions to Decisions: Interactive Effects of Outcomes and Procedures. *Psychological Bulletin* 120(2), pp. 189–208.

Buzawa, E. and Buzawa, C. 2003. *Domestic Violence: The Criminal Justice Response*. Thousand Oaks, CA: Sage.

Cassell, P. 2009. In Defense of Victim Impact Statements. *Ohio State Journal of Criminal Law* 6, pp. 611–648.

Charmaz, K. 2006. *Constructing Grounded Theory: A Practical Guide through Qualitative Analysis*. London: Sage.

Colquitt, J., Greenberg, J. and Zapata-Phelan, C. 2005. What is Organizational Justice? A Historical Overview. In: Colquitt, J. and Greenberg, J. eds. *Handbook of Organizational Justice* Mahwah, NJ: Lawrence Erlbaum Associates Publishers, pp. 3–58.

Cook, B., David, F. and Grant, A. 1999. *Victims' Needs, Victims' Rights: Policies and Programs for Victims of Crime in Australia*. Research and Public Policy Series No. 19. Canberra: Australian Institute of Criminology.

Dai, M., Frank, J. and Sun, I. 2011. Procedural Justice during Police-Citizen Encounters: The Effects of Process-based Policing on Citizen Compliance and Demeanor. *Journal of Criminal Justice* 39(2), pp. 159–168.

Davies, P., Francis, P. and Greer, C. eds. 2007. *Victims, Crime and Society*. London: Sage.

Davis, R. and Mulford, C. 2008. Victim Rights and New Remedies Finally Getting Victims Their Due. *Journal of Contemporary Criminal Justice* 24(2), pp. 198–208.

Deutsch, M. 1985. *Distributive Justice: A Social-Psychological Perspective*. New Haven, CT: Yale University Press.

Duff, R.A. 2010. Towards a Theory of Criminal Law. *Proceedings of the Aristotelian Society Supplementary Volume*, pp. 1–28.

Easton, D. 1975. A Re-assessment of the Concept of Political Support. *British Journal of Political Science* 5(4), pp. 435–457.

Edwards, I. 2004. An Ambiguous Participant: The Crime Victim and Criminal Justice Decision-Making. *British Journal of Criminology* 44(6), pp. 967–982.

Elliott, I., Thomas, S. and Ogloff, J. 2012. Procedural Justice in Contacts with the Police: The Perspective of Victims of Crime. *Police Practice and Research: An International Journal* 13(5), pp. 437–449.

Erez, E., Kilchling, M. and Wemmers, J. eds. 2011. *Therapeutic Jurisprudence and Victim Participation: International Perspectives*. Durham, NC: Carolina Academic Press.

Field, A. 2000. *Discovering Statistics Using SPSS for Windows*. London: Sage Publications.

Folger, R. 1977. Distributive and Procedural Justice: Combined Impact of voice and improvement on Experienced Inequity *Journal of Personality and Social Psychology* 35(2), pp. 108–119.

Folger, R. 1986. Rethinking Equity Theory: A Referent Cognitions Model. In: Bierhoff, H., Cohen, R. and Greenberg, J. eds. *Justice in Social Relations*. New York: Plenum, pp. 145–162.

Folger, R. and Cropanzano, R. 2001. Fairness Theory: Justice as Accountability. In: Greenberg, J. and Cropanzano, R. eds. *Advances in Organizational Justice*. Stanford, CA: Stanford University Press, pp. 1–55.

Giese, J. and Cote, J. 2000. Defining Consumer Satisfaction. *Academy of Marketing Science Review* 2000(1), pp. 1–24.

Gill, L. and White, L. 2009. A Critical Review of Patient Satisfaction. *Leadership in Health Services* 22(1), pp. 8–19.

Hall, M. 2009. *Victims of Crime: Policy and Practice in Criminal Justice*. Cullompton: Willan.

Hatfield, E., Walster, W. and Berscheid, E. 1978. *Equity: Theory and research*. Boston, MA: Allyn and Bacon.

Hauenstein, N., McGonigle, T. and Flinder, S. 2001. A Meta-analysis of the Relationship between Procedural Justice and Distributive Justice: Implications for Justice Research. *Employee Responsibilities and Rights Journal* 13(1), pp. 39–56.

Hinds, L. and Murphy, K. 2007. Public Satisfaction with Police: Using Procedural Justice to improve Police Legitimacy. *Australian & New Zealand Journal of Criminology* 40(1), pp. 27–42.

Holder, R. 2008. *The Quality of Justice: Operation of the Victims of Crime Act 1994 in the Australian Capital Territory 1996–2007*. Canberra: Victims of Crime Coordinator.

Holder, R. 2013. *Just Interests: Victims, Citizens and the Potential for Justice*. PhD thesis, The Australian National University. http://hdl.handle.net/1885/11464

Homans, G. 1961. *Social Behavior: Its Elementary Forms*. New York: Harcourt, Brace and World.

Indermaur, D. and Roberts, L. 2009. Confidence in the Criminal Justice System. *Trends and Issues* 387, Canberra: Australian Institute of Criminology.

Jackson, J. and Sunshine, J. 2007. Public Confidence in Policing: A Neo-Durkheimian Perspective. *British Journal of Criminology* 47(2), pp. 214–233.

Kelleher, C. and Wolak, J. 2007. Explaining Public Confidence in the Branches of State Government. *Political Research Quarterly* 60(4), pp. 707–721.

Laxminarayan, M., Bosmans, M., Porter, R. and Sosa, L. 2013. Victim Satisfaction with Criminal Justice: A Systematic Review. *Victims and Offenders* 8, pp. 119–147.

Lind, E.A. 2001. Fairness Heuristic Theory: Justice Judgments as Pivotal Cognitions in Organizational Relations. In: Greenberg, J. and Cropanzano, R. eds. *Advances in organizational justice*. Stanford, CA: Stanford University Press, pp. 56–88.

Lind, E.A. and Tyler, T. 1988. *The Social Psychology of Procedural Justice*. New York: Plenum Press.

MacCoun, R. 2005. Voice, Control, and Belonging: The Double-edged Sword of Procedural Fairness. *Annual Review of Law and Social Science* 1, pp. 171–201.

Maguire, M. and Bennett, T. 1982. *Burglary in a Dwelling: The Offence, the Offender, and the Victim*. London: Heinemann.

Maguire, M. and Ponting, J. eds. 1988. *Victims of Crime: A New Deal?* Milton Keynes: Open University Press.

Martínez-Tur, V., Perió, J., Ramos, J. and Moliner, C. 2006. Justice Perceptions as Predictors of Customer Satisfaction: The Impact of Distributive, Procedural, and Interactional Justice. *Journal of Applied Social Psychology* 36(1), pp. 100–119.

Matravers, M. 2010. The Victim, the State, and Civil Society. In: Bottoms, A. and Roberts, J. eds. *Hearing the Victim: Adversarial Justice, Crime Victims and the State*. Cullompton: Willan, pp. 1–16.

McDougall, G. and Levesque, T. 2000. Customer Satisfaction with Services: Putting Perceived Value into the Equation. *The Journal of Services Marketing* 14(5), pp. 392–410.

McGlynn, C. and Munro, V. 2010. *Rethinking Rape Law: International and Comparative Perspectives*. London: Routledge.

Morgan, J. and Zedner, L. 1992. *Child Victims: Crime, Impact, and Criminal Justice*. Oxford: Oxford University Press.

Murphy, K. 2009. Public Satisfaction with Police: The Importance of Procedural Justice and Police Performance in Police-citizen Encounters. *Australian and New Zealand Journal of Criminology* 42(2), pp. 159–178.

Murphy, K. and Cherney, A. 2012. Understanding Cooperation with Police in a Diverse Society. *British Journal of Criminology* 52(1), pp. 181–201.

Murphy, K., Murphy, B. and Mearns, M. November 2010a. *The 2009 Public Safety and Security in Australia Survey: Survey Methodology and Preliminary Findings*. Working Paper No. 17. Geelong: Alfred Deakin Research Institute, Deakin University.

Murphy, K., Murphy, B. and Mearns, M. November 2010b. *The 2007 Public Safety and Security in Australia Survey: Survey Methodology and Preliminary Findings*. Working Paper No. 16. Geelong: Alfred Deakin Research Institute, Deakin University.

Norris, P. ed. 1999. *Critical Citizens: Global Support for Democratic Government*. Oxford: Oxford University Press.

Pallant, J. 2011. *SPSS Survival Manual*. 4th ed. Crows Nest: Allen and Unwin.

Pattie, C., Seyd, P. and Whiteley, P. 2004. *Citizenship in Britain: Values, Participation and Democracy*. Cambridge: Cambridge University Press.

Reisig, M., Bratton, J. and Gertz, M. 2007. The Construct Validity and Refinement of Process-based Policing Measures. *Criminal Justice and Behavior* 34(8), pp. 1005–1028.

Roach, K. 1999. *Due Process and Victims' Rights: The New Law and Politics of Criminal Justice*. Toronto: University of Toronto Press.

Roberts, J. 2007. Public Confidence in Criminal Justice in Canada: A Comparative and Contextual Analysis. *Canadian Journal of Criminology and Criminal Justice* 49, pp. 153–184.

Roberts, J. and Erez, E. 2004. Communication in Sentencing: Exploring the Expressive Function of Victim Impact Statements. *International Review of Victimology* 10(3), pp. 223–244.

212   *Robyn Holder*

Roberts, L. and Indermaur, D. 2009. *What Australians Think about Crime and Justice: Results from the 2007 Survey of Social Attitudes*. Research and Public Policy Series 101. Canberra: Australian Institute of Criminology.

Rock, P. 1998. *After Homicide: Practical and Political Responses to Bereavement*. Oxford: Oxford University Press.

Ruspini, E. 1999. Longitudinal Research and the Analysis of Social Change. *Quality and Quantity* 33(3), pp. 219–227.

Sen, A. 2009. *The Idea of Justice*. Cambridge, MA: The Belknap Press of Harvard University Press.

Shapland, J., Willmore, J. and Duff, P. 1985. *Victims in the Criminal Justice System*. Aldershot: Gower Publishing.

Skitka, L. 2009. Exploring the 'Lost and Found' of Justice Theory and Research. *Social Justice Research* 22, pp. 98–116.

Skitka, L., Aramovich, N., Lytle, B. and Sargis, E. 2011. Knitting Together an Elephant: An Integrative Approach to Understanding the Psychology of Justice Reasoning. In: D. Bobocel, A. Kay, M. Zanna and J. Olson eds. *The Psychology of Justice and Legitimacy: The Ontario Symposium* (11th volume), pp. 1–26.

Skogan, W. 2005. Citizen Satisfaction with Police Encounters. *Police Quarterly* 8(3), pp. 298–321.

Stover, E. 2011. *The Witnesses: War Crimes and the Promise of Justice in The Hague*. Philadelphia, PA: University of Pennsylvania Press.

Strang, H. 2002. *Repair or Revenge: Victims and Restorative Justice*. Oxford: Clarendon Press.

Temkin, J. and Krahé, B. 2008. *Sexual Assault and the Justice Gap: A Question of Attitude*. Portland, OR: Hart Publishing.

Thibaut, J. and Walker, L. 1975. *Procedural Justice: A Psychological Analysis*. Hillsdale, NJ: Lawrence Erlbaum Associates Publishers.

Tyler, T. 1989. The Psychology of Procedural Justice: A Test of the Group-value Model. *Journal of Personality and Social Psychology* 57(5), pp. 830–838.

Tyler, T. 1990/2006. *Why People Obey the Law*. Princeton, NJ: Princeton University Press.

Tyler, T. and Blader, S. 2003. The Group Engagement Model: Procedural Justice, Social Identity, and Cooperative Behavior. *Personality and Social Psychology Review* 7(4), pp. 349–361.

Tyler, T. and Huo, Y. 2002. *Trust in the Law: Encouraging Public Cooperation with the Police and Courts*. New York: Russell Sage Foundation.

Tyler, T. and Lind, A. 1992. A Relational Model of Authority in Groups. In: Zanna, M. ed. *Advances in Experimental Social Psychology* 25. San Diego, CA: Academic Press, pp. 115–191.

Van den Bos, K., Vermunt, R. and Wilke, H. 1996. The Consistency Rule and the Voice Effect: The Influence of Expectations on Procedural Fairness Judgements and Performance. *European Journal of Social Psychology* 26(3), pp. 411–428.

Van den Bos, K., Vermunt, R. and Wilke, H. 1997. Procedural and Distributive Justice: What is Fair Depends More on What Comes First than on What Comes Next. *Journal of Personality and Social Psychology* 72(1), pp. 95–104.

Van de Walle, S. 2009. Confidence in the Criminal Justice System: Does Experience Matter? *British Journal of Criminology* 49(3), pp. 384–398.

Van de Walle, S., van Roosebroek, S. and Bouckaert, G. 2008. Trust in the Public Sector: Is There any Evidence for a Long-term Decline? *International Review of Administrative Sciences* 74(1), pp. 47–64.

Walklate, S. 1989. *Victimology: the Victim and the Criminal Justice Process*. London: Unwin Hyman.

Walklate, S. 2007. *Imagining the Victim of Crime*. Maidenhead: Open University Press.

Weitekamp, E. and Kerner, H. eds. 2002. *Restorative Justice, Theoretical Foundations*. Portland, OR: Willan Publishing.

Wells, W. 2007. Type of Contact and Evaluations of Police Officers: The Effects of Procedural Justice across Three types of Police–citizen Contacts. *Journal of Criminal Justice* 35(6), pp. 612–621.

Wemmers, J. 2013. Victims' Experiences in the Criminal Justice System and their Recovery from Crime. *International Review of Victimology* 19(3), pp. 221–233.

Wemmers J. and Cyr. K. 2004. Victims' Perspective on Restorative Justice: How much Involvement are Victims Looking for? *International Review of Victimology* 9(11), pp. 1–16.

Wemmers J. and Cyr. K. 2006. What Fairness Means to Crime Victims: A Social Psychological Perspective on Victim-offender Mediation. *Applied Psychology in Criminal Justice* 2(2), pp. 102–128.

Williams, B., Coyle, J. and Healy, D. 1998. The Meaning of Patient Satisfaction: An Explanation of High Reported Levels. *Social Science and Medicine* 47(9), pp. 1351–1359.

Zehr, H. 1990. *Changing Lenses: A New Focus for Criminal Justice*. Scottdale, PA: Herald Press.

9
Victims in the Australian Criminal Justice System: Principles, Policy and (Distr)action

Stuart Ross

The last three decades have seen sustained and comprehensive efforts to address the problems of 'secondary victimization' that are experienced by victims of crime when they are involved in criminal justice processes. Governments have introduced a range of reforms that include the provision of specialised liaison and support services at the reporting, investigative and prosecution stages; advice and practical assistance to enhance future safety; better information about justice procedures and outcomes; changes to investigative, evidentiary and witness procedures; and the use of victim impact statements in court proceedings. While reforms directed at secondary victimisation have undoubtedly bought about improvements in victims' experiences, their impact has been limited by a reluctance to cede real power to victims as participants in justice processes. More recently, victim policy reforms have become increasingly politicised, and the linkages between victim policy and punitive populism have become increasingly evident.

This chapter[1] examines the interface between victim policy processes and criminal justice policy more generally. While there is a high level of agreement about the principles that should govern responses to secondary victimisation, there is much more variability in the way these principles are implemented in policy and regulatory responses. A theme of central interest is how jurisdictions vary in the emphasis given to different elements in the secondary victimisation reform agenda, in the structural basis of reform and in the manner of implementation. The chapter concludes by arguing that recent reforms to victim compensation and parole processes represent a move away from 'rights-based' reforms that address secondary victimisation directly to one where victims are represented as consumers and participants in the politics of criminal justice policy.

Victims in the criminal justice system

Crime victims[2] play an essential and central role in the criminal justice system. The police and the courts rely on victims to report crimes promptly and honestly, identify offenders, provide evidence and act as witnesses (Shapland 2000). The actions taken by victims of crime are important in effective crime detection and prevention, the preparation of strong prosecution cases and the avoidance of delay or trial termination (Cretney and Davis 1996; Farrell and Pease 1993; Hall 2010, p. 123). Effective engagement of victims by justice agencies is especially important in relation to matters where there is a long history of victimisation or where there are countervailing pressures on victims, as is often the case in sexual assault crimes (Chung et al. 2006), family violence (Buzawa and Austin 1993; Holder 2007) and offences against children (Grubin 1998) or other vulnerable or disadvantaged groups. It has been argued that the participation of victims may also be important in achieving proportionality in sentencing, in helping perpetrators understand the effects of their actions and in promoting therapeutic jurisprudence (Erez 2000; Winick and Wexler 2003).

Beyond these instrumental reasons for promoting victim engagement, there are ethical and moral reasons why the criminal justice system should take account of victims' interests. These range from Garside's argument that as a general principle the criminal justice system should endeavour to minimise the harm that it inflicts on all parties who come into contact with it (2006, p. 26), an acknowledgement that victims have rights and legitimate interests in criminal justice processes (European Forum for Victim Services 1996), through to the achievement of specific victim outcomes, such as psychological healing (Wiebe 1996).

Secondary victimisation

The trauma of victimisation stems from the immediate injury and material loss suffered and the psychological problems (helplessness, fear, depression, anxiety) and their sequelae (substance abuse, breakdown in personal relationships and unemployment) that can extend for years after the original incident (Cook, David and Grant 1999; Hanson and

Self-Brown 2010; Macmillan 2001; Montada and Lerner 1998). Beyond these primary impacts, victims' experiences with criminal justice processes can constitute significant additional harm (Parsons and Bergin 2010). This additional harm is referred to as secondary victimization[3] and is classified in the UN Handbook on justice for victims (United Nations Office for Drug Control and Crime Prevention 1999) as one of the three impacts of crime on victims.[4] While the direct impacts of crime victimisation have been extensively studied (Cook et al. 1999; Fattah 1991; Waller 2003), the consequences of secondary victimisation are not as well understood.

The specific harmful experiences of victims that been identified include police officers not taking victims seriously and not respecting victims' preferences in domestic violence crimes (Buzawa and Austin 1993; Frazier and Haney 1996); victims having to spend long periods waiting in court and having to face the offender in court (Cook et al. 1999; Gardner 1990); difficulty in confronting the assailant and reliving the trauma of the experience by recounting the facts in court (Frazier and Haney 1996); victims' not feeling heard and validated (Koss 2000); victims' failing to receive due consideration of their experiences, concerns and expectations by prosecutors and other justice agencies (Black 2003; Erez, Roeger and Morgan 1997; Flatman and Bagaric 2001); and case processing decisions giving priority to the expeditious resolution of matters over the interests of the victim (Cammiss 2006). In opposition to these harmful experiences, a variety of benefits for victims in reporting crimes and participating in justice processes have also been reported, including improved self-esteem and the sense that their experiences have been acknowledged and validated (Parsons and Bergin 2010).

While there has been extensive documentation of what happens to victims in the criminal justice system, the consequences of these experiences are not as well understood. It is clear that many victims find their experiences in dealing with criminal justice agencies to be unpleasant and unsatisfying. While interactions with police are generally the most positively rated stage in the criminal justice process for victims, between one quarter and one half of all victims report that they were not satisfied with the way their complaint was handled by police (Van Dijk and Groenhuijsen 2007). Witnesses in criminal trials frequently report feeling unappreciated and intimidated by the process (Angle et al. 2003) resulting in dissatisfaction with the outcomes of the process and their treatment by prosecutors, judges and other professionals (Orth 2002). Vulnerable witnesses (i.e. young witnesses, victims of sexual offences and those with a disability) are especially likely to report feeling anxiety and distress, uncertainty about what will happen and unfair or discriminatory treatment (C. Edwards 2013; Hamlyn et al. 2004; Quas and Goodman 2012).

The primary consequence of secondary victimisation is generally understood to be psychological trauma (sometimes in the form of post-traumatic stress (PTSD)) and delayed or incomplete recovery from the impact of the original victimisation. Unsympathetic or hostile treatment by police can exacerbate the distress of victims and add to feelings of guilt, depression, shame and powerlessness (Campbell 2006, 2008; Norris and Thompson 1993). It is frequently argued that the process of testifying in court leads to continuing anxiety and distress for victims of domestic violence, rape and sexual assault (Parkinson 2010). However, the evidence for substantial impacts on victims' psychological health and well-being arising from secondary victimisation is 'inconclusive' (Wemmers 2013): some studies show significant consequences, and others show none at all (Parsons and Bergin 2010). Wemmers argues that this is partly the consequence of methodological weaknesses in secondary victimisation research, where studies frequently involve post-test only designs; the use of small, convenience or unrepresentative samples; the use of unvalidated measures; and a focus on certain kinds of victims (especially sexual assault victims). A prospective study of 188 Canadian victims found that those who judged that their treatment by criminal justice authorities was 'fair' (using a five-item procedural justice scale) reported fewer PTSD symptoms at the point of referral of their case to the prosecutor by police than those who judged their treatment to be 'unfair', and these differences in symptoms were maintained six months later (Wemmers 2013).

Beyond the direct impacts on victims themselves, there are also consequences of secondary victimisation for the criminal justice system. The most well known is dissatisfaction with justice agencies and loss of confidence in justice processes (Sanders and Jones 2007; Shapland et al. 1985). This may have a bearing on crime reporting and willingness to be involved in court processes – witnesses who have bad experiences with police may choose not to report subsequent experiences of victimisation, with the result that they are at continuing risk (Frazier and Haney 1996). Victims who are intimidated in court are likely to say they do not want to be a witness again (Angle et al. 2003) and vulnerable witnesses may find the pressure of testimony so great that they are unable to provide accurate or consistent testimony (Sanders and Jones 2007).

Responding to secondary victimisation

The modern era in regard to victims in the criminal justice system is often seen as starting with the adoption in November 1985 by the United Nations General Assembly of the Declaration of the Basic Principles of Justice for Victims of Crime and Abuse of Power, although the elements of the Declaration were in turn based on a wave of reforms to victims services and roles that had begun at least 15 years earlier (Doak 2008). The Declaration comprised a list of principles for the treatment of crime victims within the criminal justice system, spanning topics that included the responsibilities of criminal justice agencies towards victims, restitution and compensation for victims and the availability of social services and health services for victims.

However, in order to understand how the principles in the UN Declaration have informed victim policy, it is important to examine their underlying theoretical and empirical basis. The way that justice agencies respond to crime victims reflects fundamental ideas concerning the relationship between criminal justice institutions and the community. While these are central to the legitimacy of the criminal justice system, there is a tension on the one hand between the maintenance of long-standing rights and protections, and on the other the capacity of the system and its institutions to respond to changing circumstances and the evolving expectations of the community (Lacey 1994; Shapland 2000). Understanding these principles and their influence on criminal justice processes is critical to understanding why victims face the problems they do and to knowing what can and should be done to address them. The UN Declaration principles embody elements of three different views about what victims want in their interactions with justice agencies and processes:

- legally enforceable rights and standing (a legal perspective);
- participation and engagement (a consumer perspective);
- fair and equitable treatment (a procedural justice perspective).

The rights perspective sees the problems that victims face as arising from the way that power in the criminal justice process is allocated – in particular the focus on the interests and rights of defendants and institutional (judicial and legal) participants, with victims having peripheral standing in these processes. The UN Declaration seeks to prescribe rights for victims that address these deficiencies, including rights to be informed about case processing and their role in proceedings, to have their views and concerns considered, to receive restitution from the offender and to receive financial compensation and legal, material, medical and other assistance. However, while victims' legislation and charters routinely talk about victims' rights, there is little clarity about what actually constitutes a right and how the specification of rights translates into their implementation and enforcement (Doak 2008, p. 25). At an international level, the 'basic principles' set out in the UN Declaration can be viewed as a form of human rights and as such are inclusive statements of values that are not concerned with definitional issues (who has the rights and under what conditions?) or specific implementation or enforcement mechanisms. In the case of local legislative or policy responses, it is important to distinguish between rights that are entitlements to services, such as compensation and support, and rights that involve access to or involvement in criminal justice procedures, such as representation, evidence giving (e.g. protections from abusive cross-examination for victims of sexual assault) and victim impact statements (VIS).

One of the most significant reform paradigms in modern government is the idea that citizens are 'consumers' of government services who seek responsive participation and engagement with those services (Hood and Peters 2004). Concern about the role of victims represents one facet of a general change in the way government relates to citizens and their demands for more flexible, responsive and individualised service responses (MacCormick and Garland 1998). In this interpretation, it is not the imbalance of power within the criminal justice process that victims find distressing but rather their inability to effectively participate in those processes. Edwards (2004, p. 974) identified two broad categories of involvement: dispositive participation involves identifying and acting on victims' preferences, whereas non-dispositive participation provides for victims to have influence without that being necessarily determinative. In the UN Declaration, victim engagement with justice processes is represented in the form of provision of information and representation in justice proceedings, without specifying whether this engagement should be dispositive or non-dispositive. I. Edwards argues that a participatory approach to victims makes governments confront their relationship with victims more directly; it avoids sterile arguments associated with balancing victims' and defendants' rights; and it provides solutions that better address the expressive and affective issues that victims face. At the same time, there are significant limitations to a participatory approach to addressing victims' needs. Doak (2008, p. 157) notes that there is a lack of consensus as to what participation should actually entail, leading to an inability to specify concrete standards for determining when victims' rights to participate have been satisfied.

For many victims, their experiences (including their involvement in criminal justice process) are profoundly emotional ones (Cook et al. 1999; Maguire, 1991; Malsch and Carriere 1999). Victims also want emotional support and other nonmaterial responses, such as counselling, that are related to the emotional component of their experience. In this sense, the provisions in the UN Declaration for victims to be provided with financial compensation and counselling and other support services can also be seen as a form of participation and engagement intended to enhance victims' sense of order and justice.

Restorative justice was a key development in the engagement of victims in justice processes, and the UN Declaration includes access to 'informal dispute resolution proceedings' as an access to justice principles. The participation offered by restorative justice processes 'assists victims both in their emotional recovery and in reducing the sense of alienation that results from believing they have no control and no status' (Strang and Sherman 2003, p. 21). In addition, by providing for victims to interact directly with offenders and to receive an explanation and apology from them, restorative justice creates the conditions necessary for the 'successful resolution of the offence and the restoration of the participants' (p. 23).

The concerns and complaints of victims often revolve around the quality of the treatment they receive from criminal justice institutions. The UN Declaration enjoins criminal justice agencies to treat victims fairly and with dignity and to train personnel to deal appropriately with victims. Procedural justice theory[5] proposes that the legitimacy accorded to criminal justice institutions and processes is mainly determined by the perceived fairness of people's participation in those processes rather than by the outcomes of those processes (Tyler 2006b). A core idea is that people's perceptions about procedural fairness are critical in determining their judgements about the legitimacy of justice processes and agencies. In this analysis, it is neither inequity in the distribution of power nor a simple inability to participate but rather the quality of engagement and interaction with criminal justice agencies and the individuals in them that determine victims' satisfaction.

Originally developed to deal with processes of dispute resolution (Thibaut and Walker 1975), procedural justice theory has since been extended to cover citizens' interactions with police (Sunshine and Tyler 2003; Tyler 2002), the courts (MacCoun and Tyler 1988; Tyler 1997), problems of resource allocation (Tyler and Degoey 1995), public attitudes to punishment (Tyler 2006a; Tyler and Boeckmann 1997) and the development of children's behaviour towards legal authorities (Fagan and Tyler 2005; Hicks and Lawrence 2004). A central idea in procedural justice theory is that the relationship between an individual citizen and social institutions is strongly shaped by group processes, including the value status associated with group membership as well as perceptions about community normative values about fairness (Sunshine and Tyler 2003).

More recently, a fourth rationale for victim policy has emerged, in the form of expressing compassion for the individual and collective suffering by victims. The most striking manifestations of this can be seen in the formal expressions of compassion by governmental actors to victims of the forcible removal of Indigenous children, child migration and clerical or institutional sexual abuse (Corntassel and Holder 2008). Walklate (2012) argues that rhetorical appeals to compassion for the suffering of victims are evident in the 'rebalancing' agenda of New Labour, and similar sentiments are also evident in some victims' rights advocacy movements (Waller 2011).

Translating policy into practice

The principles in the UN Declaration have formed the conceptual basis for almost all subsequent victim policy and were repeated or reformulated across a wide range of legislated (i.e. Bills of Rights as well as Acts and Regulations) and unlegislated (charters and declarations) instruments developed over the next two decades (Fattah 2000; Reeves and Mulley 2000; Zedner 1997). A key reform was the Victims' Charter issued in the UK in 1990 (subsequently revised in 1996 before a more fundamental revision in 2003–2005), and versions of the UK model were soon found in many Commonwealth countries.[6] In the United States, the keystone policy relating to victims was the Victims' Rights Act of 2004 (part of the Justice For All Act of 2004), with all states in the country passing their own laws on victims' rights and protections.[7] European responses to crime victims were generally framed by the Council of Europe Recommendation R (85) 11 on the Position of the Victim in the Framework of Criminal Law and Procedure (Council of Europe (CoE) 1985) which restates the UN principles that relate to the actions and responsibilities of police, prosecutors, courts and enforcement bodies. The situation in Asia was more complex, but by the end of the century the primary components of the UN Declaration (support services, financial compensation and witness support) could be found in Japan, Taiwan, South Korea, Singapore and Hong Kong, with South Korea and

Japan also making provision for victim impact statements and notification of victims about bail, sentencing and release decisions (Ota 2008).

In parallel with these reforms there were developments in the institutional basis for responding to victims, in the form of compensation funds and tribunals; victim support and witness care programs; and provisions for victim impact statements in court. The obvious inadequacies in existing offender-based compensation provisions had led to the creation of state-funded victim compensation funds that in many instances preceded the UN Declaration. The first such scheme was introduced in New Zealand in 1963, and Australian state-based programs were established soon after, beginning with New South Wales in 1968 and with complete national coverage by 1983 (Cook et al. 1999). Victim support programs providing advice, counselling and advocacy for victims commenced in Australia with the establishment of the South Australian Victims of Crime Service in 1979,[8] followed by similar services in other jurisdictions over the next decade.

Neither victim compensation nor victim support programs directly address the issue of secondary victimisation, and reforms to prosecution and court processes generally lagged behind these changes. Again, South Australia was the national leader, legislating to require that VIS material should be put before courts in 1989. By 2005 VIS provisions were present in all Australian jurisdictions, although it remains the case that there is no right in Commonwealth sentencing legislation for victims to be given an opportunity to be heard. While reforms to prosecutorial, evidentiary and witness processes were proposed as early as the mid-1980s, reforms in these areas have been piecemeal and directed mainly at child victims and victims of sexual assault (Parkinson 2010; Richards 2009).

Australian victims' charters, declarations and acts

The policy basis for reforms directed at secondary victimisation in Australia has followed a convoluted path. A close adherence to the UN Declaration model was apparent in the first attempt at a national charter of victims' rights, issued by the Standing Committee of Attorneys-General in 1993 and versions of most of the UN principles can be found in state and territory victims' policy statements, although there are some notable gaps. Case processing delays are an important source of dissatisfaction for victims, but none of the states or territories includes this as a component of their victim policy. Similarly, access to appropriately trained personnel is fundamental to any effective response to victims and one that police and prosecution agencies particularly have recognised and responded to, but this principle is also absent from any of the Australian policies.[9] Another limitation is that many of these statements of rights are incomplete in the sense that they do not cover principles in the UN Declaration that are available under some other legislative mechanism – the principles relating to legal representation of victims, informal dispute resolution and restitution by offenders[10] are the most obvious examples of this.

Perhaps most importantly, there is no counterpart in any Australian charter of the provisions developed in the United Kingdom for vulnerable and intimidated victims (Ministry of Justice (UK) 2013). The UK policy requires that police and the Crown Prosecution Service identify three classes of victims (victims of the most serious crime, persistently targeted victims and vulnerable and intimidated witnesses) and provide additional protections and services (Special Measures) designed to assist them during the investigation and trial process. While Australian victims' policy statements all include some statement about the right to protection from intimidation and retaliation by the offender, this is only specified in the context of shielding victims from direct contact with offenders at court hearings, with more complex issues of witness protection left to the discretion of police. Where Australian jurisdictions have specialised witness support programs, these are typically located within the Office of the Director of Public Prosecutions and mainly concerned with information and support with court processes.

While typically described as statements of victims' rights, in Australia neither victim legislation nor unlegislated charters provide for enforcement or penalties and the powers of legislatively established bodies that deal with victims' complaints (of which only three exist among the seven jurisdictions in Australia) are limited to receiving and investigating complaints. Australian legislation has generally followed the model of the UK Victims' Charter, with provisions that are intended to 'encourage rather than bind' (Zedner 1997, p. 598). The Queensland Act prescribes that its principles are not enforceable by criminal or civil redress,[11] while the Western Australian Act refers to its principles as 'guidelines' that provide no legally enforceable rights or privileges. The Victorian Act requires that justice agencies 'have regard to the Charter principles' but at the same time specifies that its provisions neither create any legal rights or civil causes nor have any bearing on judicial or administrative decisions (see S.22). The new (2013) New South Wales Victims Rights and Support Act provides the strongest statement of the significance of its provisions relative to other legally enforceable rights in requiring that agencies or persons exercising administrative (but not judicial) functions 'must, to the extent that it is relevant and practicable to do so', have regard to the Charter of Victims Rights. Nevertheless, it remains the case that, to date, there are no recorded instances in Australia of officials being penalised for a breach of victims' rights legislation.

The future of victims' reform in Australia: New directions and challenges

From the perspective of victims, the justice system is clearly a different place compared to where it stood before 1985. In the 1980s it could reasonably be argued that victims occupied a peripheral place in the operations and decisions of the justice system. The reforms of the last two decades have brought about an improvement in this situation, although attempts to reform justice processes in order to address secondary victimisation have been less successful than reforms that address the direct service needs of victims (advice, counselling and material assistance). Referral rates to victims' service agencies by justice agencies remain low: in only about ten per cent of incidents reported to the police in the United Kingdom were the victims put in contact with Victim Support (Maguire and Kynch 2000), and in Australia it has been estimated that fewer than half of victims reporting sexual assault are referred to victim service agencies (Auditor General Western Australia 2012). There has been little change in adversarial court processes or improvement in victims' experiences in court (Angle et al. 2003; Erez 2000; Erez and Rodgers 1999; Hamlyn et al. 2004). Many of the changes made to court practices to increase support for victims have involved engaging other agents such as paraprofessionals and volunteers (Melup 1999) rather than directly addressing court practices. As a result, victims' treatment by criminal justice agencies is frequently inconsistent with the formal commitments of support set down in legislation or charter, and victims' rights charters have been dismissed as merely 'motherhood statements' (Booth and Carrington 2007, p. 384) or 'merely symbolic' (Haynes 2011, p. 299). One consequence is that public confidence in the capacity of the justice system to treat victims fairly and sensitively remains low. Only 20 per cent of respondents to the British Crime Survey who had been victims of crime or in court as witness, spectator or juror, considered that the criminal justice system met the needs of victims, and only three out of five recent witnesses said they would be willing to attend court again (Whitehead 2001). Australian data indicates similar concerns, with a survey of over 8,000 adults showing that half have no confidence or not very much confidence that courts have regard for victims' rights (Roberts and Indermaur 2009).

A fundamental problem with assessing progress in relation to victim policy reform is that there is little systematic monitoring of compliance with the requirements of Victims' Charter principles. While justice agencies routinely report detailed information about their law enforcement, judicial and correctional activities, there is little systematic reporting of activities or outcomes involving victim support (Callanan et al. 2012). A review of family violence law conducted jointly by the Australian Law Reform Commission and the New South Wales Law Reform Commission (ALRC/NSWLRC 2010) found that there was no systematic monitoring of the degree to which victims of family violence were informed about bail decisions. The impact of reform on the quality of victims' experiences is equally problematic. Victim service agencies report consistently high levels of satisfaction by their clients, but there is little regular monitoring of the experiences of justice system participants. Most agencies are unable to report on anything other than simple output measures such as applications for services received or compensation funds awarded. The Victorian Auditor-General reported that the Victim Support Agency was unable to provide 'information about outcomes' or 'clear objectives or performance indicators at the agency level' (Victorian Auditor-General's Office 2011, p. viii). A similar 2012 audit in Western Australia (WA) found that while the Victim Support Service (VSS) was able to report on service timeliness measures, neither the VSS nor WA police were able to reliably report on measures of service coverage or outcomes, and that the VSS was unable to 'evaluate whether its services improve victims' outcomes' (Auditor General Western Australia 2012, p. 18).

In the last decade a new direction in victim policy has begun to emerge that emphasises elements of the UN principles that were not central to earlier reforms. Governments increasingly view the engagement and participation of victims as important in establishing their credentials as effective managers of justice issues and as a way to maintain public confidence in the sentencing process (Englebrecht 2011). In this sense, victim policy has become more aligned with the direction of overall justice policy. The remainder of this chapter looks at two current areas of policy activity that are likely to shape the future form and effectiveness of reforms for victims: the extension of victims' rights in relation to parole and the increased use of offender restitution and compensation orders. Each of these has an important bearing on the changing relationship between victims and the larger context of criminal justice policy.

Victims and parole policy

All Australian jurisdictions provide victims with rights of access to case processing information including details of bail, prosecution decision, sentences and parole. While parole boards have always included consideration of victims' interests in their decisions, in recent years the provisions relating to victims' access to parole information and input to decision making have become increasingly detailed and prescriptive (Booth and Carrington 2007, p. 401). Victims' registers (i.e. registers specifically required to support victim engagement with release processes) have been established in all jurisdictions, beginning in South Australia (in 1995), followed by NSW (1999), Western Australia (2001), Victoria and Tasmania (2004), the ACT (2005) and the Northern Territory and Queensland (2006). While there are some variations in eligibility (four jurisdictions provide access only to victims of violent crimes), victims can get information about dates of parole hearings and parole conditions, including the offender's intended address and may be advised of any escapes. New South Wales' victims may also be advised of a change to an offender's security classification where this would allow them to be eligible for unescorted leave from custody. Most recently, Victoria enacted wide-ranging parole reforms that included enhanced notification procedures for persons on the Victims' Register.

However, as with many victims' rights in the justice system, it is unclear how often and how effectively these parole notification and submission provisions work in promoting greater safety and satisfaction by victims. Some parole boards provide basic information about submissions from victims, and these suggest that victims make submissions in only a small proportion of cases. The Western Australian Prisoners Review Board received 45 victim submissions in relation to nearly 5,000 cases considered in 2011/2012, while the Victorian Adult Parole Board recorded 95 victims' submissions in 2012/2013, during which it made over 2,000 decisions.[12] The impact of victim submissions is also debatable, with judges and parole boards generally viewing victim submissions as relevant to only the conditions imposed on parolees (Black 2003). The 'opt-in' nature of victims' registers[13] means that notification about release dates or parole conditions is likely to be uneven in its effectiveness. The Callinan review into the Victorian parole system reported that there were complaints that 'victims were not given notice...of the release of serious violent or serious sexual offenders' (Callinan 2013, p. 81); however, the review does not specify whether these cases involved persons on the Victims' Register or whether the concern was with victims in general.

Offender restitution

Another wave of criminal justice reform associated with crime victims has been directed at the perceived inadequacies of offender restitution through sentencing. The status of restitution or compensation by offenders as a sentencing outcome is problematic. There is substantial public support for sentencing that includes some form of compensation or restitution by the offender (Gelb 2011), and payment of restitution is an important factor in victims' satisfaction with court processes (Ruback et al. 2008). While all jurisdictions make provision in sentencing legislation for offenders to make restitution or pay compensation[14] to victims (ALRC/NSWLRC 2010), these provisions are rarely used. This reflects the inability of many offenders to pay and the difficulty in enforcing compensation orders and as well as the preference by jurisdictions for fines as a form of financial penalty. Civil proceedings provide an alternative avenue for seeking restitution/compensation, but these are complex, costly and rarely used unless the victim is a corporate entity. One of the earliest developments in victim policy was the establishment of state-funded crimes compensation mechanisms, in large part to address the inequities and difficulties associated with obtaining restitution or compensation directly from offenders. Interestingly, despite being one of the principles in the 1985 UN Declaration, Australian acts and charters typically omit any mention offender restitution as a component of victim policy.

Since the late 1990s there has been growing interest in restitution as a component of victim policy. In 1997 Tasmania introduced mandatory compensation orders for some offences, including a provision that, where offenders have a limited capacity to pay, compensation orders should take precedence over fines. In 2000 Victoria extended the restitution provisions in the Sentencing Act 2000 to allow courts to order offenders to pay compensation instead of, or in addition to, restitution. Further amendments in 2012 gave Victorian courts greater powers to order compensation, including the power to make an application on behalf of the victim. Victorian compensation provisions were further strengthened in 2008 through an amendment to the Corrections Act 1986 to provide for a 'prisoner compensation quarantine fund' intended to make it easier for victims to enforce compensation orders. Awards to prisoners are paid into this fund where they are held for 12 months while victims and creditors are invited to make application for them. The 2013 NSW victims' rights reforms included enhanced court-ordered offender compensation as well as provision for the commissioner to issue restitution orders against offenders to be paid from the offenders' assets or earnings (including earnings while imprisoned).

In addition to direct compensation of victims by offenders, there has been widespread adoption of offender levies and these now exist in all jurisdictions except Victoria[15] and Western Australia (Douglas and Chrzanowski 2013). Note that levies do not compensate victims directly but are intended to offset cost of the services or compensation payments to victims, although the levy introduced in Queensland in 2012 was directed to general revenue to offset generally the cost of law enforcement and administration.[16]

While victims support the principle of offender compensation, it is not clear that these orders produce substantial outcomes for victims. The Tasmanian reform of restitution laws has been of only limited efficacy in generating more reliable compensation for victims of property crime. A study by Warner and Gawlik (2003) found that compensation orders were made in 42 per cent of eligible cases in the Supreme Court and less than 25 per cent of eligible cases in the lower court, and it found that even where orders were made, the majority were either unpaid or only partially paid. In the Victorian Magistrates' Court only eight per cent of compensation amounts ordered in cases involving property loss or damage, and ten per cent of compensation in cases involving injury was received by the court, leaving the majority of victims to pursue enforcement action. Interestingly, where compensation payments are required under the Victorian Criminal Justice Diversion Scheme (i.e. where compensation is a pre-requisite for diversion out of the court system) payments rates are apparently much higher (Department of Justice (Victoria) 2009). Compensation payments can also be ordered under the Commonwealth Crimes Act 1914, but these are most commonly awarded to the commissioner of taxation or the Department of Social Security rather than to individual victims (Morabito 2000).

The politicisation of victim policy

The reforms to victims' rights in relation to parole and compensation or restitution need to be understood in the wider policy context of these issues. Both have been politically problematic for governments: parole because of concerns about public safety (Bartels 2013) and victim compensation because of the difficulty in funding these programs

(Meyering 2010). The reforms providing victims with more information about parole decisions, and the right to make submissions about those decisions, have taken place in conjunction with substantial reviews or reforms to parole systems in Victoria (2013), New South Wales (2013), Queensland (2013), South Australia (2012) and Western Australia (2010). The effects of these reforms have been a general tightening of parole eligibility rules, reductions in the length of parole terms and increased surveillance of parolees.

The relationship between victim policy and the broader scope of criminal justice policy was clearly evident in the Victorian parliamentary debate on the parole reform bill, where these reforms were presented as part of the 'rebalancing' of a parole system that had 'become too far skewed in favour of the offender and away from victims, their families, and the broader community' (Hansard, Legislative Assembly 19 September 2013, p. 3234). Similar sentiments were argued by Queensland Attorney-General Bleijie in proposing a range of criminal justice reforms (including the abolition of parole) in order to 'rebalance the scales of justice in favour of the victim and not the offender'.[17]

However, it is not at all obvious that 'rebalancing' by restricting prisoners' access to parole and providing victims with increasingly elaborate systems to access information about release and make submissions to parole boards is an effective way to address their legitimate rights to protection. Much of the concern about the failings of parole has been generated by the offences committed by parolees after their release. In most cases these involve victims who are unconnected with previous offences. The issue of protection is thus primarily one of community protection (i.e. protection of future rather than past victims), and this in turn requires the provision of effective rehabilitation programs and adequate funding of parole assessment and supervision. In recent parole reviews, all of these issues have been flagged as deficient. Reforms based on a 'rebalancing' argument do little to advance the situation of existing victims and provide only temporary protection to the community in general.

Victim compensation schemes are now an established component of criminal justice systems, but in recent years they have become increasingly politically contentious. This stems partly from a growing dissatisfaction with the constraints on eligibility (e.g. the inherent discrimination against victims of domestic violence in many schemes) and partly as a result of pressure on the financial viability of schemes as the number of applicants has grown (Meyering 2010). Recent changes to reduce the debt levels of the NSW scheme, including stricter time limits on claims and reduced maximum pay-out levels, have been the subject of a complaint to the United Nations by a coalition of legal service and victims' organisations.[18] In the recent South Australian state election, both parties pledged to double victim compensation payments in the wake of widespread criticism about the level of compensation.

As with restitution/compensation orders, offender levies appear to have support from victims as a means of 'making offenders more accountable' (Criminal Policy Unit 2010). Where victims receive compensation directly from offenders, the value of this is taken into account in setting the amount of state-funded compensation. In addition, offender levies are successful at raising revenue to offset the costs of compensation, with the New South Wales scheme generating 11 per cent of the funding for the Victims Compensation Fund (New South Wales Department of Attorney General and Justice/PricewaterhouseCoopers 2012) and the Queensland scheme $12 million in its first year. However some victims' organisations have cautioned that debt recovery proceedings in cases of domestic violence have the potential to 'jeopardise the victim centred nature of the compensation process and ... trigger new safety concerns for women', and they have argued that offender compensation orders are a more appropriate way to increase offender accountability (Australian Domestic and Family Violence Clearinghouse 2010).

National directions in the development of victim policy

Two important features can be discerned in recent reforms aimed at crime victims in the criminal justice system. The first is the increasing engagement of victim policy with the overall direction of criminal justice policy. Where this takes the form of a genuine attempt to align justice services and responses with the needs of victims this engagement can represent a significant improvement in victims' experiences and outcomes. There have been important reforms to justice process associated with the broad policy trend of making the public sector more responsive to the community, in the form of more sensitive and responsive policing, co-location of victim support services in police stations and courts and providing targeted and appropriate responses to victims of family violence and sexual violence.

However, providing victims with greater 'rights' in relation to parole processes or restitution is also consistent with the broad direction of late-modern justice policy with its emphasis on punitive responses to offenders, to individualisation of relations between victims, offenders and the state, and from 'social' to 'economic' forms of thinking about justice (Garland 2001). While there have been changes in the nature of victims' participation in justice processes, governments have been keener in general to see victims' rights extended where the burden of this was borne directly by offenders than to see reforms that involved fundamental changes in justice procedures. Provisions for victims have been seen as optional and complementary: rather than being accorded genuine rights, victims have been given access to pathways of influence that they can use if they are motivated and capable. The limited evidence we have suggests that in most cases victims choose not to use these pathways.

This focus on victims' rights vis-à-vis those of offenders also takes away the pressure to reconcile the competing demands of the adversarial system and the needs of victims, or to address the conservatism that characterises justice professions and institutions (Morgan and Sanders 1999). Innovations such as problem-solving or community courts and restorative justice have the potential to provide victims with a profoundly different experience of the justice process, but these remain on the fringe of the contemporary justice system and of little relevance to the majority of victims. In this sense, while recent reforms may have provided solutions to immediate political problems for governments, they represent a distraction from substantive reforms that address the primary causes of secondary victimisation. Until this happens, the problems of victim and community dissatisfaction with the criminal justice system are likely to continue.

The second feature of note is the variability of policy and services for victims around the country. The apparent ubiquity of the UN Declaration principles as the conceptual basis for reform does not equate to consistency in policy implementation at a national level, and the actual experiences of victims in their interactions with justice agencies vary considerably in quality and outcome. State and territory policy frameworks for victims specify embody different definitions of a victim and, as a result, different eligibility requirements for access to their provisions. Service frameworks differ in the nature of the services provided, the level of financial assistance or compensation that is available and the procedures for accessing services and compensation. Some jurisdictions provide support to only those persons who were the victim of an offence in that jurisdiction, with the result that victims who move from one jurisdiction to another may be ineligible for assistance. The absence of a general set of Commonwealth provisions for victims[19] means that victims of crimes in some Australian territories, or crimes committed outside Australia, are also disadvantaged relative to victims of crimes covered by state and territory (ACT and Northern Territory) legislation (Garkawe and O'Connell 2007).

There have been concerted attempts to improve national consistency and address structural arrangements that inhibit effective service delivery in a number of areas, including mental health (Department of Health and Ageing 2011) and disability (www.ndis.gov.au). However, as with much of the justice system, there has been little progress towards the development of nationally common arrangements in relation to victim policy. Compared with service areas such as health and education, Australian jurisdictional differences in justice system expenditure, are large and variations in output measures (e.g. court delays, imprisonment rates, program provision) are correspondingly large. These variations are primarily policy driven, and jurisdictions with similar social and economic characteristics show large variations in justice expenditure and outputs (Hanley and Ross 2013).

The National Framework of Rights and Services for Victims of Crime (Standing Council on Law and Justice 2013) represents the latest in a series of attempts at national coordination of policy and service delivery for victims. If this initiative is to proceed, it will require that Australian governments systematically examine the strengths and weaknesses of their approaches and determine the basis of the national policy framework based on a consideration of the real needs of victims. Until they do so, there will continue to be substantial deficiencies in the capacity of Australian criminal justice systems to assist victims in their recovery from the harm they have suffered.

Notes

1. Some material in this chapter draws on research conducted under an Australian Research Council Discovery Grant DP0665417.
2. The term victim refers to a person who has suffered harm as the result of the criminal actions of another person. The harm involved may be physical, psychological or material (i.e. property loss or damage). Secondary or indirect victims have been shown to experience difficulties and symptoms similar to those of direct victims and to have similar needs when dealing with the criminal justice system (Riggs and Kilpatrick 1990). Consistent with normal research practice, victim status is self-defined and does not require that the alleged crimes have been proven in a court (Doak 2008).
3. The term secondary victimization was originally coined by Sellin and Wolfgang (1964) to refer to commercial or collective victims. The contemporary use of this term dates from around 1990 (see Fattah 1991, p.13).
4. The others are the physical and financial impact and the psychological and social impact.

5. The term procedural justice is sometimes used as a synonym for due process or natural justice. In this sense the focus is on jurisprudential and evidentiary procedures that will yield fair or just outcomes (Maguire and Kynch, 2000; Rawls, 1999). This chapter is concerned with the social psychology of procedural justice.

6. The Commonwealth Secretariat also produced a set of guidelines for victims of crime (Commonwealth Secretariat, 2003); however, the UK Charter model appeared more than a decade earlier and appears to have been more influential as a model for reform.

7. For details of US policy responses, see the registry of federal, state and territory statutes relating to crime victims maintained by the US Office of Justice Programs at www.victimlaw.org.

8. Voluntary support services for victims of sexual assault had been present in many Australian jurisdictions prior to this.

9. Some state and territory policies prescribe professional requirements for persons providing publicly funded counselling and support services to victims.

10. The 2013 NSW Act is a notable exception – see below.

11. See S.7 of the Queensland Act.

12. Although not all of these cases would have involved an eligible victim.

13. The ACT Sentence Administration Board and the NT Parole Board may contact non-registered victims if they believe it appropriate.

14. Restitution is 'gains based' and involves the return of stolen property or a payment tied directly to the benefit to the offender from the crime, whereas compensation is 'losses based' and involves payment proportional to the loss or harm caused, including pain, suffering, costs of treatment, and so on.

15. A Victorian offender levy was proposed in 2010 but has not been implemented.

16. New South Wales also imposes a courts costs levy on convicted offenders, with the funds raised used to offset the costs of operating the courts and justice system.

17. Courier-Mail, 10 October 2013

18. Sydney Morning Herald, 21 May 2013.

19. The Australian Federal Police provide some victim support services, and the Commonwealth DPP provides a witness support service.

References

ALRC/NSWLRC (Australian Law Reform Commission and the New South Wales Law Reform Commission). 2010. *Family Violence – A National Legal Response.* ALRC Report 114 NSWLRC Report 128 (Vol. 1). Canberra: Australian Law Reform Commission and New South Wales Law Reform Commission.

Angle, H., Malam, S. and Carey, C. 2003. *Witness Satisfaction: Findings from the Witness Satisfaction Survey 2002.* Online Report 19/03. London: Home Office.

Auditor General Western Australia. 2012. *Victim Support Service: Providing Support to Victims of Crime.* Report 6 – May 2012. Perth, WA: Parliament of Western Australia.

Australian Domestic and Family Violence Clearinghouse 2010. *Submission to the Victim of Crime Compensation Review.* Melbourne: Australian Domestic and Family Violence Clearinghouse.

Bartels, L. 2013. Parole and Parole Authorities in Australia: A System in crisis? *Criminal Law Journal* 37(6), pp. 357–376.

Black, M. 2003. *Victim Submissions to Parole Boards: The Agenda for Research.* Trends and Issues in Crime and Criminal Justice No. 251. Canberra: Australian Institute of Criminology.

Booth, T. and Carrington, K. 2007. A Comparative Analysis of Victim Policies across the Anglo-speaking World. In: S. Walklate ed. *Handbook of Victims and Victimology.* Cullompton: Willan, pp. 380–415.

Buzawa, E.S. and Austin, T. 1993. Determining Police Response to Domestic Violence Victims: The Role of Victim Preference. *American Behavioural Scientist* 36(5), pp. 610–624.

Callanan, M., Brown, A., Turley, C., Kenny, T. and Roberts, J. 2012. *Evidence and Practice Review of Support for Victims and Outcome Measurement.* Ministry of Justice Research Series 19/12: Ministry of Justice (UK).

Callinan, I. 2013. *Report of the Review of the Parole System in Victoria.* Melbourne: Department of Justice.

Cammiss, S. 2006. The Management of Domestic Violence Cases in the Mode of Trial Hearing: Prosecutorial Control and Marginalizing Victims. *British Journal of Criminology* 46(4), pp. 704–718.

Campbell, R. 2006. Rape Survivors' Experiences with the Legal and Medical Systems: Do Rape Victim Advocates Make a Difference? *Violence Against Women* 12(1), pp. 30–45.

Campbell, R. 2008. The Psychological Impact of Rape Victims' Experiences with Legal, Medical and Mental Health Systems. *American Psychologist* 63(8), pp. 702–717.

Chung, D., O'Leary, P.J. and Hand, T. 2006. *Sexual Violence Offenders: Prevention and Intervention Approaches.* ACCSA Issues No. 5. Melbourne: Australian Centre for the Study of Sexual Assault.

Commonwealth Secretariat 2003. *Commonwealth Guidelines for the Treatment of Victims of Crime* London: Commonwealth Secretariat.

Cook, B., David, F. and Grant, A. 1999. *Victims' Needs, Victims' Rights: Policies and Programs for Victims of Crime in Australia.* Research and Public Policy Series No. 19. Canberra: Australian Institute of Criminology.

Corntassel, J. and Holder, C. 2008. Who's Sorry Now? Government Apologies, Truth Commissions, and Indigenous Self-Determination in Australia, Canada, Guatemala, and Peru. *Human Rights Review* 9(4), pp. 465–489.

Council of Europe (CoE). 1985. *Council of Europe, Committee of Ministers: Recommendation No. R (85) 11 on the Position of the Victim in the framework of Law and Justice.* Council of Europe, Committee of Ministers.

Cretney, A. and Davis, G. 1996. Prosecuting Domestic Assault. *Criminal Law Review* (March 1996), pp. 162–174.

Criminal Policy Unit 2010. *Victims of Crime Fund: A Consultation. Summary of Responses and Way Forward.* Belfast: Department of Justice (Northern Ireland).

Department of Health and Ageing 2011. *National Mental Health Reform 2011–12 .* Ministerial Statement 10 May 2011. Canberra: Commonwealth of Australia

Department of Justice (Victoria) 2009. *Reviewing Victims of Crime Compensation: Sentencing Orders and State-funded Awards: Discussion Paper.* Melbourne: Department of Justice.

Doak, J. 2008. *Victims' Rights, Human Rights and Criminal Justice: Reconceiving the Role of Third Parties*. Portland, OR: Hart Publishing.

Douglas, H. and Chrzanowski, A. 2013. A Consideration of the Legitimacy and Equity of Queensland's Offender Levy. *Current Issues in Criminal Justice* 24(3), pp. 317–339.

Edwards, C. 2013. Spacing Access to Justice: Geographical Perspectives on Disabled People's Interactions with the Criminal Justice System as Victims of Crime. *Area* 45(3), pp. 307–313.

Edwards, I. 2004. An Ambiguous Participant: The Crime Victim and Criminal Justice Decision-Making. *British Journal of Criminology* 44(6), pp. 967–982.

Englebrecht, C.M. 2011. The Struggle for 'Ownership of Conflict': An Exploration of Victim Participation and Voice in the Criminal Justice System. *Criminal Justice Review* 36(2), pp. 129–151.

Erez, E. 2000. Integrating a Victim Perspective in Criminal Justice Through Victim Impact Statements. In: Crawford, A. and Goodey, J. eds. *Integrating a Victim Perspective within Criminal Justice*. Aldershot: Ashgate, pp. 165–184.

Erez, E. and Rodgers, L. 1999. Victim Impact Statements and Sentencing Outcomes and Processes: Perspectives of Legal Professionals. *British Journal of Criminology* 39(2), pp. 216–239.

Erez, E., Roeger, L. and Morgan, F. 1997. Victim Harm, Impact Statements and Victim Satisfaction with Justice: An Australian Experience. *International Journal of Victimology* 5, pp. 37–60.

European Forum for Victim Services 1996. Statement of Victims' Rights in the Process of Criminal Justice. In: European Forum for Victim Services ed. Brixton, UK.

Fagan, J. and Tyler, T. 2005. Legal Socialization of Children and Adolescents. *Social Justice Research* 18(3), pp. 217–242.

Farrell, G. and Pease, K. 1993. *Once Bitten, Twice Bitten: Repeat Victimization and its Implications for Crime Prevention*. Police Research Group Crime Prevention Unit Series Paper No. 46. London: Home Office.

Fattah, E. 1991. *Understanding Criminal Victimization: An Introduction to Theoretical Victimology*. Scarborough, ON: Prentice-Hall Canada.

Fattah, E. 2000. Victimology: Past, Present and Future. *Criminologie* 33(1), pp. 17–46.

Flatman, G. and Bagaric, M. 2001. The Victim and the Prosecutor: The Relevance of Victims in Prosecution Decision Making. *Deakin Law Review* 6, pp. 238–255.

Frazier, P. A. and Haney, B. 1996. Sexual Assault Cases in the Legal System: Police, Prosecutor and Victim Perspectives. *Law and Human Behavior* 20(6), pp. 607–628.

Gardner, J. 1990. *Victims and Criminal Justice*. Adelaide: Office of Crime Statistics, SA Attorney-General's department.

Garkawe, S. and O'Connell, M. 2007. The Need for a Federal, Australia-Wide Approach to Issues Concerning Crime Victims. *Current Issues in Criminal Justice* 18(3), pp. 488–493.

Garland, D. 2001. *The Culture of Control*. Oxford: Oxford University Press.

Garside, R. 2006. Right for the Wrong Reasons: Making Sense of Criminal Justice Failure. In: Garside, R. and MacMahon, W. eds. *Does Criminal Justice Work? The 'Right for The wrong Reasons' Debate*. London: Crime and Society Foundation, pp. 9–39.

Gelb, K. 2011. *Purposes of Sentencing: Community Views in Victoria*. Melbourne: Sentencing Advisory Council.

Grubin, D. 1998. *Sex Offending Against Children: Understanding the Risk*. Police Research Series Paper 99. London: Home Office.

Hall, M. 2010. *Victims and Policy Making: A Comparative Perspective*. Abingdon: Willan Publishing.

Hamlyn, B., Phelps, A., Turtle, J. and Ghazala, S. 2004. *Are Special Measures Working? Evidence from Surveys of Vulnerable and Intimidated Witnesses*. Home Office Research Study 283. London: Home Office.

Hanley, N. and Ross, S. 2013. Forensic Mental Health in Australia; Charting the Gaps. *Current Issues in Criminal Justice* 24(3), pp. 341–356.

Hansard 2013. Parliament of Victoria, Legislative Assembly 19 September 2013, p. 3234.

Hanson, R.F. and Self-Brown, S. 2010. Screening and Assessment of Crime Victimization and its Effects. *Journal of Traumatic Stress* 23(2), pp. 207–214.

Haynes, S.H. 2011. The Effects of Victim-Related Contextual Factors on the Criminal Justice System. *Crime and Delinquency* 57(2), pp. 298–328.

Hicks, A.J. and Lawrence, J.A. 2004. Procedural Safeguards for Young Offenders: Views of Legal Professionals and Adolescents. *Australian and New Zealand Journal of Criminology* 37(3), pp. 401–417.

Holder, R. 2007. *Police and Domestic Violence: An Analysis of Domestic Violence Incidents Attended by Police in the ACT and Subsequent Actions*. Research Paper 4: Australian Domestic and Family Violence Clearinghouse.

Hood, C. and Peters, G. 2004. The Middle Aging of New Public Management: Into the Age of Paradox? *Journal of Public Administration Research and Theory* 14(3), pp. 267–282.

Koss, M.P. 2000. *Blame, Shame and Community: Justice Responses to Violence Against Women*. Paper presented at the 108th Annual American Psychological Association Convention, Washington DC.

Lacey, N. 1994. Government as Manager, Citizen as Consumer: The Case of the Criminal Justice Act 1991. *The Modern Law Review* 57(4), pp. 534–554.

MacCormick, N. and Garland, D. 1998. Sovereign States and Vengeful Victims: The Problem of the Right to Punish. In: Ashworth, A. and Wasik, M. eds. *Fundamentals of Sentencing Theory*. Oxford: Clarendon Press, pp. 11–29.

MacCoun, R. and Tyler, T. 1988. The Basis for Citizens' Preferences for Different Forms of Criminal Jury. *Law and Human Behavior* 12(3), pp. 333–352.

Macmillan, R. 2001. Violence and the Life Course: The Consequences of Victimization for Personal and Social Development. *Annual Review of Sociology* 27, pp. 1–22.

Maguire, M. 1991. The Needs and Rights of Victims of Crime. In: Tonry, M. ed. *Crime and Justice: A Review of Research* (Vol. 14). Chicago: Chicago University Press, pp. 363–433.

Maguire, M. and Kynch, J. 2000. *Public Perceptions and Victims' Experiences of Victim Support: Findings from the 1998 British Crime Survey*. London: Home Office Communications Development Unit.

Malsch, M. and Carriere, R. 1999. Victims' Wishes for Compensation: The Immaterial Aspect *Journal of Criminal Justice* 27(3), pp. 239–247.

Melup, I. 1999. United Nations Victims of Crime: Implementation of the Conclusions and Recommendations of the Seventh United Nations Congress on the Prevention of Crime and Treatment of Offenders. *International Review of Victimology 2*, pp. 29–59.

Meyering, I.B. 2010. *Victim Compensation and Domestic Violence: A National Overview.* Stakeholder Paper 8. University of New South Wales: Australian Domestic and Family Violence Clearinghouse.

Ministry of Justice (UK) 2013. *Code of Practice for Victims of Crime: October 2013.* London: HMSO.

Montada, L. and Lerner, M. J. 1998. *Responses to Victimization and Belief in a Just World.* New York: Plenum Press.

Morabito, V. 2000. Compensation Orders Against Offenders – An Australian Perspective. Singapore *Journal of International and Comparative Law* 4(1), pp. 59–114.

Morgan, R. and Sanders. 1999. *The Uses of Victims Statements, Occasional Paper.* London: Home Office, Research, Development and Statistics Directorate.

New South Wales Department of Attorney General and Justice/PriceWaterhouse-Coopers. 2012. *Review of the Victims Compensation Fund.* Sydney: NSW Department of Attorney-General.

Norris, F.H. and Thompson, M.P. 1993. The Victim in the System: The Influence of Police Responsiveness on Victim Alienation. *Journal of Traumatic Stress* 6(4), pp. 515–532.

Orth, U. 2002. Secondary Victimization of Crime Victims by Criminal Proceedings. *Social Justice Research* 15(4), pp. 313–325.

Ota, T. 2008. The Development of Victim Support and Victim Rights in Asia. In: Chan W.-C. ed. *Support for Victims of Crime in Asia.* Abingdon: Routledge Law in Asia, pp. 113–148.

Parkinson, D. 2010. *Supporting Victims Through the Legal Process: The Role Of Sexual Assault Service Providers.* ACSSA Wrap No. 8. Melbourne: Australian Centre for the Study of Sexual Assault, Australian Institute of Family Studies.

Parsons, J. and Bergin, T. 2010. The Impact of Criminal Justice Involvement on Victims' Mental Health. *Journal of Traumatic Stress* 23(2), pp. 182–188.

Quas, J.A. and Goodman, G.S. 2012. Consequences of Criminal Court Involvement for Child Victims. *Psychology, Public Policy and Law* 18(3), pp. 392–414.

Rawls, J. 1999. *A Theory of Justice: Revised Edition.* Cambridge, MA: Belknap Press.

Reeves, H. and Mulley, K. 2000. The New Status of Victims in the UK: Opportunities and Threats. In: Crawford, A. and Goodey, J. eds. *Integrating a Victim Perspective within Criminal Justice.* Aldershot: Ashgate, pp. 125–146.

Richards, K. 2009. Child Complainants and the Court Process in Australia. *Trends and Issues in Crime and Criminal Justice No. 380.* Canberra: Australian Institute of Criminology.

Riggs, D.S. and Kilpatrick, D.G. 1990. Families and Friends: Indirect Victimization by Crime. In: Skogan, W., Davis, R. and Lurigio, A. eds. *Victims of Crime: Problems, Policies and programs.* Thousand Oaks, CA: Sage, pp. 120–138.

Roberts, L. and Indermaur, D. 2009. *What Australians Think about Crime and Justice: Results from the 2007 Survey of Social Attitudes.* Research and Public Policy Series No. 101. Canberra: Australian Institute of Criminology.

Ruback, R.B., Cares, A.C. and Hoskins, S.N. 2008. Crime Victims' Perceptions of Restitution: The Importance of Payment and Understanding. *Violence and Victims* 223(6), pp. 697–710.

Sanders, A. and Jones, I. 2007. The Victim in Court. In: Walklate, S. ed. *Handbook of Victims and Victimology*. Cullompton: Willan, pp. 282–308.

Sellin, T. and Wolfgang, M.E. 1964. *The Measurement of Delinquency*. New York: John Wiley and Sons.

Shapland, J. 2000. Creating Responsive Criminal Justice Agencies. In: Crawford, A. and Goodey, J. eds. *Integrating a Victim Perspective Within Criminal Justice*. Farnham: Ashgate,

Shapland, J., Willmore, J. and Duff, P. 1985. *Victims and the Criminal Justice System*. Aldershot: Gower.

Standing Council on Law and Justice. 2013. *National Framework of Rights and Services for Victims of Crime: 2013–2016*. Canberra: SCLJ, pp. 52.

Strang, H. and Sherman, L.W. 2003. Repairing the Harm: Victims and Restorative Justice. *Utah Law Review* 15(1), pp. 15–42.

Sunshine, J. and Tyler, T. 2003. The Role of Procedural Justice and Legitimacy in Shaping Public Support for the Police. *Law and Society Review* 37(3), pp. 513–548.

Thibaut, J. and Walker, L. 1975. *Procedural Justice*. Hillsdale, NJ: Erlbaum.

Tyler, T. 1997. Citizen Discontent with Legal Procedures: A Social Science Perspective on Civil Procedure Reform. *The American Journal of Comparative Law* 45(4), pp. 871–904.

Tyler, T. 2002. A National Survey for Monitoring Police Legitimacy. *Justice Research and Policy* 4, pp. 71–86.

Tyler, T. 2006a. Restorative Justice and Procedural Justice: Dealing with Rule Breaking. *Journal of Social Issues* 62(2), pp. 307–326.

Tyler, T. 2006b. *Why People Obey the Law*. Princeton, NJ: Princeton University Press.

Tyler, T. and Boeckmann, R. 1997. Three Strikes and You Are Out, but Why? The Psychology of Public Support for Punishing Rule Breakers. *Law and Society Review* 31(2), pp. 237–266.

Tyler, T. and Degoey, P. 1995. Collective Restraint in Social Dilemmas: Procedural Justice and Social Identification Effects on Support for Authorities. *Journal of Personality and Social Psychology* 69(3), pp. 482–497.

United Nations Office for Drug Control and Crime Prevention. 1999. *Handbook on Justice for Victims on the Use and Application of the Declaration of Basic Principles of Justice for Victims of Crime and Abuse of Power*. New York: Centre for International Crime Prevention.

Van Dijk, J. and Groenhuijsen, M. 2007. Benchmarking Victim Policies in the Framework of the European Union Law. In: Walklate, S. ed. *Handbook of Victims and Victimology*. Cullompton: Willan, pp. 363–379.

Victorian Auditor-General's Office 2011. *Effectiveness of Victims of Crime Programs*. PP No. 6, Session 2010–2011. Melbourne: Victorian Government Printer.

Walklate, S. 2012. Courting Compassion: Victims, Policy, and the Question of Justice. *The Howard Journal* 51(2), pp. 109–121.

Waller, I. 2003. *Crime Victims: Doing Justice to their Support and Protection*. Publication Series 39. Helsinki: European Institute for Crime prevention and Control (HEUNI).

Waller, I. 2011. *Rebalancing Justice: Rights for Victims of Crime*. Lanham, MD: Rowman and Littlefield Publishers.

Warner, K. and Gawlik, J. 2003. Mandatory Compensation Orders for Crime Victims and the Rhetoric of Restorative Justice. *Australian and New Zealand Journal of Criminology* 36(1), pp. 60–76.

Wemmers, J. 2013. Victims' Experiences in the Criminal Justice System and their Recovery from Crime. *International Review of Victimology* 19(3), pp. 221–233.

Whitehead, E. 2001. *Witness Satisfaction: Findings from the Witness Satisfaction Survey 2000*. Home Office Research Study No. 230. London: Home Office (UK).

Wiebe, R.P. 1996. The Mental Health Implications of Crime Victims Rights. In: Wexler D. and Winick, B. eds. *Law in a Therapeutic Key*. Durham, NC: Carolina Academic Press, pp. 17–58.

Winick, B. and Wexler, D. 2003. *Judging in a Therapeutic Key: Therapeutic Jurisprudence and the Courts*. Durham, NC: Carolina Academic Press.

Zedner, L. 1997. Victims. In: Maguire, M., Morgan, R. and Reiner, R. eds. *The Oxford Handbook of Criminology*. 2nd ed. Oxford: Oxford University Press, pp. 577–612.

10

The Evolution of Victims' Rights and Services in Australia

Michael O'Connell

As the 30th anniversary of both the United Nations Declaration of Basic Principles of Justice for Victims of Crime and Abuse of Power and the first version of the Declaration on Victims' Rights in Australia approaches, it is difficult to imagine that just over three decades ago crime victims were often cited as the 'forgotten' or 'neglected' people in the criminal justice system. Over these past few decades, as this chapter will illustrate, interest in and concern for crime victims have steadily grown. Notably between the mid-1980s and the late 1990s many inquiries, discussion papers and the like were conducted throughout Australia, which resulted in legislative and administrative reforms and the establishment of victim assistance programmes. As this chapter will reveal, some of the reforms and programmes which were intended to improve the position of crime victims have been controversial.

Australia is an island continent with most of its population concentrated in coastal areas, especially proximate to its capital cities. Originally six self-governing colonies, in 1901 Australia became a federation of states and a Commonwealth Parliament. Two self-governing territories have since been formed. Thus, Australia today has nine jurisdictions, each with its own criminal law and criminal justice system grounded on the British common law, adversarial system. Constitutionally, the states and territories are primarily responsible for enacting and administering criminal law and thus for providing victims' rights and victim assistance. It is against this backdrop that common elements, such as a focus on primary victims of violent crime and secondary victims of homicide, as well as notable differences in victims' participatory rights, such as those fundamental to their standing in criminal proceedings, have evolved.

This chapter begins with the introduction of state-funded victim compensation schemes in the 1960s; then it describes the growth of victim support services before exploring the debate on victims' rights. Next it canvasses developments such as restorative justice, which were offered as sources of better justice for victims of crime. This chapter ends with an overview of the drivers for a national approach to harmonise victims' rights and victim assistance throughout Australia but also draws attention to the emphasis on procedural justice, especially the advent of commissioners and other reforms intended to individually and collectively give victims stronger voices in their dealings with Australia's criminal justice systems. Overall, the chapter demonstrates that the focus on improving justice for victims has shifted remarkably from monetary compensation and other victim assistance towards initially passive victims' rights and currently active participatory rights. This trend is not, however, unique to Australia.

1960s: Statutory, state-funded victim compensation

The earliest practical example of the influence of victimological concern began with the establishment of statutory, state-funded victim compensation schemes. The modern debate on such schemes dates back to a proposal in the late 1950s by British Magistrate Margaret Fry (1959). She recommended that the state compensate victims of crime because most offenders were impecunious, so they could not pay restitution. Her recommendation sat well with the post-World War II concept of the welfare state's responsibility to assist citizens in times of distress. State-funded victim compensation was therefore initially regarded as 'a breakthrough in community empathy toward victims and the taking of responsibility by governments for the adverse consequences of failed crime prevention' (Freckelton 2003, p. 1). Alternatively, such compensation could be looked upon as a 'band aid' to cover complex and challenging issues.

In the late 1960s and 1970s, Australia's states introduced state-funded compensation for the pecuniary and non-pecuniary effects of crime, especially violent crime. New South Wales was the first Australian jurisdiction to introduce a state-funded victim compensation scheme with the enactment of the *Criminal Injuries Compensation Act* in 1967, followed by Queensland's insertion of chapter LXVA in its *Criminal Code* in 1968. South Australia enacted its *Criminal Injuries Compensation Act* in 1969; Western Australia enacted an Act with the same short title in 1970 and both Victoria in 1972 and Tasmania in 1976 did likewise.

Parliamentarians in favour of state-funded victim compensation in each of the respective state parliaments proclaimed an awareness of the impact of violent offences upon victims – sometimes described as 'innocent victims of violent crime' (Office of Crime Statistics 1989). Consistent with this notion of an 'ideal victim' (Christie 1986), victims of primarily violent crimes – those who did not contribute to their victimisation but who also reported offences, co-operated with police investigators and accepted their responsibilities as witnesses for public prosecutions – have been considered worthy of state-funded compensation in all of Australia's state and territory jurisdictions. Rather than explicitly accept liability for failing to prevent crime and/or protect citizens, parliaments provided for those who suffered misfortune but also shifted some responsibility for crime and its harm from criminal to victim (Wardlaw 1979, p. 146). In South Australia, for instance, the victim must engage a lawyer, commence proceedings in the District (Civil) court, nominating the state as the first defendant and the actual offender as the second defendant, then prove the alleged offence beyond reasonable doubt as well as prove on balance the personal injury resulted from the offence.

Australia's first statutory, state-funded compensation schemes provided modest lump-sum payments intended as limited reparation rather than full compensation as might be attainable via civil prosecution for damages. Since their introduction, these schemes have varied across jurisdictions, primarily in terms of the crimes for which victims are eligible for compensation, maximum awards and methods of administration. All schemes have encountered difficulty assessing intangible or non-pecuniary damages, such as pain and suffering. In New South Wales a so-named maims table was used until reforms in 2013, whereas in South Australia a 0–50 point scale is used; in Victoria a Victim Assistance Tribunal determines the sum based on a tiered scale said to be relative to the seriousness of the offence (O'Connell and Fletcher in press).

Research in other countries, particularly the United States (see, e.g. Elias 1983), suggests that statutory, state-funded compensation schemes might not achieve their aims, such as encouraging more victims to report offences and assisting victims in distress, and may instead engender dissatisfaction as well as be counter-therapeutic (Elias 1983; O'Connell and Fletcher in press). Conversely, Australian research has shown that most victims were not alienated by the process to attain compensation and many were appreciative on receiving a payment as recognition by the state of the harm done to them (Justice Strategy Unit (JSU) 2000a and 2000b; Office of Crime Statistics 1989; Victorian Community Council against Violence 1994). According to one review of all eight victim compensation schemes in Australia, compensation can assist victims of domestic violence deal with the aftermath of such violence at both a practical and symbolic level (Barrett Meyering 2010; see also Dawson and Zada 1999), whereas other reviews, each focusing on a particular state, identified barriers preventing domestic violence victims from submitting eligible claims (New South Wales (Whitney 1997); Victoria (Lantz and D'Arcy 2000); Western Australia (Jurevic 1996); Queensland (Forster 2002)). In Australia, some critics also query whether victims' interests and the public interest in helping them would be better served if, rather than giving lump-sum compensation payments, governments spent more on counselling, other treatment and practical assistance (Freckelton 1997, 2003; Holder 1999; JSU 2000b). This debate has domi-nated much discourse on victim compensation since the mid-1990s – on which more will be said below. Suffice it to say that by the 1970s statu-tory, state-funded victim compensation had become an integral part of criminal justice policy in Australia.

1970s: Advent of the victims' movement and growth of victim assistance

Insofar as victimology is also said to be a social movement, it received its impetus from the women's movement in the 1970s that was spurred on by the civil rights movement in the 1960s. The former began to draw attention to the unenviable and essentially powerless position of victims of sexual crimes and domestic violence in particular (Law Reform Commission of the ACT 1993; O'Connell 2005; Sallman and Chappell 1982; Scutt 1982, 1983; Sumner 1991; Whitrod 1986). They exerted pressure on governments that resulted in the establishment of crisis centres for victims of rape and other sexual assault and shelters or refuges for women escaping domestic violence.

In South Australia in the mid-1970s, for instance, a rape and sexual assault service was set up in a public hospital, a women's shelter was opened and a Crisis Care Service was open 24 hours a day and 7 days a week, which was funded to, among other functions, assist police attending domestic violence incidents (JSU 1999; Paterson 1996; Sumner 1991). The growing awareness of these victims' needs coupled with victim activism served as a foundation for more generic crime victim self-help organisations to emerge.

Towards the end of this decade, families of homicide victims were able to harness the momentum in seeking support services and demanding legislative and procedural reform. In 1979, for instance, parents of homicide victims and concerned citizens gathered to form the Victims of Crime Service (VOCS) in South Australia, and during the 1980s a similar impetus led to the opening of the Victims of Crime Assistance League (VOCAL) in Victoria. Later, other organisations were set up, such as VOCAL in the Australian Capital Territory (ACT), New South Wales and Queensland. All these organisations shared a sense of injustice for victims dealing with the criminal justice system. They also often had close ties with the police; for example, the first patron of VOCS was a former Commissioner of Queensland Police and the Victoria Police Commissioner was a strong advocate for VOCAL.

Connected by common concerns and goals, these in the main volunteer organisations collaborated 'ad hoc' under the auspices of Australasia Victim Support (Paterson 1990), which is the predecessor organisation to Victim Support Australasia (VSA). There is, however, a notable difference insofar as the former membership was a mix of non-government organisations and government agencies, while the latter is dominated by government agencies. Although VSA has published several notable policies on good practice in victim assistance, it has not made the same in-roads in terms of influencing governments' policies as have peak bodies representing specific categories of victims, such as the National Association of Services against Sexual Violence. This situation contrasts to the one in Britain where Victim Support UK (a non-government organisation providing victim assistance and lobbying for crime victims) attained such success that by the turn of the century it was perceived as an active adjunct to the criminal justice system and a major source of influence on government policy in a manner that perhaps inadvertently marginalised other victim organisations, such as those for victims of sex offences (Crawford 2000; Strang 2002). Since the election of the Conservative/Liberal Democrat Coalition Government, Victim Support UK's power has eroded as funding has been reallocated to local commissioners of police and diverse victims' interests (Reeves and Mulley 2000; Victim Support UK 2012).

Professionalisation became the second phase in the development of victim assistance across Australia (O'Connell 2005). Several of the volunteer victim-based organisations employed professionals largely from the social work field. These professionals assist in the diagnosis and treatment of victims as well as in advocating for victims and agitating for victims' rights. As happened in the United States, Canada and Britain, the social work paradigm became the most influential in setting the victim service-provision agendas. That paradigm prevails throughout

Australia, no matter whether the assistance is delivered by a non-government organisation or a government agency. Limiting or reducing the adverse effects of crime became and largely remains the main objective of providing victim assistance.

The third phase in the evolution of victim assistance might crudely be described as the era of government takeovers. In the 1990s some of the non-government organisations became victims themselves of government choices about methods of service delivery and commitment of resources. The demise of VOCAL due to the establishment of the government-run Victims Referral and Assistance Scheme in Victoria (O'Connell 2000) and the reclaiming of the once outsourced victim services in the Australian Capital Territory (ACT Reference Group 2006) and Tasmania are prime examples. Governments then asserted that their responses were focused on the 'adequacy of service provision' (Keating 2001, p. 22) and improving practical outcomes for victims of crime (Griffin 2000).

Victim assistance programmes continue to be state and territory based, and they are delivered by a combination of government agencies and non-government organisations. There are some common elements. For example, all jurisdictions provide counselling services for victims of violent crimes. There are also differences in eligibility requirements. The availability of services also differs between jurisdictions. For example, while the counselling services provided by Queensland are limited to victims residing in that state, Western Australia provides services to victims of offences committed in Western Australia irrespective of where the victim resides. New South Wales Victims Services has approved counsellors in several other jurisdictions, so victims of crime in that state who return to their home state or territory can attain counselling. Adult victims of any crime in South Australia can access counselling via the Victim Support Service (VSS), which is a non-government but government-funded organisation. The VSS does not operate any victim assistance in any other state or territory, so counselling is not readily available to victims of a crime that happened in South Australia but who subsequently return to their home state or territory.

It is not uncommon for victims to experience their victimisation in a state or territory other than that in which they reside (e.g. while holidaying interstate) or to move away from the state or territory in which they were victimised. It is inequitable that a victim's ability to access victim assistance programmes is fettered by state and territory boundaries. It is in the interest of the victim's rehabilitation to have 'portable' access to services. Information, assessment, referral and therapeutic services as well as reparation should be available and accessible to victims of crime – certainly, this is a right in international law (United Nations 1985; see also United Nations 1989, 1990).

Some steps have been taken to ameliorate jurisdictional impediments to a national approach to victim assistance. For instance, Northern Territory's Crime Victim Support Unit has paid for counselling for victims who have returned to their home state; and, the authorities in New South Wales and South Australia are negotiating an administrative agreement so that New South Wales citizens who become victims of crime in South Australia can receive counselling in their home state paid from the Victims of Crime Fund in South Australia. South Australia residents who are victims of crime in other places can already receive free counselling in that state and apply for compensation (by way of *ex gratia* payment) if the place where the crime happened does not have a state-funded victim compensation scheme.

Although there is a consensus that extensive social, health and welfare services are necessary if the needs of victims are to be properly met (Grabosky 1989), there is a paucity of empirical evidence to show whether the various victim assistance programmes are meeting these needs. The one-shot victim surveys (e.g. Erez et al. 1994; JSU 2000a) available are useful but also unsatisfactory in yielding the kind of knowledge required to ensure that such programmes are well designed, properly implemented and, most importantly, matched to victims' needs that change over time.

United States' research, however, reported a mismatch between victims' needs and the range of services provided by victim support organisations, which the researchers attributed in part to the dominance of the social work paradigm. British research (Jones and Mawby 2003) also found a mismatch between the range of services offered by Victim Support UK and the expectations of some victims. The researchers suggested this might be a consequence of the manner in which Victim Support UK expanded from a localised organisation helping victims of criminal trespass on their dwellings into a national organisation endeavouring to cater to all victims' divergent needs and interests, yet remaining attached to its traditional ways of doing business.

Findings in Australia indicate the existence of a similar mismatch. For example, only four in ten victims surveyed in South Australia were satisfied with the Victim Support Service (Erez et al. 1994, p. 55); victims who identified a preference for a particular type of assistance focused on practical needs, such as help to prevent further crime, assistance in dealing with insurance companies and legal advice on entitlements (JSU

2000a). In addition, victims of theft wanted their property returned or replaced (O'Connell 2005).

Six in ten victim respondents from South Australia and Western Australia who had sought assistance did so to receive support with their role in the criminal justice process, including assistance in preparing for court and/or help with understanding the court process in particular (Ross et al. 2009, p. 110). Many of these victims had no experience with the criminal justice system, so they wanted information on their role and responsibilities. About one in five victim respondents wanted help with specific aspects of the process, such as a referral to legal services, assistance writing impact statements, help attaining information from police or help with applying for restitution or compensation. Although some victim respondents sought counselling or psychological assistance, more commonly victims wanted the opportunity to talk about their experience with other people who had experienced similar crimes. When all responses from those who mentioned support and emotional impact were combined, only about one half of victim respondents who had dealt with a victim support service had done so primarily for assistance with the emotional effects of the crime.

This ongoing debate on the mismatch between victims' perceived needs and victims' real needs is used as a valid reason to shift away from compensation schemes towards financial assistance schemes that might better cater to victims' practical needs as well as expand services like helplines (see, e.g. Holder 2002; 2008; Joint Select Committee on Victims Compensation 2000; JSU 1999; Victim Services NSW 2012; Wade 1996). This debate has served another purpose with respect to the aims of victim assistance in that most victim support agencies and organisations throughout Australia now look upon crime prevention as a part of their core business, which comes in addition to their long-standing common goal of advancing victims' rights. Unlike victimologists, however, victims and their advocates have tended to support popular policies such as declarations or charters that exalt victims' rights but might, despite their lofty intention, have little positive impact on the way public officials treat victims of crime (see later in this chapter).

1980s: Promulgation of victims' rights

During the 1980s, victims, their advocates and others moved from the initial focus on compensation and support services to reintegrating victims into the criminal justice systems across Australia. In 1981 a committee of inquiry into victims of crime in South Australia reported on providing adequate information on criminal victimisation; coordinating victim assistance programmes and other initiatives, improving and expanding victim support services; reforming court procedures; and amending laws, including those governing statutory state-funded victim compensation. The committee concluded, 'Among the most pressing needs of crime victims is the need for sympathy and understanding, qualities which do not flow from ignorance' (1981, p. 12). The findings became a road map for systemic reform, with several of its 67 recommendations becoming grounds for asserting victims' rights.

In October 1985, the Government for South Australia promulgated Australia's first version of the Declaration for Victims of Crime, consisting of 17 principles (Sumner 1985). These principles were, and now are, often called rights because a right may be guaranteed by law, a basic entitlement recognised by an international agreement or a claim grounded in social morality. Some of the principles in the South Australia Declaration were enshrined in law, such as principle 12 reflected in the *Bail Act* 1985 that requires a bail authority to take into account victims' perceived safety concerns and principle 14 augmented by the *Criminal Law (Sentencing) Act* 1988 that provides for victim impact statements. All of the principles pre-empted but also replicated many aspects of the United Nations Declaration of Basic Principles of Justice for Victims of Crime and Abuse of Power (1985), and the principles were founded on morally rooted concepts such as fairness and justice. In the context of public policy, Holder (2002) argued that such a declaration emanates from one of two perspectives. The declaration as a proclamation of rights tends to be more individualistic, and in some cases it provides for redress for those whose rights are not respected, which is a point O'Connell (2009a) traces back to the *Magna Carta*. The declaration as a statement of principles provides 'a framework and a benchmark system' that can affect, for instance, the allocation of resources and can influence the manner in which victim services are operated (Holder 2002). Perhaps, in being more consistent with the concept of systemic change, the Government of South Australia reinforced the importance of its Declaration by instructing all relevant government agencies 'to ensure that their dealings with victims were in accordance with the rights' (Sumner 1991, p. 4). Moreover, the Government did not introduce any mechanism for victims to enforce their rights.

A couple of years later, the Victorian Sentencing Committee (1987, 1988) and the Tasmanian Inter-Departmental Committee on Victims of Crime (1989) recommended similar rights in these states. The Victorian Sentencing Committee, however, did not recommend the introduction of victim impact statements, whereas a Northern Territory Report (Murphy 1989) on such statements recommended their introduction. In addition, both the Victorian Legal and Constitutional Committee on Victim Support (1987) and the New South Wales Task Force on Services for Victims of Crime (1987) recommended a range of entitlements that are tantamount to rights for victims of crime. Thus, South Australia's leadership in formulating victims' rights (Grabosky 1989) became a 'major step in victim reform' (Sumner 1991, p. 3).

A Charter of Rights for Victims of Crime was later produced by the New South Wales Government (VOCAL 1989, p. 15), while in Victoria a Statement of Principles stipulating victims' entitlements was circulated (Attorney-General's Department (Victoria) 1991; VOCAL 1990, p. 13). The former initially gave only victims of sexual assault or other serious personal violence the right to make an impact statement, whereas the latter omitted such a right for any victim of crime. A Declaration of Victims' Rights modelled on the one in South Australia was recommended as an administrative direction in Tasmania in 1989 (VOCAL 1990, p. 9), which included an entitlement for victims to have information about the harm done to them presented to a sentencing court, though that right was omitted in a later version adopted by the Government in 1991. Despite the omission, Counsel for the Crown in Tasmania reported in 1996 that impact statements were made in accordance with the original declaration and under s.385(11) of that state's criminal code.

Western Australia (s.3 and Schedule 1 of the *Victims of Crime Act* 1994) and the ACT (s.4 of the *Victims of Crime Act* 1994) in 1994 then Queensland (Division II of the *Criminal Offence Victims Act* 1995) in 1995 enshrined their declaration or charter in law, which paved the way for arguing for stronger and possibly enforceable rights. Next, in 1996 New South Wales Parliament enacted the *Victims' Rights Act 1996 (repealed)*. Several years later, South Australia's Parliament followed the Queensland Act by incorporating the Declaration of Principles Governing Treatment of Victims of Crime in the *Victims of Crime Act* 2001. Victoria's Government in 2005 released a discussion paper on a Charter of Rights in which no mention is made of that state's earlier Statement of Principles; rather, it proposes the first charter on victims' rights for that state (Department of Justice 2005). After consultation, the Victoria Parliament passed the *Victims Charter Act* 2006.

In 1990, the National Committee on Violence (1990, p. xxxviii) recommended that 'with appropriate safeguards against abuse by either the Crown or the defence, victim impact statements should be intro-duced in all jurisdictions', which has happened, except in the federal jurisdiction. The Australian Law Reform Commission (1987, 1988) did not reject the concept, and the more recent Commission of Inquiry on Sentencing Federal Offenders (2005) recommended that impact statements be admitted in sentencing these offenders. A private members bill in the Federal Parliament in 2002 that would have provided for impact statements lapsed.

The debate on victim impact statements initially centred on – and indeed in some jurisdictions still centres on – whether a criminal court when passing sentence should consider the effects of the crime on the victim, especially the victim of homicide (Booth 2005). Furthermore, even in those jurisdictions that have settled the debate in favour of courts' receiving victim impact statements, there is much controversy over whether the victim should be able to participate directly in the process as happens in some other countries – for example, the French *parte civil*. Several jurisdictions do, however, oblige prosecutors to apply for a restitution or compensation order on behalf of the victim. South Australia is the only jurisdiction to acknowledge in law that a victim can comment on the sentence itself in an impact statement (s.7C *Criminal Law (Sentencing) Act* 1988). Another issue that is not settled is whether victims should be allowed to make statements about harm that was not reasonably foreseen by offenders (Garkawe 2006; JSU 1999; Leader-Elliott 2006).

Australian research on victim impact statements has produced mixed findings. Ideological opponents have described these statements as a symbolic way of catering to victims' emotions (Douglas and Laster 1994). In contrast, Erez argues that 'to resist victims input because...it is subjective...is to suggest there is an objective way to measure harm' (1994, p. 188). In at least one state there was a consensus among police, prosecutors and defence lawyers that impact statements should be retained as a right for victims (Mansell and Indermaur 1997; see also Erez et al. 1996). Some research suggests that victim satisfaction with sentences has not improved (Erez et al. 1994), whereas other research suggests that victims who felt supported in writing their statement, were kept informed and felt the process of preparing and presenting their statement gave them 'voice' have a greater sense of procedural justice (Ross et al. 2009). Victims who felt the court did not acknowledge their impact statement were more likely to be dissatisfied (O'Connell 2009b). Professionals in criminal justice in several states have similarly observed the importance victims' place on 'having a voice', 'being heard', 'being believed' and having their version of the incident vindicated (Bluett-Boyd and Fileborn 2014; see also Holder in this volume).

Regarding the courts, Booth has observed that victims' impact statements 'allow the court to more accurately determine the seriousness of the offence, make an informed sentencing decision and enhance proportionality and accuracy in sentencing' (2005, p. 60). Surveys in South Australia (O'Connell 2009b) and Victoria (Victim Support Agency 2009) found that 73% and 66%, respectively, of the judicial respondents believed victim impact statements to be useful in most cases in which they are submitted. In the South Australia survey, only one respondent felt such statements were useful in just a few cases. Some courts have recognised the relevance of the harm done to victims in their decisions (JSU 1999; see, e.g. R v P (1991) 111 ALR 541; R v Dowlan [1998] 1 VR 123; R v Dupas [2007] VSC 305).

Victim impact statements allow victims to participate in sentencing, but some victims and their advocates seek greater participation in the criminal justice process. For instance, the founding patron of the Victim Support Service in South Australia, Ray Whitrod, expressed his disappointment that the first version of the Declaration on Victims' Rights in Australia was 'short of what is required' regarding victim participation (Whitrod 1986, p. 82). Australia's first Commissioner for Victims' Rights has argued that victims should be allowed legal counsel throughout the criminal justice process (O'Connell 2013), which other commentators have to varying degrees supported (Kirchengast 2011, 2013; Symons 2013); and, for example, a magistrate has suggested that victim statements warrant further discussion during the pre-trial conference (Cannon 2012; see also Flynn 2012). Conversely, the Victorian Sentencing Committee held that allowing the victim to be an equal party in criminal proceedings would be 'regressive' and a 'downgrading of … important principles forming part of the criminal justice system' (1988, p. 543). It took another decade before any significant advances were made in victims' participatory rights.

1990s: Consolidating victims' rights yet contracting victim compensation

As the 1980s closed and the 1990s began, two national forums examined victims' rights. Both the Australian Police Ministers Council (APMC) and the Standing Committee of Attorneys-General (SCAG) discussed papers on a National Charter on Victims' Rights. In November 1989 the South Australian commissioner of police presented the APMC with a proposal to establish a national charter of victims' rights and to minimise the risk of victimisation based on the tenets of crime prevention

(Woodberry 1989). In June 1993, SCAG endorsed a National Charter for Victims' Rights in Australia, which was modelled on the United Nations' Declaration of Basic Principles of Justice for Victims of Crime and Abuse of Power and consistent with the Economic and Social Council resolution 1989/57 that in part called for action to ensure victims are kept informed of their rights, given information on the progress of criminal proceedings and made aware of opportunities to attain restitution or compensation from the offender. The Charter sets minimum standards for the treatment of victims in the criminal justice system. It recognises that victims should

- be treated with compassion and respect for their dignity;
- be afforded access to services;
- be informed of their rights;
- be informed of the progress of proceedings;
- be allowed to present their views at the appropriate stages of the proceedings;
- be afforded measures to protect their privacy, ensure their safety and minimise their inconvenience.

The SCAG secretariat was tasked with monitoring the implementation of the Charter. In 1996, after the secretariat reported that all states and territories had taken steps towards the implementation of the Charter, victims' rights dropped off the SCAG agenda for over a decade. Whereas the momentum among politicians to advance victims' rights nationally waned, some federal agencies – in particular the Australian Federal Police and the Commonwealth Office of the Director of Public Prosecutions – were formulating victim-oriented policies and practices. States and territories continued to review aspects of their declarations or charters while re-examining their victim assistance programmes. Although each jurisdiction implemented developments across Australia, each took a state-centric approach to reform.

Several states and one territory determined to revisit their responses to crime victims' needs. One innovation which emerged from reviews was the appointment in the ACT of the first independent statutory officer dedicated to advancing the rights and interests of crime victims. The appointment of the Victims of Crime Coordinator was an important milestone in the path to enforceable victims' rights. The Coordinator could receive victims' complaints against public officials and consult on them before making recommendations to the Attorney-General. The coordinator also advised on the effective and efficient use of government resources to help victims deal with the effects of crime.

South Australia's review on victims of crime, which commenced in 1999, became a 'blueprint' for more than a decade of reform (JSU 1999, 2000a, 2000b). It also provided the government with a rationale for enshrining the administrative declaration on victims' rights into the Victims of Crime Act, as well as a platform upon which to appoint Australia's second Victims of Crime Coordinator as an independent advisor to the Attorney-General.

Meanwhile, in Victoria the Kennett Liberal (conservative) Government pointed to the recommendations made by an inquiry by the Victims' Task Force of the Victorian Community Council against Violence (1994) as justification for a major overhaul of that state's responses to victims of violent crime (Wade 1996). The Inquiry had reported on the responsiveness of the criminal justice system to crime victims' needs and their rights; queried the effectiveness of existing victim assistance programmes and support services; and highlighted the 'special needs' of certain classes of victims. Of particular concern, the Inquiry identi-fied a 'real need' for victim assistance programmes and support serv-ices to be 'grounded within the context of a strategic approach', and recommeded that 'an integrated victim assistance regime with profes-sional and community interfaces' was necessary (Victims Referral and Assistance Service (VRAS) 1998, p. 1). For this purpose, in 1997 VRAS was established as a 'single centralised referral and assistance service' primarily for victims of violent crime (VRAS 1998, p. 2).

Five years on an inquiry into VRAS and other victim services across Victoria again reported that service delivery was fragmented and poorly coordinated. A lack of coordination resulted in inconsistent service standards. A lack of standard protocols between service providers, among other factors, negatively impacted the effectiveness of a range of victim support services (Department of Justice 2002). The inquiry recom-mended 'new directions' including the establishment of the Victims Support Agency to be tasked with the responsibility of integrating the provision of victim services.

Coupled with the introduction of counselling and other thera-peutic regimes was a dramatic shift away from lump-sum compensa-tion payments for non-tangible losses resulting from violent crime. Hon Jan Wade (1996), then attorney-general in Victoria, argued that research available to her challenged the worth of lump-sum compensa-tion payments. Freckelton (2003), however, asserted that the backlash against lump-sum payments was fuelled by the government's desire to cut expenditures rather than being based on the evidence of the effects of violent crime on victims. O'Connell and Fletcher (in press) point also to the speculation that victims of violent crime exaggerate their injuries and the subsequent effects to attain compensation, which suggests some victims seek to profit from crime.

The Victorian approach has been adapted to suit local circumstances in the ACT, Northern Territory and Queensland and recently in New South Wales. The ACT Victim Support Working Party (1998) recommended a 'mixed model of service' that would include a community-based, government-funded, generic victim support service and a reformed criminal injuries compensation scheme that focuses on financial assistance for medical and psychological services and any additional sum upon completion of rehabilitative support. Holder (1999), as the statutorily independent ACT Victims of Crime Coordinator, urged the ACT Parliament's Standing Committee on Justice and Community Safety to follow the Working Group's recommendation.

Wilson et al. (2001) identified gaps in Queensland's regime of crime victim services and recommended strategies to integrate and coordinate services in that state. Rather than their establishing a new government agency, they nominated the existing Families, Youth and Community Care Queensland to be the lead agency in providing core functions but also acting as a link between victims and other support services. More recently, the Government for Queensland appointed a Victims of Crime Coordinator and established Victim Assist Queensland to assist the recovery of victims of crime who have been injured as a result of an act of violence and to administer funding for support services and the Victims LinkUp telephone service (Queensland Government 2014; State of Queensland 2009).

Although many victims and some victim advocates express ongoing support for lump-sum monetary victim compensation, others argued there is a paucity of evidence to demonstrate that such payments achieve desired outcomes for either victims or the state. O'Connell and Fletcher (in press) found little empirical research in the relevant literature that substantiates the various rationales for state-funded victim compensation. Indeed, there has been little advance in knowledge since Holder (1999) observed, 'It is very unsatisfactory that there should be no research anywhere that actually asks crime victims whether the pain and suffering component of compensation actually alleviated their trauma' (p. 13). She also concluded that a 'narrow focus on "financial compensation" for an individual's injury without consideration of the rehabilitative effect of such awards nor of the totality of victims' needs is seriously flawed' (p. 15). Yet, Fletcher and O'Connell (in press) observed that many victims perceive compensation as a right or fundamental entitlement and a means to hold offenders accountable for the harm done. Further, many victims believe the state should provide both counselling or other support and compensation (see also Joint Select Committee on Victims Compensation 1997a, b, c; Justice Strategy Unit 2000b; Victorian Community Council against Violence 1994). The debate, however, is an example of a broader debate on 'what' to provide victims with and 'how' to provide for victims' needs.

Victims have not always been the beneficiaries of such debate. Indeed, in most Australian jurisdictions it has helped fuel 'a backlash' against the expenditure involved in state funding of compensation schemes for criminal injuries (Freckelton 2003). Since the mid-1990s an era of 'victim-blaming' has played out in the majority of Australia's jurisdictions. Claims began to attain prominence that some victims contributed to their own victimisation; some victims exaggerated their injuries and the effects; and some victims do not deserve state-funded compensation. As more victims lodged applications for compensation and costs to the state increased, victims' needs became pitted against economic discourse on the financial viability of such schemes (Joint Select Committee on Victims Compensation 1997c; Justice Strategy Unit 2000b). Furthermore, according to Freckelton (2003), 'The alternative of criminal injuries compensation schemes in which the principal source for victim assistance is the offender has become swept up in the law and order movement and the movement toward restorative justice' (p.1).

The 1990s ended with the release of a national study on victims' rights and victim assistance (Cook et al. 1999). In most Australian states and territories, specialist and generic victim services existed. Common elements were referral, information provision, telephone and short-term counselling, crisis intervention and some court support. There was also, however, a lack of long-term counselling and other support options for those victims seriously affected and a short-fall in services for victims of less serious offences where victims often required practical help rather than therapy. The study in addition confirmed the importance of integration and coordination within and across jurisdictions. Moreover, a lack of coordination and, in some programmes, the misallocation of resources was perceived by respondents throughout Australia as major problems with victim assistance. In particular, the authors of the study concluded that the smaller states, such as South Australia and the Australia Capital Territory, appeared to have 'relatively good coordination and communication among services, facilitated by their smaller population size' (Graycar 1999, p. 2). Additionally the study exposed gaps in victim assistance for culturally and linguistically diverse peoples and those victims who lived in remote and rural communities (Cook et al. 1999; see also JSU 1999).

2000s: The promise of better justice by giving victims stronger rights

Connections between some elements of the victim movement and the law and order movement have been evident since the 1980s. Several victim organisations, for instance, have openly criticised sentences perceived to be lenient (Harding 1994). This is not surprising given that victim surveys often show many victims themselves believe sentences in their cases were lenient (Erez et al. 1994; JSU 2000a). Regarding offenders' sentences, victims have regularly called for tougher sentences, including greater use of imprisonment. Some victims also favoured greater use of restitution and compensation orders. Victims who perceived the sentences were not completed or enforced also expressed dissatisfaction, even anger (Erez et al. 1994; Gardner 1989, 1990; JSU 2000a; O'Connell 2006; see also Holder 2014). Many politicians succumbed to the pressure and willingly embraced the demands of disgruntled victims and public. Maximum sentences for some offences were raised and the numbers of offenders imprisoned continued to grow (ABS 2013). Between 1984 and 2012, the imprisonment rate almost doubled. One Australian jurisdiction introduced a law to allow the victim of a convicted offender up to 12 months after conviction to apply to that court for a restitution order while another introduced a law to provide for a 'mandatory' restitution whenever an offender is found guilty of a property offence. Neither has proven to be of practical assistance for the majority of victims of crime (see, e.g. Warner and Gawlick 2003).

The focus on the victim also influenced the search for alternatives to the adversarial approach to criminal justice – for instance, restorative justice. Interest in restorative justice began in the 1970s and 1980s. It was influenced by the social movements of the 1960s that identified the high levels of imprisonment of offenders, particularly of Indigenous people, and also by the lack of concern for victims of crime. By the 1990s Australia's first restorative justice programmes had begun; the concept subsequently gained much traction in the 2000s. In 2000 the United Nations Congress on Crime and Criminal Justice drafted a proposal for United Nations Basic Principles on Restorative Justice

(2002) to encourage, among other things, use of restorative justice by member-states, such as Australia, at all stages of criminal justice systems (National Justice CEOs Group 2011). In Australia several criminologists dominated the debate on the meaning of restorative justice. Braithwaite (1998,2002) emphasised the values underpinning such justice: those that constrain the process to prevent it from being oppressive (e.g. non-domination and empowerment); values that guide the process and can be used to measure success (e.g. restoration and compassion); and values that describe certain outcomes of the process (e.g. remorse and apology). Daly (2003), on the other hand, identified core elements, all of which might not be realised in practice. These elements include that the offender admits the offence, or at least does not deny responsibility, as restorative justice is not concerned with fact-finding but with the post-adjudication phase of the criminal process. In addition, the offender and the victim meet at a face-to-face meeting, which might also involve supporters of both parties and other relevant people. Furthermore, the process enables victims to tell their stories while providing opportunities for offenders to be held accountable (Garkawe 1999).

Restorative justice programmes – following the family conference approach introduced in Wagga Wagga by New South Wales Police in 1991 and embedded in South Australia's youth justice system in 1994 as well as the RISE pilot in the ACT – were implemented across Australia primarily to deal with young offenders (Daly 2003; Strang 2002; Strang et al. 1999). Inquiries, for example – the Children in State Care Commission in South Australia (2008) and the National Council to Reduce Violence Against Women and their Children (2009) – recommended exploration of the use of restorative justice to deal with sexual and family violence. As well, Australia's attorneys-general later endorsed national protocols on restorative justice. Currently, restorative justice is legislated in all states and territories.

Research yet again has produced mixed results. Offenders, victims and other participants are sometimes unable or unwilling to think and act in restorative ways (Daly 2003). Offenders may remain unmoved by victims' stories and may withhold apologies, and victims may remain angry and/or fearful and may refuse to accept that offenders are contrite or apologetic (Hayes 2006). Victim participation is also low in some jurisdictions (O'Connell and Hayes 2012; Office of Crime Statistics and Research (SA) 2000, 2005); and smaller proportions of victims are satisfied with conference outcomes (Strang et al. 1999). That said, Maxwell and Hayes (2006; see also Trimboli 2007) reported that, on balance, offenders and victims emerge from restorative programmes with a positive view of the process.

Despite the expansion of restorative justice programmes, the criminal trial remains the most visible means of tackling crime in Australia; similarly, the push for victims to have legal rights within the criminal justice system has persisted. The focus, however, in this decade included victims' rights to assistance and information as well as alienated victims asserting their participatory rights. In New South Wales and South Australia, for instance, a greater emphasis on procedural rights resulted in amendments that provide for the right to be consulted before charge decisions are varied, and in South Australia, it resulted in stronger laws on victim 'indirect' participation in bail hearings and 'direct' participation in parole hearings (see, e.g. ss.7, 9A and 10 of the *Victims of Crime Act* 2001 (SA); ss.6.5(2) and 6.16 of the *Victims Rights and Support Act* 2013 (NSW)).

Australian research revealed shortcomings in the implementation of victims' rights declarations and charters. In South Australia, two surveys (Erez et al. 1994; Gardner 1990) revealed that despite the declaration on victims' rights, many victims felt that they did not get the information they needed and that too many public officials treated them ambivalently. A review of victims of crime (JSU 1999, 2000) revealed similarly negative matters but also positive matters attributable to the declaration and steps taken to implement it. Western Australia reviews done in the same era produced both negative and positive findings (Keating 2001; Wilkie et al. 1992). Collectively, positive findings included improvements in police treatment of victims, more support during criminal proceedings and better access to therapeutic assistance, such as counselling.

The New South Wales statutory review of its victims' legislation (New South Wales Victim Services 2004; see also Curtis and Pankhurst 2003) noted that 'many victims, friends and families of victims, and victim support groups observed that the terms of the Charter are simply not being followed by government departments and agencies in their dealings with victims' (p. 47). The ACT Department of Justice and Community Safety (2008) issued a paper on the operation of the *Victims of Crime Act 1994* (ACT) and noted similar concerns. It cited the Victims of Crime Support Program Annual Report 2006–2007, in which the Victims of Crime Coordinator highlighted 'individual cases of agencies failing to adhere to governing principles contained in the Act, inconsistencies between agencies in their application or implementation of the governing principles, and problems in addressing the failures of these bodies to implement the Act's requirements' (p. 21). Likewise adverse findings have been made throughout Australia. For example, Queensland's review of operation of the *Criminal Offence Victims Act* found shortcomings and proposed three approaches to strengthen compliance: a compliance regulatory approach; an increased oversight approach; and a managerialistic approach (Department of Justice and Attorney-General 1988). Similarly, Western Australia's Auditor General (2012; see also Social Systems and Evaluation 1997) found that the West Australia Police does not have satisfactory processes and practices to ensure that victims are consistently referred to victim support and that the Victim Support Service has not ensured that other victim agencies or organisations are adequately aware of its services.

In its 2005 community consultation paper on a Victims' Charter, the Victorian Department of Justice examined monitoring and compliance models from other Australian jurisdictions and overseas. The paper concluded that 'there is a need for the provisions [of a Victims' Charter] to be clearly articulated and for a well co-coordinated implementation process and compliance mechanisms to be established' (p. 37). The Victim Support Agency was tasked to lead the implementation, to raise citizens' and practitioners' awareness on victims' right and to receive victims' grievances. Four years after the Charter was introduced, Victoria Police (2009, p. 18) conceded a compliance rate of 75 per cent, while the Aboriginal Family Violence Prevention and Legal Service (2010, pp. 139–141) in that state reported that police did not follow up adequately with many victims and that victims encountered difficulties accessing information about the progress of investigations.

All the research and inquiries revealed that there are still gaps in the ways public officials treat victims and in how the criminal justice system responds to victims. While states and territories promised reforms to strengthen victims' rights, the Commonwealth Government continued (as it had done in the 1980s during discourse on the United Nations Declaration on Basic Principles of Justice for Victims of Crime and Abuse of Power (1985)) internationally advocating for crime victims' rights. In 2005 Australia's attorney-general joined other Commonwealth Senior Law Officers in communicating a Statement of Basic Principles of Justice for Victims of Crime (Commonwealth Secretariat 2005). Notwithstanding Australia's endorsement of the United Nations Declaration in 1985, the National Charter on Victims' Rights endorsed by Australia's attorneys-general in 1996 and the Commonwealth Nations Statement in 2005, successive Commonwealth governments opposed a federal charter on victims' rights. Then in 2008, the Federal Minister for Home Affairs announced that the Commonwealth Government would introduce a charter on rights for victims of federal offences. Also that year the Federal Attorney-General's Department hosted the Summit on Justice, comprising several workgroups. The workgroup on victims of crime recommended a federal charter on victims' rights modelled on a draft convention promulgated by the World Society of Victimology (WSV) and its partners (INTERVICT 2014). However, this recommendation was not acted upon. Contrary to the pledge, Australia still does not have a federal charter on crime victims' rights.

That same year, the first independent, statutory Commissioner for Victims' Rights was appointed in South Australia. The Commissioner advises the government on how to effectively and efficiently use available resources to help victims; assists victims dealing with public agencies and the criminal justice system; reviews the effect of the law on victims; monitors the compliance of public officials and agencies with the Declaration Governing Treatment of Victims of Crime; and reports annually to Parliament. The Commissioner can also consult public officials on the treatment of victims and recommend that an official or agency make a written apology to a victim where there has been a breach of the Declaration. Having appraised the Commissioner's authorities, an ACT inquiry concluded that South Australia has the first enforceable victims' rights in Australia. Although this might be correct in general terms, South Australia, prior to the appointment of the Commissioner, enacted a law to protect the privacy of victim information maintained on the Victim Register in Correctional Services. A breach of that law is punishable by a fine of up to $10,000. That said, no Australia Charter or Declaration comprises legally enforceable rights; indeed, some specifically prescribe that violations do not give rise to either criminal or civil proceedings. Yet, all have introduced ways to resolve victims' grievances when those rights are violated. Most substantiated complaints result in disciplinary proceedings. In the ACT, New South Wales, Queensland and Victoria, for example, a public official who breaches a guideline or right can face disciplinary proceedings within his or her own agency.

South Australia's Commissioner for Victims' Rights (Attorney-General's Department (Australia) 2008) also became embroiled in the debate on a federal charter on victims' rights and victim participation at key stages in the federal criminal justice process. In addition to making a written submission to the federal attorney-general, he spoke as an expert at a meeting of the SCAG. In light of the Australian Government's expressed willingness to 'open the doors of justice' to victims of federal offences, the Commissioner proposed a national office for victims of crime, similar to the one in the United States, to help coordinate Australia's international and domestic responses to victims' needs and their rights (O'Connell 2008).

As the decade closed, Holder aptly surmised that in all Australian jurisdictions 'a pragmatic though piecemeal approach to addressing the unmet needs and rights of crime victims has resulted in law reform and service responses that traverse humanitarian, welfare and justice domains. A range of legislative and administrative instruments have been applied in the States and Territories to reflect the obligations of the UN Declaration' (2008, p. 5). States and territories faced continued demands for improvement in victim assistance and stronger procedural rights, such as a much more active role in bail hearings, in charge bargaining and in sentencing. Paradoxically, governments of states and territories knew public officials were not meeting their victims' rights obligations, in part because budgetary constraints impeded the allocation of adequate resources; yet, several governments demonstrated an unfettered desire to impose even greater and more far-reaching obligations on public officials. Attempts to promulgate a federal charter on victims' rights, however, remained stalled.

2010s: A fundamental shift towards collaboration and cooperation

As this decade began, Australia's Federal Attorney-General's Department withdrew as the chair of the National Victims of Crime Workgroup established in 2008 by Attorneys-General. The Attorney-General for New South Wales and his counterpart in South Australia agreed to co-chair the Workgroup. The Workgroup identified a number of drivers for the advent of victims' rights. They observed that underlying these drivers is the victim's lack of standing in criminal proceedings other than as witness for the state. They also determined that a major challenge is to ensure that the victims' rights reforms are mirrored in day to day administrative realities.

Contrary to the ideals underpinning victims' rights, the Workgroup reported to Attorneys-General that, across all states and territories, victims expressed concerns about the following:

- the lack of information about the process and progress of the investigation, personal safety and/or protection, the adjudication process and determination of the charge or reason for accepting a plea and the progress of the prosecution;

- the failure of authorities to involve them in key decisions that affect them, such as bail, charge bargaining, formulation of 'statements of fact' and whether to prosecute;
- the lack of opportunities for input into consideration of sentencing options and offender management;
- the ambivalent and disrespectful attitude and behaviours of police, prosecutors, court staff, judges and magistrates as well as other public officials;
- the lack of access to and availability of victim assistance, practical help and advice about prevention.

The Workgroup felt that their respective declarations or charters on victims' rights have inspired other legislative reform and served as a basis for debate on possibilities for victim participation in criminal proceedings. In addition, they concluded that improvements depend on overcoming vested criminal justice interests that, among other things, continue to relegate the victim's status to no more than a witness for the state, as investigator and prosecutor. Furthermore, victims' needs might be overshadowed by managerialism or be hi-jacked for political ends – for instance, to justify a tough-on-crime, 'law and order' agenda. The Workgroup warned that the impulse to punish offenders as a demonstration of 'justice for victims' may trump displaying respect, compassion and dignity to victims as well as assisting them to deal with the effects of crime.

Running parallel to the national agenda, several states followed South Australia's lead in providing for a Commissioner for Victims' Rights. A stronger, independent advocate was established as the Commissioner for Victims of Crime in the Australia Capital Territory. A Commissioner for Victims' Rights with authority to investigate victims' complaints but who was not statutorily independent was appointed in New South Wales. A Commissioner for victims of crime whose functions are oriented towards strategic policy advice was later appointed in Western Australia. None of these officers has the right to appear in certain criminal proceedings, which is a unique and 'interesting development' (Redmond 2007) performed by the Commissioner for Victims' Rights in South Australia. It has afforded that Commissioner with avenues to intervene in criminal proceedings in ways traditionally associated with civil (inquisitorial) criminal justice systems rather than with common law (adversarial) systems (O'Connell 2010; 2013). The Commissioner, for instance, has the authority to appear in person, or through legal counsel, before a sentencing court to make a victim impact statement (ss.7 and 7A of the *Criminal Law (Sentencing) Act* 1988; s.32A of the *Victims of Crime Act* 2001), neighbourhood impact statement or social impact statement (s.7C of the *Criminal Law (Sentencing) Act* 1988). Three neighbourhood impact statements have been made in South Australia. One was presented by the prosecutor on behalf of the women of an Aboriginal community that was negatively impacted by a male elder sexually assaulting several girls. These women wrote about the broad social ramifications and the 'fact' that the offender's crimes were contrary to both legal law and cultural lore (ABC 2007 (see also R v Ingomar District Court (SA) 11 July 2007)). Another, presented orally by legal counsel representing the commissioner, detailed the impact on teachers, administration staff, parents and students that resulted from a series of sexual assaults perpetrated on young students by an out-of-school-hours worker (R v Harvey (No. 2) (2014) SASCFC 106). No social impact statement has been made by the commissioner, although through legal counsel the Commissioner attempted to make such a statement before the Supreme Court of South Australia heard an application for release on home detention by a declared persistent sex offender (R v Marshall (2014) SASC 92); however, Her Honour Kelly J ruled that such a statement would not be acceptable in the matter but allowed the statement to be submitted as a report pursuant to other law (s.25 of the *Criminal Law (Sentencing) Act 1988* (SA)). When introduced, it was envisaged that a social impact statement could be given in cases involving the mass exploitation of children as evident when offenders are convicted of possessing thousands of images of child pornography – in so doing, these victims would be given a voice. In domestic violence cases, it was also envisaged that social impact statements could be made to draw attention to the broad social and economic costs of such violence that some victims and their advocates as well as a majority of parliamentarians believe are misunderstood or overlooked in criminal proceedings.

Perhaps the most notable development, however, is recognition of victims' right to legal counsel albeit in limited circumstances. Courts have permitted legal counsel funded by the Commissioner to intervene to uphold victims' right to privacy. Further, under South Australia law victims, as interested persons, victims can apply to appear before courts' hearing applications to revoke a licence or vary the licence conditions for mentally impaired or mentally incompetent offenders (s.269P of the *Criminal Law Consolidation Act* 1935). In Steele's case, Gray J of the Supreme Court held that the family of a killed victim were interested persons and allowed their legal counsel (funded by the Commissioner for Victims' Rights) to cross-examine witnesses and make submissions (R v Steele (No. 2) (2012) SASC [162]). Most recently, in the Supreme Court, Kelly J, as mentioned above, allowed legal counsel for the Commissioner to make submissions regarding a persistent sex offender's application for supervised release (R v Marshall 2014). In light of law that stipulates community safety is a priority factor in determining whether a persistent sex offender should be released or not, the Commissioner's counsel argued against the offender's release. Her Honour invited the Commissioner to make further submissions and in her reported decision on the case acknowledged that the Commissioner's submission was useful.

The Commissioner has also successfully intervened to protect the privacy of a child victim of sexual assault (O'Connell 2013). The court accepted the Commissioner's argument that South Australia's victims' rights law exists (as per the Preamble in Part II, Division I of the *Victims of Crime Act* 2001) to give effect to international law such as the Universal Declaration on Human Rights; the Declaration of Basic Principles of Justice for Victims of Crime and Abuse of Power; the Convention on the Rights of the Child; as well as the Guidelines on Children as Victims and Witnesses. Each of these instruments provides for the right to privacy as does South Australia's Declaration Governing Treatment of Victims of Crime. The commissioner asserted that disclosure of all information stored on a laptop hard drive would amount to an unnecessary intrusion on the child victim's privacy. Rather than allow the defence access to all data on the hard drive, the court agreed and ordered disclosure of information date-marked 24 hours before the alleged offence and 48 hours after the alleged offence.

These and other interventions demonstrate that it is possible to enhance procedural justice for victims of crime without unnecessarily encroaching on procedural justice for accused and convicted persons. As the decade closed, three reports highlighted the import of procedural justice for victims of crime in various jurisdictions. One study involving victim respondents in Western Australia, South Australia and the ACT revealed that victim satisfaction with each element of the criminal justice system is 'primarily determined by the quality of procedural experiences' in the respective element (Ross et al. 2009). Further, good or bad experiences with one element did not necessary carry over to another element. Victims' dissatisfaction with prosecution, however, appeared to be attributable to dissatisfaction with the charge bargaining process and not necessarily with the outcome per se. Another study involving respondents from New South Wales and the Netherlands investigated the concept of procedural justice for both sexual assault victims and non-sexual assault victims (Laxminarayan 2012). The researcher found that procedural justice comprising respectful police treatment, accurate and timely information and a voice impacted the psychological effects of criminal proceedings. Such was also an important determinant of victims' perceptions of 'outcome favourability'. For victims of sexual assault, procedural justice was more strongly associated with the 'outcome variable'; thus, the researcher recommended providing victims of sexual assault with means 'to voice themselves' as this would aid in their recovery.

A study in the ACT has also shown an association between voice and procedural justice (Holder 2014). Consistent with other studies (Laxminarayan 2012), this study suggested giving victims a voice (as happens in mediation (see Wemmers and Cyr 2006) and in victim impact statements (Erez 1994; O'Connell 2006)) in a manner that appears to contribute to higher confidence levels among victims, so long as such a voice is listened to and responded to appropriately. For some victims, the right to voice their views might be adequate, but others might exercise their right to voice to influence decision outcomes. Issues such as these are explored further by Holder in this volume. Many legal scholars and criminal justice professionals, among others, throughout Australia, however, reject the concept of victims having voice equivalent to a party in criminal proceedings. Instead, they would prefer to maintain the *status quo* rather than allow victims, or their legal counsel, to call or interrogate witnesses or challenge evidence (Toole 2014).

Repeatedly, cultural change within public agencies is identified as vital to ensure effective implementation obligations regarding victims' rights. With the exception of police training, there has been a lack of consistent training efforts for others who come in contact with victims. The Commissioner has therefore helped to develop, even occasionally fund, training and professional development for public officials, including judicial officers. As well, he has funded legal counsel to appear during coronial inquests to represent, as interested persons, families of deceased people. Such inquests have resulted in recommendations for systemic change in police preliminary investigation into gun crime; in transport department assessments of persons with vision impairment and diabetes to determine their entitlement to hold a driver's licence; and in recommendations for reform of mental health appraisals of patients prior to release after detention on mental health orders (O'Connell 2010; 2013).

The refreshed discourse on a national approach to victims' rights and victim assistance continued. As co-chair of the National Victims of Crime Workgroup, the Commissioner helped to distil several primary issues impacting victim assistance across Australia:

- the limitations in the availability of services beyond state and territory borders;
- the complexities of cross-jurisdiction cooperation and collaboration as well as the lack of referral protocols;
- the implications of victim mobility for victim assistance;
- the challenge for victim assistance providers to respond to the diversity of victims and of their needs;
- varying approaches to the provision of services and accreditation of service providers;
- the need for information sharing within approved guidelines between agencies at different levels;
- the lack of coordinated research into the most effective and efficient responses to facilitating victims' rights and meeting victims' needs.

Furthermore, as many victims of crime will have involvement with multiple agencies and/or organisations, victim assistance should be supported by a coordinated and well-informed interagency approach. The Workgroup concluded that government agencies (and where government services are delivered by non-government organisations, these organisations) must cooperate and collaborate for the sake of victims, and not for their vested interests, if procedural justice is to be done. To achieve practical improvements for victims of crime, the Workgroup recommended it be tasked to develop a coherent strategy that not only responds to victims' needs but also ensures commonality in service standards based on current 'good practice'; agreed upon referral protocols and processes; and appropriate monitoring and quality assurance processes. The SCAG, which later became known as the Standing Council on Law and Justice(SCLJ), approved.

The National Workgroup reported in its first progress report that a national approach to victim assistance should do the following:

- restore or improve the victim's physical, psychological and emotional well-being;
- reduce the risk that the victim will suffer re-victimisation;
- maintain, if appropriate, the victim's family and social relationships;

- minimise any negative impact on the victim's financial and social situation;
- enhance the victim's capacity to cope so that he or she can resume as normal a life as is practicable;
- foster confidence in the administration of criminal justice;
- facilitate the exercise of the victim's rights to be effectively informed and/or involved as he or she chooses;
- employ techniques and use resources to meet the victim's needs.

To address the diverse needs of victims, the National Workgroup urged that victim assistance be rendered on a multidisciplinary basis by relevant public agencies and non-government organisations in a coordinated and integrated manner. The integration and coordination must be based on joint understanding, prioritisation, resource identification and allocation, as well as use of common mechanisms relevant to a multijurisdictional (cross-border) monitoring process. Next, in 2013 the National Workgroup presented a draft of the National Framework on Victims' Rights and Victim Assistance, which the SCLJ) approved, but it also charged the National Justice Chief Executives Group (NJCEG) with monitoring the implementation of the Framework. For this purpose, the National Workgroup formulated an implementation plan that the NJCEG has since endorsed.

The ideal, as first enunciated by the Commissioner for Victims' Rights in South Australia, to devise national victims' rights laws and minimum standards exists but is no longer a priority. Instead, the Framework is an aspirational document upon which cross-jurisdictional arrangements are proposed to be built, so long as they are affordable.

Conclusion

Since the 1960s Australia's states and territories governments have enacted numerous victim-oriented laws and procedures and have established both generalist and specialist victim support services – the breadth and depth of these services is unprecedented. Victims' rights proclamations are now commonplace with the exception of the federal jurisdiction. Despite the positive developments, some of Australia's governments appear now, as they have done over more than three decades, to be satisfied by the mere existence of such a charter or declaration without checking whether or not significant practical impact and actual improvement has been achieved. That said, even if these charters or declarations have not necessarily been implemented as envisaged and desired, many victims have benefited and the cliché of the 'forgotten victim' is in general no longer the case.

There are a number of similarities across jurisdictions in the manner a victim may be treated by public officials and others as well as in how a victim may engage in Australia's criminal justice systems. Conversely, there are a number of divergences across jurisdictions that can result in inequities and injustice as victims of similar crimes are treated differently from one jurisdiction to the next. Eligibility for victim assistance varies from one jurisdiction to another. Maximums payable as either compensation or financial assistance vary also from state to state, territory to territory. Geopolitical borders constrain service delivery but not crime. These are weighty issues that require attention to help counterbalance the dehumanising and re-victimising aspects of Australia's adversarial criminal justice systems. Preventing secondary victimisation depends upon change in the attitudes and behaviours of those expected to give effect to victims' rights – changes that will enable the promise of victims' rights to be achieved more fully than at present.

Procedural justice for victims requires the means of instilling humanistic values (e.g. respect, equity and fairness) in criminal justice practitioners, prosecutors, defence lawyers, judiciaries and others in addition to expanding the role of victims beyond their role as witnesses for the state-as-prosecutor. It also must overcome the conflict which emerges between the different and opposing interests in the state-defendant contest. Remarkably, some concrete steps have been taken in at least one Australian jurisdiction to bring about such justice through greater inclusion and empowerment of victims at each stage of the criminal justice process. This advance is arguably an 'encouraging model' for all states and territories to emulate within their own criminal justice processes. The administration of just criminal justice systems across Australia necessitates no less than the proper consideration of victims' interests and appropriate action. With this in mind, it would seem that procedural justice will be central in the evolution of victims' rights and victim assistance in the next decade.

References

Acts of Parliament

Bail Act 1985 (SA)
Criminal Injuries Compensation Act 1967 (NSW), repealed
Criminal Injuries Compensation Act 1969 (SA), repealed
Criminal Law Consolidation Act 1935 (SA)

Criminal Law (Sentencing) Act 1988 (SA)
Criminal Offence Victims Act 1995 (QLD), repealed
Victims Charter Act 2006 (Vic)
Victims of Crime Act 1994 (ACT)
Victims of Crime Act 1994 (WA)
Victims of Crime Act 2001 (SA)
Victims Rights Act 1996 (NSW), repealed
Victims Rights and Support Act 2013 (NSW)

Case law

R v Dowlan [1998] 1 VR 123
R v Dupas [2007] VSC 305
R v Harvey (No. 2) [2014] SASCFC 106
R v Marshall [2014] SASC 92
R v P (1991) 111 ALR 541
R v Steele (No. 2) [2012] SASC 162

Articles, chapters and texts

Aboriginal Family Violence Prevention and Legal Service (AFVPLS). 2010. *Improving Accessibility of the Legal System for Aboriginal and Torres Strait Islander Victims/Survivors of Family Violence and Sexual Assault.* Policy Paper No. 3. Melbourne: AFVPLS. http://www.fvpls.org/images/files/FVPLS%20Policy%20 Paper%203.pdf.

ABC (Australian Broadcasting Corporation). 2007. Elder Admits in Court to Petrol for Sex. http://www.abc.net.au/news/2007-07-11/elder-admits-in-court-to-petrol-for-sex/96292.

ABS (Australian Bureau of Statistics). 2013. Recorded Crime-Offenders, 2011–12, 4519.0. Canberra, Australia: ABS. http://www.abs.gov.au/AUSSTATS/abs@.nsf/ Lookup/4519.0Main+Features12011-12?OpenDocument.

ACT Reference Group. 2006. *Review of the Victim Services Scheme – Final Report.* Canberra: Department of Justice ACT Government.

Attorney-General's Department. 1988. An Integrated Approach to Victims of Crime, unpublished. Adelaide SA: Attorney-General's Department.

Attorney-General's Department (Victoria) 1991. Declaration of Rights – Victims of Crime, Pamphlet, June. Melbourne: Attorney-General's Department, Community Services Victoria, Ministry of Police and Emergency Services and Office of Corrections.

Australian Law Reform Commission. 1987. *Sentencing Procedure.* Discussion Paper No. 29. Sydney: ALRC.

Australian Law Reform Commission. 1988. *Sentencing.* Report 44. Sydney: ALRC.

Barrett Meyering, I. 2010. *Victim Compensation and Domestic Violence: A National Overview.* Stakeholder Paper 8. Australian Domestic and Family Violence Clearinghouse, January.

Bluett-Boyd, N. and Fileborn, B. 2014. *Victim/Survivor-Focused Justice Responses and Reforms to Criminal Court Practice: Implementation, Current Practice and Future Directions.* Research Report No. 27. Melbourne: Australia Institute of Family Studies.

Booth, T. 2005. Restoring Victims' Voices: Victim Impact Statements in the Sentencing Process. *Reform* 86, pp. 59–62.

Braithwaite, J. 1998. Restorative Justice. In: Tonry, M. ed. *The Handbook of Crime and Punishment*. Oxford: Oxford University Press, pp. 323–344.

Braithwaite, J. 2002. *Restorative Justice and Responsive Regulation*. New York: Oxford University Press.

Cannon, A. 2012. The Victim is not the Person on Trial: Adapting Common Law Processes to Respect Victims. Paper Presented at the Participatory Justice and Victims: Achieving Justice for Victims in Local, National and International Settings Conference, Australian National University, 17–18 September, Canberra.

Children in State Care Commission of Inquiry. 2008. *Allegations of Sexual Abuse and Death from Criminal Conduct*. Adelaide: Government Publishing SA.

Christie, N. 1986. The Ideal victim. In: Fattah, E. ed. *From Crime Policy to Victim Policy*. Basingstoke: Macmillan, pp. 17–30.

Committee of Inquiry on Victims of Crime 1981. *Report of the Committee of Inquiry on Victims of Crime*, January. Adelaide: Government of South Australia.

Commonwealth Secretariat 2005. *Statement of Basic Principles of Justice for Victims of Crime*. London: Commonwealth Secretariat.

Cook, B., David, F. and Grant, A. 1999. *Victims' Needs, Victims' Rights: Policies and Programs for Victims of Crime in Australia*. Research and Public Policy Series No. 19. Canberra: Australian Institute of Criminology.

Crawford, A. 2000. Salient Themes Towards a Victim Perspective and the Limitations of Restorative Justice: Some Concluding Comments. In: Crawford, A. and Goodey, J. eds. *Integrating a Victim Perspective within Criminal Justice*. Aldershot: Ashgate, pp. 285–310.

Curtis, M. and Pankhurst, G. 2003. New South Wales: Phone-in Survey of Victims of Crime. *Journal of the Australasian Society of Victimology* 2(2), pp. 10–20.

Daly, K. 2003. Mind the Gap: Restorative Justice in Theory and Practice. In: von Hirsch, A. Roberts, J., Bottoms, A.E., Roach, K. and Schiff, M. eds. *Restorative Justice and Criminal Justice: Competing or Reconcilable Paradigms?* Oxford: Hart Publishing, pp. 219–236.

Dawson, M. and Zada, J. 1999. Victims of Crime: The Therapeutic Benefit of Receiving Compensation. Paper Presented to Australian and New Zealand Association of Psychiatry, Psychology and Law Annual Congress, Sydney.

Department of Justice. 2002. *Report – Review of Services to Victims of Crime*, February. Melbourne: Department of Justice, Government of Victoria.

Department of Justice. 2005. *Victims' Charter – Community Consultation Paper: Executive Summary*. Melbourne: Department of Justice.

Department of Justice and Attorney-General. 1998. *Review of the Criminal Offence Victims Act 1995 – Implementing the Fundamental Principles of Justice for Victims of Crime: Discussion paper*. Brisbane: Department of Justice and Attorney-General.

Department of Justice and Community Safety. 2008. *Review of the ACT Victims of Crime Act 1994*, Department of Justice and Community Safety, Australian Capital Territory.

Douglas, R. and Laster, K. 1994. *Victim Information and the Criminal Justice System: Adversarial or Technocratic Reform?* June. Bundoora: School of Law and Legal Studies, La Trobe University.

Elias, R. 1983. *Victims of the System: Crime Victims and Compensation in American Politics and Criminal Justice*. New Brunswick, NJ: Transaction Books.

Erez, E. 1994. Victim Participation in Sentencing: And the Debate goes on. *International Review of Victimology* 3(1–2), pp. 17.

Erez, E., Roeger, L. and Morgan, F. 1994. *Victim Impact Statements in South Australia: An Evaluation.* Series C, No. 6, August. Adelaide: Office of Crime Statistics, Attorney-General's Department SA.

Erez, E., Roeger, L. and O'Connell, M. 1996. Victim Impact Statements: South Australia. In: Sumner, C., Israel, M., O'Connell, M. and Sarre, R. eds. *International Victimology: Selected Papers from the 8th International Symposium, Proceedings of a Symposium held 21–26 August 1994.* Canberra: Australian Institute of Criminology, pp. 206–216. http://aic.gov.au/media_library/publications/proceedings/27/erez.pdf.

Flynn, A. 2012. Bargaining with Justice: Victims, Plea Bargaining and the Victims' Charter Act 2006 (Vic). *Monash University Law Review* 37(3), pp. 73–96.

Forster, C. 2002. The Failure of Criminal Injuries Compensation Schemes for Victims of Intra-familial Abuse: The Example of Queensland. *Torts Law Journal* 10(2), pp. 143–166.

Freckelton, I. 1997. A New Victim Rhetoric in Victoria. *Alternative Law Journal* 22(6), pp. 302–303.

Freckelton, I. 2003. Compensation for victims of crime: Health and financial considerations. Paper Presented at the XIth International Symposium on Victimology, 13–18 July, Stellenbosch, South Africa.

Fry, M. 1959. Justice for Victims. *Journal of Public Law* 8, pp. 191–194.

Gardner, J. 1989. Victims' Satisfaction with the Criminal Justice System. Paper Presented at the Fifth Annual Conference of the Australian and New Zealand Society of Criminology, July (unpublished).

Gardner, J. 1990. *Victims and Criminal Justice.* Series C, No. 5. Adelaide SA: Attorney-General's Department.

Garkawe, S. 1999. Restorative Justice from the Perspective of Victims of Crime. *Queensland University of Technology Law Journal* 15, pp. 40–56.

Garkawe, S. 2006. The Effect of Victim Impact Statements on Sentencing Decisions. Paper Presented at the Sentencing: Principles, Perspectives and Possibilities conference convened by the National Judicial College, 10–12 February, Canberra.

Grabosky, P. 1989. *Victims of Violence.* Monograph No. 2. Canberra: Australian Institute of Criminology.

Graycar, A. 1999. New Research on Victims of Crime in Australia – Victims' Needs, Victims' Rights – An Australian Institute of Criminology Report. Paper Presented at the Restoration for Victims of Crime Conference convened by the Australian Institute of Criminology in Conjunction with Victims Referral and Assistance Service and held in Melbourne, Australia, September. http://aic.gov.au/media_library/conferences/rvc/graycar2.pdf.

Griffin, T. 2000. Righting the Wrong – Minimising the Risk: A review of Victims' Rights and Services in South Australia with Special Reference to Preventing Victimisation. *Journal of the Australasian Society of Victimology* 2(2), pp. 6–37.

Harding, R. 1994. Victimisation, Moral Panics and the Distortion of Criminal Justice Policy: A Review Essay of Ezzat Fattah's "Towards a Critical Victimology". *Current Issues in Criminal Justice* 6(1), pp. 27–42.

272   *Michael O'Connell*

Hayes, H. 2006. Apologies and Accounts in Youth Justice Conferences: Reinterpreting Research Outcomes. *Contemporary Justice Review* 9(4), pp. 369–385

Holder, R. 1999. Victims of Crime (Financial Assistance) Bill 1998 – Submission to the Standing Committee on Justice and Community Safety. Canberra: ACT Victims of Crime Coordinator.

Holder, R. 2002. Band Aid or Big Stick: Legislation as a Means of Changing Criminal Justice Responses to Victims of Crime. Paper Presented at the Empowerment after Trauma National Conference, Brisbane, Queensland, May.

Holder, R. 2008. Victim Support in Australia – A Road Map for the Future. Paper Presented at the National Victims of Crime Conference, Adelaide, September.

Holder, R. 2014. *Satisfied? Exploring Victims' Justice Judgements* RegNet Working Paper, No. 28. Canberra: Regulatory Institutions Network.

INTERVICT. 2014. Implementing the UN Declaration – A Joint Project between INTERVICT and the World Society of Victimology. INTERVICT, Tilburg University, Netherlands. http://www.tilburguniversity.edu/research/institutes-and-research-groups/intervict/research/current/finalized/undeclaration.

Joint Select Committee on Victims Compensation. 1997a. *First Interim Report: Alternative Methods of Providing for the Needs of Victims of Crime*, May. Sydney: Parliament of NSW.

Joint Select Committee on Victims Compensation. 1997b. *Report of the Study Tour of Interstate and Overseas Jurisdictions*, October. Sydney: Parliament of NSW.

Joint Select Committee on Victims Compensation. 1997c. *Second Interim Report: The Long Term Financial Viability of the Victims Compensation Fund*, December. Sydney: Parliament of NSW.

Joint Select Committee on Victims Compensation. 2000. *Report: Ongoing Issues Concerning the NSW Victims Compensation Scheme*, February. Sydney: Parliament of NSW.

Jones, C. and Mawby, R.I. 2003. Meeting the Needs of Tourist Victims. Unpublished Paper Presented at the XIth International Symposium on Victimology, 13–18 July 2003, Stellenbosch, South Africa.

Jurevic, L. 1996. Between a Rock and a Hard Place: Women Victims of Domestic Violence and the Western Australian Criminal Injuries Compensation Act. *Murdoch University Electronic Journal of Law* 3(2), http://www.murdoch.edu.au/elaw/issues/v3n2/jurevic.html.

Justice Strategy Unit (JSU). 1999. *Review on Victims of Crime – Report One*. Adelaide: Justice Strategy Unit, Attorney-General's Department.

Justice Strategy Unit (JSU). 2000a. *Review on Victims of Crime – Report Two*. Adelaide: Justice Strategy Unit, Attorney-General's Department.

Justice Strategy Unit (JSU). 2000b. *Review on Victims of Crime – Report Three: Criminal Injuries Compensation*. Adelaide: Justice Strategy Unit, Attorney-General's Department.

Keating, N. 2001. *Review of Services to Victims of Crime and Crown Witnesses provided by the Office of the Director of Public Prosecutions – Report*, June. Perth: Office of the Director of Public Prosecutions for Western Australia.

Kirchengast, T. 2011. The Integration of Lawyers into the Adversarial Trial. In: Lee, M., Mason, G. and Milivojeic, S. eds. *Proceedings of the 4th Annual Australian and New Zealand Critical Criminology Conference*. Sydney: Institute of Criminology, Sydney Law School, University of Sydney, NSW, 1–2 July 2010, pp. 1–6.

Kirchengast, T. 2013. Victim Lawyers, Victim Advocates and the Adversarial Criminal Trial. *New Criminal Law Review: An International and Interdisciplinary Journal* 16(4), pp. 568–594.

Lantz, S and D'Arcy, M. 2000. Falling Short: The State of Crimes Compensation in Victoria. *Women Against Violence* 8, pp. 74–76.

Law Reform Commission of the ACT. 1993. *Victims of Crime*. Canberra: ACT Law Reform Commission.

Laxminarayan, M.S. 2012. *The Heterogeneity of Crime Victims: Variations in Procedural and Outcome Preferences*. Nijmegen: Wolf Legal Publishers.

Leader-Elliott, I. 2006. Guilt and Punishment: Victims and Victim Impact Statements in Sentencing, August. Adelaide: School of Law, University of Adelaide.

Legal and Constitutional Committee 1987. *Report to Parliament upon Support Services for Victims of Crime*. Melbourne: Parliament of Victoria.

Mansell, A. and Indermaur, D. 1997. Evaluation of the Use of Victim Impact Statements in Western Australia. Paper Presented at the 9th International Symposium on Victimology, Amsterdam, 25–29 August.

Maxwell, G. and Hayes, H. 2006. Restorative Justice Developments in the Pacific Region. *Contemporary Justice Review* 9(2), pp. 127–154.

Murphy, B. (1989). *Victim Impact Statements: The South Australian Experience*. Darwin: Research and Development Unit, Northern Territory Police.

National Committee on Violence. 1990. *Violence: Directions for Australia*. Canberra: Australian Institute of Criminology.

National Council to Reduce Violence against Women and their Children. 2009. *Time for Action: The National Council's Plan for Australia to Reduce Violence against Women and their Children, 2009–2021(Time for Action)*. Canberra: Australian Government.

National Justice CEOs Group. 2011. *National Guidelines or Principles for Restorative Justice Programs and Processes for Criminal Matters: Discussion Paper*. Sydney: National Justice CEOs Group.

New South Wales Task Force on Services for Victims of Crime. 1987. *Report and Recommendations*. Sydney: NSW Task Force on Services for Victims of Crime.

New South Wales Victim Services. 2004. *Review of New South Wales Victims Support and Rehabilitation Act 1996* and the *Victims Rights Act 1996*. Sydney: Attorney-General's Department NSW.

O'Connell, M. 2000. SA Victims of Crime Review. In: O'Connell, M. ed. *Victims of Crime: Working together to improve services*. Adelaide: South Australian Institute of Justice Studies, pp. 121–148.

O'Connell, M. 2005. Victimology. In: Sarre, R. and Tomaino, J. eds. *Key Issues in Criminal Justice*. Adelaide: Australian Humanities Press, pp. 192–241.

O'Connell. M. 2006. Evolving Mechanisms for Engaging Victims in the Sentencing Process: Should Victims have a Stronger Voice? Paper Presented at the Sentencing: Principles, Perspectives and Possibilities Conference, Canberra ACT, 10–12 February.

O'Connell, M. 2008. Providing the Proper Role for Victims of Crime – The Australian Government's Obligations to Treat Victims of Crime Fairly. Paper Presented at the New Voices – New Visions – New Directions, Federal Criminal Justice Forum, Canberra (Only the abstract published).

O'Connell, M. 2009a. Victims in International Law: The International Criminal Court. Paper presented At the International Criminal Courts and Tribunals – the Law @ Work, A Red Cross International Humanitarian Law Evening Seminar, Adelaide, 12 May.

O'Connell, M. 2009b. Victims in the Sentencing Process: Judges and Magistrates Give their Verdict. *International Perspectives on Victimology* 4(1), pp. 50–57.

O'Connell, M. 2010. To Do the Victim Justice Requires More than Kindness – A Case for Greater Victim Participation in Criminal Justice. Unpublished Paper Presented at the National Victim Conference, Hobart, Tasmania, November.

O'Connell, M. 2012. Financial Assistance for Australian Victims of Overseas Terrorism. Submission to the Security Law Branch, Attorney-General's Department, Australian Capital Territory.

O'Connell. M. 2013. Legal Representation for Victims of Crime – Fairer Justice. Paper Presented at the National Victims of Crime Conference, and Homicide Symposium, Adelaide, September. http://www.victimsa.org/files/michael-ocon-nell-conference-paper.pdf.

O'Connell, M. and Fletcher, S. In press. To pay or not to pay: Revisiting the Rationale for State-Funded Compensation for Crime Victims – An Australian Perspective In: Tolfenson, T. ed. *Victimological Advances in Theory, Policy and Services – Festschrift in Honour of Prof Dr John Dussich*. Mito: Tokiwa University.

O'Connell, M. and Hayes, H. 2012. Victims, Criminal Justice and Restorative Justice. In: Hayes, H. and Prenzler, T. eds. *An Introduction to Crime and Criminology*. 3rd ed. Frenchs Forest: Pearson Prentice Hall, pp. 325–342.

Office of Crime Statistics. 1989. *Criminal Injuries Compensation in South Australia*. Series B, No. 5. Adelaide: Attorney-General's Department.

Office of Crime Statistics and Research. 2000. *Crime and Justice in South Australia – Juvenile Justice*. Adelaide: Australia: Office of Crime Statistics and Research. http://www.ocsar.sa.gov.au/docs/crime_justice/JJ_Text2000.pdf.

Office of Crime Statistics and Research. 2005. *Juvenile Justice in South Australia: Where are We Now?* Information Bulletin, (40). http://www.ocsar.sa.gov.au/docs/information_bulletins/IB40.pdf.

Office of the Director of Public Prosecutions. 2000. Victims of Crime Survey 1999/2000 – Report on Survey Responses, November. Perth: Government of Western Australia.

Paterson, A. 1990. Services for Victims of Crime and Crime Prevention Programmes in Europe and the United Kingdom. Adelaide SA: Victims of Crime Service Inc.

Paterson, A. 1996. Preventing Revictimisation: The South Australian Experience. In Sumner, C., Israel, M., O'Connell, M. and Sarre, R. (eds) *International Victimology: Selected Papers from the 8th International Symposium, Proceedings of a Symposium held 21–26 August 1994*. Canberra: Australian Institute of Criminology, pp. 227–231. http://aic.gov.au/media_library/publications/proceedings/27/paterson.pdf.

Queensland Government. 2014. Victims and Witnesses of Crime. Home Page for Victim Assist Queensland. http://www.qld.gov.au/law/crime-and-police/victims-and-witnesses-of-crime.

Redmond, Hon. I. 2007. Victims of Crime (Commissioner for Victims' Rights) Amendment Bill, Second Reading Speech, House of Assembly, *Hansard*, 12 September.

Reeves, H. and Mulley, K. 2000. The New Status of Victims in the UK, Opportunities and Threats. In: Crawford, A. and Goodey, J. eds. *Integrating a Victim Perspective within Criminal Justice*. Aldereshot: Ashgate, pp. 125–145.

Ross, S., Lawrence, J., Holder, R., Politis, A. and Graham, J. 2009. *Fairness and Equity for Victims of Crime: What do they Want and Why don't they get it? Final Report*, ARC Discovery Project DP0665417, December. Melbourne: University of Melbourne.

Sallman, P.A. and Chappell, D. 1982. *Rape Law Reform in South Australia*, Adelaide Law Review Research Paper No. 3. Adelaide: Adelaide Faculty of Law, University of Adelaide.

Scutt, J. 1982. An Invasion of Privacy? Questioning Victims of Sexual Harassment and Domestic Violence. In: Beed, T. and Grabosky, P. eds. *Search Conference on Victim Surveys in Australia*, OCC Paper No. 3. Sydney: Sample Survey Centre, University of Sydney.

Scutt, J. 1983. *Even in the Best of Homes*. Melbourne: Penguin.

Social Systems and Evaluation. 1997. *A Review of the Operations and Effectiveness of the Victims of Crime Act*. Perth: Ministry of Justice, Western Australia.

State of Queensland. 2009. Victims of Crime Assistance Bill – Explanatory Notes. Brisbane: Parliament of Queensland. http://rti.cabinet.qld.gov.au/documents/2009/aug/victims%20of%20crime%20assistance%20bill/Attachments/VictimsCrAssB09%20Exp%20Notes.pdf.

Strang, H. 2002. *Repair or Revenge: Victims and Restorative Justice*. Oxford: Oxford University Press.

Strang, H., Barnes, G., Braithwaite, J. and Sherman, L. 1999. *Experiments in Restorative Policing: A Progress Report on the Canberra Re-integrative Shaming Experiments*. Australian Federal Police and Australian National University, Canberra

Sumner, C. 1985. Statutes Amendment (Victims of Crime) Bill: Second Reading Speech. *Hansard*, 29 October. Adelaide: Parliament of South Australia, reprinted, pp. 1–8.

Sumner, C. 1991. Victim Assistance in South Australia. Paper Presented at the International Workshop on Victimology and Victims' Rights, Faculty of Law, Thammasat University, Bangkok, 3 April.

Symons, S. 2013. Independent Legal Representation for Victims Of Sexual Assault: Consideration of a Proposed Amendment to the Victims of Crime Act 2001 (SA). Research Paper Submitted at School of Law, University of South Australia (unpublished).

Toole, K. 2014. Lawyers for Victims of Crime won't Guarantee Better Results. *The Conversation*, 20 June. http://theconversation.com/lawyers-for-victims-of-crime-wont-guarantee-better-results-27629.

Trimboli, L. 2007. *An Evaluation of the New South Wales Community Conferencing for Young Adults Pilot Program*. Sydney: New South Wales Bureau of Justice Statistics and Research.

United Nations. 1985. *Declaration on Basic Principles of Justice for Victims of Crime and Abuse of Power*. UN GA Res. 40/34.

United Nations. 1989. ESCOR Res. 1989/57.

United Nations. 1990. *Protection of the Human Rights of Victims of Crime and Abuse of Power*. ESCOR Res. 1990/22.

United Nations. 2002. *Basic Principles on the Use of Restorative Justice Programmes in Criminal Matters*. Resolution 2002/12. New York: United Nations. www.un.org/en/ecosoc/docs/2002/resolution%202002-12.pdf.

Victim Services NSW. 2012. *Review of NSW Victim Compensation Scheme: Issues Paper*. Sydney: Victim Services NSW, Attorney-General's Department.

Victim Support Agency. 2009. *A Victim's Voice – Victim Impact Statements in Victoria: Findings of an Evaluation into the Effectiveness of Victim Impact Statements in Victoria*, October. Melbourne: Department of Justice.

Victim Support UK. 2012. Is the Government 'Getting it Right for Victims and Witnesses'? London: Victim Support UK. https://www.victimsupport.org.uk/sites/default/files/Getting%20it%20right%20for%20victims%20%26%20witnesses_VS%20initial%20response.pdf.

Victim Support Working Party. 1998. Victim Support in the ACT – Options for a Comprehensive Response, May. Canberra ACT: victims of crime coordinator.

Victoria Police. 2009. *Annual Report 2008–09*. Melbourne: Victoria Police. Victoria-Police-Annual-Report-2008-09.pdf.

Victorian Community Council against Violence. 1994. Victims of Crime: Inquiry into Services. Melbourne: Victorian Community Council against Violence.

Victorian Department of Justice. 2005 *Victims' Charter Community Consultation Paper*. Victorian Department of Justice: Melbourne. .

Victorian Sentencing Committee. 1988. *Sentencing: Report of the Victorian Sentencing Committee*. Melbourne VIC: Attorney-General's Department.

VOCAL. 1989. Charter of Rights for Victims of Crime. *The Vocal Voice*. December, p. 15.

VOCAL. 1990. Declarations of Victims' Rights and Statements of Principles. *The Vocal Voice*. March, pp. 9–13.

VRAS. 1998. Victims Referral and Assistance Service. Melbourne: Victims Referral and Assistance Service (VRAS), Attorney-General's Department.

Wade, J. The Hon (Attorney-General). 1996. Victims of Crime Assistance Bill 1996 – Second Reading Speech, *Hansard*, Parliament of Victoria, 31 October.

Wardlaw, G. 1979. The Human Rights of Victims in the Criminal Justice System. *Australian and New Zealand Journal of Criminology* 12(3), pp. 145–152.

Warner, K. and Gawlick, J. 2003. Mandatory Compensation Orders for Crime Victims and the Rhetoric of Restorative Justice. *Australian and New Zealand Journal of Criminology* 36(1), pp. 60–76.

Wemmers, J. and Cyr. K. 2006. What Fairness Means to Crime Victims: A Social Psychological Perspective. *Applied Psychology in Criminal Justice* 2(2), pp. 102–128. http://www.apcj.org/documents/2_2_fairness.pdf.

Western Australia Auditor General's Report. 2012. *Victim Support Service: Providing assistance to victims of crime – Report 6*. Perth: Government of Western Australia.

Whitney, K. 1997. The Criminal Injuries Compensation Acts: Do they Discriminate Against Female Victims of Violence? *Southern Cross University Law Review* 1, pp. 92–119.

Whitrod, R. 1986. Victim Participation in Criminal Proceedings: A Progress Report. *Criminal Law Review* 10(2), pp. 76–83.

Wilkie, M., Ferrante, A. and Susilo, N. 1992. *The Experiences and Needs of Victims of Crime in Western Australia*. Perth: Crime Research Centre, University of Western Australia.

Wilson, P., Lincoln, R. and Mustchin, M. 2001. *Strategies to Integrate and Coordinate Victims of Crime Services: Report for Families, Youth and Community*

Care Queensland. Gold Coast: Centre for Applied Psychology and Criminology, Bond University.

Woodbery, J. 1989. *A National Charter of Victims' Rights: Minimising the Risk of Victimisation and Recognition of Victims' Rights as Fundamental Tenets of Crime Prevention.* Adelaide: Special Projects, South Australia Police.

Index

Printed and bound by CPI Group (UK) Ltd, Croydon, CR0 4YY